EXPLORATIONS IN CONNECTED HISTORY

Mughals and Franks

Sanjay Subrahmanyam

OXFORD
UNIVERSITY PRESS

OXFORD
UNIVERSITY PRESS

Oxford University Press is a department of the University of Oxford.
It furthers the University's objective of excellence in research, scholarship,
and education by publishing worldwide. Oxford is a registered trademark of
Oxford University Press in the UK and in certain other countries

Published in India by
Oxford University Press
YMCA Library Building, 1 Jai Singh Road, New Delhi 110 001, India

Oxford University Press 2005

First Edition published in 2005
Oxford India Paperbacks 2011

ISBN 13: 978-0-19-807717-6
ISBN 10: 0-19-807717-3

Typeset in Naurang 10/13
by Excellent Laser Typesetters, Pitampura, Delhi 110 034
Printed in India at Replika Press Pvt. Ltd., Haryana 131 028

For Caroline
With a weakness for Enhydra lutris

'What power does Industão have to resist 1500 Europeans in the Portuguese camp, commanded by a perfectly experienced chief, when with only 400 Frenchmen, Bussy laid down the law in Deccan, and with as many Englishmen we saw Clive conquer all Arcot and Bengal? And I do not even have to speak of the ancient prowess that was shown by the Portuguese nation in the Orient, for it is so well-known that one can do without narrating it again.'

D. António José de Noronha, *Sistema Marcial Asiático* (1772)

Mughals and Franks

Pre-colonial India—and how it was perceived in Europe at the time—has been variously written about. Of late, historians have felt the need to re-examine the sources through which this history was reconstructed. In this collection, Sanjay Subrahmanyam questions the lines of political and cultural division that traditional history writing has accepted. He demonstrates that the interface and balance of power between the Mughals and the Europeans are an integral part of a wider system of international political alliances.

Mughals and Franks reflects on two and a half centuries of Mughal–European relations, beginning with the early years of the Mughals in India, and ending with the eighteenth century. It is based on extensive research into the Portuguese, Dutch, English, French, and Persian materials of the period, both archives and published texts. The work develops the idea of 'contained conflict', which is used as paradigm to study political and commercial relations in the period.

These essays are an instance of the author's command over the resources of Indian history, and lively familiarity with archives across geographical boundaries. Like its companion *From the Tagus to the Ganges*, this work makes a major contribution to the understanding of Mughal–European relations in the early modern period. These two volumes together demonstrate that just as our notions of periodization have to be interrogated, our maps have to be redrawn to address the issues thrown up by the areas we historicize.

This will interest students and scholars of Indian and South Asian history, medieval history, early modern India, as well as politics.

Sanjay Subrahmanyam is Professor and Doshi Chair of Indian History, Department of History, Centre for India and South Asia, University of California, Los Angeles (UCLA), USA. He is also Former Professor of Indian History and Culture, University of Oxford and Former Professor of Economic History, Delhi School of Economics, University of Delhi. Also, taught at Paris as Directeur d'études in the Ecole des Hautes Etudes en Sciences Sociales.

Contents

Preface

The fate of an author who tends to publish in obscure journals and edited volumes, and often also in what are considered to be 'minor' languages, is surely not an enviable one. Since the mid-1980s, my conversations with that great French polyglot and savant Jean Aubin at times turned around this question; since I felt that those who were not fortunate enough to receive a steady stream of offprints from him often lost sight of his more important publications, buried as they were in minor French journals with a circulation that rarely went beyond the proverbial 'happy few'. Even the recent and partly posthumous publication in two volumes of his essays (under the title *Le Latin et l'Astrolabe*) has not entirely rectified this situation. My own situation was surely rather better than his, partly because of the advantages of publishing in English. Still, it has been my impression that—perhaps on account of a desire to address too large a diversity of audiences—I have at times published essays that have not quite reached their intended target. The purpose of a volume such as the present one (and its companion) is in some measure to rectify that poor aim, but it is also to bring together dispersed essays under a single roof, as it were, in the no doubt optimistic belief that both they and I will gain from this process.

When the editors at Oxford University Press initially suggested that I should bring together an 'omnibus' volume of essays, my reaction was understandably one of reticence. I felt that I had not reached the age or degree of eminence to be 'anthologized', a privilege better reserved for persons such as Romila Thapar, Ashis Nandy, or Partha Chatterjee. Then there was the issue of the quantity of essays that I have published, which—whatever their quality—is certainly considerable in terms of its sheer mass. The best solution hence appeared to be to follow a modified version of the formula adopted in an earlier work entitled *Penumbral Visions* (OUP, 2001); namely to insist on at least some semblance of thematic unity, while not forcing the issue to a point that would make it artificial. So, it came to a question of making up one (or more) coherent collection of essays from those that I had published but not yet incorporated into some other collection.

The present volume hence consists of six essays, with an introduction and brief afterword. They derive in good measure from various conference presentations made in the context of what came in the 1980s and 1990s to be constituted as the International Seminar on Indo-Portuguese History. These essays usually link up Mughal history with that of the Portuguese *Estado da Índia*, and they emerged in fair measure from reflections on the so-called Habsburg period in Portuguese history, that is the six decades from 1580 to 1640.

The latter section of the book pursues some of the issues that have been raised in the preceding part, but does so in the context of the seventeenth and eighteenth centuries. Here, the materials in use are not simply those of the Portuguese and the Mughals, but also of other 'Franks', the English and the French. The purpose in so doing is not simply to engage in a gratuitous display of erudition, but rather to demonstrate the breadth and diversity of the archival materials that are available for a study of the period. It has often been my complaint that historians of the later colonial period tend to use an astonishingly poor range of sources in relation to the riches of which they in fact dispose. It can be argued with some justice that South Asian history is simply too complex in its linguistic registers and resources to be credibly mastered by a single individual. This is undoubtedly true: but the point does remain that an opening up of the range of materials can enable one to address problems that all too often are kept artificially separate.

As is usual, these essays have benefited from the comments of a wide variety of individuals, who heard them presented in oral form, or read through draft versions. My major debt is clearly to those colleagues in Paris who heard versions of these essays at my weekly seminar in the Ecole des Hautes Etudes en Sciences Sociales between 1995 and 2002. For specific comments on, or help with, one or the other essay, I must thank Muzaffar Alam, G. Balachandran, Maria Augusta Lima Cruz, Francis Dutra, Jorge Manuel Flores (who jointly authored Chapter 5), Jos Gommans, Serge Gruzinski, Claude Guillot, Kenneth McPherson, Geoffrey Parker, Kenneth Pomeranz, Sharif Husain Qasemi, Kapil Raj, Victor Stater, and Lu-ıs Filipe Thomaz. My debts to the late Jean Aubin and Denys Lombard will also be evident to readers of their work. The doctoral thesis of Jorge Flores in Lisbon, concerning diplomatic relations between the Portuguese and the Mughals, will no doubt appear in the years to come, and will hopefully complement the present work and provide a more rigorous chronological treatment of the years from 1560 to 1660.

As someone initially trained in economics, my fondness for the essay or journal article as a form of expression is probably greater than that of many of my historian colleagues, who prefer the monograph as a privileged mode. The present work is a compromise, as it were, between the Borgesian and Nabokovian modes, in so far as it attempts to bring together dispersed essays into a more coherent and longer form.

Early in my career, I tended to publish books without dedications, and was even reproached for it. With the passage of time, and some uncertainty about how many creative years remained before me, I came to realize that this was rather a waste; and so in more recent years, such has usually not been the case. In any event, I had no difficulty finding someone to whom I could dedicate this book.

Acknowledgements

The following chapters have appeared elsewhere, in the existing or slightly modified form.

Chapter 2 as 'The Trading World of the Western Indian Ocean, 1546–65: A Political Interpretation', in Artur Teodoro de Matos and Lu-is Filipe F. Reis Thomaz, eds, *A Carreira da Índia e as Rotas dos Estreitos: Actas do VIII Seminário Internacional de História Indo-Portuguesa*, Angra do Hero-ismo: The Editors, 1998, pp. 207–27.

Chapter 3 as 'A Matter of Alignment: Mughal Gujarat and the Iberian World in the Transition of 1580–1', *Mare Liberum*, No. 9, 1995, pp. 461–79.

Chapter 4 as 'The Viceroy as Assassin: The Mughals, the Portuguese and Deccan Politics, c. 1600', *Santa Barbara Portuguese Studies*, Special Number, 1995, pp. 162–203.

Chapter 5 (jointly authored with Jorge Flores) as 'The Shadow Sultan: Succession and Imposture in the Mughal Empire, 1628–40', *Journal of the Economic and Social History of the Orient*, Vol. 47, No. 1, 2004, pp. 80–121,

Chapter 6 as 'Frank Submissions: The Company and the Mughals between Sir Thomas Roe and Sir William Norris', in H. V. Bowen, Margarette Lincoln, and Nigel Rigby, eds, *The Worlds of the East India Company*, Woodbridge: The Boydell Press, 2002, pp. 69–96.

Chapter 7 as 'Un Grand Dérangement: Dreaming an Indo-Persian Empire in South Asia, 1740–1800', *Journal of Early Modern History*, Vol. IV, Nos 3–4, 2000, pp. 337–78.

Abbreviations

AN	Archives Nationales, Paris
AN/TT	Arquivos Nacionais/Torre do Tombo, Lisbon
ARA	Algemeen Rijksarchief, The Hague
BL	British Library, London
BN	Bibliothèque Nationale, Paris
BNL	Biblioteca Nacional de Lisboa
CC	Corpo Cronológico
OBP	Overgekomen Brieven en Papieren
OIOC	Oriental and India Office Collections
VOC	Verenigde Oostindische Compagnie

1

Introduction: Mughals and Franks in an Age of Contained Conflict

[Holden] Furber sees the centuries [1600 to 1800] as an integrated period of European-Asian cooperation—a world before the establishment of empires. No one can deny the cooperation or the period's integrity. But there is more. The European used force to win privileges and exclude competition wherever he could. The native answered with non-violent chicanery.

Ashin Das Gupta (1979)[1]

It was late in the year 1605. The Wanli emperor (1573–1620) was more than halfway through his reign in China, while Shah 'Abbas (1587–1629) was at the height of his power in Iran. In India, one of the most powerful and charismatic monarchs of the early modern world lay dying, and as was so often the case in those years—whether in Ethiopia or Beijing—the ubiquitous Jesuits were not far from his court, providing a running commentary, as it were, on the proceedings. The monarch who was critically ill was the Mughal emperor, Jalal-al-Din Muhammad Akbar, and some contemporaries in the court at least believed that the immediate cause of his malady was an apoplectic fit stemming from a disastrous elephant fight between his own animal, Chanchal, and Girambar, the elephant of his estranged oldest son Salim (who was soon to take the title of Jahangir). The fight had gone badly for Chanchal and, what was worse, a quarrel had broke out between the followers of Salim and those of his son, Prince Khusrau, also a contender in the succession stakes.[2] But this was not how the

[1] Ashin Das Gupta, Review of Holden Furber, *Rival Empires of Trade in the Orient, 1600–1800*, Minneapolis, 1976, in *The Journal of Asian Studies*, Vol. XXXVIII, No. 2, 1979, p. 316.

[2] For a detailed analysis of materials, see Muzaffar Alam and Sanjay Subrahmanyam,

Jesuits, with their own politico-religious vision, saw matters. Let us consider a more-or-less contemporary document concerning the death of Akbar, and the succession thereafter: here I refer to the letter written by the Jesuit Jerónimo (Jerome) Xavier to the Provincial of the Jesuits at Goa, from Lahore on 25 September 1606, thus nearly a year after the death of Akbar.[3]

Xavier was present in Agra in the last months of Akbar's life and the first months of his son's reign, and begins his letter by noting that 'a little after I wrote to Your Reverence last year, the world revolved here (*se revolveu aqa o mundo*) with the death of the king Acbar'. He states moreover that the event had been predicted by several observers; a 'Moorish [Muslim] astrologer had given it in writing to the prince [Salim] in Agra that he would be king within three months as his father would die', while another Muslim with a saintly reputation (*tido por sancto delles*) who was resident in Lahore had also sent word to the same effect. Besides, several Gentile (*gentio*) astrologers had also gone about predicting the same. It was in early October 1605 that Akbar fell ill, but at first it was not taken to be serious. In fact, early on in this illness, in the beginning of October, he had the Jesuits sent for and proceeded to discuss matters Christian with them. On this occasion, writes Xavier, he 'gave few signs of being ill'. A few days later, word was spread that he was afflicted by dysentery, and the Jesuits began to think it was time to suggest once more that he accept 'the law of the Holy Scripture'. But, once more, when Xavier and his companion António Machado were called to pay a visit late at night ('it would have been ten hours of the night'), in the interior of the royal pavilion, they were astonished to see that he looked in good health. Akbar received them with both Salim and Khusrau present, and asked Xavier to read out and translate a letter in Portuguese that had just arrived. The emperor having formally sent off his son and grandson after a time, the Jesuits still remained there. Xavier continues:

After a time, he rose up to go into the *mahal*, the place of the women, and he went there (…) as if he were in sound health, and with even less signs of weakness than when he was well. He having retired, we remained there awaiting the time when he would return, and when it was (…) midnight, he passed through there again in order to go to the place where he used to pray. We saw him coming without anyone's support (*encosto*), and as talkative and smiling as ever, all of which we noted. In the end, the [other] Padre and I decided that it was not the right moment to talk to him, as he gave no signs of illness,

---

'Witnessing Transition: Views on the End of the Akbari Dispensation', in K. N. Panikkar, Terence J. Byres, and Utsa Patnaik, eds, *The Making of History: Essays presented to Irfan Habib*, New Delhi, 2000, pp. 104–40.

[3] British Library, London, Additional Manuscript 9854, 'Jesuit Missions in India, 1582–1693', fls 38–52, in A. da Silva Rego, ed., *Documentação Ultramarina Portuguesa*, Vol. III, Lisbon, 1963, pp. 62–91.

and he retired thereafter in order to pray. At midnight, we came away being persuaded that he was well. The next day in the morning, he showed himself at the window to the people with a very good appearance. What I have described was Saturday night, on Sunday he was well; [but] on Monday, it began to be said that the King was dying.[4]

The Jesuits now reiterate the rumour that they (and others) had already noted some years before, namely that 'the poison that he [Akbar] had been given had started to work'. Xavier and his companion thus went that morning to the *jharoka* (*ao lugar da janela*), but Akbar did not appear; instead, it was confirmed that he was unwell. The Jesuits now attempted to go into the interior of the palace, by claiming that they had a remedy (*mesinha*) for the illness, but neither they nor any of the boys whom they attempted to send in on their behalf was allowed to enter. The account continues:

In [all] this time, the prince [Salim] did not come to see his father. Some said that since the father suspected him of giving him poison, he [Akbar] did not wish to see him. Others said that he [Salim] himself did not wish to come since he did not wish to place himself behind closed doors, [because of] a Gentile captain, brother-in-law of the prince, who was aggrieved with him as his sister, who was the wife of the prince, had killed herself with poison on account of jealousy over her husband, and this captain had the King in his power, and wanted to make his own nephew, the oldest son of the prince, the king and exclude his father, and he had on his side another great Moorish captain whose daughter was married with the same son of the prince. Other Gentiles and Moors too were of the same view, and even the king was inclined towards this, so that he [Salim] was afraid to enter the fortress to see his father, since he did not know if he would be allowed to leave there.[5]

The two figures mentioned here are Raja Man Singh, Salim's brother-in-law and the maternal uncle of his son Khusrau, and Mirza 'Aziz Koka, titled Khan-i A'zam. We shall encounter these personages in the chapters that follow, but it is interesting to note that the Jesuits with their assiduously collected bazaar gossip, were not entirely off the mark here in describing the tensions and relationships of the time. Xavier then continues his account by noting that 'the king went on deteriorating'. Salim, he claims, began to think matters had now passed out of his control, 'and almost ran away one night, so badly did he see

[4] Compare the standard account in Pierre du Jarric, *Akbar and the Jesuits: An account of the Jesuit Missions to the Court of Akbar*, trans. C. H. Payne, London, 1926, pp. 203–4. Du Jarric's *Histoire*, in three volumes, completed in 1614, was largely derived for its account of the Mughals and Akbar, from Fernão Guerreiro, *Relação Anual das Coisas que Fizeram os Padres da Companhia de Jesus nas partes da Índia Oriental*, 5 Vols, Coimbra/Lisbon, 1603–11.

[5] For Jahangir's version of the death of his wife, who 'swallowed opium and killed herself', see *The Jahangirnama: Memoirs of Jahangir, Emperor of India*, translated, edited, and annotated by Wheeler M. Thackston, Oxford, 1999, pp. 50–1.

the turn of his affairs'. Though outnumbered, and also lacking control over the doors to the fort, nevertheless he did seem to have popular opinion (*o vulgo*) with him. The Jesuit states that this was because he was thought to be 'liberal [and] just', and so little by little he managed to win over the major *amîrs*. His account continues:

Even the principal Moors who wanted to give the kingdom over to the grandson consulted on the matter, and *omnibus pensatis*, they thought that it was better to give it over to him to whom it belonged, and so one of their principal members was sent by them to deal with him [Salim] and to promise him the kingdom if he swore to protect the law of the Moors (*a ley dos mouros*) and not to harm either his son or the others. He swore to it all. Immediately that evening, the Gentile uncle of the grandson of the king, and his father-in-law, came and brought him his son, and they made him touch his feet and they did the same. The prince at once ordered the fortress and its doors to be cleared, and placing his own people there, went the next day with trusted people to see the king.

The account notes that Akbar was unable to speak by that time, but was still conscious. He is said to have ordered Salim to be handed over the regalia, and signalled for him to be given the sword that he kept by the bedside to gird on. Salim is said to have performed the *sijda* (the *jezda*, in Xavier's words), after which he was told to leave. In Xavier's view then, the king died more or less alone, with only 'a few people who remained with him, and some of them took the name of Maffamede. He never responded to them, he only took the name of God a few times, nor did he die in keeping with the custom of the Gentiles. As one never knew under what religion (*ley*) he lived, nor did one know under which one he died, since he made place for all the religions and took none of them for the truth, though his usual habit was to worship God and the Sun'.

Xavier now follows up this account with a long and largely laudatory obituary notice of Akbar, providing us an image of the monarch at his death which is remarkably positive, indeed far more so than the views that were held for example by the viceroys and governors of Portuguese India. A brief passage from his letter will suffice to demonstrate this aspect:

He [Akbar] died at last on a Thursday (*sic*), on the [sixteenth] of October of the year 1605. With him died a kingly man who truly was a king, and who made sure he was obeyed and who knew how to govern. He was greatly beloved in the whole world, feared by the great, loved by the small, the same to everyone, be they natives, foreigners, small or great, Moors and Christians and Gentiles, everyone felt they had him on their side. Where God was concerned, he was so pious that he prayed four times a day without fail— that is, once at sunrise and once at sunset, at midday and midnight, without ever neglecting to do so on account of any matter, however important.[6]

[6] Xavier's letter of 25 September 1606, in *Documentação Ultramarina Portuguesa*, Vol. III, pp. 65–6.

To this Xavier then adds that no detail was too small to escape him, and that though 'he did not know how to read or write, he knew everything'. This portrait of a humanist ruler contrasts markedly with the images that would be produced half-a-century later in Europe of the Mughals, at a time when the idea of the Oriental Despot had gained firm ground in the European imagination. What is also of interest for us here is the Jesuit's description of the nature of the political transition, which precedes the long account in the same letter of the suppression of the rebellion by Prince Khusrau in April and May 1606.

The king Aqbar, that is the Great King, came to an end. The new king began to take matters in hand. He came and went from the fort in order to console his sisters who were more disconsolate than he, but he then [always] returned to his own residence. At the end of eight days, he went to the palace to take possession of the kingdom. He had the public square (*terreiro*) richly adorned, he then came out from the interior and sat on the throne, while they shouted Padja Çalamat, that is *Salve rex* [and] brought him his presents; he then went in and settled into the fortress as king. With the change in kings, the court too changed, those who had risen up now fell, and those who had fallen now rose. Much was expected of the new king for he promised much, but once things had quietened down, the promises were forgotten and the expectations were deceived.

Amongst those deceived and disappointed were the Jesuits themselves, for they apparently had thought that 'there would be a great conversion, because until then he [Jahangir] almost gave out that he was a crypto-Christian (*quasi se dava ao discoberto por christão*), and his own intimates claimed he was one'. They claim that the reason for this change lay in the politics of the court. For, in Xavier's view, at the time of his accession, Jahangir's principal worry was Man Singh ('the Gentile captain who was at the head of all the Gentiles'), and in order to counterbalance this he had had to make common cause with the orthodox Muslims.

The Moors had made him king, and he had sworn to pursue the law of Maffamede with zeal, [and] he wished to win over and keep the Moors on his side, by showing he was of their party, and so he did in the beginning of his reign. He gave out word that he would have the mosques cleaned and cleared. In the palace, Moorish prayers and orations began to be heard.

For Xavier then, as for his other Jesuit brethren located in Agra or Lahore, the main preoccupation in all this was the rise of what they understood as an official Islam, that might have repercussions for their own mission, and more generally for the treatment of Christians in northern India. A reading of their later letters demonstrates however that in their own view, these perturbations proved to be of a relative short duration, and the political system returned to a state of equilibrium. To be sure, some rose and some fell amongst the grandees of the court, but this was not for them a particularly exotic phenomenon.

The historiography of the early modern period seems to have an abiding fascination with the moment of the face-to-face encounter between the European and his Other, and its attendant *mise-en-scène*. The matter has been rehearsed time and again, whether with Vasco da Gama and the Samudri Raja in Kerala, Hernán Cortés and Moctezuma in Mexico, Pizarro and the Inca Atahualpa in the Andes, or Captain Cook and his interlocutors in the South Seas; we might well add Akbar and Xavier to that list. Evolving fashions may turn the valencies this way or that, but the *topos* itself remains dominant, freezing rather complex processes into a memorable Kodak moment, and extracting as much metaphorical juice as can be obtained from these dramatic structural oppositions. Yet much is obviously lost here. For each of these alleged 'encounters' in fact represented a chronology, and a series of events rather than a simple moment. If misunderstandings existed, they did not remain stable, and the degree of stability was even less when the two (or more) parties dealt with each other over an extended period of decades, if not centuries. This is precisely the problem that the historian must confront when dealing with the European presence in South Asia in the sixteenth, seventeenth, and early eighteenth centuries.

That the Mughal dynasty and a series of European powers enjoyed close relations in the two centuries preceding the conquest by the English East India Company of Bengal, in the 1750s, is a well-known fact. These were, however, long years of an uneasy jousting, of a jockeying for position, when no single party entirely gained the upper hand, and which in sum made up an age of 'contained conflict' whose eventual outcome could not have been read by participants in 1600 or even 1700.[7] But did proximity foster mere paranoia, or a clearer perception of the other? A few years after the westerly region of Sind had fallen into the hands of the Mughals (in 1592), the Portuguese administration in Goa began to grow nervous about the consequences of this further spread of the domains of an already too-powerful neighbour. The Mughals had taken Gujarat in the early 1570s, and Bengal later in the same decade; their imperialist intentions in respect of the Deccan were also quite clear by the early 1590s. The Portuguese viceroy Dom Francisco da Gama, Count of Vidigueira, spelt out his perception of a part of the threat in a letter to the Habsburg Crown, dated December 1598.

On the 9th of September, Jerónimo Xavier, a religious of the Company of Jesus who resides in the court of Equebar [Akbar], advised me that in some rivers that enter deep into the interior, he is making ready a great number of foists, and three large *naos*, and that it is imagined that his intention is to attack the fortress of Ormus or that of Diu. And

---

[7] Here I draw upon an earlier discussion in Sanjay Subrahmanyam, *The political economy of commerce: Southern India, 1500–1650*, Cambridge, 1990, Ch. 5, 'Europeans and Asians in an age of contained conflict'.

even though in the judgement of those who understand these matters well, there are many difficulties that stand in the way of the Mogor achieving this intent, I have fostered all of them [the difficulties], to keep myself on guard as soon as it was heard that the enemy was ready, advising the Captain of Ormus of what was required and supplying him with the necessary, and that of Diu too in the same way.[8]

The fiscal superintendent (*provedor da fazenda*) of the northern sector, a certain Luís Álvares Camelo, was hence sent out with gunpowder and other supplies to take care of the fortresses in Gujarat and the Persian Gulf, and Vidigueira equally activated his network of spies in the neighbouring courts. However, he then heard from the Jesuits that the Mughal preparations had lost momentum, since the pressing priority was now their impending war with the Uzbeks. These rumours that the Portuguese viceroy gathered paralleled in a rather curious fashion earlier rumours among the Mughals (in 1592–3), that the 'Firangi soldiers from Hurmuz' planned an attack on Sind in support of the former ruler there, Mirza Jani Beg.[9] Neither set of rumours appears to have been founded, and the historian is obliged to conclude that, in these instances at least, the neighbours and rivals were dominated by a spirit of paranoia rather than a pragmatic capacity to size up the other. We see from another letter written by the same Portuguese viceroy, this one written in late December 1599.

The king Equebar is now a little less than sixty years old, and while at his court in Laor retreated in a dissimulating manner, for he feared the king of Persia, who was approaching very close to him through the kingdom of the Uzbeques into which he had entered; now he is in Agraa, [and] he is a great, clever and devious captain. He does not trust his oldest son, for fear that he might kill him with poison. And he has called for his other son, whom he had accommodated in the part of his domains that borders Bengal. The desire that he has to approach this island [Goa] is insatiable, but since the winter [monsoon] until now, the war that he was making against the kingdom of the Melique has been suspended (...).[10]

But was the broad sense of mutual threat or menace so unfounded after all? Did the Mughals, as a massive continental power, simply shrug off whatever the 'Franks' from distant Europe could do as insignificant? The views of modern authors differ quite considerably on this question. A radical position was defined on the question a quarter-century ago by a well-known historian, who affirmed on the basis of a study of sixteenth-century Gujarat that 'control of sea trade

---

[8] Letter of the Count of Vidigueira to Philip III, Biblioteca Nacional de Lisboa, Fundo Geral, Códice 1976, fl. 94v.

[9] Abu'l Fazl, *Akbar Nâma*, Vol. III, trans. H. Beveridge, reprint, Delhi, 1989, pp. 972–3.

[10] Letter of the Count of Vidigueira to Philip III, dated 23 December 1599, Biblioteca Nacional de Lisboa, Fundo Geral, Códice 1976, fl. 141v–42r.

was (...) not a political resource essential to the operation of the Gujarati political system'. This meant that neither the Sultans of Gujarat, nor the Mughals after 1573, were really motivated to pay much attention to the European presence, since 'glory was not won at sea' but through 'horses racing over the plains'.[11] By the late 1980s, this view had become sufficiently canonical that the same author could affirm that 'contact between the two sides was minimal, the Mughal attitude especially being one of neglect and indifference', and that 'one demonstration of this [fact] is the very few references (and those casual), to the Portuguese in the very lengthy standard Mughal chronicles'.[12] Others have since questioned this view, at first hesitatingly, and more recently with greater conviction and insistence. One may admit, of course, that the Mughals were probably of greater political significance to the Portuguese than the other way around, but it does remain interesting that from the 1530s, almost all the rulers of northern India were careful to maintain diplomatic relations with Goa. This is certainly the case with Humayun, but it also is manifestly true of the Afghan Sur dynasty, which ruled for a time in the 1540s and early 1550s.[13]

A very large question also does remain open, namely of what the xenological view of the Mughals was once one turns away from the 'lengthy standard Mughal chronicles'. Can we assume that this view focused solely on the neighbours to the north and west, the Ottomans, Safavids, and Shaibanids? Some writers have argued that before the late eighteenth century, 'among the literate classes of the Mughal empire a lack of curiosity about geographical matters outside their immediate ken appears to have been the prevailing response', and that the most absurd stories concerning the world 'beyond the ocean' hence circulated.[14] While examples can undoubtedly be accumulated in favour of this view, there is also some evidence in support of the view that the literati of the Mughal court did have a view of the external world that was empirically flexible and dynamic. We might consider such texts as the rather elaborate atlas of the world prepared in the 1640s by Sadiq Isfahani, which though containing such inevitable features as Gog and Magog, is nevertheless reflective of a distinct evolution in the conception of the world that had taken place since 1500.[15] Or again, we

[11] M. N. Pearson, *Merchants and Rulers in Gujarat: The response to the Portuguese in the sixteenth century*, Berkeley, 1976, pp. 89–91.

[12] M. N. Pearson, *The Portuguese in India*, Cambridge, 1987, p. 53.

[13] See the exchange of letters between D. João de Castro and Islam Shah Sur from 1546, in Leonardo Nunes, *Crónica de Dom João de Castro*, ed. J. D. M. Ford, Cambridge [Mass.], 1936, pp. 59–65, 72–47.

[14] Simon Digby, 'Beyond the ocean: Perceptions of overseas in Indo-Persian sources of the Mughal period', *Studies in History*, (N.S.), Vol. XV, No. 2, 1999, p. 249.

[15] Irfan Habib, 'Cartography in Mughal India', *The Indian Archives*, Vol. XXVIII, 1980, pp. 88–105.

may look to the earlier work of Tahir Muhammad Sabzwari, the *Rauzat al-Tâhirîn*, from the early years of the reign of Jahangir, which includes a discussion of the circumstances leading to the disastrous North African expedition of the Portuguese king Dom Sebastião, his death there, and the ensuing political crisis in Portugal.[16] Tahir Muhammad had visited Goa as part of a Mughal mission to the Portuguese *Estado*, and it is clear that he used his time to gather together information both on the Portuguese in Asia, and the politics of Europe.

It will scarcely do, therefore, to contrast Mughal materials on the Europeans as scarce at best and fanciful at worst, while at the same time making exaggerated claims for the transparent character and empirical reliability of the materials that one finds in the European archives of the epoch. To address the second set of materials requires one equally to come to terms with the accumulated prejudices of several generations on the empirical status of the European writer on early modern India. Some years ago, it may still have been possible, and indeed even considered desirable, to read European writings on South Asia in the sixteenth and seventeenth centuries in a particular diagonal way, raiding them for 'facts' such as prices, wages, temperatures, the number of days it took for a caravan to travel from Surat to Burhanpur, or how the *hundî* (bill-of-exchange) functioned in the Mughal empire. This was the tradition in which I confess to having been trained, as an apprentice economic historian, struggling to come to terms with the vast (indeed, unmanageable) materials that the archives of Goa, Paris, Venice, Lisbon, Simancas, Madrid, Lisbon, and the Hague made available. It was a tradition in which, to quote Ashin Das Gupta, 'the world of the Indian Ocean [was]…coming into its own, and, within it, the history of trade [was] ascendant over that of politics'.[17] Then, by some alchemy that it has proved difficult to reconstruct retrospectively, all the rules of the games had suddenly changed. Rather than 'archives', one's colleagues were talking about 'texts' or 'the archive'. Rather than ambitious macroscopic overflights, close readings of particular works had become the rule. Rather than assume that in the European archives, there resided the truth about arcane matters that the South Asian language materials obstinately refused to reveal, the construction of the European materials itself was being taken apart. There was a certain initial delight to this exercise, since many who worked in, say, the Algemeen Rijksarchief (General State Archives) in the Hague had always suspected that the 'discourse'

---

[16] Cf. 'Rauzatu-t Tahirin of Tahir Muhammad', in H. M. Elliot and J. Dowson, *The History of India as told by its own historians: The Muhammadan Period*, Vol. VI, London, 1875, pp. 195–200. This is a somewhat misleading summary, and I am grateful to Muzaffar Alam for a more careful reading of the contents of Book 5, from the manuscript at the Bodleian Library, Oxford.

[17] Das Gupta's review of Furber, *Rival Empires*, p. 315.

of the factors of the VOC (Verenigde Oost-Indische Compagnie) was inherently problematic in respect to the manner in which Asian merchant communities, polities, or societies were portrayed. Certain well-known hegemonies and tyrannies were seemingly being overturned. Yet, as time has gone by, the gulf between these highly subtle analysts of texts and the diligent diggers into archives has widened in many respects.[18] The latter have more often than not refused to take up the gauntlet that was thrown down, knowing full well that they usually cannot answer for precisely which audience Jean-Baptiste Tavernier wrote, what his intellectual influences were, or even what the suitable coordinates for an intertextual reading of his travels might be.

Yet, a number of important questions have remained unanswered on the other side too. Consider a work published some years ago by Kate Teltscher analysing European and British writings on India from 1600 to 1800, that has been rather well-received in both Britain and South Asia.[19] Starting with the question: 'Who had the authority to speak for the subcontinent?', the author has gone on to analyse mainly a series of published English-language texts from the seventeenth and eighteenth centuries, but also sought simultaneously to place a healthy distance between her analysis and that in Edward Said's *Orientalism* (1978). It is suggested that 'texts about India are indeed more complex and contradictory than Said's view of such writing would allow', and that rather than necessarily reinforcing European notions of superiority, the images brought back from India and presented to an European audience contained 'troubling and ambiguous elements'. Jesuits and Lutherans saw matters differently from one another; even the servants of the English East India Company had different voices at the time of, say, the impeachment of Warren Hastings. But this period of complexity, if not cacophony, is transformed with the defeat of Tipu Sultan of Mysore in 1799. Now, 'the British start to speak for their Indian empire', or, as the concluding chapter puts it, 'the imperial pen re-inscribes India with greater assurance, and a firmer hand'.

Like some other recent works that criticize the Saidian approach while drawing on European travel-texts and related materials of the seventeenth and eighteenth centuries, such as Lisa Lowe's monograph on British and French Orientalism from Lady Mary Montagu to Roland Barthes, Teltscher's work still leaves some historians at least profoundly uneasy.[20] The avowed purpose of

---

[18] For a brave attempt to define a middle ground, see Stuart Schwartz, ed., *Implicit Understandings: Observing, Reporting, and Reflecting on the Encounters between Europeans and Other Peoples in the Early Modern Era*, New York, 1994.

[19] Kate Teltscher, *India Inscribed: European and British Writings on India, 1600–1800*, Delhi, 1995.

[20] Lisa Lowe, *Critical Terrains: British and French Orientalism*, Ithaca (NY), 1991.

such work, to put it in Lowe's mellifluous prose, is 'to challenge and resist the binary logic of otherness by historicizing the critical strategy of identifying otherness as a discursive mode of production itself'. How could Europeans possibly 'speak for India' if Lutherans and Jesuits disagreed in the eighteenth century on the status of 'idols'? The keyword in much of this sort of analysis, 'historicizing', actually means 'relativizing' for all intents and purposes. Thus, by a further step of rhetoric, the only interest that these texts on India possess is in terms of an analysis of European societies and their self-representations. This is the reason why it possible to use rather straightforward hermeneutic procedures on these texts, without any significant larger contextual knowledge of South Asia on the part of the authors of the analyses.

Or consider what it is arguably one of the strongest representatives of this genre, namely the late Sylvia Murr's long, immensely erudite, and altogether brilliant essay on the reading of François Bernier's conception of the political construction of the Mughal empire.[21] Murr writes fairly early in the essay: 'One should always begin from the principle that the information on the Mughal [in Bernier's text]…is not trustworthy in itself, and has no interest except when confirms a sufficiently large body of information that derives from independent and heterogeneous sources. In other words, one can never be sure that what Bernier says about Mughal India, which he claims to have seen between 1658 and 1666, is true (…).' This may seem an unexceptional statement, but one must take pause to wonder why Dr Bernier is being singled out for this treatment. Should one read Abu'l Fazl's *Â'în-i-Akbarî* or Seyyidi 'Ali Re'is's *Mir'at ul-memâlik* otherwise when they write of the Mughals? Does the fact that Abu'l Fazl was born of an Indian *'âlim* family make his information somehow 'fiable par elle-même' ('reliable in itself')? One may sympathize with Murr's puzzlement when she remarks, in a footnote, that 'even Indian historians who have access to sources that they clearly judge to be more reliable (in Persian or the vernacular languages)—like Jadunnath (*sic*) Sarkar, who uses the official annals and archives, the *Alamgirnamah*, and other memoirs and contemporary histories (…) nevertheless cite Bernier frequently *to support* what they say' (emphasis in original). But this is surely a matter of the prestige that an European text continued to hold in the eyes of Sir Jadunath, which takes us to the analysis of how a branch of the medieval Indian historiography functioned in late colonial times, rather than to any profound general conclusions on the relative episte-mological status of, say, the *'Âlamgîr Nâma* and Bernier's account.

In the chapters that make up this volume, I will attempt concretely to address this set of questions, and also to sketch the working out of the complex dialectical relationship between early modern south Asian society and European observers thereof in a series of broadly chronological reflections concerning the production of a series of actions and perceptions, texts, and archives. To take a long view of matters, one might start in the late fifteenth century, when the Portuguese arrived in the Indian Ocean, and from the first decade of the next century began the process of creating a maritime empire to which they only somewhat later gave the name of the *Estado da Índia*. This empire, founded during the governments of D. Francisco de Almeida and Afonso de Albuquerque, with its major Indian bases in Goa and Cochin, did not have substantial contacts with northern India though, at least in the early decades of its career. The Portuguese did periodically eye the Gujarati port of Diu covetously, but it was not until the late 1520s that they made serious moves in that direction.

The Mughals, a dynasty of Timurid and Chinggisid descent, for their part commenced the process of empire-building in south Asia a quarter-century after the arrival of Vasco da Gama in Calicut, and the Portuguese were hence privileged witnesses to their activity right from the time of Zahir al-Din Muhammad Babur (d. 1530). The Mughals were thus at one and the same time an ethnographic object for the Portuguese, as one of the three Great Empires of the western Indian Ocean (with the Safavids and the Ottomans), and potential adversaries, whose every move had to be watched and countered. Portuguese, and thus eventually European, knowledge about the Mughals was hence created at the same time that the Portuguese/Europeans acted out their at times 'Machiavellian' conceptions of politics on the Mughals and other polities in the region.

As a consequence, an altogether curious process of conceptual contamination took place. In the first instance, the theory of power politics that men like Albuquerque or D. João de Castro espoused was based on an implicit conception of similarity, in which various unitary actors were to be linked in systems of alliances and oppositions to achieve a balance. The internal makeup of different polities had little theoretical space in this construction of matters. However, the entire ethnographic exercise, to which both missionaries and laity contributed, was based on the notion of identifying, enumerating, and later theorizing about difference, and proceeded on the assumed implicit superiority of the observer over the object in terms of internal social and political constitution. How did these two notions coexist, and how did they affect each other? Historians of political thought in Europe have spent much effort in order to demonstrate how, despite the 'increasingly sinister reputation' that Machiavelli enjoyed, his ideas did spread and created a situation such that other thinkers of the sixteenth and seventeenth centuries too came to be 'inhabitants of Machiavelli's moral universe'.[22]

---

[22] Quentin Skinner, *The Foundations of Modern Political Thought: Volume One, The Renaissance*, Cambridge, 1978, pp. 248–9.

The idea that 'profitable deceit' could be engaged in, if the interests of the commonwealth were thus protected, would surely have struck a particular chord when those upon whom such deceit was to be practised were themselves not Christians.

We may thus consider a singular Machiavellian moment: the drowning in February 1537 of the Sultan of Gujarat, Bahadur Shah, in the course of parleys with the Portuguese governor Nuno da Cunha (1529–38). This is an event whose ramifications remain shrouded in mystery, for while the Portuguese had both means and motive, they never actually admitted in their writings to killing the Sultan. This death was the culmination of one process (and partly the result of Mughal pressure on Gujarat), as well as the beginning of another (the actual dismemberment of the Gujarat Sultanate). Even if Portuguese sources remain ambiguous on what precisely happened and why, chroniclers from the contemporary Islamic world were quite clear. Thus, we have the perception of a writer from south Arabia, who writes:

In this year [943 H.] on Monday, 3rd of the month of Ramazan, or the 4th of Ramazan, Sultan Bahadur Shah, Lord of Gujarat, was killed, being murdered by the Frank. It came about in this wise—that a fleet (*tajhîz*) of the Frank arrived before Diu from the south (*fi sâfil*), and when they reached Diu port, Sultan Bahadur embarked, exposing his own person to danger on Khwaja Safar Salman's grab, by way of coming to meet them, accompanied by about ten of his ministers and by the Khwaja Safar Salman. When he reached them they made a show of welcome and politeness (*ikrâm wa hismah*) towards him, and of support against his foes the Mughals who had seized his country—as was related under the year [93]7. [However] they reproached him for sending the sailing-ships to Jiddah as already mentioned, [and] that all he intended was to incite the Turks (*arwâm*) against them. He absolved himself, saying: 'My intention was merely to go on the pilgrimage in them, but nobody apart from the *wazîr* and some of my family consented to go on the pilgrimage.' They would not, however, believe him, and when he left them they sent two grabs in pursuit of him, but he fought them bravely till he and the ministers accompanying him were slain, all except the Khwaja Safar, for him they spared.[23]

The implication is that the conduct of politics and diplomacy amongst the 'Franks' was such that one could expect any degree of chicanery from them. From here, one can proceed to analyse the events leading up to the eventual Mughal conquest of Gujarat in 1573 in a relatively logical sequence. The two celebrated sieges of Diu (in 1538 and 1546) occupy a part of this intermediate space, and are also moments which produce considerable bodies of texts in Portuguese, with an implicit construct of the nature of Islamic Asian polities embedded in them. Some of these texts, such as Lopo de Sousa Coutinho's

[23] R. B. Serjeant, *The Portuguese off the South Arabian Coast: Hadrami Chronicles*, Oxford, 1963, pp. 75–6.

História do primeiro cerco de Diu or Leonardo Nunes's *Crónica de D. João de Castro* would repay closer study, as would the visual materials attached to some other texts, such as that of Jerónimo Corte-Real.[24]

I would argue that the image of a sort of Oriental Despotism *avant la lettre* was thus created and applied by these Portuguese observers to Indian Sultanates such as Gujarat, Bijapur, Ahmadnagar, and later the Mughals. Starting from the great Renaissance intellectual and chronicler João de Barros, it is necessary to look to the various voices that exist within the stream of Portuguese ethno-political discourse, namely writers of sprawling multi-volume works like Gaspar Correia and Diogo do Couto, and also relatively 'minor' voices such as António Pereira Pinto, and António Bocarro.[25] This tradition of writing continued and was developed in the seventeenth century by Dutch writers such as Johannes de Laet (*De Imperio Magni Mogolis*), Wollebrant Geleynssen de Jongh, and Francisco Pelsaert (*Kroniek en Remonstrantie*), but was brought to true fruition by the Venetian Niccolò Manuzzi in his huge five-part *Storia del Mogol*.[26] I shall focus here on a few of these figures, while rapidly surveying the corpus as a whole; the chronicler Diogo do Couto (1542–1616) would of course appear to be a particularly apposite central point for such an exercise.[27] Amongst the major political actors, it would be of interest to look in particular to one of Couto's major patrons, the viceroy of the *Estado da Índia*, D. Francisco da Gama (1565–1632), who has left behind a considerable corpus of letters and papers.[28]

The backdrop to the formulations that I shall survey comprises the unfolding of relations between Mughals, regional Sultanates, and Portuguese, Dutch, English, and French in the context of both the western Indian Ocean (Sind and

---

[24] Lopo de Sousa Coutinho, *História do primeiro cerco de Diu*, Lisbon, 1890; Leonardo Nunes, *Crónica de D. João de Castro*, ed. J. D. M. Ford, Cambridge [Mass.], 1936; Jerónimo Corte-Real, *Sucesso do Segundo Cerco de Diu*, ed. Martim de Albuquerque, Lisbon, 1991.

[25] For an analysis of some of these authors and their observations of one object, a temple complex in southern India, see Sanjay Subrahmanyam, 'An Eastern *El-Dorado*: The Tirumala-Tirupati Temple-Complex in Early European Views and Ambitions, 1540–1660', in David Shulman, ed., *Syllables of Sky: Studies in South Indian Civilization in Honour of Velcheru Narayana Rao*, Delhi, 1995, pp. 338–90.

[26] Willem Caland, ed., *De Remonstrantie van W. Geleynssen de Jongh*, The Hague, 1929; D. H. A. Kolff and H. W. van Santen, eds, *De Geschriften van Francisco Pelsaert over Mughal Indië, 1627: Kroniek en Remonstrantie*, The Hague, 1979. Neither of these texts were published in the seventeenth century, but in contrast see Joannes de Laet, *De Imperio Magni Mogolis, sive India vera, Commentarius ex variis auctoribus congestus*, Leiden: Elzevirs, 1631.

[27] Cf. António Coimbra Martins, *Em torno de Diogo do Couto*, Coimbra, 1985.

[28] For further details, see Chapters 3 and 4.

Gujarat), and the Bay of Bengal. It is, of course, necessary to contextualize these political and commercial relationships by looking at other autonomous cultural processes of importance, notably the Persianization of polities in the Indian subcontinent, and the creation of defensive ('mercantilist') mechanisms through which cross-cultural trading contacts were mediated. At the same time, it would ideally be necessary to explore the obverse of the coin set out above, namely the image of Europeans (and especially Iberians) in the Indo-Persian literature of the sixteenth and seventeenth centuries. Can the hierarchization of cultures that was part and parcel of the process of Persianization, be compared with the ethno-political discourse that is available to us in the European materials?[29] In what measure are we dealing with an asymmetrical relationship? These too are questions that are explored in the chapters that follow.

One possible 'laboratory' where many of these themes come together is the difficult, indeed tormented, relationship between the Europeans and the Mughal polity under Akbar (r. 1556–1605) and his successors. Whereas, usually, attention focuses on the Jesuit understanding of Akbar (as exemplified by figures such as António Monserrate and Jerónimo Xavier), one could as easily turn the spotlight, with archival materials, on to the 'secular' and political relationship, as well as on to the European construction of the distant Mughal past, particularly in the chronicles of Diogo do Couto and Niccolò Manuzzi. Thus, the consequences of Mughal expansion in the Deccan in the last two decades of the sixteenth century had a crucial impact on their relationship with the Portuguese; indeed, Portuguese archival documents should be counterposed to both the major Indo-Persian chronicles (Abu'l Fazl's *Akbar Nâma*, Badayuni's *Muntakhab al-Tawârîkh*, Ferishta's *Gulshan-i Ibrâhîmî*), and lesser-known texts of the period such as the reports from the Deccan in the early 1590s of Shaikh Faizi, in his letters to Akbar.

In sum, I wish to argue that the history of 'events' should not be neglected in the larger exercise of the history of 'mentalities', and one of the methodological points I will seek to make is that structural tensions and forms of perception can only be read out of the fine grain of events. At the same time, this work carries with it an implicit comparativist agenda. Over the years, a major and somewhat puzzling gap has arisen between studies of early modern Asia and the New World. Whereas writers on Latin America have skilfully shown how the political discourse of the Spaniards in the New World, and their ethnographic construction of pre-colonial and colonial societies there, were intimately intertwined,

[29] For a first approach to these problems, see Muzaffar Alam and Sanjay Subrahmanyam, 'From an Ocean of Wonders: Mahmûd bin Amîr Walî Balkhî and his Indian travels, 1625–31', in Claudine Salmon, ed., *Récits de voyage des Asiatiques: Genres, mentalités, conception de l'espace*, Paris, 1996, pp. 161–89.

historians of Asia have (with very few exceptions) failed to explicate the link between the idea of politics and the practice of ethnography in the sixteenth and seventeenth centuries.[30] It is only in the late eighteenth century, with the creation of the British empire in India, that these connections begin to coalesce in the views of most scholars. The formulations that have emerged to date are therefore heavily influenced by the agenda and methodology set out via Edward Said's powerful but tendentious statement in *Orientalism*, even in the case of those who seek to qualify or refute it, such as Teltscher and Lowe. No doubt the comparison between South Asia and Spanish America has its limits, notably because powerful independent political and cultural structures persisted long after the sixteenth century in the former case, unlike in the latter. This is precisely why we need to counterbalance the European materials on south Asia not with *La Vision des Vaincus* ('the vision of the vanquished', as Nathan Wachtel's classic work of a quarter-century ago put it), but with a rather more complex and, frequently, self-confident perspective.

My purpose here is thus at one and the same time to suggest in very preliminary outline a 'prehistory' of institutionalized Orientalism, contribute to the debate on the beginnings of notions of Oriental Despotism as applied to India, and link this to the emerging conception of *Realpolitik*, both as conceived and theorized in Europe and as practised in Asia. While my primary materials will remain textual, the discussion of visual materials ought not to be wholly neglected either. Portuguese were often portrayed in Mughal miniatures, and also appear in the major Mughal chronicles as the quintessential 'hat-wearers' (*kulah-poshân*). Equally, many of the European texts of the epoch contain elaborate illustrations, and several free-standing pictorial representations also exist, depicting the south Asian scene for a European audience.

In this context, a crucial place should be accorded to a particular, and rather neglected work, that of the Venetian Niccolò Manuzzi (1638–1717), who wrote the voluminous text called *Storia del Mogol*, and who is conventionally used by Indian historians as one of the major 'sources' for the history of the later Mughal empire.[31] Leaving Venice in November 1651, and passing through Ragusa,

[30] Cf. Serge Gruzinski, *La colonisation de l'imaginaire: Sociétés indigènes et occidentalisation dans le Mexique espagnol, XVIe–XVIIIe siècle*, Paris, 1988; Anthony Pagden, *European Encounters with the New World: From Renaissance to Romanticism*, London, 1993.

[31] Niccolao Manucci [Niccolò Manuzzi], *Mogul India, or Storia do Mogor*, tr. William Irvine, 4 Vols, London, 1907–8 (reprint, Delhi: Low Price Publications, 1990). Unfortunately, the full original text of Manuzzi has never been published, only the earlier sections thereof. For these sections (which do not include Vols III and IV of the translation), see Piero Falchetta, ed., *Storia del Mogol di Nicolò Manuzzi veneziano*, 2 Vols, Milan, 1986.

Smyrna, Erzurum, Tabriz, and a number of other centres in the Middle East, Manuzzi arrived in the western Indian port of Surat in January 1654. In the early part of his Indian sojourn, he was in the service of the Mughal prince Dara Shikoh, the older brother and unsuccessful rival of Aurangzeb. After Dara's violent death, Manuzzi spent a long period of nearly a quarter-century in search of stable patronage and employment. One of his patrons at this time was the Mughal prince Shah 'Alam, by whom he was employed as a physician, despite his rather meagre training in this sphere. The last three decades of his life from 1686 onwards were then spent in southern India, in the English territory of Madras, and the French possession of Pondicherry.

Manuzzi wrote his text, as he informs us, 'for the benefit of voyagers, merchants and missionaries' (*per benefisio dy caminanty, mercanty y mission-ary*), and justifies it in the following fashion. 'Though other authors (...) have produced some accounts of the empire of the Mugole, but as it is known that they were not well informed, and besides did not have the necessary time to know the greatness, riches, dominion, power, politics and the rest—as can be seen in my account which I have sent and continue to send—all these reasons have obliged me to send this curiosity [work] of mine to France'. The implicit critique is above all of the influential French traveller and writer François Bernier. Yet, paradoxically, a first, and rather distorted, version of some parts of the work was published in French by the Jesuit François Catrou as early as 1705, and it is only recently that the first volumes of Manuzzi's original text have been edited and published by Piero Falchetta, with the very valuable illustrations that Manuzzi commissioned, some of them rather poorly executed but interesting copies of Mughal miniatures, others strikingly original examples of 'ethnographic' representation, probably painted by Indian artists in the Madras region.

An analysis of Manuzzi's approach to politics, religion, and the 'indigenous' perceptions of these and other questions, his gratuitous use of Persian citations to prove his authentic knowledge of the country (in which he reminds us of a downmarket version of the earlier Italian traveller, Pietro della Valle), and his marginal position both with respect to the Mughals and the European commercial empires that were being established at the time, all merit a full-scale study.[32] Perhaps some hints of what such a study might entail could be given here, by suggesting that Manuzzi's is very much a hybrid text, a product of a multiple series of *métissages*, across European cultures, between Indian and European

[32] On Della Valle, see for example John D. Gurney, 'Pietro Della Valle: The Limits of Perception', *Bulletin of the School of Oriental and African Studies*, Vol. XLIX, 1, 1986, pp. 103–16; also Ettore Rossi, 'Versi turchi e altri scritti inediti di Pietro della Valle', *Rivista degli Studi Orientali*, Vol. XXII, 1947, pp. 92–8.

elements, and between Persian and vernacular textual and representational traditions. Little wonder that even historians of art have been hard put to know whether to classify many of the paintings that accompany his volumes as 'Mughal', 'South Indian', or 'early Company' painting.

I would hence argue that Manuzzi is the counterpart, in some respects, of the westernized Indian gentleman of Persianized upbringing who authored xenological texts in the eighteenth century, the period when the first Indo-Persian travel-accounts of Europe begin to make an appearance. Even though these texts have received far greater attention than travel texts in Persian within Asia itself, partly because Indian 'xenologists' remain preoccupied with the problem of Indian identity as defined in an European looking-glass, much work still remains to be done with them.[33] As we know, British writers of the early colonial period themselves were particularly interested in how they and their civilization were viewed by Indians, a fact that must explain the early notoriety enjoyed by, say, Mirza Abu Talib Khan Isfahani's *Masîr-i Tâlibî fi bilâd-i afranjî* ('Talib's travels in the land of the Franks'), translated into English by Charles Stewart in 1810.[34] The writer, who travelled between 1799 and 1803, provided a view that was not always flattering to the English, but congenial enough all in all, in that it contrasted Albion's vigour to Indian decadence. Also quite well-known is Mirza Shaikh I'tisam al-Din, *Shigraf-nâma-i wilâyat* ('Wonder Book of England'), written in 1785, but recounting its author's travels two decades earlier, in the months from January 1766 to October–November 1769.[35] In this case, interestingly, the Persian text was never published, but Urdu and English translations enjoyed fairly wide circulation. Still more recently, Simon Digby has drawn our attention to an unpublished manuscript in his possession, namely Munshi Isma'il's *Târîkh-i jadîd* (or 'New History'), for its part relating the author's voyage to England in the early 1770s.[36] From the same decade, Digby also notes

---

[33] Cf. Tapan Raychaudhuri, 'Europe in India's Xenology: The Nineteenth-Century Record', *Past and Present*, No. 137, 1992, pp. 156–82.

[34] Mirza Abu Talib Khan Isfahani, *Masîr-i Tâlibî fi bilâd-i afranjî*, eds, Mirza Husain 'Ali and Mir Qudrat 'Ali, Calcutta, 1812; also Charles Stewart, tr., *The Travels of Mirza Abu Talib Khan in Asia, Africa and Europe during the Years 1799–1803*, 2 Vols, London, 1810.

[35] J. E. Alexander, *Shigurf namah-i-velaët: Or excellent intelligence concerning Europe; being the travels of Mirza Itesa Modeen, translated from the original Persian manuscripts into Hindostanee, with an English version and notes*, London, 1827; for a more recent translation from Persian into English (via Bengali), see Mirza Sheikh I'tesamuddin, *The Wonders of Vilayet: being the Memoir, originally in Persian, of a visit to France and Britain in 1765*, tr., Kaiser Haq, Leeds, 2001.

[36] Munshi Isma'il, *Târîkh-i jadîd*, Mss, Simon Digby Collection (completed November 1773); for a discussion, see Simon Digby, 'An eighteenth century narrative of

the existence of another Indo-Persian text (equally unpublished), namely Mir Muhammad Husain bin 'Abd al-Husaini's *Risâla-i ahwâl-i mulk-i Firang-o-Hindustân*, which recounts travels to Lisbon and London from Calcutta, in around 1774.

The bulk of these accounts was written by writers who accompanied Englishmen back to their native land, in some capacity or the other, as *munshîs*, as envoys, but also (as with Abu Talib) as gentlemen of leisure. One may imagine that the production of these texts would in part have been indirectly encouraged by the British, since they served to stress the 'wonders' of *Wilâyat*, and the superiority of western technology, even if they equally contained disparaging remarks on food, manners, social functioning, or even climate. However, the texts must be separated from other accounts, also written by Indians in the late eighteenth and early nineteenth centuries, as forms of political or economic intelligence for the British. Here, the purpose was far more pressing and functional, and the texts may themselves follow the form set out by an implicit questionnaire, that forces their authors willy-nilly to observe certain matters, as required by the colonial information-gathering machinery. Within this category fall a good number of texts concerning the trade routes linking northern India to Central Asia, both the westerly salient to Afghanistan, and Iran, and the easterly one, headed towards Yarkand; there are also accounts of trade routes within northern India itself, that parallel the travel accounts of colonial writers such as Francis Buchanan.[37] From such accounts derive the first attempts by the Company at mapping out the economic geography of South Asia, as also the major and minor centres from which military resistance could be anticipated. Paradoxically, these texts, the product of the exigencies of early colonial rule, wind up resembling—in a formal sense, at least—certain Chinese gazetteer-

---

a journey from Bengal to England: Munshi Ismâ'îl's *New History*', in Christopher Shackle, ed., *Urdu and Muslim South Asia: Studies in Honour of Ralph Russell*, Delhi, 1991, pp. 49–65.

[37] Cf. by way of example, P. D. Henderson, trans., *Travels in Central Asia by Meer Izzut Oollah, 1812–1813*, Calcutta, 1872; Mohan Lal, *Journal of a Tour through the Panjab, Afghanistan, Turkistan, Khorasan and Part of Persia, in Company with Lieut. Burnes and Dr Gerard*, Calcutta, 1834; Ahmad Shah Naqshbandi, 'Narrative of the Travels of Khwajah Ahmud Shah Nukshbundee Syud', *Journal of the Asiatic Society of Bengal*, Vol. XXV, 4, 1856; and *Idem.*, 'Route from Kashmir, via Ladakh to Yarkand by Ahmad Shah Nakshahbandi', *Journal of the Royal Asiatic Society of Great Britain and Ireland*, Vol. XII, 1850. For a recent discussion, also see Maria Szuppe, 'En quête de chevaux turkmènes: Le journal de voyage de Mîr 'Izzatullâh de Delhi à Boukhara en 1812–13', in *Inde—Asie Centrale. Routes du commerce et des idées*, Cahiers d'Asie Centrale Nos 1–2, 1996, pp. 91–111.

style travel accounts, written by official literati in the Ch'ing period and even earlier.[38]

To conclude this brief introductory text then, I have attempted to argue that a number of interpretational strategies are available to us today, that allow us on the one hand to avoid the pitfalls of the 'diagonal' reading techniques that I have lightly caricatured at the outset, without necessarily falling into the trap of the type of textual analysis that focuses exclusively on the author rather than his ostensible object. Some of these remarks no doubt run the risk of sounding pedestrian to at least some of my readers, who probably implicitly already practise what I have set out self-indulgently to preach. Equally, some of the materials that will be dealt with in the chapters that follow may seem all-too-familiar to historians of the Mughal empire or of the European presence in late pre-colonial India. If this is the case, an effort has also been made to mix a reading of published texts with archival materials, and to draw upon sources of as diverse a provenance as possible. The pages that follow are not written in ignorance of the analyses of such materials made by literary scholars, whether of the Iberian world or that of Tudor and Stuart England. But they deliberately choose a different angle of attack, one that is better suited to the skills and predilections of the archivally-oriented historian. For the history of European interactions with early modern south Asia is hardly exhausted by looking to Camões, Shakespeare, or Dryden; on the contrary, one may be far better off looking to Abu'l Fazl , Khafi Khan, Diogo do Couto, or Francisco Pelsaert, to gain a sense of what was really at stake when Mughals and Franks confronted each other over several centuries.

---

[38] Cf. for instance Claudine Salmon, 'Wang Dahai et sa vision des 'Contrées insulaires' (1791)', *Études chinoises*, Vol. XIII, Nos 1–2, 1994, pp. 221–57.

2

The Trading World of the Western Indian Ocean, 1546–65: A Political Interpretation

What I affirm to Your Highness is that I shall put such a curb on those of the Strait of Mequa, and of Ormuz and Balaguate, and thus on any other parts to which they [the spices] go, and I shall impose such order on their sale, that each year both in these and those parts, their price shall go on expanding, as will the treasury of Your Highness. The grandeur that the city of Goa hopes to attain with this *Casa de Drogas*, and the expansion of its customs, one may believe, will be such that it shall cause great envy in the powers that are Venice and Turkey.

Governor Francisco Barreto to D. João III (1557)[1]

Introduction

In late May 1546, as the monsoon drew near, and the affairs in Diu too were beginning to attain a certain elevated temperature (a month-and-a-half after the arrival there of a besieging force under Khwaja Safar al-Salmani Khudawand Khan), the isolated and rather frightened Portuguese factor in the Konkan port of Dabhol, a certain Francisco Brito Chanoca, wrote to the governor's son D. Álvaro de Castro, with a report of the political situation in the Deccan and Gujarat. This brief letter, mentioned by Georg Schurhammer S. J. in his well-known *Quellen* (Q 2219), provides an interesting panorama of the situation at the time of the second siege of Diu.[2] The letter's main purpose is to complain of oppressions on the part of the local *tanadar* (Governor), appointed by Ibrahim

---

[1] Arquivos Nacionais/Torre do Tombo (hereafter AN/TT), Lisbon, Corpo Cronológico (henceforth CC), I-100-74, letter from Francisco Barreto at Bassein to D. João III, 11 January 1557.

[2] Georg Schurhammer, *Die zeitgenössischen Quellen zur Geschichte Portugiesisch-Asiens und seiner Nachbarländer zur Zeit des Hl. Franz Xaver (1538–1552)*, reprint, Rome, 1962.

'Adil Shah I of Bijapur (r. 1535–58), and to ask the governor either to write to the Bijapur ruler and demand redress, or to withdraw the Portuguese factory altogether. But mention is also made in some detail of the situation in the Gujarati port of Surat, which was to emerge within decades as *the* major centre of trade from Mughal India to the Red Sea and Persian Gulf. Chanoca had a trusty informant in a Malay Christian (*hum Jao cassado*), who had returned to Dabhol after a two-month-long absence in Surat. This Malay, for his part, had friends in the garrison of Surat, particularly amongst the artillerymen; they had reported to him that there were 30 Portuguese being held prisoner there, while the none-too-substantial garrison numbered some 200, including 40 Rumis, and 30 Malays (mostly in the artillery). The captain of the fort was a Rumi, he reported, and the local tanadar an Abyssinian. The fortress was undermanned, with only four foists to guard it, since all the other Rumis had gone to Diu, in view of the impending hostilities there.

Chanoca saw his role not only as providing strategic information on Surat, but also to link this up with the politics of the Deccan. The same Malay, he reported, had returned to Dabhol overland, via Daman, where he had found the Gujarat notable Burhan al-Mulk Bambani (*ho Bramaluco*), who was notionally considered to pose a threat to the Portuguese possessions at Bassein. However, he was assured by men in Burhan al-Mulk's pay that until the monsoon had passed, no real threat was to be apprehended on that front. The panoramic view now passes therefore to commercial matters.

This *Jao* says that when he arrived in Çurate, which was in the beginning of April, two large ships (*naos*) of 1200 *candys* each, belonging to a merchant called Melyque Mamenad, left Reinell [Rander] laden with goods for Dachem [Aceh], where they were going to lade on pepper, in order to go from there on the route to Meca, and from there to return to Curate, where this April there also arrived two very rich ships from Tanaçarym; one of them was of Coja Çofar, and the other of this same Melyque Mamenade.

The letter equally reports the departure that year from Cambay of many large and richly laden ships to the 'Straits of Meca', which would return from there in about early August. It then goes on to mention the despatch by Ibrahim 'Adil Shah of military contingents to different parts of the Deccan (to aid the Barid Shahis and to Sholapur), as well as rumours that the 'Adil Shah himself would soon march against Jamshid Qutb Shah of Golkonda.[3]

A second letter, from the same Chanoca (Schurhammer, *Quellen*, Q 2511), but dated some six months later, on 21 November 1546, continues to insist on the fear and despair in which he lives, and to request that the factory be wound up as quickly as possible. The news of the Portuguese victory (*a vytorya grande do Senhor Governador*) at Diu provides him with some consolation though, and

---

[3] AN/TT, Casa Forte No. 38, fls 41–42v.

he assures D. Álvaro de Castro that the 'Adil Shah and the other rulers of the Deccan have been greatly affected and impressed by these tidings, which they had initially found almost impossible to believe.[4]

Men like Chanoca (or for that matter the chroniclers Leonardo Nunes or Diogo do Couto) understood a rather simple fact that has escaped many later historians: to comprehend the problems of trade and élite politics that are so often the concern of historians of Portuguese Asia, the local level in the western Indian Ocean finds meaning only iteratively, in relation to a set of concentric circles, or larger wholes.[5] The trading politics of Dabhol had to be tied up on the one hand to 'Adil Shahi political concerns in the Deccan (that which led Sultan Ibrahim to make 'unreasonable' demands on the Portuguese factor, for supplies of coir and sulphur), and on the other to affairs in Gujarat and beyond. Reading these letters, we enter directly into some of the key questions of the day, for example:

• Gujarati mediation between Aceh and the Red Sea, and the pepper trade

• The growing role of the Surat–Rander complex, in comparison to the older prestigious centres of Diu and Cambay

• The complex part paid by mercenaries and imported military elites—Rumis, Abyssinians, even Malays—in the Sultanates of western India in the mid-sixteenth century

Now, the middle years of the sixteenth century, years of 'crisis' for the *Estado da Índia*, remain obscure from a number of different points of view.[6] Exhaustion sets in among nationalist Portuguese historians once they are done with the second siege of Diu, to which they continue to refer with pride as 'one of the most important feats of arms of the Portuguese in the sixteenth century'.[7] However, we are aware that between 1546 and 1560, a number of rather significant processes took root in respect of Portuguese Asia. The Society of Jesus established itself as an important force; the Counter-Reformation and, concomitantly, the Inquisition reached out to define a new set of relations between Christianity and the other religions, whether Judaism, Islam, or 'Hinduism', in Asia; the

[4] AN/TT, Casa Forte No. 38, fls 43–44v.

[5] Cf. Leonardo Nunes, *Crónica de D. João de Castro*, ed. J. D. M. Ford, Cambridge [Mass.], 1936, for a valuable account, with materials relating to the second siege of Diu, and relations between the Portuguese and disgruntled Afghan notables from the Gujarat court.

[6] For an overview of these questions, see Sanjay Subrahmanyam, *The Portuguese Empire in Asia, 1500–1700: A Political and Economic History*, London, 1993.

[7] José Manuel Garcia and Maria João Quintans, 'O segundo cerco de Diu visto por D. João Mascarenhas: Uma carta e o seu contexto historiográfico', *Mare Liberum*, No. 5, 1993, p. 139.

Portuguese established at first tenuous footholds in civil-war-torn Japan, and then gradually developed a set of regular trading relationships with the Far East. These are significant years, then, hardly deserving of the contempt reserved for them by traditional historians, who saw the end of the halcyon days of the *Estado* already in these decades, and looked out for telltale signs of the beginnings of *decadência*, little realizing that the same complaints, the same *murmuração* (back-biting) could equally be found as early as 1515 or 1520.[8]

From the point of a larger space such as the western Indian Ocean, however, the significance of the mid-century processes briefly set out above is not altogether clear. True, the Jesuits came to be a force in Cochin, Goa, and the *Província do Norte*; equally true, precious metals began to trickle in from the Far East; but the logic of change seems to have lain elsewhere. In this chapter, I propose a primarily political reading of events in this maritime space, arguing that between the successful second defence of Diu by the Portuguese in 1546, and the definitive taking of Daman by them late in the following decade, one of the keys to understanding changes is the slow collapse of the earlier structure of the Gujarat Sultanate, and the failure of the Ottomans to fulfil the expansionist promise that had seemed theirs for the taking in about 1530. In other words, the middle decades of the century are a period of a curious 'vacuum' in the politico-economic history of maritime Gujarat, which is eventually resolved by Mughal consolidation in the early 1570s.

This is not without significance for another grand theme that has preoccupied historians, namely the relationship between the 'old' and the 'new' routes linking Europe and Asia in the sixteenth century and thereafter: in other words, the trade from India and beyond to the Red Sea and the Persian Gulf, on the one hand, and the trade of the *Carreira da Índia*, on the other. I shall argue that a regional perspective, taking the western Indian Ocean as the logical unit of analysis, helps us to defuse a certain set of false problematics that have for long dogged the literature. For, with the arrival of the second Portuguese fleet in the western Indian Ocean in 1500, a problem was invented: that of the rivalry between the Red Sea route and that of the Cape of Good Hope (or the *Carreira da Índia*). This rivalry or competition has been much misunderstood. Modern writers have usually seen it as quintessentially economic in character, that is, of which of the two routes would supply the European market with Asian pepper and spices. From this has flowed a second proposition, even more misconceived than the first: the notion that of the two routes, only one—the more 'efficient'—

---

[8] 'E portamto, senhor, nam m'espanto aver muitos juyzos e dizeres que a Índia era já perdida, porque a estes taes nam lhe minguariam Rezões afiguradas pera isso poder ser...'; letter from Afonso de Albuquerque to Duarte Galvão (1514), in R. A. de Bulhão Pato, ed., *Cartas de Afonso de Albuquerque*, Tomo I, Lisbon, 1884, p. 395.

could survive. Nothing could be further from the truth. The Portuguese attempts at blockading the Cape route were essentially political in character, aimed at undermining a part of the fiscal resources of first the Mamluks and then the Ottomans, their geo-political rivals; it was believed, but only secondarily, in some circles that by so doing, the procurement price of pepper in Kerala would drop for the Portuguese. As the history of the Red Sea trade shows us as late as the eighteenth century, the two commercial routes could perfectly well coexist, once this political problem had been defused and transformed by a larger set of circumstances. The Cape Route by, say, 1700, supplied western Europe with Asian goods, while the Red Sea (and the Persian Gulf) did the same for west Asia, north Africa, a part of eastern Europe, and Russia. This made perfect sense geographically: for who would dream of supplying the demand for Asian pepper or textiles in the Ottoman domains by first carrying these goods to Amsterdam, Lisbon, or London?[9]

Our historiography carries the heavy burden of a narrative, developed by Frederic Lane, Vitorino Magalhães Godinho, Fernand Braudel, and Niels Steensgaard: of Portuguese domination over the pepper and spice markets of Europe from 1500 to 1530, of a recrudesence of rival routes after 1530, and a full-fledged challenge from 1570 spearheaded by the Acehnese and Gujaratis.[10] Underlying this narrative is a second one, of an initial Golden Age, giving way to *decadência* in Portuguese Asia. Hopefully, this will further the building of a more nuanced, and contingent history, to replace the once provocative, but now stultified, narrative summarized above, and in broad support of the quantitative reinterpretation suggested by C. H. H. Wake as early as 1979, but which is still studiously ignored by most of our colleagues.[11]

[9] For a sense of the 'survival' of the trade from the Red Sea to India into the eighteenth century, see Sanjay Subrahmanyam, 'Precious metal flows and prices in western and southern Asia, 1500–1750: Some comparative and conjunctural aspects', *Studies in History*, (N.S.), Vol. VII (1), 1991, pp. 79–105. Also see the useful account in Bruce Masters, *The Origins of Western Economic Dominance in the Middle East: Mercantilism and the Islamic Economy in Aleppo, 1600–1750*, New York, 1988.

[10] The central text is Frederic C. Lane, 'The Mediterranean spice trade: Its revival in the sixteenth century', in Lane, *Venice and History*, Baltimore, 1966; but also see Vitorino Magalhães Godinho, 'O Levante e a Rota do Cabo', in Godinho, *Mito e mercadoria, utopia e prática de navegar, séculos XIII–XVIII*, Lisbon, 1990, pp. 411–26, where we find the claim that between 1554 and 1565, between 20,000 and 40,000 quintais of pepper reached the Mediterranean via the Red Sea and Persian Gulf *every year*.

[11] C. H. H. Wake, 'The changing pattern of Europe's pepper and spice imports, ca. 1400–1700', *The Journal of European Economic History*, Vol. VIII (2), 1979, pp. 361–403. This is not to deny that many of Wake's conclusions are tentative, requiring further archival research.

The Rise of Surat

In the early sixteenth century, of the numerous ports that dotted the Gujarat coastline, most historians are agreed that the dominant centres were Khambayat (Cambay) and Diu. The latter, and its enveloping region of Sorath, were dominated by the figure of Malik Ayaz, whose career has been studied with some care by Jean Aubin; the former port, on the other hand, appears to have been the privileged area of interest of the Brahmin trader-administrator Gopinath (or Malik Gopi), who though a native of Surat, seems to have centred his trade largely on Cambay.[12] The port of Surat itself, though inevitably mentioned by writers like Tomé Pires and Duarte Barbosa, was in these years overshadowed by its twin, Rander, on the other bank of the river Tapti, and a city distinguished by its considerable community of Navayat Muslims, who were prized in the western Indian Ocean as pilots and navigators. Rander appears to have benefitted in the late fifteenth and early sixteenth centuries from the gradual decline of Cambay, in evidence in these years on account of silting of the Gulf of Cambay; but these benefits were shared with Diu, whose aggressive commercial expansion was piloted by Malik Ayaz. Once the Portuguese were ceded the right to construct a fortress in Diu in 1535, by the harried Sultan Bahadur Shah Gujarati, it was inevitable that the commercial activities of Asian traders would seek other outlets in Gujarat. The figure of Khwaja Safar al-Salmani, who had arrived in India in the late 1520s as part of the abortive expedition of the sometime Ottoman auxiliary Salman Re'is, thus emerged into prominence in order to build up Surat into an alternative to Diu (by now in Portuguese hands), and to Cambay (whose viability was seriously in question).

The role played in this decision to shore up Surat by the court of the Sultan of Gujarat, Mahmud Shah (r. 1537–54), is unclear, as is the situation in the court itself. In the early years of Mahmud Shah's reign (and during his minority), it would seem that the court was dominated by the figures of Darya Khan and 'Alam Khan Lodi, neither of whom was quite indifferent to maritime affairs. However, historians of Gujarat, such as M. N. Pearson have suggested from a reading of contemporary documents that the fortification of Surat from about 1539 was the decision of Khwaja Safar alone, in pursuit of his own politico-mercantile ambitions.[13] It is likely in any event that this decision was taken after the failed Gujarati–Ottoman siege of Diu in 1538, when Hadim Süleyman Pasha's Ottoman fleet returned to the Red Sea with little or nothing achieved

[12] Cf. Jean Aubin, 'Albuquerque et les négociations de Cambaye', *Mare Luso-Indicum* t. 1, 1971, pp. 3–63, especially pp. 5–12.

[13] Michael N. Pearson, *Merchants and Rulers in Gujarat: The response to the Portuguese in the sixteenth century*, Berkeley, 1976.

in India. The Indo-Persian chronicles insist that the defence of the fortress of Surat was assured in large measure by cannon taken from the fleet of the Pasha, and that the construction of the fortress was a personal achievement of Khudawand Khan (the title of Khwaja Safar). Thus, writes 'Abd al-Qadir al-Badayuni, in the late sixteenth century:

They say that the reason for Khudawand Khan's building this fort was, that the Portuguese used to exercise all kinds of animosity and hostility against the people of Islam, and used to occupy themselves in devastating the country, and tormenting the pious. At the time of the commencement of the building, they ceased not to throw the builders into confusion, firing continually at them from their ships but they could not prevent them (...). On the bastions which overlooked the sea they made a gallery, which in the opinion of the Europeans is a speciality of Portugal and an invention of their own. The Europeans were very much opposed to the building of that *chaukandi*, and endeavoured to prevent it by force of arms. But at last they resorted to peaceful measures, and agreed to pay a round sum of money, if they would leave off building that *chaukandi*. But Khudawand Khan, through his love and zeal for Islam gave the reins to his high spirit, and would not consent, and in spite of the Christians soon carried out his purpose of completing that building.[14]

The building of this fortress, one of the few major maritime redoubts on the Indian west coast in the sixteenth century that was not in Portuguese hands, has perhaps not received the attention it deserves. However, the fact remains that even after the death of Khwaja Safar, in the course of the second siege of Diu, Surat continued to grow and to resist Portuguese control. Control of the port, and its fortress, passed after 1546 to Khwaja Safar's successor in the title of Khudawand Khan Rumi, and then in the late 1550s was seized by Chengiz Khan (son of the notable 'Imad al-Mulk Aslan al-Turki), after killing Khudawand Khan. In turn, after Chengiz Khan's violent death in 1567, the fortress was taken over by the Timurid Mirzas (the Central Asian cousins of the Mughal dynasty, who played a destabilizing role in the politics of the period), before being besieged and captured eventually by Akbar, as part of his Gujarat campaign in 1573. In this entire time, we must not lose sight of the fact that Surat continued to grow and prosper. The Mughals may have contributed to its effloresence after the 1570s, by linking Surat directly to the rich hinterland of the Gangetic *doâb*, but there is a sense in which they seized hold of a port that was already in a formidable position in relation to its rivals. Thus, it is useful to distinguish three phases: a *first*, when Rander and to a lesser extent Surat benefited from the slow decline of Cambay in the late fifteenth century; a *second*, and crucial one, when

---

[14] 'Abd al-Qadir al-Badayuni, *Muntakhab al-Tawârîkh*, Vol. II, tr. G. S. A. Ranking, reprint, New Delhi, 1990, pp. 149–50. Compare Abu'l Fazl, *Akbar Nâma*, Vol. III, tr. H. Beveridge, reprint, Delhi, 1989, pp. 39–41.

Surat came to be fortified and emerged as the major alternative to not only Cambay but also to Diu, which after 1546 was definitively seen as in Portuguese hands; and a *third*, relatively well-known phase, that commences after the Mughal conquest.

To have a sense of where matters stood by the end of the second phase, the following description from Couto's *Década Oitava* may be helpful. In 1568, he notes, the viceroy D. Antão de Noronha sent D. Luís de Almeida with six ships to Daman, 'to go in August to Surrate, to prevent the ships that leave there for Achém without *cartazes*, and those which were to come back from Meca to that river, which always return laden with silver and rich goods'. The fleet is reported to have sighted one large ship (*huma fermosa nao*), which managed to evade them and to unload its goods in haste, and two others from Jiddah, whose booty is said very easily to have exceeded 100,000 *cruzados*, 'besides another equal sum that was robbed', presumably by the Portuguese soldiers and captains involved in the action.[15] In brief, *before* its capture by the Mughals, Surat had already emerged into a position of major importance for the maritime trade of Gujarat, a role in which it was aided by the politico-commercial activities of Khwaja Safar and his successors, Khudawand Khan (the second), 'Imad al-mulk, and Chengiz Khan.

The Ottoman 'Threat'

The middle decades of the sixteenth century are a particularly interesting and neglected phase in the history of western India. The Gujarat Sultanate, regarded up until the 1520s as a true rival to Delhi for the general domination of the Indo-Gangetic heartland, found itself struggling for survival by the early 1540s. However, the *coup de grâce* could not be delivered by the Afghans who controlled northern India in the 1540s and early 1550s, allowing a political situation of a curious and remarkable fluidity to come into existence. Elite political factions came to develop partly on ethnic lines, but partly on even more narrow bases. In this, a major role was played by the 'Rumis' who had arrived in Gujarat in successive waves: some descendants (or survivors) from the time of Mahmud Begadh, others (a prominent group) who had accompanied Salman Re'is and Mustafa Bairam, and still others from the late 1530s and early 1540s.[16]

---

[15] Maria Augusta Lima Cruz, *Diogo do Couto e a Década 8ª da Ásia*, 2 Vols, Lisbon, 1993–4, Vol. I, pp. 365–8.

[16] An important source for these years is the anonymous Portuguese chronicle, often attributed to Diogo de Mesquita, but for which no satisfactory edition exists; AN/TT, Colecção São Vicente, Vol. XI, pp. 91–111, 'Capítulo das cousas que passarão no Reyno de Guzarate depois da morte de Sultão Modafar'. Extant editions are by Ethel Pope, *Boletim do Instituto Vasco da Gama*, Vols 21 and 24, 1934, and by Francisco A.

All in all, these 'Rumis' formed a part of the group of west Asian migrants whom the Portuguese were wont to call *estrangeiros*, borrowing on the local notion of *âfâqî*.

The élite struggles that beset the Gujarat Sultanate in these years are well reflected in the fates of the Sultans themselves. After the (natural) death of Sultan Muzaffar Shah in 1526, his son Bahadur succeeded only after a long struggle that pitted him against his brothers, of whom one, Sikandar Shah, even briefly sat the throne; and, as is well-known, Bahadur himself came to a violent, if watery, end in February 1537 (producing the well-known witticism and chronogram: *Sultân al-bar shahîd al-bahr*, 'Sultan ashore, Martyr at sea'). Bahadur's successor, Mahmud Shah, ascending the throne at the age of 11 years in 1537, died some 17 years later, also assassinated, by a certain Burhan. In turn, his brother Ahmad Shah, who succeeded him in 1554, was equally assassinated some seven years later, by the notable I'timad Khan: Muzaffar Shah, who came to the throne after him, was defeated by the Mughals in 1573, and led a vain rearguard action culminating in his own suicide in the early 1590s. Behind this increasingly sanguinary action that occupies centrestage are a set of formidable notables, jockeying for power backstage, 'Imad al-Mulk and I'timad Khan, then 'Imad al-mulk's son Chengiz Khan, still later the Fuladi Afghans and Timurid Mirzas.

But there was also a rather complex external context to be considered. By the late fifteenth century and the reign of Mahmud Begadh, it is clear that the Sultans of Gujarat did not recognize the superiority of the Delhi Sultans; in point of fact, the elder brother and rival of Sikandar Shah Lodi was given refuge in Gujarat by them, in the expectation of better days to come for him. At the same time, there are hints that the Gujarat Sultans recognized, at least ritually, the superiority of the Mamluks and the Caliphs, resident in Cairo, over themselves. Thus, in December 1512, there arrived in Cairo an ambassador of Muzaffar Shah (who had just succeeded in Gujarat), requesting a confirmation of investiture from the Caliph.[17] It is my impression that after the seizure of Egypt and Syria by the Ottomans, this notional relationship of subordination was transferred to the latter. This places in a mildly different light the negotiations between Bahadur Shah and the Ottoman Pasha of Egypt in the mid-1530s, in which the former sent the latter a substantial 'gift' to solicit Ottoman intervention in Gujarat against the Portuguese.

Mendonça, S. J., *Chrónica Geral dos Sucessos do Reyno de Gusarate a Qm. Chamão Cambaya: General Chronicle of the events in the Kingdom of Gujarat which is called Cambay*, eds, S. C. Misra and K. S. Mathew, Baroda, 1981.

[17] Gaston Wiet, tr., *Journal d'un bourgeois du Caire, Chronique d'Ibn Iyâs*, Paris, 1955, Vol. I, pp. 268–9, entry for 30 Ramazan 918 AH.

How were these dealings between Champaner and the Sublime Porte in fact carried out? It seems very likely that the 'Rumi' notables in Gujarat would have had a role to play, both during the time of the two sieges of Diu and thereafter. A decent prosopography is not possible at this stage, but let us note that besides Khwaja Safar and Mustafa Bairam (alias Rumi Khan), we may also see a role of prominence being played for instance by Mustafa Qaramani, who held the title of 'Adil Khan under the rule of Sultan Ahmad Shah (r. 1554–61), and held partial control of the Broach region in that period. He belonged to the political faction led by 'Imad al-Mulk Arsalan al-Turki, the same who finds repeated mention in the Portuguese documents of the 1550s, as 'Madre Maluquo' (but who is not to be confused with members of the 'Imad Shahi dynasty of Berar). In 1559, when 'Imad al-Mulk was killed in the fortress of Surat by his brother-in-law Khudawand Khan Rumi (not to be confused with Khwaja Safar!), Mustafa Qaramani too died in the fracas.

Still another personage of importance, and also of 'Rumi' origin, was Qara Hasan (known as Jahangir Khan, during the reign of Sultan Mahmud [1537–54]), and a close associate of Khwaja Safar during the second siege of Diu. Unlike his patron, he survived the event, and was later the *wazîr* of Chengiz Khan (son of 'Imad al-Mulk), as well as an informant of Diogo do Couto on the court-politics of Gujarat.[18] These men, and others—survivors for example of the ill-fated expedition of Seyyidi 'Ali Re'is in the mid-1550s—probably represented the single most important nucleus of 'Rumi' penetration into the politics of the Indo-Islamic states in the sixteenth century. To be sure, a sprinkling of such Rumis could be found further south, in Ahmadnagar and Bijapur, but one gathers the impression that the latter states were primarily oriented towards an external relationship (equally not without certain elements of ritual subordination) with the Iran of Shah Tahmasp Safavi.[19]

The question nevertheless remains of the real extent of Ottoman interest in India affairs after about 1546. No doubt the Portuguese *Estado da Índia* periodically apprehended a direct threat, both at the time of Sultan Süleyman and that of his immediate successors; equally, it was believed that the powerful 'Jewish lobby' at the Sublime Porte had a role to play in this. But the seriousness of Ottoman military intentions in India (as distinct from Iraq and the Persian Gulf)

[18] These data can be pieced together from 'Abdullah Muhammad al-Makki Hajji al-Dabir, *Zafar al Wâlih bi Muzaffar wa Âlihi*, 2 Vols, tr., M. F. Lokhandwala, Baroda, 1970–4; and Shaikh Sikandar ibn Muhammad urf Manjhu, *The Mirât-i-Sikandarî*, eds, S. C. Misra and M. L. Rahman, Baroda, 1961.

[19] Cf. M. A. Nayeem, *External Relations of the Bijapur Kingdom (1489–1687)*, Hyderabad, 1974, as also Riazul Islam, *A Calendar of Documents on Indo-Persian Relations (1500–1750)*, 2 Vols, Karachi/Teheran, 1978–82.

is open to question, for even in 1538, when some real military resources were committed, they were left in the hands of the aging Hadim Süleyman Pasha, who in any event showed no great enthusiasm for the task that had been given him.[20]

What did the Ottomans really want by the middle years of the sixteenth century, in relation to the Indian Ocean? The limited works by specialists of the Ottoman archives, notably Cengiz Orhonlu and Salih Özbaran, leave us with a distressingly large set of mysteries at a conceptual level.[21] Behind the series of expeditions mounted by Piri Re'is, Seyyidi 'Ali Re'is, Sefer Re'is, and Mir 'Ali Bey, one sees a set of actions mainly directed at policing the Persian Gulf; and the extended flirtation with the Acehnese Sultans seems to have involved the commitment of few serious resources on the part of the Ottomans.[22] A frequently cited essay on the question, from the distinguished pen of the late Luís de Albuquerque, appears to me to further confound matters. He begins with the premise that 'The disaster that the failure of the first siege of Diu represented for the Turks (...) may have disillusioned them, for some time at least, from the possibility of reconquering the domination of the Indian Ocean trade, which they had been deprived of in the beginning of the sixteenth century'; this is based on a misunderstanding of some dimensions, since the 'Turks' had never controlled the trade of the Indian Ocean in the early sixteenth century, and is based, besides, on the assumption of a perfect congruence between Mamluks and Ottomans.[23] In fact, the Ottomans did not even have direct access to the ocean until 1517. He then goes on to argue that the disastrous expedition to the Red

[20] A key piece of evidence is AN/TT, CC, III–14–44, letter from Hadim Süleyman Pasha to the *wazîr* Ulugh Khan, or 'Olucão Gozil' (the lost original is dated 10 December 1538, and the Portuguese translation 7 May 1539) (Schurhammer, *Quellen*, Q 345). In this letter, written at Aden and dated 18 Rajab 945, Süleyman Pasha reports his expedition to India, and his own considerable reticence concerning the Gujaratis. For a discussion of this expedition, also see Muhammad Yaqub Mughul, 'The Expedition of Suleyman Pasha al-Khadim to India (1538)', *Journal of the Regional Cultural Institute* (Teheran), Vol. II, 1969, pp. 146–51. For the context, see Palmira Brummett, *Ottoman Seapower and Levantine Diplomacy in the Age of Discovery*, Albany, 1994, and the review of this book by Rhoads Murphey, *Bulletin of the School of Oriental and African Studies*, Vol. LVIII (3), 1995, pp. 561–3.

[21] For the bulk of Özbaran's writings, see Salih Özbaran, *The Ottoman Response to European Expansion: Studies on Ottoman-Portuguese Relations in the Indian Ocean and Ottoman Administration in the Arab Lands during the Sixteenth Century*, Istanbul, 1994.

[22] There are, however, rare references to Ottoman attacks on Portuguese shipping in Sind (Thatta and Lahori Bandar); cf. AN/TT, CC, I–100–28, letter from Francisco Pereira de Miranda at Chaul to D. João III (fl. 2v).

[23] Cf. in this context, Jean Aubin, 'La politique orientale de Selim Ier', in *Res Orientales VI: Itinéraires d'Orient, Hommages à Claude Cahen*, 1994, pp. 197–216.

Sea in 1541 of D. Estêvão da Gama was 'at the origin of the forceful intervention with which the Turks some years later pressurised the Portuguese empire in the Indian Ocean in an alarming fashion'.[24] It is my impression, on the contrary, that the Sublime Porte never had clear ambitions beyond the Persian Gulf, and that once the world-conquering ambitions of Süleyman had subsided by the early 1550s, it was the 'Rumi' diaspora and other external agents who attempted in vain to agitate a reluctant Porte into action, over an enlarged sphere. On the contrary, the Ottomans, who had begun to send out feelers for a *modus vivendi* with the Portuguese, periodically revived this project, not from hypocrisy, but from pragmatism. The major frontier that the Ottomans wished to leave open for future action was the Swahili coast, where their intentions clearly were to guard the southern flank of the province of Habesh. It was while in the pursuit of such an action that Sefer Re'is himself died off Aden in 1565, while at the head of a fleet of 10 galleys.[25]

Numerous gaps exist in our knowledge of the politico-commercial negotiations between the Ottomans and the Portuguese monarchs during the reigns of D. João III and D. Sebastião. At least two moments, when a near-agreement was reached, present themselves from the literature: the first in the early 1540s, and the second in the late 1550s and early 1560s. But we may suppose that more-or-less continuous relations of one or the other sort existed, both before and after, in view of the networks of espionage and overland trade that run like a persistent thread through the epoch. Besides Duarte Catanho, whose career has been studied at some length, and who served as an intermediary in these relations, another figure whose actions merit attention is the Italian Nicolau Pietro Cuccino, who first comes to our notice in the late 1550s.[26] Cuccino, incidentally, was later to have a rather successful career as *provedor* of the *Casa da Índia*, and then *vedor da fazenda* in Cochin under the Habsburgs.[27] An

[24] Luís de Albuquerque, 'Alguns aspectos de ameaça turca sobre a Índia por meados do século XVI', *Biblos*, t. LIII, 1977.

[25] AN/TT, CC, I-107-101, letter from Matias Bicudo Furtado at Cairo to D. Fernando de Meneses, 18th January 1566; also see the earlier letter from Tomás de Cornoça to D. Fernando de Meneses, dated 12 March 1565, AN/TT, CC, I-107-64.

[26] Cf. António da Silva Rego, 'Duarte Catanho, espião e embaixador (1538–42)', *Anais da Academia Portuguesa de História*, IIª Série, vol. IV, 1953, pp. 119–40.

[27] AN/TT, Chancelarias D. Sebastião e D. Henrique, Doações, Livro 43, fl. 41, letter naming Cuccino *provedor* of the *Casa da Índia*, dated 3 July 1578; AN/TT, Chancelaria D. Filipe I, Livro 6, fls 37–8, letter naming him *vedor da fazenda* in Cochin, dated 1 April 1582. Cuccino, born in about 1527, was still alive and serving as *provedor* of the *Casa da Índia*, in 1602; cf. Francisco Paulo Mendes da Luz, *O Conselho da Índia: Contributo ao estudo da história da administração e do comércio do ultramar português nos princípios do seculo XVII*, Lisbon, 1952, pp. 48–9.

anonymous document ('Memorial sobre as pazes') from about 1564, at the time when D. Francisco Coutinho, Conde do Redondo, was still viceroy of the *Estado da Índia* (his triennium lasted from 1561 to 1564), sets out a global view of matters. It begins in fact implicitly by regretting the absence of a peace between the Portuguese and the Ottomans.

In the past years, the issue of peace between the Turk and the King who is with God [D. João III] was treated through Duarte Catanho, Dioguo da Mizquita and Gaspar Palha, whom His Highness sent for this purpose, and even though it was gathered that the desire of the Turk and his Pashas was to accept the said peace, it was God's will that it should not be concluded. At the time that Lourenço Pyrez de Tavora resided as His Highness's ambassador in Rome, an Italian who is here, called Cochyno, offered his services to His Highness in this affair of a peace with the Turk, and His Highness gave him accreditation to be able to parley on this...[28]

Cuccino was thus sent to Istanbul, with letters for Süleyman and his chief Vizier (*wazîr-i â'zam*) and son-in-law (*dâmâd*), Rüstem Pasha, and in the meanwhile letters also arrived from the Conde do Redondo reporting that 'Ali Pasha, the Ottoman *beylerbey* in Basra, had for his part approached him to make peace, sending his emissary Khwaja Nasrullah Basri to Goa, via Hurmuz, in November 1562. A *casado* from Hurmuz, one António Teixeira de Azevedo was thus sent to Istanbul via Basra in 1563, and on arriving at the court in November that year, found Cuccino already present. The arrival of the two envoys at first created some confusion (especially since Azevedo carried no proper accreditation), but the matter was eventually resolved, with Süleyman sending back letters to Portugal via Cuccino, and to Goa via Azevedo. We are aware that this negotiation did not result in any lasting *entente*, and a rather elaborate discussion in the (recently edited) complete text of Couto's *Década Oitava*, gives us a sense of Portuguese foot-dragging in the affair.[29] On the other hand, it seems likely that both Rüstem Pasha and his mother-in-law, the celebrated Hurrem Sultan (or Roxelane), were not averse to an agreement with the Portuguese. Indeed, even Diogo do Couto's chronicle reflects this in the relatively favourable view held by the Portuguese of the harem-favourite Roxelane. It was thus probably in the aftermath of the failure of these embassies of the late 1550s and early 1560s, and after the death of Süleyman (1566), that the celebrated petition of the Sultan of Aceh, 'Ala al-Din Ri'ayat Syah al-Kahhar (r. 1539–71) was received in the Porte, with its demand for aid against the Portuguese, even though contacts between Aceh and Istanbul dated back to an earlier period.

[28] AN/TT, Colecção São Vicente, Vol. III, fl. 306.
[29] Maria Augusta Lima Cruz, *Diogo do Couto e a Década 8*, Vol. I, pp. 123–8, 199–217.

To resume, the objective existence of a persistent and stable Ottoman threat to western India, that runs all the way from 1517 to the close of the sixteenth century, cannot be shown. On the contrary, as I have argued elsewhere, Ottoman ambitions may have been at their highest in the time of Ibrahim Pasha (d. 1536), and in the decade following his death.[30] The conquest of Basra in late 1546 thus marks the end of an epoch, and Ottoman actions thereafter are directed in the main at the two shores of the Persian Gulf (Bahrein, but also Masqat, in the broad region). Any involvement beyond, whether in western India or in Aceh, was on the one hand episodic, and the product of external pressures (petitions, pleas from Ottoman subjects in diaspora), and on the other hand based on a minimal commitment in terms of military resources. We should not confuse the existence of 'Rumis' in diaspora, including disgruntled deserters from Sefer Re'is's fleet, with a coherent Ottoman policy of expansion.

Western India and the Red Sea Route

This brings us to the third step in our construction, namely the politico-commercial relationship between the Red Sea (in Ottoman hands) and western India, and the relationship between the 'old' and the 'new' routes between Asia and Europe. Consider the rather well-known letters of Gaspar and João Ribeiro, written from Venice in the 1560s. In one of these, dated 27 August 1564, and addressed to the Portuguese Crown, they note:

We understand from letters of the last 6th of June that more than 18,000 *quintais* of pepper and 3000 *quintais* of other drugs had arrived in Cairo, which came to the port of Juda [Jiddah] in ships from Dachem [Aceh] and also ships from Batequalla [Bhatkal], and that there were 23 ships in all that brought these spices, and these Dachens [Acehnese] are the one who mostly frequent this commerce and navigate, and who send presents to the Turk as they have their ambassadors in the court, and one has information on them through the Jews [*hebreos*] who come here...[31]

However, it is noted, the Acehnese have got little out of the Ottoman court: a mere six artillerymen and six other military specialists. Their intention was to have expert cannon-founders, but the few men they have managed to get hold of have been at the price of a rather generous present, including a large string of pearls, and many diamonds and rubies. The letter equally adds a rider on the subject towards its closing. The Ottomans are not interested in pursuing matters in the Indian Ocean, the Ribeiros write, because they are still hopeful of a peace

[30] For a further discussion, see Chapter 3.

[31] AN/TT, CC, I–107–9 (1 folio), letter dated 27 August 1564. A partial transliteration may be found in Luís Filipe Thomaz, *Os Portugueses em Malaca (1511–80)*, tese da licenicatura, Universidade de Lisboa, 1964, Vol. II.

with the Portuguese. In this they have been encouraged by the celebrated Jewish magnate José Nassi (or João Micas), who at the same time has made it clear to the Portuguese that such a peace would serve no purpose for them: 'since the Turks will come to know every nook and cranny of India and thus can conquer it more easily'![32]

The Ribeiros now return to a discussion of the spice trade, noting the departure from Venice for Tripoli in Syria of three large (but poorly laden) galleys, as well as another three for Alexandria (the latter carrying 275,000 ducats, besides silks and other textiles). Little or no spices have arrived at Tripoli via the Red Sea, they note, but the situation in Cairo is rather better, the price of pepper having come down to 24–30 cruzados a *quintal*. Yet, the letter-writers make it perfectly clear that this is a reactive phenomenon, the result of poor Portuguese pepper and spice cargoes in those years. Thus:

Last year, sixty thousand *cruzados* worth was sent [to Alexandria] and many Genoese came to this city [Venice], and they go in these galleys with a great quantity of money, for they have information from a certain António Calvo who lives in Lisbon that the *nao Tigre* brought back no more to the Kingdom [Portugal] than 500 *quintais* of pepper....

In sum, the phenomenon that is being described is precisely that set out by C. H. H. Wake in his important (but usually neglected) paper of nearly three decades ago. Ships from the Kanara port of Bhatkal, and others, notionally from Aceh—but undoubtedly including Gujarati ships from Rander and Surat of the type described by Chanoca as early as 1546—brought certain quantities of pepper and spices into the Red Sea. However, Venetian and Genoese interest in these spices was strictly a function of the arrivals in Lisbon. In years in which Lisbon was well-supplied, it made no sense for them to buy up the spices that came via Jiddah. In years such as 1563–64, when matters were perceived to be otherwise, a rush on Red Sea arrivals was remarked.

Two years earlier, in 1562, we already have clear indications of how these circuits of information and commercial speculation worked. In a letter from Venice, dated 22 August 1562, Tomás de Cornoça, the Portuguese consul there, noted the arrival in that city of word from Flanders concerning the fleet from India, which carried the returning viceroy D. Constantino de Bragança. Six ships had apparently left India in late 1561, of which three had reportedly failed to double the Cape, being forced to remain on the east coast of Africa awaiting

[32] For a recent reconsideration of the relations of Nassi and others with Portugal and the *Estado da Índia*, see José Alberto Rodrigues da Silva Tavim, 'Os Judeus e a Expansão Portuguesa na Índia durante o século XVI: O exemplo de Isaac do Cairo: Espião, 'língua' e 'judeu de Cochim de Cima'', *Arquivos do Centro Cultural Calouste Gulbenkian*, Vol. 33, 1994, pp. 137–260, especially pp. 164–7, *passim*.

favourable winds. D. Constantino himself was in the Azores with two ships, but these were poorly laden; one carried 1400 *quintais* of pepper and some 100 *quintais* of cinnamon, while the other carried about 3500 *quintais* of pepper. Of the sixth ship, there was no word to be had. When this news arrived in Venice, he reports, the price of pepper and the other spices at once rose.[33]

Cornoça now turns perfectly naturally to the other route. Meanwhile, word had come from Alexandria that the 'Moorish ships from India' (*los navjos moros de la India*) had begun to arrive in the Red Sea. But these too brought little by way of spices, whether pepper, cloves, or cinnamon. Indeed, one vessel from Aceh ('Asi') that carried 7000 *quintais* of pepper had been sunk by Portuguese fleets, all trace had been lost of another, and a third had arrived with some difficulty at Aden. Meanwhile, in Aleppo, a few camel-loads of spices (mostly cinnamon) had arrived via Hurmuz and Basra. The letter concludes by noting fears in Venice that Portuguese squadrons would intercept ships to the Red Sea with greater frequency; but, he concludes significantly, 'how felicitous it would be if, together with this, our ships did not fail to arrive by the usual way'.[34]

In this case, once more, the precise nature of the interrelationship is brought home forcefully. Venice and Flanders awaited news of the *Carreira da Índia*; and very often, this news was less than positive, because ships failed to complete the voyage, because the number of ships fell below that expected, or because capital for the pepper and spice cargoes was lacking. In such an event, recourse was taken to the overland route, principally via the Red Sea, but also to a limited extent through Hurmuz, Basra, and Aleppo. If the *Carreira* failed in a given year, and ships arrived in the Red Sea, funds would be rushed to Alexandria. But if, at the same time, because of the surveillance by Portuguese fleets (or some other reason), arrivals in the Red Sea too fell below expectations, the market went through the roof. However, this was a question of annual fluctuations, rather than a neat division of the market. In those years when the ships on the *Carreira* met expectations (i.e. 25,000 to 30,000 *quintais* of pepper, a few thousand *quintais* of assorted other spices), Venice and Genoa saw no sense in investing precious funds in the overland spice trade.

An enclosure to Cornoça's letter adds further useful details on actual and potential arrivals in the Red Sea and especially Jiddah ('Alcide'). These included

---

[33] Some of the documents of this period are discussed and summarized in Maria do Rosário de Sampaio Themudo Barata de Azevedo Cruz, *As Regências na menoridade de D. Sebastião: Elementos para uma história estrutural*, 2 Vols, Lisbon, 1992, Vol. II, pp. 189–203, *passim*. However, the discussion is more often than not confused, and full of basic errors (the author assumes, for example, that Surat was a Portuguese fortress).

[34] AN/TT, CC, I–106–8. There is an extensive correspondence around Cornoça from this period.

one ship from Cambay, two from Surat, two from Dabhol, two from Bhatkal, as well as the three Acehnese vessels that had had such mixed fortunes. In 1565, arrivals at Jiddah included eight ships from Bhatkal and three from Calicut; in the following year, there were three ships from Bhatkal, and five from Aceh.[35] It is my impression, however, that Portuguese officialdom in India sometimes tended to confuse cause and effect in the affair, and this has further muddied the waters of the analysis of modern historians. The viceroy D. Antão de Noronha, in a letter to the Crown dated December 1566, insisted that the problem lay at the supply side: that the rivals of the Portuguese had easy access to sources of pepper that the *Estado* did not. His solution was thus to shift the focus of pepper procurement partly from Kerala to Kanara, and he thus inaugurated a policy that endured into the seventeenth century.[36] This shift eventually helped justify the Portuguese capture of Honawar, Basrur, and Mangalore in 1568–9, and their destruction of the commercial potential of Bhatkal. But the reasoning used was nevertheless faulty. The viceroy argued that while 20,000 to 25,000 *quintais* of pepper went to the Red Sea annually (an exaggeration, anyway), a mere 10,000 to 12,000 *quintais* found its way on the bottoms of the ships of the *Carreira da* *Índia*. He implied that if the Portuguese cargoes were smaller than those to the Red Sea, it was because the pepper was drained away into other channels, and lured away from the Portuguese factories. Many modern historians have accepted this view. But it is my impression that the real source of the problem lay elsewhere. European demand for pepper and spices via Aleppo, Tripoli, and Alexandria was, we have seen, formulated in *reaction* to the cargoes expected at Lisbon, not the other way around. In any event, the total quantity of 37,000 *quintais* (proposed by D. Antão) does not enhaust Kanara and Malabar production in the epoch, far from it. The problem lay elsewhere, in the fact that the Crown part of the *Carreira da Índia* was often under-capitalized, and that the Portuguese factors in Cochin and elsewhere tried to hold procurement prices too low.

These aspects are made clear in a letter from a certain António Mendes de Castro, returning to Portugal in 1563, and written to the Queen from the Azores, in August of that year. Castro was captain on board the ship *São Vicente*, which

[35] For a discussion, see Sanjay Subrahmanyam, *The Political Economy of Commerce: Southern India, 1500–1650*, Cambridge, 1990, pp. 129–33. For the importance of Bhatkal in the 1560s, see AN/TT, CC, I–106–50, letter from Manuel Travassos at Cochin to the Queen, 20 January 1563, where mention is made of 'onze ou doze naos que se carregavão no Reino de Batecala e outros rios da costa de pimenta e hiam pera Meca todolos anos'.

[36] AN/TT, CC, I–108–15, letter dated Goa, 17 December 1566, in A. da Silva Rego, ed., *Documentação para a história das missões do padroado português no Oriente: Índia*, Vol. X, pp. 158–9.

had left Cochin in late January, together with the ships *Rainha* and *Frol de la Mar*. The last of these had broken its rudder off the Cape, and made for São Tomé; in any event it carried little or no pepper. The two other ships mentioned above are reported to have had 7700 *quintais* of pepper on board, while the Captain-Major's vessel and the *Esperança* (which only left in mid-February) are said to have had some 6000 or 7000 *quintais* on board. And finally, there is notice of two other vessels of the returning fleet of the year, one the *Tigre* (mentioned in the Ribeiros' letter) with a very small cargo of pepper, the other *Cedro*, with no pepper at all. A total fleet of as many as seven ships then, but a pepper cargo of less than 15,000 *quintais*.[37]

What reasons may be given for this? According to Castro himself, the problem was that the Malabar rulers (*os Reis do Malavar*) had not delivered what they had promised. Indeed, the Conde do Redondo himself had made his way from Goa to Cochin in November 1562 in a fleet of some 50 sails, 'since he had news that the pepper was not flowing' (*por ter nova que a pimenta não coria*). En route, in Quilandi ('Coulete'), he had even met and made peace with the Samudri Raja of Calicut, Manavikrama (r. 1562–74) to this end. But the problem had not been solved, since immediately after the viceroy's departure from Cochin, hostilities had broken out with the Raja's agent (*regedor*) there, a certain Rama, in which some 20 or 30 Portuguese and local Christians were killed. This tense atmosphere, provoked moreover by a failed Portuguese assassination attempt on Rama, had hardly helped matters where pepper procurement went.

The official Portuguese attitude towards pepper procurement in Kerala had been a rather curious one, from the very beginning. They insisted on seeing the matter as a political question, rather than a commercial one, and refused for the most part to pay market prices (based on an application of their notional 'monopoly' of pepper). Since the Portuguese factors expected to receive pepper below market prices, it was not surprising that they were constantly undersupplied, while pepper found its way overland across the Ghats, in private Portuguese ships, to Bengal and elsewhere and also to the Red Sea and Persian Gulf. In this situation, the Portuguese *Estado* had two solutions: a commercial one, to raise prices of procurement; or a politico-military one, to coax and coerce pepper out of local rulers by a mixture of bribes and threats. They consistently chose the latter solution, leading to a chronic shortage of pepper in their factories, for the former solution would have required larger outlays of capital than the Crown thought it could afford, besides being a blow to Portuguese prestige. A third solution, closer in spirit to the Dutch perhaps, would have been to apply a far higher degree of coercive force, but here the *Estado da Índia* fell short of its

---

[37] AN/TT, CC, I–106–80, António Mendes de Castro on the ship *São Vicente* to the Queen, 1 August 1563.

ambitions. Coercive force was applied, but mainly in an extensive rather than intensive fashion, to try and intercept the ships of rivals (whether Asian merchants, or Portuguese 'smugglers') in the Indian Ocean, and this was a strategy that had only limited success. There were many who felt by the 1560s that the *Estado* had turned its back on Cochin, leaving it to turn into a mere centre of private trade; the former captain of Chaliyam and *vedor da fazenda* at Cochin, D. Jorge de Castro, who had a way with words, even cited the Scriptures (the *Lamentations*) with respect to his city of residence: 'She who was once the Mistress of Peoples, declines and becomes a widow and tributary' (*Feyta e caye veuva he trebutarya a que hera Senhora das gentes*).[38]

Conclusion

Thus, in a sense, the Ottomans were really a red herring, a false threat in the middle years of the sixteenth century. Offered peace by the Porte on a number of occasions, the Portuguese Crown spurned the offer, confusing the flow of pepper to the Red Sea with a political rivalry.[39] In fact, the pepper and spices that came into the Red Sea served two purposes at once. One part of it fed the west Asian, North African, and eastern European markets, and as such was no threat to the commercial viability of the *Casa da Índia*. The remaining part, which made its way to Venice and Genoa, only did so to the extent that the Portuguese failed to meet western European demand via the *Carreira da Índia*. This was a result, as we have seen, of the nature of Portuguese claims to monopoly, and their peculiar pepper and spice procurement policies.

In the early sixteenth century, the *Carreira da Índia* had been meant, amongst other things, to provide the Portuguese Crown a way of outflanking the Mamluks and blockading trade to the Red Sea. Even after the campaign against Egypt (and the desire to recapture the Holy Land) had been given up, Portuguese policies with respect to the Red Sea failed to 'modernize', save in the very last years of the sixteenth century, when a regular and pragmatic policy of granting *cartazes* to ships from the Indian west coast was finally adopted. The Red Sea, as the 'home' of Islam for the Portuguese (and it is no coincidence that they persisted in using the phrase *Estreito de Meca*), continued through the 1550s and the 1560s, to be viewed with alarm and suspicion. In late 1556, D. João da Costa, writing to D. João III, to convince him of the importance of Daman, made it a point to note that if the Portuguese did not take the town, the 'Turk' would,

---

[38] AN/TT, CC, I–106–52, D. Jorge de Castro to the Cardinal D. Henrique, Cochin, 24 January 1563.

[39] See, in this context, the rather significant letter from D. Pedro de Sousa, captain of Hurmuz, to the Crown, AN/TT, CC, I–106–135, 25 May 1564.

'for it is the principal spot where he can gain a foothold'.[40] Nor was his voice an isolated one. D. Diogo de Noronha, writing in late 1557 to Pêro de Alcáçova Carneiro, equally insisted that the real justification for taking Daman from 'Imad al-Mulk was to prevent the Ottomans from doing so. He wrote:

This port of Damão that they are giving now to His Highness is one of the most important of Cambaia, and amongst the most appropriate and necessary for this *Estado*, and we can keep and sustain it better than any other through all these changes. And with it, we become masters of all the wood of Cambaya, and we take it away from them, and this fortress is so much in the throat of that bay that we shall come to control it, and can keep a strict account of all the ships that enter and go out of it, and a thousand other profits and benefits that it would require a great deal of writing to set out. Besides everything else, this is the only port of Cambaia that if the Turks come to these parts, they could occupy and fortify, and they would then have all the wood for their fleets.[41]

This rather devious piece of writing conceals two crucial points. First, to take Daman had been a Portuguese ambition since at least the 1530s, when it had been more or less ceded to them by the short-lived Timurid 'ruler' of Gujarat, Muhammad Zaman Mirza.[42] Second, the control of the 'bay' (*enseada*) in question reflected a recognition by the Portuguese of the crucial role played by Surat, from which 'Imad al-Mulk himself sent out his trading ships.[43] The ostensible reason given, namely the Ottoman threat, may or may not have appeared genuine to the letter's author; but we for our part have no reason to give it more than a negligible weight.[44]

---

[40] AN/TT, CC, I–100–31, D. João da Costa to D. João III, 20 December 1556 (1 fl.).

[41] AN/TT, CC, I–102–47, letter dated Goa, 17th December 1557. This letter contains a valuable account of negotiations with 'Imad al-Mulk through the emissary Diogo Pereira.

[42] Cf. AN/TT, CC, I–58–73, a treaty of March 1537 between the governor Nuno da Cunha and Mirza Muhammad Zaman, reproduced with some errors in Luciano Ribeiro, 'Em torno do primeiro cerco de Diu', *Studia*, Nos 13–14, 1964, pp. 52–4.

[43] A richly laden ship returning to Surat from the Red Sea, with a *cartaz* from the governor Francisco Barreto, is reported in a letter from Chaul of 1556; cf. AN/TT, CC, I–100–28, letter from Francisco Pereira de Miranda to D. João II, 18 December 1556. In 1557, it is noted that letters from the Portuguese agent João de Lisboa in the Middle East, were brought to Goa via the ships that returned to Surat from the Red Sea; cf. AN/TT, CC, I–102–47, letter from D. Diogo de Noronha of December 1557. Also see AN/TT, CC, I–99–135, for a letter from João de Lisboa at Cairo to D. Afonso de Lencastre at Rome, dated 26 October 1556.

[44] For another view of the political situation in the Indian Ocean from about this period, see Luís Filipe F.R. Thomaz, 'A Crise de 1565–75 na História do Estado da Índia', *Mare Liberum*, No. 9, 1995, pp. 481–519.

In a characteristically insightful essay published in the mid 1980s, the Indian maritime historian Ashin Das Gupta pointed to the crucial nature of the (partly oppositional) relationship between Dabhol and Surat in the history of western Indian Ocean trade in the early seventeenth century. Das Gupta argued that Dabhol, relatively closely identified with the Portuguese *Estado*, suffered in the early seventeenth century transition, while Surat emerged in a position of even greater strength: in the 1620s, he noted, 'Dabhol was destroyed and Surat became the most important base for Indian shipping'.[45] The present chapter has attempted, among a number of tasks it set itself, to shed light on the 'prehistory' of the relationships surveyed by Das Gupta. We have seen that the role of Surat emerged over several stages in the course of the sixteenth century, and was the consequence of a series of actions and oppositions, some real and others imagined, by the protagonists. One need hardly stress, by way of conclusion, that we see once more that even in the sixteenth century, and even in an area such as western India (where the Portuguese *Estado* concentrated so much of its resources), the dynamics of maritime trade were determined by a number of factors, and not by the Portuguese alone. This was a fact that would be emphasized even more after 1573, when the Mughal state made its entry into the western Indian Ocean scene. Indo-Portuguese historians thus need to ensure that in their vision of matters too, the Portuguese do not appear to act in a vacuum, against a historical *tabula rasa*.

[45] Ashin Das Gupta, 'Indian Merchants and the Western Indian Ocean: The Early Seventeenth Century', *Modern Asian Studies*, Vol. XIX (3), 1985, pp. 481–99.

3

Mughal Gujarat and the Iberian World in the Transition of 1580–1

I don't know if it has ever struck you, but the fact is there has never yet been an opposition that didn't change its tune when it took over the helm. And, you know, that isn't as one might think, just something that goes without saying. On the contrary, it is most important. The fact is, it's the cause of what I call the hard core, the thing one can count on, the continuum, in politics!

Robert Musil, *The Man Without Qualities* (1930)[1]

Introduction

Historians of the early modern period have returned in recent years to a serious reconsideration of the significance of the press of events and the confluence of intricate processes, after a long flirtation with a form of structuralist-inspired disdain for *l'histoire événementielle*. As part of this reconsideration, the repeated recourse by writers on early modern Euro-Asian interaction to the related notions of 'crises' and 'turning points' as key concepts to explain the giving way of one 'structural complex' to another is now far more open to question than it was, say, two decades ago. This chapter is concerned with a potentially 'dramatic' moment of transition in the Iberian world, namely the takeover of Portugal and her empire by the Habsburgs in 1580–1, as seen from the perspective of a region peripheral from the viewpoint of the Iberian world—that is, western India under the Mughals. It addresses itself both explicitly and implicitly to the need to go beyond the methodological position that one can choose points in time and a space, and refract whole institutional complexes through them, taking out

[1] Musil, *Der Mann ohne Eigenschaften,* translated as *The Man Without Qualities, Two: The Like of It Now Happens (II)*, tr. Eithne Wilkins and Ernst Kaiser, London, 1979, p. 415. The words are spoken by a character, Count Leinsdorf.

from the tangled web of history, dramatic but often chimerical notions about 'revolutions' and 'structural crises'.

The conquest of the western Indian region of Gujarat by the Mughals in 1572 undoubtedly contributed to a quickening of relations between that state and the Portuguese *Estado da Índia*, which had established a presence there in the first half of the sixteenth century. Closer contact did not necessarily mean more cordial relations, and the history of Mughal–Portuguese dealings right to the end of the seventeenth century can at best be called a mixed one.[2] Moments of outright hostility were few, but could be dramatic: one might think of the intermittent warfare between Jahangir and the *Estado* between 1613 and 1615 as a minor example; the capture of Hughli in 1632 by Shahjahan's general Qasim Khan is still more striking, and was a theme to inspire Mughal painters of the epoch. On the other hand, there was also a certain pressure for the two entities to collaborate in that 'Age of Contained Conflict', not least of all because the price of sustained hostility was simply too high in material terms for both parties, and the benefits not at all evident.

Nevertheless, we must understand that the nature of the relationship was such, that probings for mutual weaknesses and a tendency for each of the two parties to take advantage of shifts in a larger conjuncture were an inevitable part thereof. At stake was not only, from the Portuguese viewpoint, the trading network of Chaul, Surat, Khambayat, and Diu, and the land revenue and customs collections from Diu, Daman, and Bassein, whose importance is testified to by the *orçamentos* (budget statements) of 1574, 1581, and 1588; there was also the question of the prosperity of Surat from the Mughal viewpoint, the thorny problem of the *hajj*, and the jockeying for prestige *vis-à-vis* third parties, most notably the Safavids and Ottomans, to a lesser extent the Uzbeks. Further, a very real ideological tension existed between the claims of Counter-Reformation Christianity and the heterodox Sunnism that the Mughals espoused in the late sixteenth century, which well-meaning, modern-day propagandists of the *Dîn-i Ilâhî* (*sic*: for *Tauhîd-i Ilâhî*) have been unable to paper over. It is in this wider context that I shall examine the impact of the transition caused by the Habsburg annexation of Portugal in 1580–1 on the Mughal–Portuguese relationship, with a particular view to its implications for Gujarat, and a passing look at the context of the *Prov-incia do Norte*.

The Context of the Transition

On 31 January 1580, the first Jesuit mission to the court of the Mughal ruler Jalal al-Din Muhammad Akbar was witness to a lunar eclipse at about 11 p.m.,

---

[2] See, for example, Sanjay Subrahmanyam, 'The *Estado da Índia* and the Merchants of Surat, c. 1700', *The Indian Ocean Newsletter*, Vol. VIII, 1986.

en route from Surat to Mandu. The event, otherwise of no particular import even in the century of Nostradamus, thus a century obsessed with apocalyptic signs and portents, was later invested by one of the Jesuits, António Monserrate, with great significance: for he found that at that very time the Cardinal-King Dom Henrique had breathed his last in Lisbon. 'This eclipse', he wrote, 'may also be reckoned to have foreshadowed the trials and griefs which came upon Portugal after the death of King Henry'.[3] The contemporary Portuguese doggerel wished the pious King ill in the afterlife: '*Viva El-Rei Dom Henrique/no inferno muitos anos/Pois deixou em testamento/Portugal aos Castelhanos*'.[4] Akbar, on the other hand, in conversations with the Jesuits in his court in late 1581, made it clear that he had held him in esteem; indeed, Monserrate writes, he 'was wont to praise and respect King Henry's sanctity, fortitude and constancy, as though he had been a second St. Sebastian'.[5] If Dom Henrique's birth had been marked by an unusual sign, namely snow in Lisbon, his death was no less remarked it seemed in the heavens, and even in a distant court.

The 1580–1 transition is a well-known and much debated one in Portuguese history: to some, it is the beginning of the 60 years of Spanish 'Captivity', to others no more than the inauguration of the rule of another dynasty in Portugal, the Habsburgs.[6] Were we to see the matter purely from the perspective of the

---

[3] S. N. Banerjee and John S. Hoyland, tr., *The Commentary of Father Monserrate S. J. on his Journey to the Court of Akbar*, London, 1922, p. 14. For a discussion of another celestial sign endowed with political significance, namely the comet of 1576–7, see Shaikh Abu'l Fazl, *Akbar Nâma*, tr. H. Beveridge, Vol. III, reprint, New Delhi, 1989, pp. 315–18. Abu'l Fazl links the comet with political disaster in Iran, where it is associated with the deaths of Shah Tahmasp, Sultan Haidar, and Shah Isma'il II.

[4] Cited in J. Augusto Ferreira, 'O Prior do Crato em o norte do Pais, onde teve uma vitória efémera, e a sua fuga para França...', in *Congresso do Mundo Português*, Vol. VI, Part I, 1940, pp. 105–16. A loose translation is: 'Long live King Dom Henry/ for years and years in hell/ for he left poor Portugal/ to the Castilians in his will'.

[5] *The Commentary of Monserrate*, ed. Hoyland and Banerjee, p. 129.

[6] For a somewhat mediocre survey, see Ronald Cueto, '1580 and All That...: Philip II and the Politics of the Portuguese Succession', *Portuguese Studies*, Vol. VIII, 1992, pp. 150–69. Also compare Queiroz Velloso, 'A perda de independência: Factores internos e externos, que para ela contribuiram', *Congresso do Mundo Português*, Vol. VI, Part I, 1940, pp. 9–40. As yet we lack a global study of this phase, or even a compendium of essays of the sort devoted recently to the English 'Glorious Revolution' of 1688 in Jonathan I. Israel, ed., *The Anglo-Dutch Moment: Essays on the Glorious Revolution and its World Impact*, Cambridge, 1991. But see, in the interim, Geoffrey Parker, 'David or Goliath? Philip II and his world in the 1580s', in Richard L. Kagan and Geoffrey Parker, eds, *Spain, Europe and the Atlantic World: Essays in Honour of John H. Elliott*, Cambridge, 1995, pp. 245–66.

logic of a 'domino' theory of international relations, we would certainly not disdain the potential significance of this transition. After all in 1578, when Dom Sebastião embarked on his ill-fated North African expedition, Portugal and Spain were both implicated in an elaborate set of international alliances, involving France, Venice, the Ottomans, and the Safavids, amongst other actors. The amalgamation of the two into one, at the level of international politics, may have had a significant destabilizing and realigning effect on the system of alliances. Portuguese nationalists, for example, have often claimed that it was the wedding of Portugal to Spain which triggered off Dutch and English attacks on Portuguese shipping in the Atlantic in the 1580s, and eventually led these North Atlantic powers after 1590 to infringe on the Portuguese monopoly of the Cape Route. This view, supported by a few of the more crass modern historians of empires as well, is based on the somewhat naive expectation that had Portugal remained independent, the Dutch and English would have accepted the logic of the Tordesillas Treaty (1494), despite their own pressing economic compulsions and disdain for the Papacy. From our perspective, it seems on the contrary that for the Dutch and the English, Portugal's attachment to the Habsburgs was in the instance a handy *casus belli*, but scarcely a great deal more than that.

It is useful here to distinguish this naive 'political' interpretation of the transition of 1580–1 summarized above, from the far more sophisticated view of Fernand Braudel in his classic study of the Mediterranean in the Age of Philip II, even though the latter has written, with a characteristic flourish, that the transition of 1580–1 (and more generally the years 1578–83) was from the viewpoint of the Mediterranean the 'turning point of the century'.[7] While the logic of international politics plays a role in Braudel's explanation of the shift from the Mediterranean to the Atlantic in about 1580, it is underpinned by a sense of the enormous inertial momentum of the longer-term shifts of economic balance in Europe, that led to the rise in importance of the Low Countries and England. Thus the plate-techtonics at the level of a slow-moving substratum of forces is *manifested*, in his view, at the level of events in a dramatic political climax, which is at once a 'crisis' and a 'turning point'.

Returning to the political dimension, it is evident to any student of the epoch that the weakness of several of the other actors aided the Spanish Crown to consolidate its position. An obvious example is France, which under Henri III (operating in turn under the watchful eye of Catherine de Médicis) found itself unable, on account of its own Wars of Religion, to provide more than half-hearted support to the pretender Dom António, Prior of Crato, who had proclaimed himself King of Portugal on 19/20 June 1580. Expelled by the Spanish

---

[7] Fernand Braudel, *The Mediterranean and the Mediterranean World in the Age of Philip II*, 2 Vols, tr. Siân Reynolds, New York, 1972, Vol. II, pp. 1176–7.

army of the Duke of Alba after a defeat on 25 August at Alcântara, Dom António fled to the Azores, then to France, and after two unsuccessful French-supported expeditions against the Spaniards, to England.[8] Not even the fact that he had offered the French the territory of Brazil as a bait, could allay the cold feet of the Valois ruler, as we see from the unfortunate history of the Florentine Filippo di Pietro Strozzi (1541–82), sent out by the French to the Azores in June 1582 as a support to Dom António, and then disclaimed by them as a privateer.[9]

Internal opposition to Spanish rule in Portugal seemingly did not constitute a truly formidable obstacle to Philip II's designs. The most serious military opposition was, interestingly enough, provided by Dom Diogo de Meneses, a returned former governor of the *Estado da Índia* (1576–8), who was killed after a defence of the Cascais fort. The Venetian ambassador Gioan Francesco Morosini described him in his correspondence to the Senate as 'il miglior uomo da guerra di tutto Portogallo' ('the best warrior in all Portugal'), and decried his execution after his capture, 'a person of noble blood and important position not meriting such an ignoble death for having served his country (*sua patria*) and his master against a King to whom he as yet had no obligation'.[10] There was another reputed military figure, of whom it was said that had he but accompanied Dom Sebastião, the disaster of Alcácer-Quibir could have been avoided, and who had sufficient charisma to draw together elements of an opposition: but this was Dom Lu-ıs de Ata-ıde (1517–81), Conde de Atouguia, who was at that very time viceroy of the *Estado* at Goa. As for concerted opposition from the clergy or nobility, this was well taken care of by Philip's agents like Don Juan de Silva, Conde de Portalegre, and Cristóvão de Moura, who had begun to act already from late 1578, when the ransom of captives in North Africa was to be arranged. Families like the Gama, the Távora, the Mascarenhas, and even the Castro were too insecure, politically and even perhaps financially, by 1580 to resist the Habsburgs, and the few who resisted like Dom Francisco de Portugal, putative Conde de Vimioso, were soon in exile with the Prior of Crato.

Nevertheless, the actual annexation of Portugal drew upon the military re-serves of the Habsburgs, which were already stretched thin across much of western Europe. It was hence necessary for them, tactically speaking, to ease

[8] On Dom António in England, and his troubled dealings with Exeter and Devon merchants, see John W. Blake, 'English Trade with the Portuguese Empire in West Africa, 1581–1629', *Congresso do Mundo Português*, Vol. VI, Part I, 1940, pp. 313–35.

[9] Cf. Hermann Taffin Sieur de Torsay, *La vie, mort et tombeau de haut et puissant seigneur Philippe de Strozzi…*, Paris: G. Le Noir, 1608.

[10] 'Relazione di Gioan Francesco Morosini, 1581', in Eugenio Alberi, ed., *Le Relazioni degli ambasciatori veneti al Senato durante il secolo decimosesto*, Serie I, Vol. V, Florence, 1861, pp. 281–338, especially p. 308.

the pressure by means of diplomacy on at least some fronts, and this goes some way to explaining their eagerness to arrive as rapidly as possible at a confirmation by treaty of the series of truces agreed on with the Ottomans in March 1577, February 1578, and March 1580.[11] On the other hand, the French ambassador at the Sublime Porte, Jacques de Germigny, made it abundantly clear to the Ottomans that the Habsburg occupation of Portugal was a threat to them above all. In a letter of 17 May 1580 from Istanbul, he noted:

I remonstrated with them concerning the expansionary designs of the King of Spain, to the extent of occupying the kingdom of Portugal and the countries in the Levant that depend on it, which is to say Ormus and others that border of this Seigneur, [and] that he would not hold back afterwards, having expanded in such a fashion, from making war on this empire and plotting its ruin...[12]

But it is interesting to note that the Ottoman court, with the exception of a few like Lala Mustafa Pasha (who had led the successful expedition against Cyprus in 1571), was not enthusiastic; we may recall that the Ottoman polity was suffering the political after-effects of the assassination of the Grand Vizier Sokollu Mehmed Pasha in October 1579. A Bosnian Serb of Christian origin, who had been recruited into the Ottoman *devshirme* system, Mehmed Pasha had effectively dominated the court from 1565, the last year of Süleyman's reign, through the reign of Selim II (1566–74). In turn, he continued to determine to a large extent the making of policy in the first years of Murad III, so that the Ottoman polity found itself notably divided in the face of the new conjuncture. The significance of Mehmed Pasha's influence is shown for example by his role in encouraging the English to trade in the Ottoman domains, which facilitated the eventual formation of the Levant Company in 1581. Even if we do not accept the conventional judgment that 'once Sokollu was dead, the first signs of decline appeared', the fact of some turbulence in the Ottoman polity cannot be wished away.[13]

[11] Cf. S. A. Skilliter, 'The Hispano-Ottoman Armistice of 1581', in C. E. Bosworth, ed., *Islam and Iran: In Memory of V. Minorsky*, Edinburgh, 1971, pp. 491–515. The 1581 agreement, piloted on the Spanish side by Giovanni Margliani, was signed in late January that year. For a wide-ranging examination of Ottoman-Spanish relations in North Africa, also see Andrew C. Hess, *The Forgotten Frontier: A History of the Sixteenth Century Ibero-African Frontier*, Chicago, 1978.

[12] E. Charrière, ed., *Négociations de la France dans le Levant, ou Correspondance, Mémoires et Actes Diplomatiques*, Vol. III, Paris, 1853, pp. 908–10.

[13] Jean-Louis Bacqué-Grammont, 'L'apogée de l'Empire Ottoman: Les événements (1512–1606)', in Robert Mantran, ed., *Histoire de l'Empire Ottoman*, Paris, 1989, p. 157. The historiographically-minded reader may go back a century-and-a-half to the classic studies of Leopold von Ranke, *Die Osmanen und die spanische Monarchie im 16. und*

Besides, as Braudel has shown, Ottoman calculations rested not on Europe and North Africa alone. Rather they had, from as early as the time of Selim I, made heavy weather of the management of the eastern front with the Safavids as well. The weight of the two polities was obviously highly unequal, but the fact remains that despite their victory at Chaldiran in 1514, the Ottomans were unable comprehensively to defeat the Safavids (as they had the Mamluks in Egypt in 1517), and that Shah Tahmasp (r. 1524–76) remained throughout his long reign a problematic figure for Süleyman and his successors. We are aware from the work of Jean Aubin and others that in the mid-1560s, the Habsburgs and Maximilian II had been attempting to build an anti-Ottoman alliance with Tahmasp. The problem at that time was the lack of cooperation from the Portuguese, since emissaries had to pass through the *Estado da Índia* en route to Iran.[14] These were the very years, we should recall, that the Ottomans had opened independent negotiations with the Portuguese for the first time since the early 1540s, when Dom João III had mooted abortive discussions with a view to exchanging limited quantities of pepper for wheat from the Ottoman domains. Unlike in the 1540s, the initiative in the 1560s came from the Ottomans; in 1562, an ambassador had arrived from Basra at Hurmuz, and in 1563, the Portuguese sent a return envoy, António Teixeira de Azevedo, to Istanbul, besides another emissary from Lisbon, the mysterious Nicolau Pietro Cuccino, much later to be *vedor da fazenda* in charge of pepper cargoes at Cochin. Received by Süleyman on 14 November 1563, Azevedo made his way to Portugal in 1565, where he put the possibility to the court of a *modus vivendi*, in which the Ottomans would be permitted free trade in the Indian Ocean, with establishments in Sind, Gujarat, Dabhol, and Calicut, and the Portuguese would in return be allowed trade in Basra, Cairo, Alexandria, and the Red Sea.[15] The suggestion was eventually

---

17. Jahrhundert, 2 Vols, (Sämmtliche Werke, Vols XXXV and XXXVI), Leipzig, 1874 (first published c. 1830) and Joseph von Hammer-Purgstall, *Histoire de l'Empire Ottoman depuis son origine jusqu'à nos jours*, tr. J. J. Hellert, 18 Vols, Paris, 1835–43, especially Vol. VII (translated from his *Geschichte des osmanischen Reiches*, 10 Vols, Budapest, 1827–35).

[14] Jean Aubin, 'Per viam portugalensem: Autour d'un projet diplomatique de Maximilien II', *Mare Luso-Indicum*, t. IV, 1980, pp. 45–88.

[15] *Diogo do Couto e a Década 8ª da Ásia*, ed. Maria Augusta Lima Cruz, Vol. I, Lisbon, 1993, pp. 123–8, 199–217. Of particular relevance among the documents cited by the editor in the notes to that text is a letter from Süleyman to D. Sebastião, Istanbul, 14 November 1563, in A. da Silva Rego, ed., *As Gavetas da Torre do Tombo*, Vol. IV, Lisbon, 1964, pp. 464–5. Later letters from November 1564 and August 1565, with a far more hostile tone, may be found in Ottoman Turkish in the *Başvekâlet Arşivi*, Istanbul, Diwan-i Humayun, Mühimme Defterleri, Vol. 6, fl. 166, and Vol. 5, p. 70 (No. 161)

rejected by Dom Sebastião's court, but we may nevertheless sense here the distance between Spanish and Portuguese perspectives in the mid-1560s.

The reasons for which the Portuguese court rejected the Ottoman overtures seem, with the benefit of hindsight, to have been based on an anachronistic perception, of which many modern-day historians are still victims. Still thinking in terms of Diu, which they had defended at such cost against the Ottomans, locally-implanted Rumis and Gujaratis, the Portuguese perception as late as 1563 was that Süleyman was an omnivorous World-Conqueror, and that to give the Ottomans even an inch of room would be a fatal error. As Cornell Fleischer has recently demonstrated though, the nature of Süleyman's ambitions and self-perception had changed rather extensively between the 1540s and the 1560s. Earlier inclined to designate himself *Sâhib-Qirân*, 'Lord of the Conjunction', and even *Mujaddid*, or 'Renewer (of the Age)', Süleyman after 1550 is increasingly seen by himself and his courtiers less as a conqueror (now the prerogative of Fatih Mehmed and Selim I) and more as a preserver of internal order (thus, the title *Pâdshâh-i 'Âlampanah*, Emperor, and Refuge of the World, and later *Qânûnî*, the Law-Giver).[16] From an earlier tendency systematically to destabilize the Safavid regime by using dissident members of the royal family like Tahmasp's brother Alqas Mirza, the post-1550 Süleyman sought increasingly to demarcate boundaries and signed treaties with at least his Asian neighbours. If the Ottomans had schemed in the 1530s and early 1540s of gaining at least a foothold in Gujarat, this seems to have been very little on their minds by the time of Azevedo's embassy. Their adventurism in respect of Masqat and the Persian Gulf in the 1550s, and then again in the early 1580s, should not be confused with dreams of an Indian empire; it has been argued, with some conviction, that once they took Basra in late 1546, the major preoccupation of the Ottomans was its preservation and the recovery of the costs of occupation. They seem, if anything, to have been eager in the late 1540s to promote trade with Hurmuz and even Goa.[17] Of course, the Ottomans could not abandon the

---

respectively. For details, see Naimur Rahman Farooqi, *Mughal-Ottoman Relations: A Study of Political and Diplomatic Relations between Mughal India and the Ottoman Empire, 1556–1748*, Delhi, 1989, pp. 144, 156–7, 162, 170.

[16] Cornell Fleischer, 'The Lawgiver as Messiah: The Making of the Imperial Image in the Reign of Süleyman', in Gilles Veinstein, ed., *Soliman le Magnifique et son temps*, Paris, 1992, pp. 159–77. Also the earlier discussion in Barbara Flemming, 'Sahib-kiran und Mahdi: Türkische Endzeiterwartungen im ersten Jahrzehnt der Regierung Süleymans', in Gyorgy Kara, ed., *Between the Danube and the Caucasus*, Budapest, 1987, pp. 43–62.

[17] See Dejanirah Potache, 'The commercial relations between Basrah and Goa in the sixteenth century', *Studia*, No. 48, 1989, pp. 145–62. Of obvious importance among the documents cited there is a collection from 1547–8, *Biblioteca da Ajuda*, Lisbon, Codex

tactical building of alliances with Indian and south-east Asian potentates, and even sent out the odd (and usually abortive) maritime expedition in the 1560s, especially to Aceh, but this must be seen in the context of longer-term developments.

Thus, all in all, we may conclude that the excessive and dramatic importance given to Lepanto, and its aftermath, both by near-contemporary and later writers, obscures the fact that in the course of the late 1570s, a relatively stable European frontier between the Spanish Habsburgs and the Ottomans was defined for the last quarter of the sixteenth century. In a sense, by 1580–1, the generalized fear of an Ottoman threat to Europe was a thing of the past; the real enemies for the Spanish Habsburgs were to be from now on the ones within Christendom— namely England, and above all the Netherlands. To be sure, a war of sorts— sometimes hot and sometimes cold—continued intermittently with another branch of the Habsburgs in Central Europe; under Rudolph II, the Ottomans were defeated at Sziszek in 1593, while later Mehmed III in 1596 for his part conquered the strategic fortress of Erlau. The culmination of this phase may be thought to come with the Treaty of Zsitvatorok (November 1606) in which the Ottomans made significant symbolic and actual concessions to their adversaries, recognizing them finally as equals rather than subordinate. One can see, thus, that the idea of Ottoman 'decline' was in fact the slowly crystallizing counterpart of the receding of the Ottoman threat; and contributing to this was a new structure of alliances, which saw an implicit marriage of convenience between the Spanish Habsburgs and Ottomans that may even have helped seal Habsburg control over Portugal and her overseas territories.[18] The later skirmishes over Mombasa in the late 1580s and early 1590s should be seen as local

---

51–VII–19, 'Pareceres de Baçora', fls 194–331. Also see the regulations of the Basra customs-house under the Ottomans, in Robert Mantran, 'Règlements Fiscaux Ottomans: La Province de Bassorah', *Journal of the Economic and Social History of the Orient*, Vol. X, Nos 2–3, 1967. And finally, see the useful overview in Salih Özbaran, 'The Ottoman Turks and the Portuguese in the Persian Gulf, 1534–81', *Journal of Asian History*, Vol. VI, no. 1, 1972, based on both Portuguese and Ottoman materials.

[18] It is instructive in this context to read the reports from the early seventeenth century of the Venetian representative in Constantinople, in Nicolò Barozzi and Guglielmo Berchet, eds, *Le Relazioni degli Stati Europei lette al Senato dagli Ambasciatori Veneziani nel secolo decimosettimo: Turchia*, 2 Vols, Venice, 1871–2. Particularly striking is the account by Ottavio Bon, 'Massime essenziali dell'Impero Ottomano notate del bailo Bon', Vol. I, pp. 116–24. For an analysis of these reports, see Lucette Valensi, *Venise et la Sublime Porte: La naissance du despote*, Paris, 1987; and for a very useful overview, Cemal Kafadar, 'The Ottomans and Europe', in Thomas A. Brady Jr., Heiko A. Oberman, and James D. Tracy, eds, *Handbook of European History, 1400–1600: Late Middle Ages, Renaissance and Reformation*, Vol. I, Leiden, 1994, pp. 589–635.

manoeuvres rather than part of a grand scheme; Braudel, depending too heavily it seems on Joseph von Hammer's mid-nineteenth century account, surely exaggerates when he asserts that the momentum of 1580–1 'flung Turkey (*sic*) towards Persia and the depths of Asia, the Caucasus, the Caspian, Armenia and, later, the Indian Ocean itself'.[19] As for the Portuguese belief that the Ottomans were fomenting trouble as late as the 1590s in places as distant as Burma and Thailand, there is little evidence that has turned up so far in the Ottoman archives to support it.[20]

To the extent that the Habsburgs understood this shift in Ottoman policy, it meant that Safavid Iran had a somewhat diminished role to play in Philip II's calculations, when compared either to those of Dom Sebastião or, later, to those of Philip III—whose case is rather special, since he was actively sought out and wooed for a time by Shah 'Abbas I. But there was also a gap between Habsburg perceptions and Ottoman realities, and this helps explain Philip II's concern to encourage Iran in its struggle against the Ottomans in the 1580s, and his sporadic, as well as rather anachronistic, interest in Prester John of Ethiopia.[21] The turmoil that followed Shah Tahmasp's death in 1576 had helped precipitate a new, but largely improvised, conflict between the Ottomans and Safavids. Tahmasp's successor (after the brief intervening reign of Haidar), Isma'il II, launched on a policy that—had it borne fruit—might have profoundly affected the course of regional politics. Rejecting the Twelver Shi'ism of his forbears, he embraced Sunnism with some vigour, and sought to make common cause with the orthodox Islamic ruler of Kabul, Mirza Muhammad Hakim, the rival and half-brother of the Mughal ruler, Akbar. But Isma'il had miscalculated the extent of opposition to his new regime, and his early (and probably unnatural) death in 1577 opened Iran up to external turmoil, with attacks by the Ottomans on the one hand, and the Uzbeks on the other, making severe inroads. In turn, this meant that Iran's notional satellites on the Indian subcontinent, the Deccan Sultanates, which recognized the Safavids' ritual suzerainty over themselves,

[19] Braudel, *The Mediterranean*, Vol. II, p. 1165 (emphasis added). Again, Braudel surely exaggerates the importance from an Ottoman point of view of Mir 'Ali Bey's activities on the Swahili coast (*Ibid*, pp. 1175–6), relying partly it seems on W. E. D. Allen, *Problems of Turkish Power in the Sixteenth Century*, London, 1963.

[20] For an example of this belief, see Manuel de Abreu Mousinho, *Breve Discurso em que se conta a conquista do Reino do Pegu*, ed. M. Lopes de Almeida, Barcelos, 1936, pp. 17–18.

[21] Cf. the useful summing up of Philip II's policy towards Iran, the Ottomans and Ethiopia, in João Paulo Oliveira e Costa and Victor Lu-is Gaspar Rodrigues, *Portugal y Oriente: El Proyecto Indiano del Rey Juan*, Madrid, 1992, pp. 321–6. However, there are some minor divergences between my interpretation of the politics of the period and that of the authors of this study.

were left adrift in large measure. The death, in early 1580, of the Sultan of
Bijapur 'Ali 'Adil Shah, helped bring about one of the more dramatic transfor-
mations of the epoch. From a belligerent, Shi'i polity under 'Ali 'Adil, who had
besieged Goa on at least one major occasion, Bijapur under his successor
Ibrahim 'Adil Shah (r. 1580–1627) turned towards a heterodox form of Sunnism,
and showed little or no further interest in attacking the *Estado da Índia*. Both
Ibrahim and Goa were more preoccupied it seems by a new threat in the 1580s,
the lengthening Mughal shadow in the Deccan.

The Mughal Perspective

Between 1572–3, when Akbar personally ensured the incorporation of Gujarat
into his domains and made a brief and celebrated sea voyage, and the end of
the 1570s, the Mughal perspective on the world at large changed in substantial
measure. As has been argued elsewhere, Akbar's half-century-long reign can
schematically be divided into four phases: an apprenticeship of Bairam Khan
and the *atka khail* (foster-brothers), when the consolidation of Humayun's
legacy was the main preoccupation; a phase occupying the latter half of the
1560s and the 1570s, when massive territorial expansion and fiscal tightening
were accompanied by a relatively orthodox politico-religious outlook, including
hostility in the late 1560s to non-Sunni practices; a third period, beginning in
the late 1570s, and marked by the famous *mahzar* (document) of 1579, when
Akbar's own universal pretensions emerged, and were accompanied by a changed
policy of internal political alliances; and a final one, beginning in the late 1580s,
which saw the flowering of the mature Akbarian ideology as defined by the great
ideologue, Abu'l Fazl.[22] These shifts, and especially the transition from the
second to the third phase, must be kept in mind for the analysis that follows.

By the mid-1570s, a loose arrangement had been reached to manage the
external affairs of still-turbulent Gujarat; the trade of Surat was dealt with by
the *hâkim*, or local governor, in these years Qilij Muhammad Khan Andijani,
and revenue collection in and around the port city largely carried out through
the mediation of local elites, who were given the position of revenue farmers
(*mustâjirân*).[23] In this system, private Portuguese traders at Surat or Khambayat

[22] This interpretation draws on but differs in several respects from that of Iqtidar Alam
Khan, 'Akbar's personality traits and world outlook: A critical reappraisal', *Social
Scientist*, Vol. XX, nos 9–10 (No. 232–3), 1992, pp. 16–30. Also see, for an earlier
argument, Iqtidar Alam Khan, 'The Nobility under Akbar and the Development of His
Religious Policy, 1560–80', *Journal of the Royal Asiatic Society of Great Britain and
Ireland*, 1968, Nos 1 and 2, pp. 29–36.

[23] Farhat Hasan, 'Surat in the reign of Akbar', paper presented to a seminar on *Akbar
and His Age*, Aligarh, 9–11 October 1992.

were able to carry on their commerce with Goa and Cochin; the *Estado da Índia* continued to collect revenues from ships that were obliged to put in at Diu; the Mughals, for their part, were placated by the giving of *cartazes* for their vessels destined to the Red Sea carrying *hâjîs*.

Beneath this tranquil surface, however, certain changes of importance were taking place. For one, the 1570s saw the extension of fiscal centralism in the Mughal state, causing stirrings among large sections of the nobility, which saw its privileges as under threat; among those who were highly perturbed were the Central Asian (or Turani) nobles, led by Mirza 'Aziz Koka, son of Shams al-Din Atka Khan, and named governor of Gujarat almost immediately after the Mughal conquest. At the same time, a definitive attempt was made to shift the ideological basis of Akbar's rule by redefining his image in keeping with the messianistic expectations of the times.[24] In early September 1579, a group of theologians, including the *Shaikh ul-Islâm* were pressurized into signing a text claiming for Akbar a special status of *Pâdshâh-i Islâm*, beyond that even of a *Sultân-i 'Âdil*. From the writings of Abu'l Fazl, we gather that one of the epithets used for him was now *Mujtahid*, as also *Imâm-i 'Âdil*, the latter startlingly close to the usages favoured at one time by Süleyman.[25] Indeed, the challenge was directed in good measure at the Ottomans, who had claimed superior status as the *Khalîfas* of the east, with their conquest of Egypt. But other relatively orthodox Sunni rulers, from Mirza Hakim at Kabul, to 'Abdullah Khan Uzbek, could not ignore the implications of such claims. And Akbar's relations with the Portuguese too had to be redefined in this new context.

The crucial issue of these years in Mughal–Portuguese relations was the *hajj*. Before defining his new ideological stance which we have sketched out above, Akbar had sent away some of the members of his own family—including his aunt Gulbadan Begam who would almost certainly have been opposed to such a shift—for a pilgrimage of the Holy Cities. At this stage, the tensions inherent in dealing with the Portuguese *Estado da Índia* became even more marked. It was one thing, after all, to send Haji Habibullah Kashi to Goa in 1575 to seek

---

[24] It is possible that this shift was also influenced by Akbar's contacts with the Mahdawi followers of Sayyid Muhammad Jaunpuri in Gujarat in the 1570s; cf. John F. Richards, *The Mughal Empire* (*The New Cambridge History of India*, I.5), Cambridge, 1993, p. 38. Also see S. A. A. Rizvi, *Muslim Revivalist Movements in Northern India in the Sixteenth and Seventeenth Centuries*, Agra, 1965. The key texts of this period are the *Târîkh-i Alfi* by various hands, and Muhammad 'Arif Qandahari's *Târîkh-i Akbari* (c. 1580–1) (for which see Note 47).

[25] Mulla 'Abd al-Qadir al-Badayuni even suggests that Akbar was termed *Insân-i Kâmil* at the suggestion of Shaikh Taj al-Din of Ajodhan, as well as *Sâhib-i Zamân*; cf. his *Muntakhab ut-Tawârîkh*, Vol. II, tr., George S. A. Ranking, reprint, New Delhi, 1990, pp. 265–6, 278–80, 295. See also Abu'l Fazl, *Akbar Nâma*, Vol. III, pp. 390–3.

out 'clever craftsmen', but it was quite another to test whether in reality 'the governors of the European ports had become shakers of the chain of supplication', after the Mughal conquest of Gujarat.[26] Gulbadan's party thus had a difficult time, embarking from Surat in October 1576, after a stay of almost a year in Gujarat. Monserrate in his account suggests that Gulbadan had given over the territory of Bulsar, near Daman, to the Portuguese in order to ensure her safe passage to the Red Sea. The fact that such a gift had to be made rankled: it must have seemed to the Mughal court that its inflated claims for Akbar's status in the Islamic world were given the lie directly by this flagrant compromise with the *firangîs*. Orthodox Sunni elements like Mulla 'Abdullah Sultanpuri, titled Makhdum ul-Mulk, were quick to seize the opportunity to taunt Akbar for his acceptance of such an arrangement.[27]

In 1579, then, Akbar and his advisers were caught in a cleft stick. Their strategy of promoting heterodox religious debate—both within Islam and outside it—led them in the direction of encouraging the first Jesuit mission to Fatehpur Sikri from Goa. This window to Europe was also, we can gather, meant to outflank the Ottomans, and to an extent is hence a precursor to Shah 'Abbas's European strategy of the early 1600s. In the case of Shah 'Abbas, there was a concrete military and commercial purpose that lent his dealings with Spain some urgency (even if they bore no real fruit); with Akbar the play was more at the level of the symbolic and of prestige. Yet, the Portuguese *Estado* was in turn viewed with great reticence, for its Christianity, and for the fact that it held the key to the sea-lanes of the *hajj*. Akbar may have been drifting towards a heterodox, messianically-flavoured Islam, but in the late 1570s and early 1580s, he was still concerned with the significance of the *hajj* and the importance of the Holy Cities. Gulbadan's pilgrimage thus underlined the central problem: if the Ottomans were hostile to her party, the Portuguese too were an irritant.

Akbar's dilemma of these years is nicely captured in a letter sent by him to 'Abdullah Khan Uzbek, the powerful ruler of Transoxania, in 1586, and carried by Hakim Humam. In 1577, let us recall, 'Abdullah Khan had sent an ambassador to Akbar suggesting a joint expedition against the Safavids.[28] Akbar had shown his lack of interest in the venture, leading 'Abdullah Khan to gravitate first towards a possible alliance with Mirza Hakim, in the years 1579–81, and still later to the Ottomans. Nevertheless, as late as 1586, Akbar felt it necessary to justify himself before the Turani ruler, and especially to delineate his policy

---

[26] Abu'l Fazl, *Akbar Nâma*, Vol. III, p. 207.

[27] Badayuni, *Muntakhab ut-Tawârîkh*, Vol. II, pp. 205–6.

[28] Mansura Haider, 'Relations of Abdullah Khan Uzbeg with Akbar', *Cahiers du Monde Russe et Soviétique*, Vol. XXIII (3–4), 1982, pp. 313–31, on pp. 317–20. Haider suggests that the proposal was a ploy, rather than a serious venture.

with respect to the Portuguese; a particular problem was 'Abdullah Khan's accusation, in view of the developments of 1579 and thereafter, that Akbar had ceased to be a good Muslim. To this Akbar (and his amanuensis Abu'l Fazl) responded by posing the Mughal ruler precisely as an Islamic conqueror. Thus:

Places which from the time of the rise of the sun of Islam till the present day had not been trod by the horse-hooves of world-conquering princes and where their swords had never flashed, have become the dwelling-places and the homes of the faithful. The churches and temples of the infidels and heretics have become mosques and holy shrines for the masters of orthodoxy. God be praised! What we wished for has been accomplished, and arrangements have been made in accordance to our desires. All the leaders and stiff-necked ones of the hosts of Hindus and others, have placed the rings of obedience in their ears and been enrolled among the victorious armies.[29]

Thus, the Mughal armies are shown as not merely laying the foundations of justice and irrigating 'the garden of men's hopes and peace', but 'bringing to book' both Christians and Hindus, and establishing an order not simply based on any form of Islam, but on that of the *sunnat-o-jamâ'at* (the adherents of the first four Caliphs). In this idyllic picture, the Portuguese could not but be the fly in the ointment. Therefore, the letter continues:

I have kept before my mind the idea that when I should be entirely at liberty from these [other] tasks, I should, under the guidance of God's favour, undertake the destruction of the *firangî* infidels who have come to the islands (*sic*) of the ocean, and have lifted up the head of turbulence, and stretched out the hand of oppression upon the pilgrims to the holy places. May God increase their glory! They [the *firangîs*] have become a great number and are stumbling-blocks to the pilgrims and traders. We thought of going there in person and cleansing that road from thorns and weeds.

But other pressing matters had, alas, interrupted. The Safavid ruler Muhammad Khudabanda faced rebellions from provincial governors (the reference is probably to the attempt by 'Ali Quli Khan Shamlu, governor of Khurasan, to raise 'Abbas Mirza to the throne in 1581), and the Mughal ruler felt obliged to go to his aid, the more so since the Ottomans were preying on him. Here then is how the events from 1572–3 to 1586 were presented retrospectively for the edification of 'Abdullah Khan. Naturally, Akbar did not speak of the widespread rebellions in his own territories (in Bihar and Bengal) in 1579–80, or the elaborate expe-

---

[29] Abu'l Fazl, *Akbar Nâma*, III, p. 757. For earlier and later correspondence between Akbar and 'Abdullah Khan, see Riazul Islam, *A Calendar of Documents on Indo-Persian Relations (1500–1750)*, 2 Vols, Karachi/Teheran, 1978–82, Vol. II. The major themes of the 1586 letter are already rehearsed in letters of the late 1570s. This letter is briefly mentioned but dismissed as empty rhetoric in M. N. Pearson, 'The Estado da Índia and the Hajj', *Indica*, Vol. XXVI, Nos 1–2, 1989, p. 118.

dition in 1581 to attack his brother Mirza Hakim in Kabul. These tests to the Mughal polity had been passed by that time, and the unfortunate Mirza Hakim had fallen into 'the whirlpool of destruction' in 1585. The Portuguese were thus posed in their appropriate context, the conduct of international affairs, along with the Safavids, Ottomans, and—indeed—the Uzbeks themselves.

The Estado da Índia, 1580–1

We may return now to early 1580, when Monserrate and his companions were making their way to the Mughal court. It is a curious fact that the *Akbar Nâma* records the sending of Qutb al-Din Muhammad Khan at almost precisely the same time (18 Bahman 987) 'to capture the European ports', and also 'to remove the Firangis who were a stumbling block in the way of the pilgrims to the Hijaz'.[30] Let us note that the motives given are almost exactly the same as in the later letter to 'Abdullah Khan Uzbek. Let us note too that Qutb al-Din Muhammad Khan was no ordinary noble, but rather a member of the *atka khail* or 'foster-brother battalion' (which we have already encountered), so named because of the special relationship of fictive kinship between *his* brother Shams al-Din Muhammad Atka Khan and Humayun, whose life he had once saved. A high *mansabdâr* with the rank of 5000, Qutb al-Din Khan's *jâgîr* of Broach was located within striking distance of Daman. But before the battle could be joined, some matters remained to be settled.

The most immediate problem was of Gulbadan's party, which still remained in the Hijaz, but whose return was imminently expected. Akbar had instructed the *Mîr Hajj*, Khwaja Yahya Naqshbandi, to urge the party to return, after they had been in the Holy Cities for over three years and had created a series of embarrassing situations, with their 'strange activities', which were deemed 'contrary to the Shariat' by the local authorities. The Ottoman Sultan, Murad III, had in fact issued repeated *farmâns* to the *beylerbey* of Egypt and the Sharif of Mecca, to urge Gulbadan's party to depart. The first of these, dated October 1578, notes that the presence of the party had led to overcrowding in the Ka'ba Sharif, and to a shortage of provisions. Their expulsion was hence ordered, but not carried out, probably for fear of committing a diplomatic impropriety. The *farmân* had hence to be reiterated, in February and March 1580,

---

[30] Abu'l Fazl, *Akbar Nâma*, Vol. III, pp. 409–10.

[31] The relevant *farmâns* from the *Basvekâlet Arsivi*, Istanbul, Mühimme Defterleri, are translated in N. R. Farooqi, 'Six Ottoman Documents on Mughal-Ottoman relations during the reign of Akbar', in Iqtidar Alam Khan, ed., *Akbar and his Age*, New Delhi, 1999, pp. 209–22. For earlier discussions, see Farooqi, *Mughal-Ottoman Relations*, pp. 113–14, and Suraiya Faroqhi, *Pilgrims and Sultans: The Hajj under the Ottomans, 1517–1683*, London, 1994, pp. 129–33.

and then again in August of that year.[31] The party finally embarked in two ships, probably from Jiddah, in that year, but were wrecked off Aden, where they had to endure harrassment from the local governor during a seven-month stay.[32] It was thus only in 1581, at a date that cannot be precisely determined, that they returned to Surat, eventually making their way back to Fatehpur Sikri only in April 1582.

Between the moment that instructions were issued, in early 1580, to Qutb al-Din Khan, and the clearing of the ground for hostilities therefore, a year had to pass. This was, as it happens, the same fateful year when the Prior of Crato was first proclaimed king, and then expelled, and when Philip II was in turn proclaimed ruler of Portugal. The same year too, when 'Ali 'Adil Shah met an unfortunate end at the hands of a palace slave, and the same year as well when Ibrahim Qutb Shah of Golconda died on 5 June, from a violent bout of typhoid. Further east, it was the year when the short-lived Sultan Zain al-'Abidin, the third successor in the brief space of a year to 'Ali Ri'ayat Syah of Aceh, met his end. Kings, it seemed, were dying like flies, but not always with the same consequences. The transition in Golconda to Muhammad Quli Qutb Shah was smooth, that in Bijapur far more contested, claiming numerous victims along the way, including the veteran Iranian-born diplomat Mustafa Khan Ardistani.

And how did the *Estado da Índia* work its way through the transition that followed the change of regime in 1580? The historian who seeks an answer to this question has a natural tendency to turn to the great chronicle of Diogo do Couto, whose *Década Décima* begins precisely with this moment of transition.[33] And this is no coincidence, for we know that it was Couto's original intention to begin his work with the proclamation of Philip II in the *Estado da Índia*, and it was only subsequently that he decided to start his chronicle much earlier, in continuation of Barros.[34] One part of this transition, the purely administrative, passed off with far less difficulty than might have been imagined. The Habsburgs and their agents had suspected Dom Lu-ıs de Ata-ıde of being a supporter of the Prior of Crato, and were prepared to offer him a superior title, perhaps that of

---

[32] For Gulbadan at Aden, see Bayazid Bayat, *Tazkira-i-Humâyûn wa Akbar*, ed. M. Hidayat Hosain, Calcutta, 1941, pp. 355–6. For a discussion also see Annette S. Beveridge, 'Introduction', in *The History of Humayun (Humâyûn-Nâma) by Gul-Badan Begam*, reprint, New Delhi, 1989, pp. 74–5. Finally, for a general overview (albeit a rather pedestrian one) of Mughal dealings with the Hijaz, see M. N. Pearson, 'The Mughals and the Hajj', *Journal of the Oriental Society of Australia*, Vols XVIII–XIX, 1986–7, pp. 164–79.

[33] Diogo do Couto, *Da Ásia, Décadas IV–XII* (reprint, Lisbon, 1974–5. from the Régia Oficina Tipografica edition, 1778–88).

[34] Cf. António Coimbra Martins, 'Sobre a génese da obra de Couto (1569–1600): Uma carta inédita', *Arquivos do Centro Cultural Português*, Vol. VIII, 1974, pp. 131–74.

Marques de Santarém, for his allegiance. His position in rumour was analogous to that of Dom Constantino de Bragança earlier: after the death of Dom João III in 1558, it was widely believed that the *Estado da Índia* and its viceroy might secede from Portugal.[35] It was hence decided, in late 1580, to send out a handpicked successor, with the personal prestige to provide the Habsburgs legitimacy, and whose loyalty was also unquestionable: the person chosen was Dom Francisco Mascarenhas, named Conde de Vila da Horta.

Choosing Mascarenhas was politically rather astute. As the defender of Chaul in 1570–1 against the Nizam Shahi forces, he had a formidable military reputation; further, he had accompanied Dom Sebastião to North Africa, and had even sensibly advised him to hold his position rather than advance on the eve of the battle of Alcácer-Quibir. Captured, he was ransomed as a 'plebeian' rather than a nobleman; when the question of succession arose, he threw his weight solidly behind the Habsburgs, receiving titles (Count of Vila da Horta and then, in 1593, Count of Santa Cruz), donatory-captaincies on the Atlantic islands (Flores, Corvo, and Santo Antão, in 1596), and even being named one of the governors of Portugal in 1593 in place of Archduke Alberto. On 8 April 1581, when he embarked with his fleet from Lisbon, it was with ample powers of negotiation (he reputedly carried, as Couto puts it, 'signed and blank *alvarás*', as well as memberships in the military orders to distribute as largesse), in case there was resistance in the *Estado da Índia* to the Habsburg succession; he also had a limited agenda of reform, particularly in respect of the customs-houses of Chaul and Cochin.[36]

The situation on his arrival was an anti-climactic one. On 10 March 1581, the viceroy Dom Lu-ıs de Ata-ıde had died, still having received no news of the succession. In his place, as governor, was Fernão Teles de Meneses, reputedly one of the Prior of Crato's sympathizers. Due back from Melaka later that year or early next year, at the end of his term as captain was the ambitious, and somewhat unscrupulous, Dom João da Gama, grandson of Vasco da Gama. His solidarity with Meneses was less than clear, as indeed was that of his brother Dom Miguel da Gama, himself returned from making the China–Japan voyage. Waiting in the wings was the captain of Diu, Dom Pedro de Meneses, who had hoped to be named governor at the death of Dom Lu-ıs de Ata-ıde, and who was not about to support Fernão Teles in any political adventurism. The position of

---

[35] Aubin, 'Per viam portugalensem', p. 49, citing a letter from Lourenço Pires de Távora at Rome to Dom Sebastião, dated 19 July 1561, in *Corpo Diplomatico Portuguez*, Vol. IX, pp. 306–7.

[36] Sanjay Subrahmanyam, *The Political Economy of Commerce: Southern India, 1500–1650*, Cambridge, 1990, pp. 218–20, based in good measure on Couto, *Década Décima*, Parte I, pp. 472–80.

other powerful noblemen like Matias de Albuquerque, who had also recently returned from Melaka where he had served as *capitão-mor do Sul*, and eager to go to Hurmuz where he was to be captain, was equally unclear. The close association of Albuquerque with Dom Diogo de Meneses at an earlier stage of his career might weigh with him against the Habsburgs; on the other hand, Albuquerque's dislike for Dom Lu-ıs de Ata-ıde (as also possibly for Fernão Teles himself), and his flagrant opportunism career-wise could well lead him in the other direction.[37] In the final analysis, therefore, Teles de Meneses decided to opt for the safe course. When letters finally arrived for him overland, informing him of the succession, he swore the loyalty of the *Estado da Índia* to Philip II, on 3 September 1581.

There are a few indications that it may have been his intention right from March to await the outcome of events in Portugal, and go along with whatever was decided there. The report of the Venetian ambassador Morosini, written in late 1581, suggests as much:

It is believed that in the East Indies, His Majesty will not meet any opposition, because the captain of the fleet that returned just now went of his own will to present himself to His Majesty, saying that he had orders from the Governor of those Indies to obey whoever would be declared King by the governors of the kingdom...[38]

Did Fernão Teles de Meneses then have other reasons that led him to suppress his personal preferences? While we have no means of knowing for certain, a collection of documents from the transition period helps us to clarify matters to some extent at least. These include the 'Act of Transfer' (*auto da entrega*) by which Fernão Teles handed over the government to Dom Francisco Mascarenhas on 28 September 1581, as well as several letters and certificates dating from November and December 1581, addressed in their great majority to Philip II, and meant to be sent back to Portugal with the ships of winter 1581–2.[39] These papers include several signed by the *vedor da fazenda* and

[37] *Biblioteca Pública e Arquivo Distrital*, Évora, Codex cxv/1–13, 'Vida de Mathias de Albuquerque', Part I, Chs 3, 4, and 11, fls 9v–17v, 41v–45.

[38] 'Nelle Indie orientali non si crede che S. M. abbia ad avere alcun contrario, poiche il capitano della flota ultimamente venuta s'è volontariamente andato a presentar a S. M., dicendo d'aver ordine dal governador di esse Indie di ubbidire a chi sara stato dichiarato rè dai governatori del regno, siccome egli ancora voleva fare; di modo che, superata la difficolta delle Terzere, restera S. M. pacifico possessore di tutto il regno di Portogallo...'; cf. Alberi, ed., *Relazioni degli ambasciatori*, Vol. V, p. 310.

[39] Bibliothèque Nationale de France, Paris (henceforth BN), Fonds Portugais, No. 23, fls 115–16v, 'Treslado do auto da entregua da governança da Índia que fez o Senhor Governador Fernão Telez de Meneses ao Senhor Viso Rey Dom Francisco Mazcarenhas Conde de Viladorta'.

provedor-mor dos contos, Simão do Rego Fialho, who is also the author of the budget (*orçamento*) of 1581, published two decades ago by Artur Teodoro de Matos.[40]

Let us begin however with Fernão Teles himself, and his evaluation of the situation in the *Estado da Índia*, place by place in the 'Act of Transfer'. Goa, he declares, is at peace, save for some residual tension with the 'Adil Shahs, who are yet to honour a few clauses in a treaty signed by them;[41] there is also some unrest in Salsette as a consequence. Bassein, on the other hand, is rather unquiet (*desinquieta*) on account of difficulties with a neighbouring chief (*Rey dos Coles*), and the same is true of Asserim and Manora. Daman again is full of unrest. Further, 'from the letters of the Padres who are in the Court, it is understood that Equebar has ordered that people be brought together to take the said fortress by siege'. The situation in Colombo, on the contrary, is on the mend; the Raju has been defeated in February 1581, but has now built a large and strong city four leagues from Colombo, so that renewed troubles were possible. Hurmuz was at peace, but there were troubles with the ruler of Lar, who had taken Kamaran (Gombroon), leading to an interruption in the caravan traffic into Hurmuz. We note in passing that Fernão Teles had apparently not been advised of the activities of four Ottoman galleys under the 'corsair' Mir 'Ali Bey (sent out by Cighalazade Sinan Pasha to raid Masqat in September that year).[42] Diu, Chaul, and Karanja were incident-free. The Mappilas were reported active near Nagapattinam, where the Nayaka of Tanjavur had recently expelled the resident Portuguese *casados*; as for Malaca, Ambon, and Tidore, there was no recent news from there. Teles de Meneses concludes this rapid *tour d'horizon* by noting: 'All of these fortresses are largely lacking in munitions and other things that are needed for their defence, and all the captains demand supplies with great

[40] The document from Arquivos Nacionais/Torre do Tombo, Lisbon (henceforth AN/TT), Fundo Antigo, No. 845, is published integrally in Artur Teodoro de Matos, *O Estado da Índia nos anos de 1581–88: Estrutura administrativa e economica, alguns elementos para o seu estudo*, Ponta Delgada, 1982, pp. 51–191. Matos did not however use the Paris papers of 1581 cited in this chapter, though they are cited sporadically in Vitorino Magalhães Godinho, *Les Finances de l'Etat Portugais des Indes Orientales (1517–1635)*, Paris, 1982.

[41] Also see BN, Paris, Fonds. Ports. No. 23, 'Treslado do asemto que se tomou sobre as pazes deste estado com o Idalxá', fls 473–4, copy made by Manuel Botelho Cabral, 4 October 1581. Also relevant is a letter on fls 399–99v, from Yusuf Khan to Philip II, dated 3 December 1581, proposing that Ibrahim 'Adil Shah II be deposed.

[42] For details of this raid, see Couto, *Década Décima*, Parte I, pp. 84–99. Also R. B. Serjeant, ed. and trans., *The Portuguese off the South Arabian Coast: Hadrami Chronicles*, Oxford, 1963, p. 111.

[43] BN, Paris, Fonds. Ports. No. 23, 'Treslado do auto da entregua...', fl. 116.

insistence, which should be sent to them.'[43] The conclusion might well be that the governor had some doubts about the military strength of the *Estado*, a good reason to opt for a conservative strategy.

Financially, affairs can be gauged from the 1581 *orçamento*, as also other treasury papers. A certificate from the *vedor da fazenda*, Diogo Corvo, suggests the following 'cash-flow' position.

The Estado da Índia's Finances, 1581 (in *pardaos*)[44]
Treasury balance on 10/3/1581: 61,500–4–40
Addn. Revenues to 28/9/1581: 196,803–0–27
Expenditure from 10/3 to 28/9: 128,562–4–33
Treasury Balance on 28/9/1581: 129,741–0–34

There were, of course, other more complicated calculations to be made; a sum of 21,898 *pardaos* from the Goa customs-house that was allocated directly to expenditure without entering the treasury; from the annual revenues of Salsette and Bardes, a sum of over 50,000 *pardaos* was allocated to the payment of old state loans and debts; in sum there were a number of transactions that allocated revenue to expenditure without entering central finances.

The view of Simão do Rego Fialho suggests a far more pessimistic picture. Having noted that besides the expenditures that enter into the usual calculations, there is a large category of *extraordinárias*, intended to sustain widows, orphans, poor cavaliers, and *fidalgos* waiting to claim a benefice, he concludes: 'The *Estado* spends more than it collects on a regular basis to the amount of 29 *contos* of *reis* from one year to another, besides the matters of chance for which one cannot make a certain calculation.' Not only this, in his view, most *fidalgos* in the first part of the careers, before they were given a benefice (*mercê*), routinely ran up substantial debts.

Each one of them has eight or nine thousand *pardaos*, fifteen or twenty thousand *pardaos* of debts, which they incur from when they begin to serve to the time they enter the said *mercês*, and unless they are greatly favoured, cannot get rid of their debts or improve themselves.[45]

This suggests an altogether precarious situation as much for the nobility as for the Crown, which is puzzling; it might seem that everyone was losing money on the enterprise! There were, of course, the direct returns on commerce, whether to the *casados*, or indeed to the nobles and officials in a private capacity. But

[44] BN, Paris, Fonds. Ports. No. 23, fls 465–65v, Certidão de Diogo Corvo, vedor da fazenda, 22 November 1581.
[45] BN, Paris, Fonds. Ports. No. 23, fls 414–14v, Simão do Rego Fialho to the King, 23 November 1581.

the point which Fialho makes can be reinterpreted more meaningfully: the *fidalgo*'s career was based on a sort of cycle of not merely service (and the periodic presentation of *cartas de serviço* and *consultas de partes* at different phases of the career), but on a financial cycle, in which the first part of the career required the incurring of debts, to support clients, or to underwrite what were normally state expenses, so as to be able to recoup them later on. This elaborate logic, based on a dependent relationship between the *Estado* and its constituent parts on the one hand, and the Crown on the other, could simply not be called into question by its participants; from this perspective, an autonomous *Estado da Índia* was a non-issue. But there was still the possibility of a fair amount of autonomous initiative within the system as it existed, as we see from the numerous cases of fleets of *aventureiros* sent out in these years, and which included one to Gujarat in 1581. With this fleet, the logic we have been developing comes full circle; the internal mechanisms of the *Estado da Índia* and the Mughals both emerge into the full light.

The Gujarat Trade Tussle of 1581–3

In his well-known work of the mid-1970s, *Merchants and Rulers in Gujarat*, M. N. Pearson devotes considerable attention to the Mughal–Portuguese conflict in and around the major port of Surat in the years 1581–5. To Pearson, relying largely on the chronicle of Diogo do Couto, the conflict resulted from the peculiar predilections of the 'captain of Surat fort' Qilij Khan Andijani, who as 'a proud man, a strict sunni Muslim, a Turk of the Jani Qurbani tribe, and a confidant of the Emperor', could not tolerate the Portuguese system of *cartazes*. Thus, he is said to have decided to send a ship to the Red Sea without a *cartaz*, and entered headlong into conflict with the Portuguese *Estado*, which sent a fleet to stop him. Skirmishes on land followed, in which the Mughal forces were commanded by Qilij Khan's brother. Then, in order to break the stalemate, Qilij Khan 'without saying anything to Akbar... got the captain of Broach to undertake a diversionary attack on Daman'. The Broach captain, it seems, acted only to get the Portuguese fleet to lift the blockade of Surat, to allow Qilij Khan's ship to sail. Unfortunately, the merchants of Surat showed no desire to support Qilij Khan, and refused to send goods on his ship; to make matters worse, 'Akbar was furious with him for arranging the attack on Daman without his permission'.[46]

Couto's account continues in the same vein, to speak of retaliatory attacks

---

[46] M. N. Pearson, *Merchants and Rulers in Gujarat: The Response to the Portuguese in the Sixteenth Century*, Berkeley-Los Angeles, 1976, pp. 57–60; the account derives from Couto, *Década Décima*, Parte I. It is noteworthy that Pearson has used neither the account of Monserrate nor Bayazid Bayat, nor even the document cited in Note 50, in his work.

by a later Portuguese fleet on other vessels returning from the Red Sea in 1582; one ship of Akbar was allowed to pass, but another Surat vessel partly plundered. The last episode in the series extends to 1585, and the 'villain' is still the same. Qilij Khan on this occasion, writes Couto, sent a well-armed ship to Jiddah without a *cartaz*, once more as a challenge to the Portuguese. On its return however, it ran aground near Surat, and was destroyed by a Portuguese fleet. Qilij Khan, it seems, lost both his ship and his 'reputation'.

The whole portrayal is typical of Couto, with his penchant to reduce everything to the high drama of the clash of personalities. Here then is Qilij Khan, a chivalrous and foolhardy Turk, forever with his hand on his scabbard (to assert that his sword is the best *cartaz*), and who—single-handedly defying the Mughal state as much as the *Estado da Índia*—is overtaken by the logic of *hubris*. In order to do so, he mobilizes his family (his brother, in 1581) and friends (the captain of Broach). Couto, quite characteristically in his gossipy style, describes Qilij Khan's family at some length, goes on to speak of how he was a childhood companion of Akbar, and even estimates the extent of his private fortune. Akbar is seen as, by turns, innocent of the doings of his own captains, and unable to control them. But do our other sources, both Mughal and Portuguese, square with this picture?

Let us begin by recalling that, according to the *Akbar Nâma*, Qutb al-Din Muhammad Khan (the 'Captain of Broach') had already been ordered by Akbar in early 1580 to move against Daman. Further, the evidence of Fernão Teles de Meneses cited above suggests that in September 1581, the Portuguese in Goa apprehended such a threat, emanating not from local initiative but from the Mughal court and Akbar. Third, the story of Qilij Khan does not quite add up, for he was no novice at negotiations. As *hâkim* of Surat, probably in 1576, he is reported for example to have negotiated with the Portuguese for *cartazes* for the *hajj* vessels: in the words of 'Abd al-Qadir al-Badayuni, he went 'together with Kalyan Rai Baqqal an inhabitant of Cambay to the port of Surat to obtain an agreement from the Europeans, so as to set free the ships of Sultan Khwajah [the *Mîr Hajj*], which for want of such an agreement lay idle'.[47] The reader of the Mughal chronicles discovers still another minor anomaly: during most of 1581, Qilij Khan was with Akbar in the Punjab and later at Kabul, participating in the campaign against Mirza Hakim. Further, on the execution of Shah Mansur Shirazi, he was briefly named *wazîr*, before returning to Gujarat,

---

[47] Badayuni, *Munta<u>kh</u>ab ut-Tawârî<u>kh</u>*, Vol. II, p. 249, where these events are placed in 1576 (i.e. Rajab 984 AH), suggesting that the *hajj* party was that of Gulbadan. It is strange that another account suggests that 'Abd al-Azim Sultan Khwaja was *Mîr Hajj* in 1577 (985 AH); see Muhammad 'Arif Qandahari, *Târî<u>kh</u>-i Akbarî*, tr. Tasneem Ahmad, Delhi, 1993, pp. 278–80.

possibly only in early 1582. Is it likely that he would, at the same time, have launched such a risk-prone, anti-Portuguese venture purely on his own personal initiative?

A rather valuable account from 1580 helps set the affairs of 1581–3 in perspective. This is the memoir of the veteran Mughal official, Bayazid Bayat, who set sail in that year from Surat for Jiddah, in the ship *Muhammadî*, belonging to Qilij Khan and Qutb al-Din Muhammad Khan. Accompanying him was Khwaja Yahya Naqshbandi, whom we have already encountered in our earlier discussion. Bayazid managed to get permission from the court to depart only with great difficulty, and after his personal effects had been closely examined. As it happened, the sum of 100,000 rupees was found on him, but Akbar dismissed the idea that these were the proceeds of embezzlement, and allowed him to embark with his three sons on the *hajj*. As Bayazid describes it, the ship having set sail from Surat put in at Daman, to pay the Diu-toll (*'ushûr-i Dîv*) to the *firangî* revenue-farmers (*ijâradârân*) there. This arrangement was apparently seen by Surat shipowners as more convenient than putting in at Diu itself. Once in Daman, a complicated negotiation ensued; the revenue-farmers were unwilling to step on board the ship to value the cargo, unless a hostage was sent ashore. One of Bayazid's sons was finally sent to serve this purpose, a settlement was reached after evaluation, and since the other passengers did not have ready cash, Bayazid advanced the sum 10,000 *mahmûdîs* on behalf of all of them with the intention of recovering it at Jiddah. Mention is made in these negotiations of a Surat official Hasan Chunu, titled *nâkhudâ-yi jahâzât-i Sırat*, who carried back a document on Bayazid's behalf to Tehpal, the *chaudhuri* of the port. Once these affairs had been settled, the voyage seems to have been a rapid and uneventful one; leaving Daman on 1 Safar 988 AH, the ship sighted the mountains of Aden after 14 days.[48] Bayazid remained in the Hijaz for three years, and the *firangî*s find little further mention in his account. Nevertheless, his memoir gives us a straightforward view of the inconveniences and negotiations involved in prosecuting any Surat-Red Sea voyage in the epoch.

A careful reading of the Jesuit Monserrate's account is equally a salutary corrective to Couto's highly coloured portrayal. From his perspective in the Mughal court, the Jesuit saw the conflict of 1581–2 as having three causes. First, he mentions the episode of Gulbadan's *hajj*, and the consequent conflict over Bulsar; other Jesuit sources, including a letter of 1582 cited below, confirm that Gulbadan was very ill-disposed to the Portuguese, and accuse her of spreading false rumours about an Ottoman fleet on her return from the *hajj*. Second,

[48] Bayazid Bayat, *Tazkira-i-Humâyın wa Akbar*, ed. M. Hidayat Hosain, pp. 355–6. I am grateful to Professor Sharif Husain Qasemi of the Department of Persian, University of Delhi, for reading this section of the text with me.

Monserrate like other observers notes the the vexed issue of *cartazes*, which created ill-feeling between the Portuguese and Mughal officials. Third, the *casus belli* on the occasion if we are to follow his account, was an unprovoked Mughal attack on the soldiers on board a Portuguese fleet commanded by Diogo Lopes Coutinho. Monserrate poses this last in essentially religious terms; nine of the soldiers—including a certain Duarte Pereira de Lacerda—were, he reports, dragged to Surat, and asked to convert to Islam, with a promise they would be given 'riches, honours and beautiful wives'. When they refused to do so, they were executed. This was followed by an attack by Qutb al-Din Khan and his son on Daman, which was defended in turn by Martim Afonso de Melo, captain of Daman, with the aid of Fernando de Castro, captain of Chaul; Manuel de Saldanha, captain of Bassein; and Fernão de Miranda, who commanded a fleet sent from Goa. The Mughal attack was beaten off after a stiff fight.[49]

Monserrate now addresses the issue of Akbar's complicity or lack thereof in the affair and arrives at a conclusion radically different from that of Couto. At first, he reports, Akbar 'swore that the war had been started without his knowledge', and that Qutb al-Din Khan and Shihab al-Din Ahmad Khan (*sûbadâr* of Gujarat from 1577 on) had begun the campaign of their own initiative as they were anti-Christian. An anonymous Jesuit letter of 1582 even claims that Akbar sent a message to Goa, saying that the *Estado* was free to attack Gujarat, and that he would be glad if Qilij Khan and Qutb al-Din Khan got their come-uppance ('the king himself advised the *Estado* that they should do as much harm as they could to these Captains').[50] But, soon enough, the Jesuits at the court began to doubt this version (which is in essence also that found in Couto). Monserrate for his part states that the Mughals were secretly planning an attack on Diu in 1582, which was foiled by the captain there, Dom Pedro de Meneses. His conclusion is thus that Akbar was perfectly cognizant of the anti-Portuguese activities in Gujarat, but preferred to conceal his hand for the time being.

Monserrate's own visit to Surat in 1582, *en route* from the Mughal court to Goa, confirmed his opinion. Anti-Portuguese feeling ran very high on the way, he reports: 'the mere name of Christian or Frank is horrible and hateful'.[51] Monserrate was accompanied on the voyage, which was the first leg of an abortive embassy from Akbar to Philip II, by Sayyid Muzaffar, a Turani noble who was closely related to Qutb al-Din Muhammad Khan, and whom the Jesuit

[49] *Commentary of Monserrate*, ed. Hoyland and Banerjee, pp. 166–9.

[50] AN/TT, Livro 28 de Jesuitas, fls 162–171v, reproduced in A. da Silva Rego, ed., *Documentação para a história das missões do padroado português do Oriente*, Vol. XII (1572–82), Lisbon, 1958, pp. 779–82, for a version rather close to that of Couto.

[51] *Commentary of Monserrate*, eds, Hoyland and Banerjee, pp. 185–91, especially, p. 186.

deeply distrusted.[52] Yet Monserrate could pass through Surat with the permission (even if reluctantly given) of Qilij Khan, was even feted with some ceremony, and went on board Fernão de Miranda's blockading fleet at the mouth of the Tapti. He even persuaded Miranda to release a large number of captives from the Red Sea-returned vessel that he had captured, thus somewhat helping defuse tensions in the port.

Monserrate's impressions, while at Fatehpur Sikri and then Surat, concord well with the other materials, in particular the evidence of the *Akbar Nâma*. Reading his account together with that of Abu'l Fazl, it is possible to obtain a sense of the intricate manoeuvrings that lay behind the Luso-Mughal conflict of these years, and which Couto apparently failed to grasp. It is clear from Abu'l Fazl and Badayuni that there were indeed differences between Akbar and the powerful Turani nobles in Gujarat such as Shihab al-Din Khan, Qutb al-Din Khan, and Qilij Khan. And this may well have emanated in turn from the opposition of these men, one of whom—Qutb al-Din Muhammad Khan—was 'Aziz Koka's uncle, to the new politics and ideological formation then gaining force in the court. It is thus not inconceivable in turn that Akbar was playing a dual game: on the one hand, he wished to show to the orthodox within his court (including his aunt, Gulbadan), to the Uzbeks, and even to the Ottomans, that he was firmly opposed to the *firangîs*; on the other, he was willing to use the Portuguese against those of his nobles who were politically suspect. One is put in mind of the celebrated letters from Abu'l Fazl to Mirza 'Aziz Koka in the early 1590s (after the latter abandoned the Mughal domains in 1593, in a huff, for the Hijaz), in which he threatened that he would turn both the Ottomans and the Portuguese *Estado* on him.[53] An empty threat in the event, but one that shows the complex nature of calculations in Mughal politics of the 1580s and 1590s.

Other circumstantial evidence also casts doubt on the view that Portuguese actions were merely a reaction to Qilij Khan's eccentric and intemperate behaviour. This includes the account of Diogo Corvo concerning the fleets sent

[52] There is a large literature on this embassy. We may content ourselves by noting the letter that accompanied it, drafted by Abu'l Fazl, and dated March–April 1582, translated by E. Rehatsek, 'A letter from the Emperor Akbar asking for Christian Scriptures', *The Indian Antiquary*, April 1877, pp. 135–9; for the general context, M. S. Renick, 'Akbar's First Embassy to Goa: Its Diplomatic and Religious Aspects', *Indica*, Vol. VII, 1970, pp. 32–47.

[53] The letter is to be found in the second *daftar* of the *Inshâ-yi Abû'l Fazl*, or *Mukâtabât-i 'Allâmî* (lithograph, Lucknow, 1863–4), a collection discussed in Saiyid Athar Abbas Rizvi, *Religious and Intellectual History of the Muslims in Akbar's Reign, 1556–1605 (with special reference to Abu'l Fazl)*, New Delhi, 1975, pp. 318–20.

out by Fernão Teles de Meneses during the six months of his governorship, which details the circumstances of the departure from Goa of the fleet of Diogo Lopes Coutinho, which features so significantly in Monserrate's relation.[54] Fernão Teles, we may note, adopted a particular strategy with respect to the sending out of patrolling fleets, which killed two birds with one stone. Under pressure to cut down expenses from the treasury, and at the same time anxious to meet the clamour of *fidalgos* so well evoked by Simão do Rego Fialho, the governor seems to have encouraged the practice of what were called *armadas de aventureiros*, private fleets under the command of *fidalgos*, which were sent out with the clear intention of taking prizes and conducting raids. One such *armada*, under the command of Gonçalo Vaz de Camões, was sent out by him just after the monsoon, to attack ships from Aceh and Burma at the Golconda port of Masulipatnam.[55] Still another, of eight *navios ligeiros*, he prepared to send to the north, under the command of Dom Simão da Silveira; when the latter fell ill and later died, the fleet's departure was delayed, so that it finally left Goa on 14 November 1581, under the command of Diogo Lopes Coutinho. It was this fleet which provided, as we have noted, the *casus belli*; its explicit, and thus provocative, intention was to go out for prizes (*andar às presas*). The difficulties encountered by Coutinho, and the aggravated situation in Daman, eventually led to the sending out of reinforcements, which Couto describes in some detail.

Neither the Mughals nor the Portuguese emerge covered in glory therefore: but nor do Qilij Khan's actions appear simply as the peculiar doings of someone who was 'a little slow to understand the system' on account of being 'a devout Sunni Muslim' and hence 'less inclined to submit to the Portuguese than would a Muslim who wore his religion more lightly'.[56] The Mughal context is important here: as long as Akbar's pretensions to being the *Imâm-i 'Âdil* and the *Insân-i Kâmil* lasted, which seems to have been to the late 1580s (indeed fairly close to the Islamic millennium in 1591–2), contradictions were bound to appear in his image. Some of the Jesuits persisted in seeing in him, to his death in 1605,

---

[54] BN, Paris, Fonds. Ports. No. 23, fls 477–77v, 'Das Armadas que deitou fora e como nenhuma era saida quando chegou'. On the *armadas de aventureiros*, also see the letter to Philip II from Dom Jerónimo Mascarenhas, Goa, 2 December 1581, BN, Paris, Fonds. Ports. No. 23, fls 423–23v: '…tenho busquado novos modos de o servir como foi Navios avintureiros que emventei em que andei dous anos que foi meio mui conhecido de por o Malavar no estado em que esta…'.

[55] Cf. Subrahmanyam, *Political Economy of Commerce,* p. 155; the account is based on Couto, *Década Décima,* Parte I, pp. 74–83, and AN/TT, Manuscritos da Livraria, No. 1104, fl. 105.

[56] Pearson, *Merchants and Rulers,* pp. 84–5.

a crypto- (or perhaps proto-) Christian, a Prester John in the making; on the other hand, the *Estado da Índia* saw in him an *inimigo encuberto*, or secret enemy, as both Matias de Albuquerque and Dom Francisco da Gama insisted in the 1590s. In the context of the transition of 1580–1, this internally inconsistent image contributed to the confusion in the *Estado*, the external relations of which were already in turmoil in view of the larger realignments taking place in Europe. Still fearful of a 'Turkish threat' that was really a chimera east of Masqat, barely privy to the shifts in Deccani politics of the time, the tangled logic of trade and pilgrimage in the Mughal domains was beyond the ken of both Couto and—in all probability—Fernão Teles de Meneses. As with Shah 'Abbas later in the same century, the Portuguese response to Akbar seems to have been one of awe mixed with loathing, and neither emotion made for the conduct of good politics.

Conclusion

There are two substantially opposed views in the recent historiography on the effects of the change of regime in Portugal in 1580–1. Most institutional and legally-minded historians, including those of an explicitly Marxist bent, have argued that Portugal and her empire were allowed by the Habsburg system of conciliar government to preserve a large degree of autonomy in the first half of Habsburg rule. In this interpretation, which is rather in the spirit of Robert Musil's character Count Leinsdorf, it is only midway through the reign of Philip III, and then particularly in the reign of Philip IV (and the period of dominance of the Count-Duke of Olivares), that Habsburg centralism begins to make its impact felt, eventually leading to a 'conservative' response in the form of the Portuguese Restoration.[57] In this view still, the changes of the years 1580–1610 are generally the result of large, impersonal, and principally economic forces: the rise of Brazil, the decline of the Mediterranean *vis-à-vis* the Atlantic, the imported inflation and consequent shifts in wealth and income distribution in

[57] This is represents a schematic reading of the complex argument in the work of Fernando Bouza Alvarez, 'Portugal en la monarqu-ıa hispanica (1580–1640): Felipe II, las Cortes de Tomar y la génesis del Portugal catolico', Ph.D. thesis, Univeridad Complutense, Madrid, 1987, which also forms the basis for a good part of António Manuel Hespanha, 'O governo das Austrias e a 'modernização' da constituição pol-ıtica portuguesa', *Penélope*, No. 2, 1989, pp. 49–74. Also see, for an earlier portrayal in similar terms, Patrick Lincoln Williams, 'The Court and Councils of Philip III of Spain', Ph.D. thesis, University of London, 1973; and most recently, the works of Antonio Feros, *Kingship and favoritism in the Spain of Philip III, 1598–1621*, Cambridge, 2000, and Jean-Frédéric Schaub, *Le Portugal au temps du comte-duc Olivares (1621–1640): Le conflit de juridictions comme exercice de la politique*, Madrid, 2001.

Portugal, and so on.[58] By implication, in the views of these historians, the transition of 1580–1 means nothing for the *Estado da Índia* except perhaps indirectly, as a marker in the longer-term process of the 'Atlantic turning'.

A more event-oriented and purely political interpretation, to which we have already referred above, would point directly to the political costs of 1580 for the Portuguese, and would argue that it was no coincidence that the first English expeditions into the Indian Ocean via the Cape route, as well as the beginnings of systematic Dutch attacks on the *Carreira da Índia*, date to after 1580. Further, from such a perspective, the years 1580–1610 bring about a fundamental weakening in the military and fiscal position of the Portuguese in Asia, and eventually lead to their delegitimization in the eyes of the Mughals (to the benefit of the English, and to a lesser extent the Dutch).

Fernand Braudel's model of the 'turning point of the century' may be said to combine elements of both these views, while leaning largely towards the first. However, he introduces what appears to be a somewhat irrelevant thread into the analysis in terms of a purported Ottoman thrust leading to a resumption of the 'war for control of the Indian Ocean' as a consequence of the 1580–1 transition. In his view, the energy earlier focused on the Mediterranean had to be transferred using a sort of parallelogram law of forces (or what he himself calls the 'physics of international relations') to two external zones: the Atlantic and the Indian Oceans.[59] In fact, the so-called eastern drive of the Ottomans turned out to be of little long-term consequence even where their land frontier was concerned: the gains in Georgia, western Iran, and Azarbaijan could simply not be sustained. As for the Indian Ocean, which Braudel disarmingly admitted was to him 'an unknown quantity', our effort has been to show, inter alia, that it makes little sense to see changes there in the period as largely (or even significantly) the consequence of a Portuguese-Ottoman struggle.

The approach followed in this chapter has attempted a variant tack from those set out above: that of exploring the interaction between domestic political and ideological shifts in several polities, and the wider system of international political alliances, taking as points of focus the Portuguese and the Mughals. This has brought us to consider 1580–1 as a moment not merely in Iberian history, but far more generally. One major motivation for this reconsideration, as stated at the outset, is persistent dissatisfaction with the neo-Weberian, structural-functional approach that gained currency in the 1970s in the study of

[58] The principal points of reference here would be the works of Frédéric Mauro and Vitorino Magalhães Godinho, especially the latter's '1580 e a Restauração', in *Ensaios*, Vol. II, Lisbon, 1968, pp. 255–92. But also see Braudel, *The Mediterranean*, Vol. II, pp. 1181–85.

[59] Braudel, *The Mediterranean*, Vol. II, pp. 1166, 1174–6.

the *Estado da Índia* and Indian Ocean trade more generally, with its confident assertion of immutable categories such as 'the Portuguese', 'the Dutch', 'the Ottomans', 'the Mughals', 'merchants', 'rulers', 'redistributive enterprises', and so on. The motives of all agents and actors in this world of trade and politics need to be examined, in terms not only of how we retrospectively slot them into binary functional and developmental schema (pedlars versus princes, merchants versus rulers, redistributive enterprises versus productive ones, the inexorable march of the dynamic and 'rational' principal actor over his sluggish Other) but through a reconstitution of both the ideational and the material contexts of actions. Seen in these terms, 1580–1 represents a set of unresolved tensions, in Mughal India, in Portuguese Asia, and in their interaction. This is precisely why it may be important.

4

The Portuguese, the Mughals, and Deccan Politics, c. 1600

Reason of State (*la razón de Estado*) can commonly be defined as a special doctrine which, by means of various rules, renders a prince skilful either in maintaining in his own person the States that he possesses, or in conserving in the same States the original form and greatness that they have, or in improving and increasing through new additions the ancient mass of which they are formed.

Pedro Barbosa Homem, *Discursos* (c. 1627)[1]

Introduction

Though there has been welcome emphasis in recent times on the biographies of the relatively 'little people' (*gente miuda*) in sixteenth- and seventeenth-century Portuguese Asia, it is in fact clear enough that even the 'great figures' of the epoch are somewhat ill-served. Mediocre biographies existed of men like D. João de Castro, somewhat better ones for Afonso de Albuquerque, D. Francisco de Almeida, Tristão da Cunha, Diogo Lopes de Sequeira, or António de Saldanha, but none at all that were worth mentioning for, say, Nuno da Cunha or D. Lu-ıs de Ata-ıde. Thus we were very far from a position wherein we could curl our collective lips with disdain, and declare biography itself to be passé, for the genre had barely been explored, since what passed for biography in Portuguese Asia was more often than not mere secular hagiography.[2] Of course,

---

[1] Citation from Pedro Barbosa Homem, *Discursos sobre la verdadera y jur-ıdica razón de Estado*, Coimbra, c. 1627, in Javier Peña Echeverr-ıa, ed., *La razón de Estado en España, Siglos XVI–XVII*, Madrid, 1998, p. 181.

[2] In the early 1990s, Kenneth McPherson and the current author co-directed a project entitled 'From Biography to History: Essays in the Social History of Portuguese Asia, 1500–1800', which appeared in a truncated form, as 12 essays but without its introduction,

there were the inevitable exceptions to this sweeping generalization, particularly once one takes into account the works of some of the major figures in modern Luso-Asian historiography, above all C. R. Boxer (on André Furtado de Mendonça), Jean Aubin (who devoted important essays to Duarte Galvão, Duarte Pacheco Pereira, and Francisco de Albuquerque), Panduronga Pissurlencar, Lu-ıs de Albuquerque, as well as (with all his limitations as a historian) Georg Schurhammer S. J. on Francis Xavier. But the revival of 'social biography' as a genre for Portuguese Asia nevertheless continues to be a desideratum, indeed precisely to advance along the path of a meaningful social (and even cultural and political-institutional) history.[3]

This serves in part to justify the pages that follow. In recent years, I have begun a leisurely and somewhat desultory investigation into the life and world of a Portuguese *fidalgo*, Dom Francisco da Gama (1565–1632), fourth Count of Vidigueira, and twice viceroy at Goa, from 1597 to 1600, and again from 1622 to 1628. This parallels two projects, one of my own, the other of Anthony Disney. My own other, rather more pressing, project has been a study—published in 1997—of the founder of the house of Vidigueira, Vasco da Gama himself.[4] Disney, for his part, has over the years published a number of essays as part of a project on another Portuguese viceroy, Dom Miguel de Noronha, Count of Linhares (at Goa from 1629 to 1635).[5] Disney's work has been substantially aided by the existence of extensive documents in Goa, in the two main archives in Lisbon, and at Simancas, besides Linhares's public diary which has survived in fragmentary form. For Vidigueira, while we are relatively well-served for his second viceroyalty of the 1620s, the first triennium from 1597 to 1600 seemed

---

in *Mare Liberum*, No. 5, 1993. The same idea was then 'borrowed' in a volume of *Arquivos do Centro Cultural Calouste Gulbenkian*, Vol. XXXIX, 2000, entitled 'Biographies', characteristically without acknowledgement of the earlier project.

[3] This is not to mention the parallel work in the equally neglected domain of prosopography; for a useful example of which see Santiago de Luxán Meléndez, 'Los funcionarios del Consejo de Portugal: 1580–1640', *Cuadernos de Investigación Histórica*, No. 12, 1989, pp. 197–228.

[4] Cf. Sanjay Subrahmanyam, *The Career and Legend of Vasco da Gama*, Cambridge, 1997.

[5] Cf. Anthony Disney, 'The viceroy Count of Linhares at Goa, 1629–35', in Lu-ıs de Albuquerque and Inácio Guerreiro, eds, *Actas do II Seminário Internacional de História Indo-Portuguesa*, Lisbon, 1985, pp. 301–15; Disney, 'The Viceroy as Entrepreneur: The Count of Linhares at Goa in the 1630s', in Roderich Ptak and Dietmar Rothermund, eds, *Emporia, Commodities and Entrepreneurs in Asian Maritime Trade, c. 1400–1750*, Stuttgart, 1991, pp. 427–44; and Disney, 'On attempting to write an early modern biography: My encounter with the life of Dom Miguel de Noronha, Fourth Count of Linhares (1588–1656)', *Indica*, Vol. XXIX (2), 1992, pp. 89–106.

to pose a far greater problem.[6] The standard series simply did not yield his letters or papers from these years. On the basis of earlier research on diplomatic correspondence of the late sixteenth century between Asian rulers and Goa, however, it was possible to piece together some of the Asian political context for Vidigueira's activities in his first term as viceroy.[7]

Vidigueira belonged to one of the important noble families of sixteenth- and seventeenth-century Portugal, and was the great-grandson of the celebrated Vasco da Gama, the 'discoverer' of the all-sea route to Asia via the Cape of Good Hope in 1498. Other members of the family too played a part of some prominence in the history of Portuguese Asia, including Dom Vasco's sons Estêvão da Gama and Cristóvão da Gama, the former briefly governor of the *Estado da Índia* in the early 1540s, and the latter the 'martyred' leader of an unsuccessful expedition to Ethiopia in 1541.[8] The third Count of Vidigueira, and grandson of Vasco da Gama, was Dom Vasco Lu-is da Gama, who besides

[6] António da Silva Rego, 'O in-icio do segundo governo do vice-rei da Índia D. Francisco da Gama, 1622–3', *Memórias da Academia das Ciências de Lisboa, Classe de Letras*, Tomo XIX, 1978, pp. 323–45, especially pp. 323–8. I have earlier dealt with Vidigueira's career in passing in my essay, 'An Augsburger in Ásia Portuguesa: Further Light on the Commercial World of Ferdinand Cron, 1587–1624', in Ptak and Rothermund, eds, *Emporia, Commodities and Entrepreneurs*, pp. 401–25, and in my *The Portuguese Empire in Asia, 1500–1700: A Political and Economic History*, London, 1993, pp. 234–6. For the period of Vidigueira's career between his two viceroyalties, useful materials may be found in Francisco Paulo Mendes da Luz, *O Conselho da Índia: Contributo ao Estudo da História da Administração e do Comércio do Ultramar Português nos princ-ipios do século XVII*, Lisbon, 1952, pp. 153–97, *passim*.

[7] Interestingly, the life of Vidigueira's contemporary and political rival, the Augustinian churchman-governor D. Frei Aleixo de Meneses (1559–1617), is far better documented, on account of ecclesiastical records. For a sample, see Padre Avelino de Jesus da Costa, 'Acção missionária e patriótica de D. Frei Aleixo de Meneses, Arcebispo de Goa e Primaz do Oriente', *Congresso do Mundo Português*, Vol. VI, Part I, Lisbon, 1940, pp. 209–47; and a number of articles by Carlos Alonso O.S.A., notably 'Documentación inédita para una biografia de Fr. Alejo de Meneses, O.S.A., Arzobispo de Goa (1595–1612)', *Analecta Augustiniana*, Vol. XXVII, 1964, pp. 263–333. Once more, though, we see the imperceptible slide here from biography to hagiography; also see Sanjay Subrahmanyam, 'Dom Frei Aleixo de Meneses (1559–1617) et l'échec des tentatives d'indigénisation du christianisme en Inde', *Archives de Sciences Sociales des Religions*, No. 103, 1998, pp. 21–42.

[8] During Vidigueira's second viceroyalty, in 1626, he managed with some effort to recover the relics of his granduncle Cristóvão da Gama from Ethiopia, showing once more how much store he set by his family's reputation; cf. *The 'Itinerário' of Jerónimo Lobo*, tr. D. M. Lockhart, ed. M. G. da Costa, annot. C. F. Beckingham, London, 1984, pp. 208–17.

his hereditary position of Admiral of the Indies, was also closely associated, successively, with the households of the Kings D. João III and D. Sebastião, as *estribeiro-mor*. He married into the politically powerful family of the Counts of Castanheira, with his wife Don Ana de Ata-ıde being a daughter of the first Count, António de Ata-ıde, the close confidant of Dom João III. The Gama–Ata-ıde alliance was an old one, though Vasco da Gama's own wife, deceptively named Catarina de Ata-ıde, did not belong to the same branch as the Counts of Castanheira. Dom Francisco da Gama's maternal uncle was the powerful Bishop of Viseu, Dom Jorge de Ata-ıde (1539–1611), who from 1579 held a series of positions of crucial political importance in Portugal and Spain, including president of the Council of Portugal under the Habsburgs. This relationship stood Dom Francisco in good stead at various points, when his career prospects came under a serious cloud.[9]

A crucial, and even determining event, in Dom Francisco da Gama's life was his participation in the ill-fated North African campaign of the Portuguese King Dom Sebastião, in 1578. This ruler, ignoring the advice of many both within Portugal and at the Habsburg court, embarked in July of that year with an expeditionary fleet in order to support one of two rival candidates of the Sa'di dynasty then ruling over Morocco. With him were the cream of the Portuguese nobility, including the Dukes of Bragança and Barcelos, the Count of Vidigueira and his 13-year-old son Dom Francisco da Gama, Dom Duarte de Meneses (later viceroy of Portuguese Asia from 1584 to 1588), and Cristóvão and Álvaro Pires de Távora, brothers of Rui Lourenço de Távora (also viceroy of Portuguese Asia from 1608 to 1612). Most of those mentioned above were either killed or captured in a celebrated battle at Wad al-Makhazin or al-Qasr al-Kebir (Alcácer-Quibir to the Portuguese) on 4 August 1578. The Count of Vidigueira was among those killed, and his son was made captive together with over 370 other *fidalgos*, ranging from Dom Duarte de Meneses to Dom Francisco de Portugal (son of the Count of Vimioso).[10] Eighty of these captured *fidalgos* were eventually ransomed from the Sa'di ruler for a sum of 400,000 *cruzados*, and Dom Francisco da Gama was among them. The man who arranged the ransom negotiations was one of the captives, Dom Duarte de Meneses (1537–88), who held the post in the 1578 campaign of *mestre-de-campo geral*. It was his daughter, Dona Maria de Vilhena, whom Dom Francisco da Gama married sometime in 1583–4, once

---

[9] On Dom Jorge de Ata-ıde, see British Library, London, (henceforth BL), Additional Manuscripts, Addn. 28,428, fos 156r–174v, *Memorial de la vida y muerte del Il^{mo} y R^{mo} Señor Don Jorge de Atayde...*; and on his early career, BL, Addn. 20,957, *Livro terceiro do Senhor Bispo Dom Jorge de Ata-ıde*.

[10] BL, Addn. 20,846, fos 17r–23v, *Rol dos fidalgos que cativarão em Africa o ano de 1578 aos quatro dias de agosto(...)*.

more showing how the 'Generation of Alcácer' had a profound impact as a collective on Habsburg administration in Portuguese Asia.[11]

After his return to Portugal from North Africa, Dom Francisco was confirmed in his position as Count of Vidigueira, and Admiral of the Indies by Philip II of Spain, who had by then become King of Portugal in 1580. A letter of 10 January 1581, addressed to him by Philip II at Elvas, enjoins him to attend the *cortes* (a general assembly for the acclamation of Philip as ruler of Portugal), or to send an agent empowered to swear loyalty on his behalf to Philip.[12] Other letters from the King in the 1580s and early 1590s confirm that Vidigueira was among those charged to perform a number of minor tasks in connection with Habsburg rule, and that the link between ruler and subject was strengthened through the latter's membership of the Order of Christ, of which Philip was the Master.

As heir to a substantial estate, Dom Francisco remained in Portugal through the 1580s and early 1590s, unlike some of his siblings who had to seek employment overseas. His brother Dom Jorge da Gama was, we note, killed in Asia in these years, 'honourably, in the service of the King my Lord', as a letter of condolence of September 1587 addressed to Vidigueira notes.[13] Two other brothers entered the church: one—Dom António—became a Capuchin friar, and the other Dom João da Gama attained the post of Bishop of Miranda. Still another brother, Dom Lu-ıs da Gama (or Dom Vasco Lu-ıs da Gama, as he appears in the standard genealogies of the family), had long service in Asia, both in the 1590s and thereafter, being implicated for example in the loss of the fort of Kamaran (or Gombroon) in September 1614 to Shah 'Abbas of Iran.[14]

---

[11] Arquivos Nacionals/Torre do Tombo, Lisbon (henceforth AN/TT), Convento da Graça, Tomo III [Cx. 2], p. 1, letter from the Cardinal D. Alberto to the Count of Vidigueira, 27 February 1585, which refers to 'o Viso Rey dom Duarte, vosso Sogro'.

[12] AN/TT, Convento da Graça, Tomo III [Cx. 2], p. 7.

[13] On condolences for D. Jorge da Gama's death, see the letter from the Cardinal D. Alberto to Vidigueira, AN/TT, Convento da Graça, Tomo III [Cx. 2], p. 3. D. Jorge's presence in Asia is noted already in 1583 by Diogo do Couto, *Da Ásia, Décadas IV–XII*, reprint, Lisbon, 1974–5, from the Régia Oficina Tipográfica edition, 1778–88, *Década Décima*, Parte I, p. 425, where D. Jorge is mentioned as one of the captains of the Malabar patrol fleet that year. He is described as 'D. Jorge da Gama, son of the Count of Vidigueira, D. Vasco da Gama, who had come this year from Portugal with 1,000 *pardaos* each year as a maintenance allowance'. His death near Masqat, while fighting the forces of 'Nequilús' in 1585, is reported in *Década Décima*, Parte II, pp. 253–5.

[14] For details of the family, see Felgueiras Gayo, *Nobiliário de Fam-ılias de Portugal*, Tomo XV, Braga, 1939, pp. 75–6; also the study by A. C. Teixeira de Aragão, *Vasco da Gama e a Vidigueira: Estudo Histórico*, Lisbon, 1898. On D. Lu-ıs da Gama at Hurmuz and Kamaran, see AN/TT, Convento da Graça, Tomo II-E [Cx. 6], pp. 161–73.

Then, in 1595, at the age of 30, and with no prominent service in any administrative capacity, the Count of Vidigueira was named viceroy of Portuguese Asia. The appointment had not been long contemplated. In 1593, for example, when the question was raised in the Council of Portugal in the context of a replacement for Matias de Albuquerque (who had been viceroy since May 1591), the strongest candidates seemed to be Fernão Teles de Meneses (who had served as interim governor at Goa for seven months in 1581), Fernão da Silva (Governor of the Algarve), and the Count of Linhares.[15] The last-named was eventually chosen but refused to accept, and Matias de Albuquerque was hence given a second three-year term, to 1597. It was in August 1595 that Vidigueira was chosen by Philip II, against the advice of the governors of Portugal, to succeed Albuquerque, and it was decided that he would embark in the spring of 1596, to take charge of the government by late that year.[16]

One can scarcely find two more diametrically opposite types than Matias de Albuquerque and Francisco da Gama among the viceroys of Portuguese Asia. The latter came to the viceroyalty almost purely as a right defined by his birth and family connections, with the prestige of not merely his great-grandfather but also his late father-in-law behind him. The reasons behind an appointment such as his can be found in a letter from the Count of Portalegre to the Marquis of Castel Rodrigo, Cristóvão de Moura, written on the occasion of the Count of Linhares's refusal to go to Asia as viceroy under the terms that were offered to him, in November 1594. He wrote, 'India also has an extreme need for everything that is necessary to conserve itself, money, men, munitions, leadership, authority, brio, and the expectation of rewards for feats of arms. Of these things, the most necessary and the one which it lacks the most is cavaliers and particular [prestigious] persons(...)', going on to add that 'it has already been said that the Count [of Linhares] can command [the loyalty of] more cavaliers than any other man in Portugal'. The conclusion then was that if Linhares would not go, whoever was in fact sent should be a nobleman of the same status, and

---

[15] BL, Addn. 20,929, letter from D. João da Silva, Count of Portalegre to Philip II, August 1593, fos 49r–49v; on Linhares's refusal, see the letter from the Count of Portalegre to Dom Cristóvão de Moura, Marquês de Castel Rodrigo, fos 74v–77r, November 1594.

[16] AN/TT, Colecção São Vicente, Vol. XII, pp. 119–20, letter from the governors of Portugal to Philip II, dated Lisbon, 8 August 1595. Also see *Memorial de Pero Roiz Soares*, ed. M. Lopes de Almeida, Vol. I, Coimbra, 1953, p. 319; Soares, a contemporary diarist, describes the appointment as follows: 'In April 1596, the King sent as viceroy to India the Count of Vidigueira, Admiral, son-in-law of the Viceroy Dom Duarte de Menezes, who at that time was a widower and youthful and from a well-connected family, given that he had no experience and had never been to India(...)'.

thus able to take along with him a retinue that would make an impact on Portuguese Asia.[17]

In marked contrast to Vidigueira was Matias de Albuquerque, whom we have encountered in an earlier chapter, a relatively petty nobleman, and whose main virtue was that he had served a number of captaincies in Asia in the 1570s and 1580s, and also commanded various fleets, before being appointed viceroy. In the late 1570s, for example, he commanded the 'southern fleet' in south-east Asian waters, combating the Acehnese; then, in the early 1580s, he headed the patrol fleet on the Malabar coast for several seasons, before acceding to the captaincy of Hurmuz. We find the high points of his career summarized in an obscure chronicle, probably by a certain Miguel de Lacerda, entitled *Vida e Acções de Mathias de Albuquerque* ('Life and Actions of Mathias de Albuquerque').[18] This text is a defence of Albuquerque's record in Asia—in the face of attacks on his reputation after his return to Portugal. The pattern is a common one during the 60 years of Spanish rule over Portugal (1580–1640); more than one viceroy or governor had to face charges of corruption or cowardice on returning to Europe, and several had small chronicles written to defend their conduct.[19]

Vidigueira, it is likely, did not resort to this after his first viceroyalty (even though it ended in somewhat unhappy circumstances), because his relations with the official chronicler, Diogo do Couto, were already sufficiently close that he

[17] Letter from the Count of Portalegre to Dom Cristóvão de Moura, BL, Addn. 20,929, fos 75r–76r, November 1594. Compare the later discussion on choosing a viceroy, in 1603, in BL, Addn. 28,432, fos 66r–81r, with the opinions of Francisco Nogueira, Henrique de Sousa Godinho, the Count of Vila Nova, the Viceroy of Portugal Dom Pedro de Castilho, and Dom Jorge de Ata-ıde. The reference is to the third Count of Linhares, D. Afonso de Noronha.

[18] For a discussion of this text, also see Subrahmanyam, *From the Tagus to the Ganges*, Chapter 6. In 1603, Matias de Albuquerque was turned down for the post of viceroy, because, in the opinion of Dom Jorge de Ata-ıde, 'besides having yet to free himself from the many charges in the investigations conducted against him, it is only recently that he was viceroy so that the loves and hates that were held in those parts are still very much alive, from which there are bound to follow many inconveniences in that Estado'; cf. BL, Addn. 28,432, fo. 80r. Some papers relevant to this question (including a letter by Matias de Albuquerque defending his own record) may be found in the James Ford Bell Library, University of Minnesota.

[19] For instance, see Lu-ıs Marinho de Azevedo, *Apologéticos discursos, offerecidos à Magestade del Rey Dom Joam N.S. quarto do nome entre os de Portugal, em defensa da fama e bona memória de Fernão d'Albuquerque...*, Manoel da Sylva, Lisbon, 1641. The text was written as a polemic directed at a Castilian chronicler, Gonzálo de Céspedes y Meneses, *Primera Parte de la Historia de D. Felippe el IIII, rey de las Españas*, Pedro Craesbeck, Lisbon, 1631.

was sure of getting a 'good press' in the latter's *Décadas da Ásia*.[20] He was right of course, even though Couto's relatively hagiographic account was later contradicted by the far more acerbic view of Vidigueira in Manuel de Faria e Sousa's *Ásia Portuguesa*.[21] On the other hand, since the only published edition of Couto's 12th *Década* is an abridged draft, the chronicler could not do full justice to the events of the period (as distinct from the personality of the viceroy, which receives a quite full treatment); we thus have no more than some glimpses of the Asian context of Vidigueira's viceroyalty.

The other standard sources are not particularly helpful in this respect either. All of them refer to one or two major events, and pass over in silence most of the rest, as we can see for example from the summary view in Pedro Barreto de Resende's *Tratado de todos os Visoreis e Governadores* (written in 1635):

Dom Francisco da Gama, Count of Vidigueira, Admiral of the Seas of India, the first time that he went to govern there as sixteenth viceroy and thirty-third amongst those who governed the *Estado*, left Lisbon on the 10th of April of the Year 1596 with six *naus*, he wintered at Mombassa, and arrived at Goa, which he reached in some foists on 22nd May 1597, he governed three years and seven months and then left for Portugal. He sent Lourenço de Brito with a fleet to the South, where the Jaos captured three galleys from him with all the people in them and killed him, he sent his brother Dom Lu-ıs da Gama against the Cunhalle with more than four hundred Portuguese who also returned defeated, and in the year 1599 again sent against the same Cunhalle André Furtado de Mendoça who brought back the Lord of the Land [Kunjali] to Goa, below in a galley, after having put everything to fire and sword, [and] in Goa they cut off his [Kunjali's] head and quartered him. [T]he Count-Admiral was elected as viceroy this first time at the age of thirty-one years.[22]

[20] See Charles R. Boxer, 'Diogo do Couto (1543–1616), Controversial Chronicler of Portuguese Asia', in R. O. W. Goertz, ed., *Iberia—Literary and Historical Issues: Studies in Honour of Harold V. Livermore*, Calgary, 1985, pp. 49–66; also António Coimbra Martins, 'Pelos Vidigueira e Dom Francisco' in Albuquerque and Guerreiro, eds, *Actas do II Seminário*, pp. 721–47, and Coimbra Martins, 'Diogo do Couto et al. la famille Da Gama: Un traité inédit', *Revue des Littératures Comparées*, 1979, pp. 279–92.

[21] Manuel de Faria y Sousa, *The Portugues Asia: Or, the History of the Discovery and Conquest of Asia by the Portugues*, tr. Capt. John Stevens, Vol. III, London, 1695, pp. 93–124; also the comments in Silva Rego, 'O in-ıcio do segundo governo'. For another particularly damaging assessment by a contemporary of Vidigueira, see *Comentarios de D. Garc-ıa de Silva y Figueroa de la Embajada que de parte del Rey de España Don Felipe III hizo al Rey Xá Abas de Persia*, ed. Manuel Serrano y Sanz, 2 Vols, Madrid, 1903–5, Vol. II, pp. 587–603.

[22] Bibliothèque Nationale de France, Paris (henceforth BN), Fonds Portugais, 36, *Primeira parte deste livro do Estado da Índia...*, fos 71v–72r, with a portrait of Vidigueira on fo. 71v. The passage cited here, like all citations from the Portuguese in this chapter, is in my translation.

The stress is thus on the one major success of the viceroyalty from the Portuguese point of view: namely, the successful attack that was mounted, with the connivance of the Samudri Rajas of Calicut, on the position of the Mappila leader Muhammad Kunjali Marikkar. The growing Dutch presence in south-east Asia is naturally passed over in discreet silence, but what of the rest of India, the hinterland of Goa itself, for example, or Gujarat, in brief the areas where the Portuguese came into contact with the Mughals?

Portuguese and Mughals

Much has been written on Mughal–Portuguese relations during the reign of Akbar, particularly after the Mughal conquest of Gujarat in 1573. Three clear strands are visible in the historiography, even though they often appear intertwined. First, it is pointed out that the Mughal ports of Gujarat and Portuguese-controlled ports like Goa and Hurmuz enjoyed important trade links in the last quarter of the sixteenth century, and that an accomodation of interests was necessary if the coastal *cáfilas* along the west coast or the annual fleets to the Persian Gulf were to ply. Both parties had an interest in the matter, the Mughals because Surat was thus supplied with silver *reales* and other goods, the Portuguese *Estado* because it received customs revenue, and Gujarati textiles brought to Goa could be carried back to Europe. Portuguese private traders settled at Surat, Rander, Cambay, and other centres also formed a sort of pressure group which acted on the Goa administration.

A second aspect of relations stemmed from the *hajj* traffic in which the Mughal state interested itself. Here, the Portuguese, as *cartaz*-issuing authorities, and the Mughals, whose ships received the safe-conducts, had to enter into dealings (paralleling those between the Portuguese and the Deccan rulers for the same purpose). Such dealings were of course a source of conflict, as the Mughals evidently did not accept *cartazes* with good grace, and Portuguese officials for their part did not miss opportunities to squeeze benefits out of the arrangement. At the same time, an alignment with the realities of the balance of maritime power was necessary, if the *hajj* from Surat and other ports was to be maintained.

A third aspect, perhaps the best known, can be traced to the late 1570s, with the beginnings of the Jesuit presence in Akbar's court, and lent a religious dimension to the dealings. The Fathers hoped, in vain, to convert the ruler, or at least some of his prominent nobles. But they also served as a conduit between the authorities at Goa and the Mughal court, and were thus a convenient presence since the *Estado da Índia* and the Mughals did not maintain permanent diplomatic missions in each other's domains.

It is evident even from the bald summary presented above that relations between the Mughals and the Portuguese were potentially as much of conflict as of collaboration, since their basic interests were by no means congruent. We have to look no further than the *Mongoliecae Legationis Commentarius* of the Catalan Jesuit António Monserrate for a confirmation of this, for his account contains a detailed mention of the difficulties between Mughals and Portuguese in Gujarat and off the Konkan coast in 1581–2.[23] Abu'l Fazl's official chronicle, *Akbar Nâma* is no less explicit on the question, as has been noted in an earlier chapter.[24]

The Mughal–Portuguese equation, then, was an ambiguous one, even if we take only Gujarat into account. Mughal expansion in other directions was not all that well-received by the Portuguese either, as we see from Diogo do Couto's account of Raja Man Singh's expedition to the east in the 1590s, in *Década XII* of his huge chronicle, *Da Ásia*. It is all the more disappointing therefore that the surviving section of his chronicle says so little about the major Mughal expansion of the years 1597 to 1600, namely the incorporation of large parts of the Deccan, and in particular the Ahmadnagar Sultanate.[25] This is in evident contrast to the detailed attention Couto pays to Nizam Shahi affairs in earlier parts of *Da Ásia*; the struggle for succession at the death of Burhan Nizam Shah (r. 1508–54), the siege of Chaul in 1570–1, earlier Mughal threats to Ahmadnagar in the 1580s, and Portuguese–Nizam Shahi relations in the viceroyalty of Matias de Albuquerque (1591–7) all receive their fair share of attention.

The present chapter is largely based on the chance rediscovery of some letters from the Portuguese viceroy at Goa, Dom Francisco da Gama, Count of

---

[23] H. Hosten, ed., 'Mongoliecae Legationis Commentarius', in *Memoirs of the Asiatic Society of Bengal*, Vol. III, 1914, pp. 513–704; S. N. Banerjee and John S. Hoyland, tr. *The Commentary of Father Monserrate S. J. on his Journey to the Court of Akbar*, London, 1922. For a discussion of the context in 1580–1, see Chapter 3.

[24] Abu'l Fazl, *Akbar Nâma*, Vol. III, tr. H. Beveridge, reprint, Delhi, 1989, pp. 409–10 (personal names have been modernized). Akbar's anti-Portuguese posture at this time is also echoed in his letter to 'Abdullah Khan Uzbek, for details of which see Mansura Haider, 'Relations of Abdullah Khan Uzbeg with Akbar', *Cahiers du Monde Russe et Soviétique*, Paris, Vol. XXII, Nos 3–4, 1982, pp. 313–31. A later letter to 'Abdullah Khan, from 1586, again stressing the desire to expel the Portuguese, may be found in *Akbar Nâma*, Vol. III, pp. 754–60. It is somewhat puzzling that the relationship between the *hajj* of Gulbadan Begam's party, and Akbar's attitude towards the Portuguese, is ignored in M. N. Pearson, 'The Estado da Índia and the Hajj', *Indica*, Vol. XXVI (1/2), 1989, pp. 103–18, esp. pp. 117–18.

[25] Diogo do Couto's *Década Duodécima* is divided into five books, and a total of 63 chapters, all dealing with the viceroyalty of the Count of Vidigueira (1597–1600). Of these, Malabar affairs dominate by far, but four chapters are Mughal-related. Two of these (pp. 24–39) are devoted to the affairs of Man Singh ('Manacinga'), and another two to the conversion of a prince of Badakhshan ('Abadaxam'), son of Mirza Shahrukh, to Christianity by the Augustinians at Hurmuz (pp. 483–505).

Vidigueira, to Philip III from 1599. The letters exist in at least two copies, one preserved in the Altamira collection (which forms part of the Additional Manuscripts) at the British Library's Manuscript Room in London, and the other at the Biblioteca Nacional in Lisbon. In what follows, I shall largely concentrate on one letter, written by Vidigueira late in 1599, and concerned essentially with Deccan politics and the place of the Mughals therein.[26] It reveals what appears to be a hitherto unsuspected Portuguese hand in the events of the epoch, but also clearly sets out the geo-strategic concerns of the Portuguese *Estado* in the years immediately preceding the arrival of the Dutch and English in India.

Mughal Expansion and the Deccan

There is a retrospective inevitability about Mughal expansion in India, but contemporaries did not wholly share this sense until the late sixteenth century. From our perspective, the history of the Mughal state from its very creation in the 1520s in northern India, to the early eighteenth century, is one of expansion in every direction from its core at the Ganges–Jamuna *doâb*, but especially southward. After the early 1590s, once Sind had been captured and the last gasp of organized resistance by Muzaffar Shah III snuffed out in Gujarat, the west remained relatively stable; on the other hand, the expansionary campaigns to the east came to a halt only in the 1660s, with the fall of Chittagong. As for the north and northwest, they continued to harbour potential for expansion into Shahjahan's reign, as the unsuccessful campaign into Balkh shows.

But it was the south, first the Deccan, then the Karnatak, where the Mughals fought a true war of attrition, expanding step by step from the late sixteenth century to the early eighteenth century, when the furthest southern limits were defined under Zu'lfiqar Khan Nusrat Jang and Da'ud Khan Panni. It was here that Mughal expansion seemed most uncertain, as a host of challengers from Malik 'Ambar in the early seventeenth century to Shivaji Bhosale later in the same century, arose to halt the advancing tide. The Portuguese, who had arrived in India a quarter-century before Babur turned his attention to Hindustan, were uneasy observers of Mughal expansion from their coastal enclaves, and invented in this process the collective myth of the omnivorous triumvirate of giants of south and south-west Asia, the Great Turk, the Great Sufi, and the Great Mughal.[27]

---

[26] BL, Addn. 28,432, fos 13r–16v; Biblioteca Nacional, Lisbon (henceforth BNL), Códice 1976, fos 117r–121v. The latter volume contains several other letters of interest for Mughal–Portuguese relations.

[27] Elements of this portrayal, in respect of the Ottomans and the Safavids, may already be found in João de Barros, *Da Ásia, Décadas I–IV*, reprint, Lisbon, 1973–4, and the legend of the 'Grand Turk' itself, of course, goes back at least to the fifteenth century;

In the first quarter of the sixteenth century, when the Portuguese initially established themselves at Cochin and Goa, the Vijayanagara state in peninsular south India had given them far less cause for anxiety, even if relations between Goa and Vijayanagara were not always amicable. From the era of Vasco da Gama and Afonso de Albuquerque, when the Portuguese king Dom Manuel had even dreamt of a marriage alliance between the royal houses of Portugal and Vijayanagara, things began to sour in later decades. The idea of using Vijayanagara as a counterweight to keep the 'Adilshahi rulers of Bijapur in check, and thus protect Goa's internal frontier, was the principal focus of Albuquerque's own geo-political conception of the Deccan, but other considerations were to modify this. First, between 1520 and 1560, there was no very serious attempt by the Sultans of Bijapur to retake Goa; this limited the extent of their conflict. Second, official Portuguese policies brought them into conflict with the trading settlements of the Kanara coast, which were controlled (or at least protected) by Vijayanagara. The ports of Bhatkal, Basrur and Honawar, as also Mangalore, were seen as allied to the Mappila opponents of the Portuguese, who hence used every opportunity to harass their shipping. Third, the relative tolerance shown under Dom Manuel for Vijayanagara—which was after all a 'Gentile', that is, a Hindu, kingdom to them—did not survive into later decades, when the Counter-Reformation spirit at Dom João III's court prompted him, among other things, implicitly to permit the governor Martim Afonso de Sousa in the 1540s to essay an attack on the Tirupati temple.[28] The attack did not come off, but the fact that it was contemplated—despite the awareness that the Vijayanagara kings were major patrons of this temple—suggests that the *Estado da Índia* cared little about hurt feelings at the inland court.

The revival of Vijayanagara as a military power under Aravidu Rama Raya in the 1550s and early 1560s may have caused the Portuguese to take pause. But they were quick to seize the opportunity, when in 1565, Rama Raya was defeated and killed by the Deccan Sultans. Their 'share' of the spoils were the ports of Mangalore, Basrur and Honawar, which they took in series of attacks

---

cf. Lucette Valensi, *Venise et la Sublime Porte: La naissance du despote*, Paris, 1987. For one of Couto's earliest uses of the term 'Grão Mogor', see *Década Oitava*, p. 39, the context being a Mughal attack on Daman.

[28] For the most detailed account, see Gaspar Correia, *Lendas da Índia*, ed. M. Lopes de Almeida, reprint, Oporto, 1975, Vol. IV, pp. 299–305, 324–5; also the anonymous 'Verdadeira enformaçam das coisas da Índia (1544)', in A. da Silva Rego, ed., *As Gavetas da Torre do Tombo*, Vol. III, Lisbon, 1963, pp. 199–234. The Tirupati affair is also referred to, oddly enough, by Henrique de Sousa Godinho in 1603, while discussing nominations for the viceroyalty; cf. BL, Addn. 28,432, fo. 72r.

in 1568–9, thus assuring Goa of a stable supply of rice, and also giving them easy access to Kanara pepper.[29] It was left to the Italian Filippo Sassetti in the 1580s to point to how the decline of Vijayanagara had been detrimental to the Portuguese at Goa; there is little evidence that many other contemporary Portuguese thought so, with the arguable exception of Diogo do Couto.[30]

Sassetti's argument, like that of Couto later, was an economic one: Goa's trade had, he felt, been crucially dependent on the market for imports at Vijayanagara. Other arguments of a more political and military nature could be added. The fact that in the late 1560s and early 1570s, the Portuguese settlements of the Konkan and Goa itself were attacked by the Sultans of Ahmadnagar and Bijapur, was evidently no coincidence; relieved of the pressure from Vijayanagara, these rulers could now turn their attention coastward, and also use the momentum and goodwill of their earlier anti-Vijayanagara alliance against the *firangî* enemy. True, when under siege from the land, Goa's lifeline was now secure so long as the rice-fleets from Kanara came in, but on balance the geo-political shifts of the 1560s seem to have been unfavourable to the *Estado*.

It is however difficult to link these events directly to Mughal expansion into the Deccan, which, while it may have been contemplated as early as 1577, in fact began only in the 1590s. Conventional accounts link Akbar's decision to expand into Ahmadnagar with the quarrels between the ruler Murtaza Nizam Shah (r. 1565–88) and his brother Burhan, which led the latter, after a brief sojourn in Bijapur, to take shelter with the Mughals, who incorporated him in 1584 into their own hierarchy of notability, and made him a *mansabdâr-jâgîrdâr*. It seems likely, however, that the Mughals would have turned their attention to the Deccan sooner or later, once they had secured the conquests of Bengal and Gujarat, and consolidated their northern and north-western frontiers. Besides, it is useful to bear in mind that the succession struggle that ensued at Ahmadnagar on Murtaza's assassination in 1588 only set the seal on a process of fragmentation that had deeper roots; the effort by the *habashî* element in the state to assert its autonomy, the recourse by others—especially Deccani notables—to a form of Mahdawi millenarianism, in view of the approach of the Hijri year

[29] Portuguese relations with the Kanara coast have been extensively discussed in Sanjay Subrahmanyam, *The Political Economy of Commerce: Southern India, 1500–1650*, Cambridge, 1990, especially pp. 120–35, 260–5.

[30] Diogo do Couto, *Década Oitava*, pp. 93–4; Vanni Bramanti, ed., *Lettere da Vari Paesi, 1570–1588, di Filippo Sassetti*, Milan, 1970. For general Portuguese official indifference to the fate of Vijayanagara, see José Wicki, 'Duas relações sobre a situação da Índia Portuguesa nos anos 1568 e 1569', *Studia*, No. 8, 1961, pp. 133–220; also the earlier letter from the viceroy D. Antão de Noronha to the King, 17 December 1566, in A. da Silva Rego, ed., *Documentação para a história das missões do padroado português do Oriente*, Vol. X, Lisbon, 1953, especially p. 161.

1000, all of these point to a political situation fraught with tension.[31] The reader of the two great chronicles of the epoch, the *Burhân-i Ma'asir* of Sayyid 'Ali bin 'Azizullah Tabatabai, and the *Gulshan-i Ibrâhîmî* of Muhammad Qasim Hindushah Astarabadi (better known by his *nom de plume* of Firishta), is left in no doubt as to this.[32] Both writers were witness to the situation in the late 1580s, and Firishta left Ahmadnagar for Bijapur soon after Murtaza Nizam Shah's death, apparently fearing the rise of the Mahdawis and its implications for Shi'as like himself.

Burhan returned to Ahmadnagar as Burhan Nizam Shah II in 1591. He did so with Akbar's blessings, but took the aid of Raji 'Ali Khan Faruqi, ruler of Khandesh, rather than that of the Mughals themselves, in order to improve his own legitimacy once in Ahmadnagar. On his return, he displaced and imprisoned his own son Isma'il, who had ruled for two years with the support of the Mahdawi leader Jamal Khan.[33] However, Mughal expectations that he would be little more than a quisling once in power were soon denied. Abu'l Fazl, in his

[31] Mahdawi movements in the region are conventionally traced to Sayyid Muhammad Jaunpuri (1443–1505), who was born in the Sharqi Sultanate of Jaunpur, and after performing the *hajj* in 1495–6, settled down in western India, where he attracted numerous followers and sympathizers in Gujarat, and Ahmadnagar, including—it is claimed—Sultan Mahmud Begarha of Gujarat and Ahmad Nizam Shah. He was however expelled from the area by Sultan Mahmud, and died (or was killed) in Afghanistan. For details, see S. A. A. Rizvi, 'The Mahdavi movement in India', *Medieval India Quarterly*, Vol. I (1), 1950, pp. 10–25; M. M. Saeed, *The Sharqi Sultanate of Jaunpur: A political and cultural history*, Karachi, 1972, pp. 284–92. Professor Derryl N. Maclean of Simon Fraser University, Burnaby (Canada), is preparing a definitive monograph on the subject. For further discussion, see Subrahmanyam, *From the Tagus to the Ganges*, Chapter 5.

[32] See T. Wolseley Haig, tr., *The History of the Nizâm Shâhî Kings of Ahmadnagar*, Bombay, 1923, pp. 201–3, an abridged translation of the third *tabaqa* of Sayyid 'Ali bin 'Azizullah Tabatabai of Samnan's chronicle, *Burhân-i Ma'asir* (the Persian edition is from Hyderabad, 1936–7). Tabataba was first in Qutb Shahi and then in Nizam Shahi service; his work goes on to the negotiations between Chand Sultana and the Mughals, ending 27 Rajab 1004 (14 March 1596), when the author was probably present. For the *Gulshan-i Ibrâhîmî* or *Târîkh-i Firishta*, by Muhammad Qasim Hindu Shah, born in Astarabad (1552), and died at Bijapur (1623), see John Briggs, tr., *History of the Rise of Mahomedan Power in India*, 4 Vols, reprint, New Delhi, 1989; earlier editions London, 1829, and Calcutta, 1908–10, in which Volume III deals with the five post-Bahmani Deccan Sultanates. A third, as yet unpublished, chronicle is the *Tazkirat al-mulûk* of Rafi' al-Din Ibrahim Shirazi (1540/41–c. 1620), written between 1608 and 1612; for a discussion of which see Iqtidar Alam Khan, 'The Tazkirat ul-Muluk by Rafi'uddin Ibrahim Shirazi: As a source on the History of Akbar's Reign', *Studies in History* (N.S.), Vol. II (1), 1980, pp. 41–55.

[33] Firishta, in Briggs, *History of Mahomedan Power*, Vol. III, pp. 168–71.

Akbar Nâma, expresses great disapproval of Burhan throughout his four-year reign, as the following passage demonstrates:

When Burhan al-Mulk prevailed over Ahmadnagar, he should have increased his devotion and gratitude, and been an example of obedience to other rulers in that quarter. The wine of success robbed him of his senses, and he forgot the varied favours he had received from the Shahinshah. In his evil fortune he set himself to oppress the weak, and considered that his profit consisted in the injury of others.[34]

To force him back to a more submissive posture, Abu'l Fazl's brother Abu'l Faiz 'Faizi' was sent on a mission to the Deccan in the years 1591–3, but could achieve little, beyond expressing his disdain for the city of Ahmadnagar, 'full of noise and evil (*shor wa sharr*)... where the dissolute and libertines (*fitnasâzân wa aubâshân*) abound'.[35] Faizi in his letters of 1591–3 expresses Mughal designs clearly enough though, referring to the Nizam al-Mulk and 'Adil Khan as mere Mughal *hâkim*s and *jâgîrdâr*s, and pointing to how Burhan had been 'lifted up from the very dust (*az khâk bardâshta*)' by Akbar in his generosity. For reasons that await detailed analysis, the Mughals still held back militarily though, but did not conceal their amusement at Burhan's military failures—in respect of not only Bijapur but the Portuguese. One possible reason for Mughal reticence may have been the difficulties they faced in the early 1590s in Gujarat, where Muzaffar Shah once more led a resurgence of local chiefs, including those of Jamnagar, Junagadh, Sorath, and Kacch. Akbar's foster-brother Mirza 'Aziz Koka, newly appointed *sûbadâr* of Gujarat, set about crushing this move, in a military action that endured from 1591 until well into 1592.

In the next year, 1593, Mirza Koka began to threaten the Portuguese settlements in Gujarat, in particular Diu. Thereafter, apparently disgruntled with the lack of favour shown him by the Mughal court despite his military success, he began to display rebellious tendencies, and eventually embarked in a Mughal pilgrim ship for the *hajj*, returning only in 1594.[36] This was the very year when Burhan Nizam Shah II entered into headlong conflict with the Portuguese over a fortress he had built on a tongue of land, overlooking their settlement

---

[34] Abu'l Fazl, *Akbar Nâma*, tr. Beveridge, Vol. III, p. 909.

[35] H. K. Sherwani, *History of the Qutb Shâhî Dynasty*, New Delhi, 1974, pp. 352–3. Also see *Inshâ'-i Faizî*, ed. A. D. Arshad, Lahore, 1973, pp. 95, 101–3, *passim*. An extensive discussion of this text may be found in Muzaffar Alam and Sanjay Subrahmanyam, 'A Place in the Sun: Travels with Faizî in the Deccan, 1591–3', in François Grimal, ed., *Les sources et le temps/ Sources and Time: A colloquium*, Pondicherry, 2001, pp. 265–307.

[36] Abu'l Fazl, *Akbar Nâma*, tr. Beveridge, Vol. III, pp. 979–82, 1006; 'Abd al-Qadir Badayuni, *Muntakhab al-Tawârîkh*, tr. George S. A. Ranking, W. H. Lowe, and T. W. Haig, 3 Vols, Calcutta, 1884–1925; reprint, New Delhi, 1990, Vol. II, pp. 400–1, 412.

of Chaul in the Deccan. It is here that Vidigueira's letter of 1599 begins its analysis of events.

The Morro and its Aftermath

Rather than consider the viceroy's account, however, let us return to the Persian chronicler Muhammad Qasim Firishta, and his view of affairs (which adopts a perspective from within the Deccan):

In the year AH 1001 [AD 1592–3], Burhan Nizam Shah marched his army against the Portuguese of Rewadanda; and despatching a large force to the sea-port of Chaul, ordered that a fort should be built to prevent the entrance of the Portuguese into the harbour of Rewadanda, and this fort he called Korla. The Portuguese sailing during the night effected their escape, but they returned with reinforcements from many other ports which had also fallen into their hands (...). Burhan Nizam Shah now sent a body of about four thousand men, under Farhad Khan, to reinforce Korla; and as other troops were expected from Daman and Bassein, he appointed one Bahadur Khan Gilani, at the head of all the foreign troops, governor of the fortress of Korla, to blockade Rewadanda.[37]

The chronicler goes on to describe how the Ahmadnagar forces nearly got the Portuguese to capitulate; however, the 'tyranny' of Burhan caused many of his commanders to desist from taking the enterprise to its conclusion. The Portuguese meanwhile arrived in a fleet, carried out a landing, and after a prolonged fight in which 12,000 of the Ahmadnagar forces were killed, 'reduced the fort to ashes'. This event, according to Portuguese sources, took place in early September 1594; Burhan himself died on 18 April 1595 (13 Sha'ban 1003 AH). Thus far Firishta, who—in keeping with his disapproval of this particular monarch—does not tell us what prompted Burhan to act in such a manner, and so contravene the agreement that his brother Murtaza and the Portuguese had arrived at after the earlier siege of Chaul in the 1570s. Now Couto, whose chronicle contains a quite detailed description of these events, is not much more helpful than Firishta in explaining what prompted the 'Melique' (i.e. Malik, the title by which he refers to Burhan and the Nizam Shahs in general), to build the fortress of the 'Morro' (the hilltop—referring here to Korla).[38] Vidigueira, on the other hand, has a clear and acerbic view of matters:

[T]he principal cause from which has resulted the perilous state in which the kingdoms of the Deccan are, and from which other worse effects are feared as well, is a wholly

---

[37] Firishta, in Briggs, *History of Mahomedan Power*, Vol. III, pp. 172–3 (proper names have been modernized). For Mughal responses to Burhan's defeat, see Abu'l Fazl, *Akbar Nâma*, Vol. III, pp. 1023–5.

[38] Couto, *Década XI*, pp. 164–73; Biblioteca Pública e Arquivo Distrital, Évora, Códice CXV/1–13, Part II, which is entirely devoted to the taking of the *Morro de Chaul*.

pointless and notorious action which was moved against the King Melique, of a ship of his that was captured, and it was even worse not to return it to him, though this King asked for it with much insistence, and requested that Your Majesty's judges in the High Court [of Goa] determine the rights of the matter, since he agreed to abide by their judgement, and since none of these things was conceded, moved by despair, he decided to make war on Chaul and to fortify the Moro, devoting himself to this to such an extent that when he had news that it had been captured from him, he died of rage...[39]

The message is clear enough: behind Burhan's actions lies a malevolent Portuguese hand, that of Vidigueira's predecessor Matias de Albuquerque, who had permitted the looting of one of Burhan's vessels, called *Husainî*, wrecked off the west coast near Bassein, on its return to Chaul from the Red Sea. This, to Vidigueira's mind, was only a part of Albuquerque's faulty geo-strategic conception, and his inability to tell friends from enemies. His letter goes on to blame the former viceroy, the captain of Diu, Pero d'Anhaya, the financial superinten-dent Francisco Paes, and the captain-major of the fleet patrolling the Gujarat coast Fadrique Carneiro d'Aragão, for losing a great opportunity in future negotiations with the Mughals, by not making a 'prize' (*preza*) of 'Aziz Koka when he embarked for the *hajj*. The Mughals, for Vidigueira, did not have an ambiguous status: they were a 'concealed enemy' (*enemigo encuberto*) and had to be dealt with as such. The death of Burhan Nizam Shah thus, in Vidigueira's view, opened the floodgates to Mughal expansion, which had been on the cards already for a decade or more in the Portuguese perception. He continues, after his account of the death of Burhan from rage (*paixão*):

[A]nd as the King who succeeded him was a child, and handed over to a woman who shut herself up with him in a fortress (fearing that some vassals of his would seize him and tyrannise him as is the custom among these people), there arose such a division in the kingdom that Equebar profiting from this facility has subjected most of it, which would not have happened nor would the Mughal have attempted it had the King Melique been alive...[40]

The reference is to the minor Bahadur Nizam Shah, placed on the throne under the control of Chand Bibi (or Chand Sultana), the sister of Burhan and the widow of 'Ali 'Adil Shah of Bijapur. Bahadur succeeded his father Ibrahim, who

[39] BL, Addn. 28,432, fo. 13r. For the capture of this ship, also see BL, Addn. 28,432, fos 124r–31r, *Lembrança dos galeões, galés, galeotas, fustas e manchuas que mandey com provimentos e socorros...*', by Matias de Albuquerque.

[40] BL, Addn. 28,432, fo. 13r. I am unable to trace when the Portuguese began terming the Nizam Shahs, whom they had earlier termed Nizamaluco (Nizam al-Mulk), Nizamoxá, or Izamaluco, as 'Melique'. My initial surmise that it dated after the rise of Malik (thus 'Melique') 'Ambar, is obviously not borne out here. Couto does not use the term 'Melique' until his chronicle comes to the late 1580s (i.e. in *Década Décima*).

died in battle against Bijapur forces a mere four months after acceding, and was initially confined in the fort of Chawund. Later, Chand Bibi moved him to Ahmadnagar fort, and it was at this stage that Vidigueira was in correspondence with her; the evidence of some of her letters to Goa which have survived in the archives suggests that she wished the Portuguese to aid her principally against the *habashî* (Abyssinian) element in Ahmadnagar, particularly a certain Abhang Khan Zangi (sometimes, confusingly, termed Farhang Khan)—who supported the candidacy of Miran 'Ali, reputedly the son of Burhan Nizam Shah I, against Bahadur. Abhang Khan managed to gather a sizeable force around himself; the later-to-be-celebrated Malik 'Ambar, on his return to Ahmadnagar in these years after a sojourn in Golconda and Bijapur, found service for example with him as a commander of cavalry, and took part in his successful attack on the Mughals at Bir in 1599.[41] One of her letters, written to Vidigueira in August 1598, runs as follows:

To the most enlightened, and powerful, feared and obeyed by all, full of much justice and prudence, chosen of the law of the Messiah [Christ], Admiral Dom Francisco da Gama Viceroy of India, after my many salutations and greetings, Your Lordship will be aware how at present some of the slaves and servants of this royal house have turned rebel, and disobedient to it, and to all the enemies that there are of this house has been added Abancão, rising in rebellion against the service of his King, sending men to the Conquão to make himself master of it on account of which I ask Your Most Illustrious Lordship to keep in view the ancient friendship, and write to the Most Magnificent Captain of Chaul that he may give all the assistance in terms of men, and aid, that he can to Faemocão, Governor of the Concão, so that with it the rebels may be prevented from mistreating the said lands and may be expelled from them forcibly. The rest Agisinay, who is a trustworthy man, will tell Your Lordship in words, and he carries some notes that he will present. Written on the 5th of the Moon of August of [15]98.[42]

The letter was followed however by another, written barely a week later, acknowledging a reply from Vidigueira, and assuring him that now that the Almighty had brought him to the *Estado*, she was sure that the friendship between the two parties would grow apace. However, Vidigueira had his own plans, and these did not comprise solely of dealings with Chand Bibi. Among his other correspondents were the merchants of Murtazabad-Chaul (*Chaul de cima* to the Portuguese), and his letter-book of the period preserves at least one letter from a certain Sa'dullah, who styles himself *malik al-tujjâr* of that port.[43]

[41] Sherwani, *Qutb Shâhî Dynasty*, pp. 274–7.

[42] AN/TT, Convento da Graça, Tomo III [Cx. 2], p. 295.

[43] AN/TT, Convento da Graça, Tomo III [Cx. 2], p. 237, *Treslado de huma carta que escreveo Sadola Maliqe toyar e os mais mercadores de Chaul de cima a V.S.*, dated November 1597.

The letter concerns references to the captain of Portuguese Chaul, António de Sousa, with whom the writer declares himself most satisfied in general; since his arrival in the port, De Sousa has 'worked at once to conserve and effect this friendship (…) by sending assurances to the merchants who were in other ports and he has brought all of them to this one where they have made houses and ennobled this port'. However, difficulties have arisen in the recent past, ever since the local governor (*tanadar*) appointed by Ahmadnagar, a certain Khwaja Haidar, was replaced by another Khwaja Fath al-Din, who 'gets along badly with the merchants and with everyone and is a man who never tells the truth, and writes many falsehoods'. The new *tanadar* had complained to Vidigueira about De Sousa, alleging that he took bribes and that he had seized many villages in the vicinity from the Nizam Shahs; De Sousa, by way of revenge in a familiar vein, chose to seize a ship returning from the Red Sea to Chaul and which notionally pertained to the 'Melique and the merchants'. Now Sa'dullah had written to request the vessel's release so that it could 'go upriver in order to unload, and to prepare it in order to make a return voyage'.

Evidently then, the Portuguese had their own troubles to attend to at the local level in the Konkan, besides helping keep the peace for Chand Bibi. Besides, Vidigueira was not at all anxious to fall in with the regent's plans with respect to Abhang Khan, whom he saw as a useful ally rather than a rebel against legitimate rule. In his later letter of 1599, he explained his strategy to Philip III as follows:

To Chande Bibi, who with the boy King is shut up in the fortress of Madaneguer, I have written many times, keeping up her spirits and persuading her to show confidence in her vassals so as to oblige them to be united and treat of their defence, making many offers to her and promising to help her in everything that is due to her from this *Estado*, and despite continuing in this way with her ever since I have governed this *Estado* it has not added up to anything, and being a woman, she is so variable and inconstant that at times she shows signs of allowing herself to be persuaded but soon changes, principally as she has conceived a great hatred for some captains who are her vassals and it is believed that if only to have satisfaction of them, she is trying and working to hand herself with the King and all the rest to the Mogores, who at present face no other resistance in that Kingdom than that which is offered them by Abancão, a forceful and valorous captain, who recently has had some goodly successes against them, I am trying to animate him and have to this end sent to attend on him Belchior Diaz, an Armenian, as an intermediary (*homen de negoceo*) as I have found him zealous and with the talent and ability for these matters, I have word from him that Abancão gets along well with him and listens to him, may God help him, even though as he is alone and the kingdom is divided and Chande Bibi mistrusts him, he will not be able to do all that is needed, and I no longer write to him nor can I support him more openly, for fear that Chande

Bibi will wind up mistrusting [me] and may commit some indiscretion that cannot be remedied.[44]

The Bijapur Factor

There was one other factor through which the Portuguese viceroy could operate, in order to attempt a shift in the balance of power in the Deccan. This was the Sultanate of Bijapur, the erstwhile mortal enemies of the Portuguese, whose rulers (in their Lusitanized form of Idalxá or Idalcão) played the role of chief bogeymen to the Portuguese in the sixteenth century, until that mantle passed on to the Sultans of Aceh and the Kunjali Marikkars. Relations had touched a particularly low point in the early 1570s, when the Bijapur Sultan had attacked Goa as part of what the Portuguese believed to have been a larger alliance against the *Estado da Índia*; at the same time, the Nizam Shahs had attacked Chaul, the Samudri Raja of Calicut the Portuguese fort of Chaliyam, and the Sultans of Aceh had attacked Melaka.[45] The 'Adil Shahi attack cannot be counted a great success, and in its wake, negotiations were mooted between Sultan 'Ali 'Adil Shah and the Portuguese *Estado*. A preliminary truce was signed at Goa in January 1575 with the viceroy D. Antão de Noronha, and thereafter—in what was an unprecedented move—the Bijapuri ambassador Zahir Beg actually was sent to Lisbon, to be presented to Dom Sebastião. He left Goa on 23 January 1575 on the *nau Santa Barbara*, arrived in Lisbon on 13 August, and after cooling his heels for almost two months at Cacilhas, finally had an audience at Sintra, on 10 October.[46] He then left by the return fleet of the same winter, and signed a final version of the treaty in Goa in October 1576, by which the permanent presence of a Portuguese factor at Dabhol was confirmed,

[44] See BL, Addn. 28,432, fo. 14r. Compare the letter from Vidigueira to the King, dated April 1599, in BNL, Códice 1976, fos 99r–99v.

[45] There are few good conjunctural studies of the 'alliance' of 1568–71; but see Lu-ıs Filipe F. R. Thomaz, 'A Crise de 1565–75 na História do Estado da Índia', *Mare Liberum* No. 9, 1995, pp. 481–519. Also P. M. Joshi, 'The Portuguese on the Deccan (Konkan) coast: Sixteenth to seventeenth centuries', *Journal of Indian History*, Vol. LXI (1), 1968, pp. 65–88 for the 'Adil Shahi and Nizam Shahi attacks, and Pierre-Yves Manguin, 'Of Fortresses and Galleys: The 1568 Acehnese Siege of Melaka, after a Contemporary Bird's-Eye View', *Modern Asian Studies*, Vol. XXII (3), 1988, for south-east Asia.

[46] For a description of the audience at Sintra, see the letter from Fernão Guerreiro S. J., reproduced in Josef Wicki and John Gomes, eds, *Documenta Indica*, 18 Vols, Rome, 1948–88, Vol. X (1575–7), pp. 1057–61. Another version of the encounter, less probable, claims that the Portuguese King received the ambassador while lying in bed, in order not to reveal how young he was! For this, see Joaquim Ver-ıssimo Serrão, ed. *Itinerários de El-Rei D. Sebastião*, 2nd edn, Lisbon, 1987, p. 367.

and the 'Adil Shahis assured a certain number of *cartazes* for their ships to the Red Sea and Persian Gulf.[47]

This agreement, though it may eventually have formed the basis for a changed relationship between Bijapur and Goa in the last two decades of the sixteenth century and the early seventeenth century, could not be implemented until 1579. Hostilities resumed in the late 1570s, after some troubles at Dabhol between the 'Adil Shahi *thânedâr* and Portuguese soldiers; in retaliation, a punitive expedition under D. Pedro de Meneses captured two Dabhol vessels on their return from the Red Sea.[48] In another version, it is claimed that Dom Sebastião had given clear instructions to the viceroy, Rui Lourenço de Távora who returned with Zahir Beg to Asia in 1576, but the viceroy dying *en route*, his successors did not properly pursue the peace, and war resulted.[49] It was only with the return of Dom Lu-ıs de Ata-ıde as viceroy in 1578 that effective peace could be concluded. The treaty was eventually finalized in August 1579 with the sending of Fernão Gomes Cordovil to the 'Adil Shahi court, with the 'Adil Shahi side being represented not only by Zahir Beg, but the veteran diplomat Mustafa Khan Ardistani.[50]

Thus, by the 1580s, the Bijapur rulers were hardly seen as a major threat to Goa any longer, with the long reign of Ibrahim 'Adil Shah II (1580–1627) being particularly remarkable for its low level of hostility. Ibrahim had emerged as ruler on the assassination of his uncle 'Ali 'Adil Shah in 1580 under particularly scandalous circumstances; however, being a minor, power was controlled by a series of regents, in a tussle with 'Ali's wife, the Ahmadnagar princess Chand Bibi.[51] The regents were, in succession, Kamil Khan Dakhni, Kishwar Khan, Ikhlas Khan, and finally—after 1583—Dilawar Khan Habashi, and they had taken care to imprison Ibrahim's brother Isma'il in the fort of Belgaum. From

---

[47] For the text of this agreement, between the 'Adil Shahi ambassador Zahir Beg, and the governor António Moniz Barreto, dated 22 October 1576, see J. H. da Cunha Rivara, ed., *Archivo Portuguez-Oriental*, 6 Fascicules in 10 Vols, Goa, 1857–76; reprint, Delhi, 1992, Fasc. V, (2), pp. 921–30.

[48] M. A. Nayeem, *External Relations of the Bijapur Kingdom (AD 1489–1686): A study in diplomatic history*, Hyderabad, 1974, pp. 226–7.

[49] BN, Fonds Portugais, No. 23, fo. 397r, Simão Vaz Telo to the King, Cochin, 1 January 1582.

[50] This was the Iranian noble Mustafa Khan Ardistani, who served Ibrahim Qutb Shah until 1566, and then came over to 'Adil Shahi service. He was assassinated soon after, in Malabar in 1580, on the orders of a rival faction of the Bijapur court.

[51] For 'Ali 'Adil Shah's death, see Diogo do Couto, *Década Décima*, Parte I, pp. 8–9; Abu'l Fazl, *Akbar Nâma*, Vol. III, tr. Beveridge, pp. 440–1. Interestingly, Abu'l Fazl gives credit to Shah Fathullah Shirazi, at that time in Bijapur, for Ibrahim's accession to the throne.

this imprisonment, he was released only in the 1590s, but almost immediately led a rebellion against Ibrahim which was crushed.[52]

By 1583, when Dilawar Khan had emerged as the central figure of the regency, those opposed to him sought to find a rival candidate to Ibrahim. Now the family of 'Mealecão' (Miyan 'Ali Khan), younger son of Yusuf 'Adil Khan (and brother of Isma'il 'Adil Shah), had resided in Goa, more or less voluntarily, since the 1540s, in anticipation of a day when they would be placed back on the Bijapur throne as vassals of the Portuguese Crown.[53] On Meale's death around 1567, the mantle of pretender descended on his only 'legitimate' son Yusuf Khan, who thus wrote to Philip II in December 1581, asking that he be aided in a bid against the 10-year old Ibrahim, and claiming support from Ahmadnagar and Golconda.[54] Besides, it would appear that a faction of Bijapur nobles, such as 'Ain al-Mulk, also actively canvassed for his candidacy. The project was not supported; the ink was too fresh on the treaty to consider such a move.[55] Of course Ibrahim in these years was insecurely placed, but this insecurity may have been seen by the Portuguese as a positive rather than a negative feature. The fact that Ibrahim supported a far milder form of Sunni-inflected Islam than 'Ali 'Adil Shah (who was a militant Shi'a) may have also tempered his attitude towards the Portuguese.[56] Besides, Bijapur had become a centre of Portuguese private trade in these years, replacing the city of

[52] Cf. Firishta in Briggs, *History of Mahomedan Power*, Vol. III, pp. 107–12.

[53] The article by B. S. Shastry, 'Identification of "Mealecão", the rebel prince of Bijapur', *Indica*, Vol. XX (1), 1983, pp. 17–24, based largely on the chronicles, is now superseded by Sanjay Subrahmanyam, 'Notas sobre um rei congelado: O caso de Ali bin Yusuf Adil Khan, chamado Mealecão', in Rui Manuel Loureiro and Serge Gruzinski, eds, *Passar as fronteiras: II Colóquio Internacional sobre Mediadores Culturais, séculos XV a XVIII*, Lagos, 1999, pp. 265–90. Portuguese support for Mealecão had created difficulties for their relations with the 'Adil Shahs in the 1540s, leading to attacks by Bijapur forces on Salsette, and a Portuguese raid on Dabhol, both in 1546–7; cf. Couto, *Década Sexta*, Parte I, pp. 402–8, 416–21.

[54] BN, Fonds Portugais, No. 23, fos 399r–99v, letter from Isufucão to Philip II.

[55] Eventually, Dilawar Khan, fearing that Yusuf Khan would come to be a threat, is reported to have lured him into Bijapur, blinded him, and imprisoned him, so that he died in 1584; a major part was played in this by a Portuguese mercenary in Bijapur pay, called Diogo Lopes Baião. For details, see Couto, *Década Décima*, Parte I, pp. 11–13, 454–7. Couto also claims (p. 461) that two other notables of Bijapur, Sayyid 'Ali and Bibi 'Acilá', tried to persuade Dom Francisco Mascarenhas in 1583–4 to help them place Meale's 'bastard' son, Muhammad Khan, on the throne, but he refused. These notables eventually went over to Akbar, after a sojourn at Goa.

[56] Richard M. Eaton, *Sufis of Bijapur, 1300–1700: Social roles of Sufis in Medieval India*, Princeton, 1978, pp. 67–75.

Vijayanagara (now in decline), and these private traders could easily be held hostage against any rash move by Goa. Such then were the new considerations of the early 1580s.

Among the Sultans of Bijapur, it is Ibrahim whose court attracted the largest number of Europeans, ranging from jewel traders and dilettantes, to painters like the Haarlem-based Cornelis Claeszoon de Heda.[57] Despite this, European accounts of Bijapur during the reign of Ibrahim 'Adil Shah can hardly be said to have attracted the sort of attention scholars have devoted to the chronicle of Asad Beg Qazwini, the Mughal emissary to Ibrahim in the early seventeenth century.[58] Most remarkable among the Portuguese and Spanish-language portrayals of Ibrahim and his court is the account (in Spanish) of the Flemish jeweller from Bruges, Jacques de Coutre, who claims to have known the monarch closely (*con mucha familiaridad*) between 1604 and 1616, but is nevertheless bitingly sarcastic, referring to him by turns as a coward, tyrant, arbitrary, and obsessed with his harem of over 900 concubines 'who served him carnally when he wished'.[59] Indeed, Ibrahim's major virtue in Coutre's eyes is that he paid up his debts promptly (*era... puntual en lo que comprava*), besides being harsh in punishing bandits, and regular in paying his soldiers and household.

[57] Cf. the interesting, and little explored letters, of and about Heda, in Algemeen Rijksarchief, The Hague, Overgekomen Brieven en Papieren, VOC. 1055 and VOC. 1056. The first mention of him occurs in a letter from Jan van Wesick and Antonij Schorer at Masulipatnam to Jacques l'Hermite de Jonge, dated November 1610, and speaks of how Heda has been favoured at Bijapur by Ibrahim 'Adil Shah, and wishes to remit money to his mother in Holland (cf. VOC. 1055, unfoliated volume of loose papers). There is also a later letter by Heda himself at Nauraspur, addressed to Wemmer van Berchem at Masulipatnam, dated 30 November 1613, VOC. 1056, fos 237r–38r. Finally, see the brief mention in Mark Zebrowski, *Deccani Painting*, Berkeley, 1983, pp. 95–6.

[58] Cf. P. M. Joshi, 'Asad Beg's mission to Bijapur, 1603–4', in S. N. Sen, ed., *Mahamahopadhyaya Prof. D.V. Potdar Sixty-First Birthday Commemmoration Volume*, Poona, 1950, pp. 184–96; also Joshi, 'Asad Beg's return from Bijapur and his second mission to the Deccan, 1604–6', in V. D. Rao, ed., *Studies in Indian History: Dr. A.G. Pawar Felicitation Volume*, Bombay, 1968, pp. 136–55. Curiously, neither a full translation nor even a complete edition of Asad Beg's account, the *Waqâ'i'-i Asad Beg*, exists. Manuscripts may be found in the OIOC, London (Or. 1887, and Or. 1996); at the Aligarh Muslim University (Abdus Salam Collection No. 270/40); at the Andhra Pradesh Government Oriental Manuscripts Library and Research Institute, Hyderabad (Asafiyah Collection); at the Rampur Raza Library, and several other centres. Excerpts may be found in H. M. Elliot and J. Dowson, eds, *The History of India as told by its own historians: The Muhammadan Period*, 8 Vols, reprint, Delhi, 1990, Vol. VI, pp. 150–74.

[59] Jacques de Coutre, *Andanzas asiáticas*, eds, Eddy Stols, B. Teensma and J. Verberckmoes, Madrid, 1991, pp. 174–98, 287–98; the quotation is from p. 297.

We are thus some distance away from the notion of Ibrahim the aesthete-king, the composer of the *Kitâb-i Nauras*, and the patron of the poet Zuhuri.[60]

Particularly troublesome to Coutre was Ibrahim's alleged cowardice, especially in respect of the Mughals, to whom he is supposed to have given 'gross gifts and tributes'. The Flemish jeweller reported that 'Adil Shah had justified this to his own vassals by claiming that instead of spending money and lives in making war, which always carried the risk of a loss, he would 'rather send him [the Mughal] the money in offering, and make him content, and be his friend, and remain in my house with my peace and quiet (*quedarme en mi caza con mi quietud y sossiego*)'.[61] This account was written, however, much later than the events with which we are concerned; indeed, it refers to Ibrahim throughout in the past tense, making it clear that he was already dead at the time of the writing. And yet, elements of the same portrayal can be found already in Vidigueira's correspondence, suggesting that Coutre in fact partook of a widely held opinion of Ibrahim in Portuguese India. Thus, we have Vidigueira's own evaluation of Ibrahim in the following passage:

Finding matters in this state when I took charge of this government and being particularly aware of this matter as its importance deserves, I at once attempted to persuade the Idalcão of how much it was worth to him to aid the kingdoms of the Melique before it became necessary to defend his own after the enemies had entered his house, [and] I wrote him many letters about it, but they amounted to no more than that he thanked me with others of his own for the good counsels I was giving him; on account of which I resolved this winter to send him an ambassador in which [post] I appointed António d'Azevedo who was [there] at the time of Mathias d'Alboquerque, since he knows the manners and proceedings of those people and is known there and since, although very old, he still has the talent to perform this task well; he advised me that this King, besides the other vices that he earlier had, now was given to another greater and more damaging one than all the others which is not to admit anyone's counsel on any matter and to decide everything by his own opinion alone, giving some absurd and baseless reasons for this, it being understood that what obliges him [to do this] is the great mistrust which he has of his vassals in such an extreme fashion that he [Azevedo] doubts whether he can change this notion of his, due to which I have written to him with great emphasis that he should

---

[60] Cf. Eaton, *Sufis of Bijapur*, pp. 98–100 for a discussion; among contemporary texts, see Nazir Ahmad, ed., *Kitâb-i Nauras by Ibrâhîm Adil Shâh II*, New Delhi, 1956; also the *hindavî* text by 'Abdul Dihlawi, *Ibrâhîmnâmâ*, ed. D. V. Chauhan, Bombay, 1973.

[61] Coutre, *Andanzas*, pp. 296–7; for Ibrahim's relations with the Mughals in the early 1610s, see Khursheed Nurul Hasan and Mansura Haidar, 'Letters of Aziz Koka to Ibrahim Adil Shah II', *Proceedings of the Indian History Congress*, 27th Session, 1965, pp. 161–7, containing a calendar of some diplomatic documents in 'Abd al-Wahhab bin Muhammad Ma'muri al-Husaini, *Gulshan-i Balâghat*, for a manuscript of which see Asiatic Society of Bengal, Calcutta, Curzon Collection, II, 312 (IvC 131).

employ in this matter all the good offices he can, but since this King knows little and applies himself even less to what is needed, and Equebar is solicitous and full of artifice, and does not lose any occasion (having at present an ambassador in the court of the same Idalcão through whom he makes him great promises and offers, which is the means and dissimulation in which he usually enters with everyone), I hope that God does not permit that all the exertions that António d'Azevedo has been charged to make in this matter may not suffice to bring him around as they should.[62]

Ibrahim had of course already recently intervened once before in Ahmadnagar affairs, at the invitation of Chand Bibi. This was after the treaty of March 1596, signed between Ahmadnagar and the Mughals in the aftermath of a long siege, when the Mughal armies had withdrawn temporarily from the region after having been ceded Berar. However, they re-entered the fray soon enough, against an Ahmadnagar army that was supported by a Golconda contingent under Mahdi Quli Sultan, and a force from Bijapur under Suhail Khan Habashi. In the battle that resulted at Sonepat, in late January 1597, the Bijapur general was isolated, suffered heavy losses, and made his way back to Ibrahim's territories only with difficulty. This experience may have decided Ibrahim against further intervention, and prompted him to begin negotiations with the Mughals instead. The vision of a united Deccani front against the Mughals was thus, in Vidigueira's view, an unattainable one by early 1599.

The Final 'Solution'

There remained one other possibility. The Mughals were, it was known, themselves divided. Charge of expansion into the Deccan had been given by Akbar in 1594 to his second son Shah Murad (b. 1570), reputedly a highly competent general despite his young age; however, Murad's powers were curbed by the presence of the veteran courtier and general 'Abd al-Rahim, titled Khan-i Khanan, who had recently completed the successful conquest of Sind from the Tarkhans. From late 1594, when the campaign began, the two were at cross-purposes, and Abu'l Fazl's account in the *Akbar Nâma* tends largely to blame the Khan-i Khanan in the quarrel, though at the same time speaking of Murad's hauteur, want of experience, and 'evil' advisers. Conventional accounts stress the role in these divisions of Murad's tutor (*atâlîq*) Sadiq Muhammad Khan Herati, whose death in 1597 did not however help mend fences between Murad and 'Abd al-Rahim. We gather instead that after the victory in early 1597 over Suhail Khan (in which 'Abd al-Rahim commanded the Mughal forces), matters deteriorated further; the Khan-i Khanan asked to be recalled, while Murad wrote

[62] See BL, Addn. 28,432, fos 13v–14r. Also see BNL, Códice 1976, fo. 147v, another letter dated 23 December 1599 from Vidigueira to the King.

letters of complaint against him to Akbar. Eventually, on reaching Agra, 'Abd al-Rahim appears to have defended his own conduct, leading Akbar to send Abu'l Fazl himself to the Deccan in order to persuade Murad to return, leaving Deccan affairs in the hands of the Timurid prince, Mirza Shahrukh. Abu'l Fazl set off in early 1599 for Shahpur, where Murad had set up headquarters. Matters were thus delicately balanced in mid-1599.

These divisions and problems were not wholly unknown to Vidigueira, although we do not know what precisely the sources of his information were. On the other hand, the differences were public enough, for Firishta refers to them in some detail, even if his chronology is at times somewhat confusing. The affair was given a decisive twist however, as Abu'l Fazl advanced to meet Murad in his camp; not wishing to meet him, the prince shifted camp, and advanced into the Deccan. What followed is summed up by Abu'l Fazl, who though not an eyewitness, arrived at Murad's camp soon after what he describes:

Owing to the wickedness of selfish and presumptuous men, some vexation arose, and some leaders of the army set themselves to hamper work. He [Murad] returned unsuccessful from Ahmadnagar and fell into chronic grief(...) When his son [Rustam] died, the jewel of wisdom grew dim, and he set himself down to drink in the company of foolish sensualists. Excessive drinking brought on epilepsy, and he did not apply his mind to getting better. He concealed his pains and did not digest his food(...) When he heard of the arrival of the Shahinshah at Agra, and of his being summoned to court, he became excessively melancholy, for out of shame for his drunkenness he could not make up his mind to kiss the threshold. His officers suggested another course, and when news came of the approach of the writer of the book of fortune, he marched on 9th Isfandarmaz towards Ahmadnagar. His sole idea was to make this expedition a reason for not going [to Agra]. The New Year's feast of this year he celebrated at Tamurni. On the 16th Ardibihisht he was seized with violent fits near Dihari on the banks of the Purna, 20 *kos* from Daulatabad, and on the 22nd he died in an unconscious state.[63]

Abu'l Fazl arrived too late to see the prince alive, having already received news of his grave illness from Mirza Yusuf Khan Rezawi, Murad's new tutor, while 30 *kos* from the camp. To him fell the charge of sending the body to Shahpur, and of setting the army and administration in order. The news was eventually conveyed to Akbar through his wife Miriam Makani.

In Jahangir's memoirs, a brief account of Murad occurs quite early in the text, and presents what is in summary a similar account to that of Abu'l Fazl. Murad, it is stated, had 'taken to excessive drinking through associating with unworthy persons, so that he died in his 30th year, in the neighbourhood of Jalnapur, in the province of Berar'. What is more, Jahangir follows this with a more detailed account of the death in early 1605 of his youngest brother, Daniyal, who he notes

---

[63] Abu'l Fazl, *Akbar Nâma*, Vol. III, tr. Beveridge, pp. 1125–6.

also 'took to improper ways, like his brother Shah Murad'.[64] The role of moralist on the question of course sits somewhat uneasily on Jahangir's shoulders (in view of his own passion for wine), as does his posthumous award to these two princes of the titles of *Shâhzâda maghfûr* and *Shâhzâda marhûm* (the 'pardoned prince', and the 'prince admitted to mercy')!

Vidigueira's version of the affair is rather different, indeed quite startlingly so. A translation of the relevant passage is appended below, and its significance is then discussed. The letter, we note once more, was written on 18 December 1599, some seven-and-a-half months after Murad's death.

[The Mughal's] army has been held back so far this winter because of the recent death in it of the Prince Xâmorad, his son, who commanded it, and though it is rumoured that this death was caused by the Prince Xêcogi [Shaikhu-ji, ie. Salim] his brother, I had to undertake many efforts to cause it, spending a good bit on it, but by such occult means that it can never be imputed to this *Estado*, although some persons are of the view that it would have been better for this *Estado* if Xâmorad had not died, for on account of the ill-will that he and his older brother bore each other there would have been such wars among them and they would have gone at each other so much after the death of the father that they would have had no opportunity to trouble this *Estado*, which is the principal purpose of these people, and the same reasons would have also put a halt to the conquest of the kingdom of the Melique on account of secret dealings that the Prince [Salim] had with Canacam, the general of the soldiers of Xaa Morad, who on the orders of his father accompanied him on this enterprise, but as against these reasons, of which I was aware, I always found that there were in this state of affairs certain inconveniences of greater importance, for if one had to wait for the death of Equebar for these two brothers to come out with their differences this could have taken an indefinite time, [and] it was better to prevent by the death of this [prince] the evil that threatened this *Estado* most immediately than to take into consideration that the wars that might in time take place after the father's death would divert them from disturbing us, especially because Equebar having called back Canacan on account of the dealings he had with the Prince [Salim], with his absence there remained nothing to impede the conclusion of this conquest with such a powerful army against disorganised people unable to defend themselves, and [our] experience has shown how significant the death of Xaa Morad was, for he dying in the beginning of May when Equebar was making a great show of coming with great power to put a finish to this enterprise, not only did he [Akbar] not do so, but since then the greater part of this army has diminished(...)[65]

[64] *The Tûzuk-i Jahângîrî, or Memoirs of Jahângîr*, tr. A. Rogers, ed. H. Beveridge, reprint, Delhi, 1989, Vol. I, pp. 34–5.

[65] See BL, Addn. 28,432, fos 14r–14v. Compare the view of Deccan politics in a letter dated 9 December 1597, written by the Archbishop of Goa, D. Frei Aleixo de Meneses to Philip II, published (regrettably with numerous errors) in Arthur Beylerian, 'Cinq lettres inédites de D. Frei Aleixo de Meneses, Archevêque de Goa', *Arquivos do Centro Cultural Português*, Vol. VIII, 1974, pp. 580–6.

Vidigueira's statement is thus most matter-of-fact: it is *he* who has caused Murad's death, but by means so 'occult' that he and the Portuguese *Estado* would never be blamed. In the latter part of the statement, he was certainly right, for no blame has ever been laid at the door of the Portuguese for this affair! The strategic reasons compelling him have also been set out with Machiavellian clarity: to observers in Goa, 'Abd al-Rahim was an agent of Prince Salim, whose main purpose was to prevent Murad from attaining too conspicuous a military success; hence his recall from the Deccan freed Murad's hand militarily. Vidigueira now goes on to dilate on the further consequences of his actions, namely the defeat of some Mughal forces by Abhang Khan Zangi:

Abancão in the end of September attacked these people and killed fifteen hundred cavalry and a great captain, and captured others with a small loss on his part, as a result of which he began to take heart, and I am advised that there is now some possibility of friendship between him and Chandebibi, which I try hard to promote, because with that one can have hope of the restoration of those kingdoms at this time when the Mogor is greatly troubled by fear of the Xaa ['Abbas].[66]

Here, once more, Vidigueira's larger geo-political calculations came into play, for he was well aware that the situation on the Safavid–Mughal border was somewhat unstable at this time. He writes, later in the same letter, in the context of trading fleets (*cáfilas*) from Hurmuz to Goa:

[I]n my time, one [*cáfila*] was diverted, for it came with an ambassador of the Xaa to the Mogor in the company of another who had been sent to him ['Abbas], and he brought with him around five thousand persons and he wished that Dom António de Lima embark him in the fortress of Ormuz. [C]ouncil was held on this, in which it was decided that if they wished to embark themselves and with their servitors (for there was place for no more) there, they could do so, but otherwise they could not enter and I approved this resolution, for given the intentions of these people [to capture Hurmuz] it was not a bad occasion to implement them, and with this reply which they did not accept they took the land route, passing through very difficult regions for fear of Abdulacão, King of the Usbeques, whom, had he not died at that time, none of them would have escaped on account of the great differences there were between him and Equebar, for whom his death was a great good fortune, for there was much trouble between them. [T]he Xaa has captured most of his kingdoms, approaching through those regions so close to Equebar that he forced him to retreat from Laor, and they are today not as great friends as they used to be for they have clashed in that ambition.[67]

---

[66] BL, Addn. 28,432, fo. 14v.

[67] BL, Addn. 28,432, fos 16r–16v. Compare other letters on Hurmuz affairs from Vidigueira to the King, dated April 1598 and December 1599, in BNL, Códice 1976, fos 92r, 107v, and 141v. For Persian materials on Portuguese-Safavid relations and the

The reference is probably to the Safavid embassy to the Mughals, led by Mirza 'Ali Beg Qurchi, which arrived at Agra in early 1599, in order to verify Akbar's intentions in respect to 'Abdullah Khan Uzbek's erstwhile territories. In late 1594, a series of ambassadorial exchanges had been set in motion, when the Safavid representative Yadgar Sultan Rumlu was permitted to return to Iran. Along with him, Akbar sent Mirza Ziya al-Din (accompanied by Khwaja Abu Nasir) to Iran as his ambassador, with the idea that they should go from Lahore to Lahori Bandar, and then to Hurmuz. Then in 1598, a certain Minuchihr Beg was sent back by 'Abbas as his ambassador, with rich presents, and eventually in 1599 another embassy also comprising Mirza 'Ali Beg Qurchi (Karamilu).[68] The Portuguese evidently kept close track of these exchanges, in particular because they so often passed through Hurmuz. Vidigueira's calculation evidently was that the Safavid front would preoccupy Akbar, and that—when added to Murad's death—would suffice to take the pressure off the Deccan.

There was also another factor: namely his poor opinion of Akbar's other sons. This is made evident in the same letter, in a passage immediately following the discussion of Murad's death:

Besides the Prince Xaamorad, Equebar has another younger son Danniel by name whom he had accomodated in the part of his kingdoms that borders on Bengal, and as soon as he heard of the death of Xâmorad, fearing the Prince [Salim] who planned to give him poison, he called for this other son, and now has him with himself, and with this [son] the Prince [Salim] may have more difficulties than were expected would occur between him and Xaamorad, mainly because the father has him close by and trusts him more, even though this prince is not believed to be a man of war or of talent who can cause any changes, it being understood that on the death of Equebar there will be many [quarrels] between the captains of greatest importance, who do not get along at all (...)[69]

Few of these prognostications turned out to be true, of course. Instead of keeping Daniyal with him, Akbar sent him to the Deccan, with 'Abd al-Rahim—now his father-in-law—to keep him company. Eventually, Akbar himself moved south, asking Daniyal to leave the conclusion of matters to him and not hasten unduly

---

Portuguese presence in the Persian Gulf in the period, also see Jahangir Qa'im Maqami, *Asnâd-i fârsî 'arabî wa turkî dar ârshîv-i millî-yi purtughâl, darbâr-i hurmûz wa khalîj-i fârs*, Vol. I, Teheran, 1354 Khurshidi.

[68] See Riazul Islam, *A Calendar of Documents on Indo-Persian Relations (1500–1750)*, 2 Vols, Karachi/Teheran, 1978–82, Vol. I, pp. 123–33. There is some variation in the precise names of ambassadors between these documents and the *Akbar Nâma*, and I have generally preferred the former versions.

[69] Cf. BL, Addn. 28,432, fos 14v–15r. Compare another letter, dated 23 December 1599, from Vidigueira to the King, in BNL, Códice 1976, fos 141v–142r.

in the campaign. As Mughal pressure increased, Abhang Khan Zangi fled the region in about April 1600; Chand Bibi was killed by dissenters within Ahmadnagar a few months later; the fort of Ahmadnagar eventually fell in August 1600 and Asirgarh in January of the next year. Resistance was left to a certain Miyan Raju Dakhni, and perhaps more importantly to the Habashi leader, Malik 'Ambar (1548–1626), who—as students of Deccan history well know—continued to hold back the tide of Mughal expansion for almost another quarter-century.[70]

Doubts and Questions

The Count of Vidigueira returned to Portugal in late May 1601, after handing over the post of viceroy to a caretaker governor, the Archbishop D. Frei Aleixo de Meneses on 9 December 1600. He embarked from Goa on 26 December in the ship *São Francisco*, leaving behind much discontent—both visible and concealed.[71] Vidigueira's overall record as a viceroy in relation to his subjects in the *Estado da Índia* is not the concern of this chapter; we may leave that for another discussion. His relations with the *Estado*'s neighbours are another matter, and we may look at how he himself evaluated his record, in an undated letter written from Cascais, soon after his return to Portugal.

I handed over [the government] on the 9th of December, being in a state of universal peace and quietude with the Neighbouring Kings, and free of that old discredit and notorious damage that was received from Cunhale, of whose capture and destruction I advised His Majesty overland, and later I had him publicly brought to justice in Goa, and after having prepared and despatched the fleets to Malabar and the North, and having in September sent two galleys and two covered galliots to Malaca against the Dutch who continue in those parts, and having sworn the terms of peace with the Samorin, who sent his nephew to Goa with sufficient powers for that effect, and having made peace with

---

[70] The standard accounts are Radhe Shyam, *The kingdom of Ahmadnagar*, New Delhi, 1966; and also by the same author *Life and times of Malik Ambar*, Delhi, 1968. The loosely-structured and confused book of B. G. Tamaskar, *Life and work of Malik Ambar*, Delhi, 1978, which uses a small sprinkling of Portuguese sources, can only be consulted with extreme caution. His assumption that the term 'Melique' always means Malik 'Ambar, for instance, makes nonsense of much of the discussion in his chapter 7, pp. 153–76. Also note the interesting point made in B. P. Saksena, 'A few unnoticed facts about the early life of Malik Amber', *Proceedings (Transactions) of the Indian History Congress*, 5th Session, 1941, pp. 601–3, that in 1599–1600, Malik 'Ambar wished to enter Mughal service, but was not accepted by Abu'l Fazl; this is based on Asad Beg's travel account cited above.

[71] For the documents of the administrative transfer of late 1600, see BNL, Códice 1976, fos 531r–538v. For a brief discussion, see Subrahmanyam, 'An Augsburger in Ásia Portuguesa', p. 412.

the King of Travancor, who demanded it through his ambassador as soon as he knew of the destruction of Cunhale (...)[72]

The conduct of foreign affairs has been reduced here to a one-point programme: the success against the Mappila chieftain, credit for which was, incidentally, a matter of great dispute between Vidigueira and another *fidalgo*, André Furtado de Mendonça, who actually led the expedition.[73] In fact, the successful attacks on the Mappila stronghold (carried out from December 1599, and brought to a conclusion on 7 March 1600) provided a much-needed triumph for Vidigueira, whose own brother, Dom Lu-is da Gama, had led an earlier disastrous assault on the same target. Basking in the glory of this victory, Vidigueira strategically neglected to mention his Mughal policy, for the fall of Ahmadnagar to the Mughals had made an absurdity of his letter of late 1599.

Nevertheless, some doubts linger. Mughal historians, jealous of their own 'domains', are bound to accept with reluctance the idea that Prince Murad was done away with by a Portuguese directed 'foreign hand'. The objection that no such hand is to be detected from a reading of the usual sources, the Persian chronicles, is to my mind an inadmissible one; the writers of the Persian chronicles, including Abu'l Fazl who was not far from the scene, possibly were simply unaware of it (and even if they caught a hint of gossip to this effect, were unlikely to reproduce it). It is a pity that the resolutely gossipy account of Mulla 'Abd al-Qadir Badayuni does not take us as far as 1599, for it is he above all who might have retailed such a rumour or suspicion. At any rate, it is little short of fetishism to insist that only those 'facts' of Mughal history that are retailed in Persian are true and all others false!

But could Vidigueira in fact have confessed (rather pathologically) to a crime he did not commit? There are certainly two possibilities to be taken into consideration. One is that while he had the *intention* of having Murad assassinated, he did not realize that it was Nature and not a Portuguese assassin which had done for the prince. The second possibility is that Vidigueira simply, and opportunistically, took credit for an event with which he had no connection (either actual, or even in terms of intention). The latter seems unlikely, for such a claim was not to be made lightly, particularly in view of its ambiguous moral nature, even in terms of contemporary arguments relating to 'reason of State'. Besides, from whatever we know of Vidigueira's later career in Portugal, and

---

[72] Copy of a letter from Vidigueira to the Marquês de Castel Rodrigo, sent from Cascais, BL, Addn. 28,432, fos 17r–18r.

[73] See C.R. Boxer and Frazão de Vasconcelos, *André Furtado de Mendonça (1558–1610)*, reprint, Macao, 1989; 1st ed. 1955, with Mendonça's own account being reproduced there on pp. 97–104. Also the letter from Vidigueira to Philip III, dated April 1600, BNL, Códice 1976, fos 100v–103r.

then again in India, he was not given to outright fabrication of this sort. On the other hand, assassination was a tactic he used at least once more, in the 1620s during his second viceroyalty; on this occasion, the target was a Portuguese renegade who was employed by Ibrahim 'Adil Shah to make cannon in Bijapur.[74] In his rule-book then, assassination was an extension of politics by other means.

We can, of course, never prove beyond all doubt that the Portuguese arranged Murad's death. There is, as the phrase goes, no 'smoking gun', only pieces of paper. What is important is that they thought of doing so, and that one viceroy— an inexperienced, ambitious, and particularly quarrelsome *fidalgo*—actually claimed to have done so. This claim alone sets a different tone to our understanding of Mughal–Portuguese relations in the latter part of the reign of Akbar.

What of larger implications for Mughal history? We are aware that the succession of Prince Salim ('Xêcogi') to the throne in late 1605 with the title of Nur al-Din Muhammad Jahangir was facilitated considerably by the death in the preceding decade of his brothers, Murad and Daniyal (the latter on 11 March 1605, a bare seven months before Akbar). The only serious alternative contender remaining besides Salim, was his own son Khusrau, whose rebellion was crushed in the aftermath of Akbar's death. It is not my intention here to speculate what would have happened had Murad remained alive; this is the business of crystal-ball-gazers rather than historians. But it is nevertheless worth remembering that the age was one in which individuals (and especially members of the elite) were seen as important sources of historical agency, and the temptation to assassination was naturally strongly present as a consequence.[75]

In the early 1580s, members of Akbar's entourage are reported by Abu'l Fazl to have suggested the elimination of his troublesome half-brother Mirza Muhammad Hakim, whose claims to sovereign status were recognized by the Safavids, as well as possibly the Uzbeks.[76] Mirza Hakim's fortuitous death

---

[74] See Subrahmanyam, *The Portuguese Empire in Asia*, p. 255. On other Portuguese renegades in the Deccan, in the service of Malik 'Ambar (and at his court), see W. Ph. Coolhaas, ed. *Pieter van den Broecke in Azië*, 2 Vols, The Hague, 1962–3, Vol. I, pp. 140–51. The incidents described took place in November 1617, when Malik 'Ambar was at Khadke (Kirkee), near Daulatabad.

[75] For a parallel reflection, on a rather more well-known event, see Ronald Mousnier, *The Assassination of Henry IV: The Tyrannicide Problem and the Consolidation of the French Absolute Monarchy in the Early Seventeenth Century*, tr. Joan Spencer, New York, 1973.

[76] On the proposal to assassinate Mirza Hakim, see Abu'l Fazl, *A'în-i Akbarî*, Vol. III, tr. H. S. Jarrett, rev. Jadunath Sarkar, reprint, Delhi, 1989, pp. 428–9; Abu'l Fazl, *Akbar Nâma*, Vol. III, tr. Beveridge, pp. 541–2. For Safavid and Uzbek attitudes towards him, see respectively 'Abd al-Husain Nawa'i, *Shâh Tahmâsb Safawî: Majmû'a-i asnâd wa*

(from Akbar's viewpoint) in 1585, did away with the necessity in this particular instance, but not necessarily with the idea, as such. Akbar himself is reported for example, by 'Abd al-Qadir Badayuni, to have suspected Salim at least once of having poisoned him.[77] If Prince Murad was indeed the victim of a Portuguese hand then, there is little that would have been surprising in such a world. For pious thoughts aside, there was always the pressure of a certain version of *razón de Estado*, which men like the Count of Vidigueira had learnt in a hard school. But this meant in turn that the events of May 1599 did not augur well for the future Mughal–Portuguese relationship; the eventual beneficiaries were to be the English and the Dutch East India Companies. For even if the Mughals did not succeed in expelling the Portuguese from Goa, Daman, or Diu, the veiled but deeply entrenched hostility between the two in the age of Akbar can be ignored by the historian only at his own peril.

---

makâtabât târîkhî hamrâ ba yâddâshtha-i tafsîlî, Teheran, 1989, pp. 503–5, and Tanish ibn Mir Muhammad Bukhari, *Sharaf-Nama-ii Shakhi: Kniga Shakhskoi Slavy*, ed. and tr. M. A. Salakhetdinova, 2 Vols, Moscow, 1983.

[77] Badayuni, *Muntakhab al-Tawârîkh*, Vol. II, p. 390. This incident took place in AH. 999 (AD 1591), and Akbar accused not only Salim but also the physician Hakim Humam. This was also the occasion for increased tensions between Salim and Murad. Letters from Jerónimo Xavier S. J. suggest that Akbar continued to harbour such suspicions even later; cf. his report on Akbar's death in his letter from Lahore of 25 September 1606, in A. da Silva Rego, ed., *Documentação Ultramarina Portuguesa*, Vol. III, Lisbon, 1963, pp. 62–5. The same suspicion even finds mention in letters from Philip III to the viceroy Aires de Saldanha of 1601 and 1604, cited in Tamaskar, *Life and Work of Malik Ambar*, pp. 29–30.

5

The Legend of Sultan Bulaqi and the Estado da Índia, 1628–40[1]

One of these men is Genius to the other;
And so of these: which is the natural man,
And which the spirit? Who deciphers them?

Shakespeare, *The Comedy of Errors*, Act V, Scene[1]

Introduction

Early modern historiography has in the past decades devoted considerable attention to emerging notions of personal identity, which in turn are linked to theories of historical trajectory of the idea of the 'individual' in various cultures. To be sure, some elements of this problem can be traced back to medieval (or even older) reflections on self-knowledge, and it has even been argued from this perspective that 'the discovery of the individual was one of the most important cultural developments in the years between 1050 and 1200' in western Europe.[2] The issue has also been posed from a rather different angle, namely that of the specificity of the individual, which in turn takes us to the very widespread theme of the 'impostor' or 'double', of which an outstanding example may be found in Akira Kurosawa's 1980 film *Kagemusha* ('The Shadow Warrior').[3] The film is situated in Japan's sixteenth-century warring states period, and narrates how a condemned thief is saved from execution by agreeing

[1] This chapter was co-authored with Jorge Flores. I am grateful to him for permission to use it here.

[2] Colin Morris, *The Discovery of the Individual, 1050–1200*, Toronto, 1972, p. 158; also more recently, the related reflection in Aaron Gurevich, *The origins of European individualism*, tr. Katherine Judelson, Oxford, 1995.

[3] Cf. David Desser, *The Samurai Films of Akira Kurosawa*, Ann Arbor, 1983.

to serve as a double for the powerful warlord Takeda Shingen (1521–73) of Kai. In this case, the key elements are somewhat particular: the 'double' is in a sense authorized by the original to substitute for him, and the tensions revolve largely around the difference in the social status of the two. But a series of other questions also emerge from such materials. Can one person somehow 'become' another? Can one think of historical cultures in which personal identity was effectively subordinated to social identity, and, by an extension of the same logic, to social function? Can a person simply be produced as a social actor, in the sense that some have argued that authors are produced?[4] What notions of proof of identity do different historical cultures demand, and can we assume that we are moving historically from more credulous cultures to others where ever-more rigorous ideas of proof are being set down by an intrusive state apparatus?

India has had its fair share of Tichborne Claimants and Martin Guerres who lend themselves to this type of reflection, of which one of the most celebrated modern cases is that of the so-called Kumar of Bhawal in Bengal, that has recently been studied in considerable detail by Partha Chatterjee.[5] Though the Bhawal case, which was brought to trial in the 1920s and 1930s, is unusual for the fact that a considerable moment of forensic material was brought to bear on the matter, Chatterjee and others have noted that it also followed on a longer Indian trend, of which a notable earlier figure is that of the so-called 'False Pratapchand', an instance referring to a claimant to one of the zamîndârî estates in Bengal in the first half of the nineteenth century.[6] However, if we cast our glance back as far as the sixteenth or seventeenth centuries, we can already find such instances, of which one well-known case concerns Shah Shuja', the son of the Mughal emperor Shahjahan who was apparently killed in Arakan in the 1660s, but who turned up periodically in quite diverse parts of the Mughal domains. Chatterjee's purpose in his work is complex, but one of his intentions is to juxtapose 'modern Western philosophical discussion on identity', with what he terms 'Indian philosophical discussions on identity and recognition', arguing that these produced quite different notions of both personhood and proof.[7] An

---

[4] Michel Foucault, 'What is an Author?', in Vassilis Lambropoulos and David Neal Miller, eds, *Twentieth-Century Literary Theory*, Albany, NY, 1987, pp. 124–42; and the further discussion in Anthony Grafton, *Forgers and Critics: Creativity and Duplicity in Western Scholarship*, Princeton, 1990, and Roger Chartier, *The Order of Books: Readers, authors, and libraries in Europe between the fourteenth and eighteenth centuries*, tr. Lydia Cochrane, Stanford, 1994, pp. 25–60.

[5] Partha Chatterjee, *A Princely Impostor? The Kumar of Bhawal and the Secret History of Indian Nationalism*, New Delhi, 2002.

[6] See John R. McLane, *Land and Local Kingship in Eighteenth-Century Bengal*, Cambridge, 1993, pp. 316–22; also Gautam Bhadra, *Jâl râjâr kathā*, Kolkata, 2003.

[7] See the discussion in Chatterjee, *A Princely Impostor*, pp. 115–37.

examination of the situation in the seventeenth century may demonstrate that this opposition was by no means quite so radical, in particular if one moves from the realm of philosophical reflection to the methods actually used by states to separate the sheep from the goats, as it were.

The question of the 'impostor' may of course exist at various levels in a society: the long-absent merchant, the renouncer who returns after a long interval, and so on. Yet the issue takes on a particular charge when the personage in question, like the Kumar of Bhawal, has a function in guaranteeing social order by virtue of his or her association with royal power. Now the theme of the royal 'double' is a powerful one that potentially possesses the capacity to transcend cultural divisions, but nevertheless seems more anchored in some cultures than in others. The central idea is quite simple. A royal figure, who could be a reigning or former monarch or is at any rate close to the throne, possesses an exact double, who resembles him or her perfectly—and is either a perfect stranger or an identical twin. In a variant, the 'double' is in fact an impostor, a false claimant who will either be unmasked for what he or she is, or again will manage successfully to impose this false claim on a credulous population. The first of these broad lines of development gives us popular literary themes such as that of Louis XIV's identical twin, developed by Alexandre Dumas (or his ghost-writers) in *The Man in the Iron Mask*. The most recent literary version, albeit not concerned with a royal double, is the work entitled *O homem duplicado* by the Nobel Prize winning novelist José Saramago, who adds a further twist by making his 'hero' a professor of history.[8] In an extensive post-Dumas sub-literature, we already have examples such as Anthony Hope's late nineteenth-century work, *The Prisoner of Zenda*, to which Saramago incidentally does refer. The second line is far more fecund from a historical point of view. For instance, we know that in Tsarist Russia, a vast number of claimants purporting to be this or that prince existed from the sixteenth century on, and that this tradition even continued after the Russian Revolution, with several persons claiming to be Aleksei or Anastasia, or other members of the Tsar's family who had survived the mass execution by the Bolsheviks.[9] Again, in England in the late fifteenth century, the nascent Tudor dynasty had to face a challenge in the form of various rival claimants who stated that they descended from the Yorkist kings. One of these claimants, Lambert Simnel, was dealt with relatively easily by Henry VII, but the other, Perkin Warbeck, posed a rather more major threat and was hence eventually hanged for treason in 1499 after mounting several unsuccessful attacks and rebellions with the aid of a number of European monarchs who recognized his

---

[8] José Saramago, *O homem duplicado*, Lisbon, 2002.

[9] Gyula Szvák, *False tsars*, tr. Peter Daniel, Boulder, 2000.

claims.[10] What makes the case of Warbeck particularly curious is his Portuguese 'connection'; for though he was probably born in the Flanders, he had spent time in Portugal, and one of his major supporters was a Jewish adventurer of Portuguese origin, Duarte Brandão or Edward Brampton.[11]

Closer geographically to the case we shall examine presently, we have an important incident in late sixteenth-century Iran, namely of a *qalandar* called Muzawwar who appeared in 1580, claiming to be the recently deceased monarch Shah Isma'il II. This man had managed at a certain stage to gather together as many as 20,000 supporters, and to defy the Safavid regional governors, until his movement was brutally repressed.[12] A less well-known instance that is relevant to the subject of this essay is narrated by the Portuguese official chronicler Diogo do Couto, in his account of the Sultanate of Gujarat in the sixteenth century, and draws upon a number of other sources. In this view, the life of Sultan Bahadur of Gujarat (r. 1526–37) followed a certain familiar pattern. Couto writes:

[The Sultan] Modafar(...)had many sons, and the first-born was called Bador, and not Badur, as the chronicles of India call him. When he was still a boy, either because the astrologers told his father that that kingdom would be lost in the hands of his oldest son, or (as seems more likely) because he wanted to give it over to a younger son for whom he had more affection, it seems that he [Modafar] became ill-disposed towards Bador, who—either because he knew of this or because he feared that his father would have him killed—escaped bodily and went around that Industão as a pilgrim, or what is called a *calandar*, and in this fashion wandered many years, learning different languages, observing and noting new rites and customs, and many new and fugitive things.[13]

So we have the theme of the royal exile, who becomes a renouncer (Persian *qalandar*), and wanders about incognito. Couto then develops the logically necessary second part of this theme as follows.

While he was going about in this manner, his father died, and the brother to whom the father wanted to give the kingdom succeeded, but this lasted only a short while, and he left the kingdom to another younger brother, but we do not know their names. When news

[10] Ian Arthurson, *The Perkin Warbeck conspiracy, 1491–1499*, Stroud, 1994; also, more recently, the popular work by Ann Wroe, *Perkin: A story of deception*, London, 2003.

[11] Jean Aubin, 'D. João II et Henry VII', in Aubin, *Le Latin et l'Astrolabe, Vol. II: Recherches sur le Portugal de la Renaissance, son expansion en Asie et les relations internationales*, Paris, 2000, pp. 83–92.

[12] See Roger M. Savory, 'A Curious Episode in Safavid history', in C. E. Bosworth, ed., *Iran and Islam: In Memory of the late Vladimir Minorsky*, Edinburgh, 1971, pp. 461–73.

[13] Diogo do Couto, *Década Quarta da Ásia*, ed. M. Augusta Lima Cruz, Lisbon, 1999, Vol. I, p. 55.

of the death of Modafar travelled through that Industão, it reached Bador, who at once returned in order to come and demand his kingdom, and—so they say—still in the clothes of a *calandar* entered the court of Amadaba, where his mother was still alive, as well as her son the king, who was still a boy, and without identifying himself to anyone, he [Bahadur] went in to see his mother and revealed himself to her, asking her that she should give the necessary orders for him to have his kingdom. The queen (and it may well be that she was not his mother but his stepmother, and that the Guzarates who recount this got it mixed up) told him that he should leave, for if his brother were to find out about him, he would have him killed, from which we may infer that she was the mother of the king and not of Bador. He, on being disillusioned, went to the king of Mandou, and revealed himself to him (*se lhe descobrio*), asking him for help and favour in order to recover his kingdom. And since, with the great people of the world, there is nothing that moves them so much as the miseries of an exiled prince, he promised him every favour and even that he would go in person to help him: and to this end, he asked some of the neighbouring kings that they should join him with great might.

Sultan Bahadur thus recovers his throne either with the help of the ruler of Mandu, or (in a variant that Couto also recounts) through the help of the Queen of Chitor. However, once he is on the throne, 'as he was evil, cruel and weak' he loses no time in attacking those who have helped him. The origins of a part of this narrative, in which Bahadur wanders in exile, may already be found in an anonymous Portuguese text of the mid-1530s, that describes how 'the said Bador became a *calamdar*, going about barefoot and dressed in skins'.[14] Couto, who clearly had a fondness for this theme, subsequently uses it somewhat indiscriminately in his text, in relation, for example, to an ancestor of the Mughals whom he seems to have largely invented. In his view, then, one of the sons of Timur called 'Umar Shaikh ('Haomarxac') also had a similar career. Couto thus writes of how in the course of a political sibling rivalry in fifteenth-century Central Asia, 'Haomarxac, who is called Balobo by some, was a boy (...) and was left with nothing, because the two other brothers took hold of everything they could'. Faced with these circumstances, the inevitable took place: 'This Haomarxac, or Balobo, on seeing himself disinherited, decided to serve Mafamede and leaving those states that had belonged to his father in the clothes of a *calandar* (which is to say a pilgrim) went off in the direction of India, and traversed all of Industan, and eventually halted in the kingdom of Deli, where he decided to stay'.[15] Couto then goes on to describe how he became popular amongst the other *calandares* there on account of the 'fame of his life and religion, which was wonderful'; he thus built up this following into a sizeable

---

[14] Sanjay Subrahmanyam, 'A Crónica dos Reis de Bisnaga e a Crónica do Guzerate: Dois Textos Indo-Portugueses do século XVI', in Jorge Manuel Flores, ed., *Os Construtores do Oriente Português*, Lisbon-Oporto, 1998, pp. 131–54.

[15] Couto, *Década Quarta*, Vol. I, pp. 544–5.

army, and eventually attacked and killed the king of Delhi, seizing power there himself and creating a sizeable domain through a series of conquests. Couto even tells us that this Balobo 'who entitled himself king of the Magores' was the founder of Mughal rule in India, and the grandfather of Babur, who eventually came to rule in the sixteenth century.

The manifest inaccuracy of Couto's account, which confuses Mughal history with that of the Afghan ruler Bahlul Lodi (almost certainly the 'Balobo' of the account) need not concern us here; what is of interest is that the theme was clearly a common and widespread one and that Couto made use of it while drawing upon a vein of 'folklore' in his chronicle.[16] It is clear then that by the sixteenth century, a tradition already existed in northern India of wandering princes in exile who might make claims to a throne while appearing ostensibly to be mere *calandares*. Whether these claimants were true or false is not a theme that concerns Couto much, for he assumes that in general they were authentic—whether with Sultan Bahadur, or with his account of Balobo. But in the case that we shall consider below, matters appear far more complex, and lead us in the direction of a different variant, namely one where 'false' and 'true' claimants appear in the same political panorama.

Mughal Succession and the Case of Bulaqi

Mughal succession had been much contested in the early phase of the dynasty which had established itself in India in the 1520s. At the death of the first emperor, Zahir-al-Din Muhammad Babur, his sons fought for years over the succession, with the designated heir Humayun being forced to contend time and again with his brothers Hindal, 'Askari, and especially Kamran, who operated from a base in Kabul. Eventually, Humayun was able to put an end to this threat only by blinding Kamran. However, if we return to the moment of Babur's death, we note that some sources suggest that this fact was initially kept secret for a certain time in order to avoid the social turmoil on account of which such moments were particularly feared. The account of Babur's own daughter, Gulbadan Begam, in her *Humâyûn Nâma*, makes this clear enough; she suggests that only after the lapse of some time was it eventually announced that the emperor had 'become a dervish (*Hazrat Bâbur Bâdshâh darwîsh shudand*)', and

---

[16] Compare this with the account of 'Ballu', as Bahlul Lodi is termed, in the sixteenth-century text of Shaikh Rizqullah Mushtaqi, *Waqi'at-e-Mushtaqui of Shaikh Rizq Ullah Mushtaqui: A Source of Information on the Life and Conditions in Pre-Mughal India*, trans. Iqtidar Husain Siddiqui, New Delhi, 1993, pp. 1–15; for the Persian text, see Shaikh Rizqullah Mushtaqi, *Wâqi'ât-i Mushtâqî*, eds Iqtidar Husain Siddiqui and Waqarul Hasan Siddiqi, Rampur, 2002, pp. 3–16.

that he had left his domains to his oldest son, Humayun.[17] On Humayun's own death, a quarter-century later in 1556, matters proved somewhat complicated as well. The designated heir was Jalal-al-Din Muhammad Akbar, but he too had a half-brother, Mirza Muhammad Hakim, who though an infant at the time also had his own partisans. The Ottoman admiral, Seyyidi 'Ali Reis, who was present at the time of Humayun's death in Delhi (in January 1556), claims that a ruse had to be used in order to conceal the emperor's death for a certain time, while Akbar returned to the capital. He writes:

Amongst those close to the emperor [Humayun], there was a person called Munla Bi-kesi who had a certain resemblance to him, but who was somewhat smaller. Finally, on Tuesday, he was installed on the throne that had been placed under an arch that overlooked the river, he was dressed up in the emperor's clothes, his face and eye were covered in bandages, Khushhal Beg stayed close to him and the Mir Munshi directly in front. All the Sultans, Mirzas, the subjects and the common people arrived, saw the emperor from the bank of the river and made prayers for him. Joyful music was played, the physician was given a robe of honour, and it was asserted that the emperor was in good health.[18]

On Akbar's eventual return, this imposture could finally be dispensed with, and the death of the emperor was at last announced to the public. Akbar's own death, a half-century later, was attended by somewhat less subterfuge. His successor Nur-al-Din Muhammad Jahangir had seen his brothers and major potential rivals, Daniyal and Murad, die in quick succession, and his only serious rival was his own son, Khusrau, whose ambitions were initially suppressed by deft political alliance-building in 1605. It turned out, however, that the enthronement of Jahangir had by no means resolved his problems with Khusrau. The prince rebelled in 1606, and besieged Lahore; imperial armies had to be sent into the Punjab to quell the movement, which apparently enjoyed quite extensive popular support. Khusrau was captured, and others around him were meted out exemplary punishments. A year later, a fresh 'conspiracy' was unearthed, with the alleged intent of assassinating Jahangir and placing his son on the throne; the conspirators were again severely castigated. This time, Khusrau himself was partially blinded and placed under strict guard. But then, in late April 1610, a further strange incident occurred. A man—later identified as a certain Qutb from Uchh—appeared in the eastern Indian province of Bihar in the guise of a *faqîr*,

[17] Gul-Badan Begam, *Humâyûn-Nâma*, ed. and tr. Annette S. Beveridge, reprint, Lahore, 1974, p. 109 (text, p. 25).

[18] Seyyidi 'Ali Re'is, *Le miroir des pays: Une anabase ottomane à travers l'Inde et l'Asie centrale*, tr. Jean-Louis Bacqué-Grammont, Paris, 1999, pp. 90–1. For the original text, see Seydi Ali Reis, *Mir'âtü'l-Memâlik*, ed. Mehmet Kiremit, Ankara, 1999, pp. 120–1.

and managed to gather together a fair degree of armed support in the region of Ujjainiya by claiming to be Khusrau—who had escaped from prison.[19] The provincial governor, Afzal Khan, was absent from his post at the time, and when the rebel army, which was supported by some *zamîndârs*, approached the provincial capital of Patna, the other officials took fright at their numbers and fled without offering too much resistance. The 'false Khusrau' and his supporters were able to help themselves liberally to the treasury, and thus gain even greater popular support. Eventually, five days later, Afzal Khan returned and a pitched battle ensued, in which the rebel forces were defeated, and the impostor himself was executed by the governor. The imperial court for its part was greatly displeased, not least of all by the behaviour of its officials who, it seemed, were all-too-ready to believe rumours of rebel princes and draw unwarranted conclusions therefrom. Some of these officials were hence publicly humiliated, with 'their heads and beards shaved(...), dressed in women's head coverings, mounted on donkeys, and paraded around the city and marketplace to serve as a warning to others'.[20] Afzal Khan himself barely escaped punishment on account of the intervention of his friends.

Yet, even if the rest of his life was spent in obscurity, the figure of Khusrau had not quite lost its aura. We see this some two decades later, in 1627, when Jahangir lay on his deathbed. On 28 October that year, when he died in Rajauri, in the outskirts of the city of Lahore, several rival claimants to the throne existed. Even if the robustness of the political institutions of the Mughal empire was sufficient to ensure no truly deep crisis at a moment such as the death of a monarch,[21] there is little doubt that such periods of transition were always somewhat disturbed. The succession to the throne of Shahjahan (r. 1628–58) was no exception to this rule. The Dutch East India Company employee, Dirck van der Lee, reported from Surat that the Company's factors in Agra had reported conflicting rumours concerning Jahangir's state of health. This had led 'some of the more important persons in the city to leave the town with their costly

---

[19] For a detailed account, see Mirza Nathan, *Baharistan-i-Ghaybi: A history of the Mughal wars in Assam, Cooch Behar, Bengal, Bihar and Orissa during the reigns of Jahangir and Shahjahan*, tr. M. I. Borah, 2 Vols, Gauhati, 1936, Vol. I, pp. 89–91; also Khwaja Kamgar Husaini, *Ma'asir-i Jahangiri: A contemporary account of Jahangir*, ed. Azra Alavi, Bombay, 1978, pp. 129–31, section entitled: 'The rising of the dust of sedition in the city of Patna, and its quelling by the irrigation of imperial fortune'.

[20] *The Jahangirnama: Memoirs of Jahangir, Emperor of India*, tr. Wheeler M. Thackston, New York, 1999, pp. 112–13; for the Persian text, see *Toozuk-i Jahangeeree*, ed. Syud Ahmud, Aligarh, 1864, pp. 83–4.

[21] Cf. Muzaffar Alam and Sanjay Subrahmanyam, 'Witnessing transition: Views on the end of the Akbari dispensation', in K. N. Panikkar *et al.*, eds, *The Making of History. Essays presented to Irfan Habib*, New Delhi, 2002, pp. 104–40.

belongings; others employed guards in their houses'.[22] Besides, the roads had become unsafe, and the price of provisions too had risen unusually.

Now, the attention of historians has usually focused on a brief period of three months, dominated by a marked degree of political instability caused by the succession. Prince Parwiz, the eldest son of Jahangir and principal claimant to the throne in the eyes of some, had already died a year earlier, in October 1626. Khusrau himself had died in prison in early 1622, under obscure circumstances. The contest thus seemed to centre essentially on the rivalry between Shahryar, the youngest son of Jahangir, who was married to a daughter of Nur Jahan, and Prince Khurram, who had rebelled against his father in 1622, and who some suspected in the convenient deaths of his two brothers. In the succession struggle, a central role was to be played by Asaf Khan, brother of Nur Jahan and *wazîr* of the empire. While Nur Jahan seems to have preferred Shahryar, Asaf Khan own preferences clearly lay with Khurram. Yet, given the fact that the latter found himself in the distant Deccan, and was some days' march from Lahore, and the need was felt to neutralize Shahryar, Asaf Khan seems to have found a temporary solution in order to gain some time. With the support of a sizeable party of Mughal nobles, he organized the crowning of Dawar Bakhsh, the son of Khusrau, who had meanwhile been kept in prison. According to the chronicler Muhammad Hadi:

Asaf Khan, a loyal supporter of Shahjahan, conspired with Iradat Khan to release Khusraw's son Dawar Bakhsh from prison and give him the good news of a phantom rulership. However, he would not believe it until they swore solemn oaths that it was so. Then Asaf Khan and Iradat Khan put Dawar Bakhsh on a horse, raised the royal parasol, and set out for the next station. No matter how many messengers Nurjahan Begam sent to summon her brother, Asaf Khan made excuses and did not go to her.[23]

In this way, Shahryar, who for his part had also declared himself emperor and taken over the imperial treasury at Lahore, was obliged to react and to combat this unexpected rival. The battle took place near Lahore itself, and Asaf Khan managed to capture Shahryar alive, obliging him to submit formally to Dawar Bakhsh. This latter prince, also known in popular parlance as Sultan Bulaqi,[24]

---

[22] Van der Lee's report is summarized and paraphrased in Om Prakash, 'Archival source material in the Netherlands on the history of Gujarat in the early modern period', in Ernestine Carreira, ed., *Sources européennes sur le Gujarat*, Paris, 1998, pp. 144–5.

[23] *The Jahangirnama*, tr. Thackston, pp. 456–7; for the Persian text, see *Toozuk-i Jahangeeree*, ed. Syud Ahmud, p. 421.

[24] Bulaqi, which is also written at times in Safavid texts as 'Bulaghi', seems to be a name of Turkish rather than Persian origin. It does not seem to have any relationship with Bulaq, a small town near Cairo.

seems to have benefited from the reflected glory of his father's charisma, and had also been somewhat favoured by Jahangir in the latter years of his reign.[25] Thus, in 1623, Dawar Bakhsh had been named governor of Gujarat, and in the same year had also received the high *mansab* of 8000/3000.[26] But, in the strategic conception of the *wazîr*, Bulaqi was a figure whose prime significance was decorative, and he is even described by the Mughal chroniclers as no more than a 'sacrificial goat' (*gosfand-i qurbânî*).[27]

Roughly 20 days after the death of Jahangir, Prince Khurram in the Deccan received news of his father's demise. He left immediately for Agra, but first sent a *farmân* to Asaf Khan, ordering him to eliminate Shahryar, Dawar Bakhsh, as well as other possible candidates to the throne who might represent a potential threat. Thus, on 19 January 1628, Bulaqi was made prisoner, at the same time that the Friday prayers were read in the name of Khurram, who was now proclaimed ruler with the title of Shahjahan. Some days later, we hear of the execution of Shahryar, Dawar Bahksh, and his brother Gurshasp, as well of two sons of the deceased prince Mirza Daniyal (Tahmurs and Hoshang), brother of Jahangir.[28] Yet, even the official Mughal tradition attributes a certain *sang-froid* and gallows humour to the unfortunate Bulaqi. Khurram, so it is reported, had sent a certain Riza Bahadur to Lahore, with orders that 'he should cleanse the world from the contamination of the existence of sundry princes who were the source of disturbance'. The account then continues:

They say that Sultan Dawar Bakhsh known as Sultan Bulaqi—whom Asaf Khan had placed upon the throne for some days out of certain considerations of policy—was playing chess (*shatranj mî bâkht*) with his brother Sultan Gurshasp. When he heard the noise of Riza Bahadur's arrival, he divined his object and said to his brother: 'Virtue (*Rizâ*) has not come, it is your and our Fate (*Qazâ*) that has arrived.' Yamin-ud-Daula

[25] Cf. John F. Richards, *The Mughal Empire* (*The New Cambridge History of India*, Vol. I. 5), Cambridge, 1993, p. 103, where the author notes that 'Khusrau universally was seen as a tragic and popular figure both by the populace at large and by the royal harem women who resented Nur Jahan's power'.

[26] *Jahangirnama*, tr. Thackston, p. 397; also *Toozuk-i Jahangeeree*, ed. Syud Ahmud, p. 361.

[27] *Toozuk-i Jahangeeree*, ed. Syud Ahmud, p. 422 (addendum by Muhammad Hadi); Kamgar Husaini, *Ma'asir-i Jahangiri*, p. 484; also the later reference in Shahnawaz Khan, *Ma'asir-ul-Umara, being biographies of the Muhammadan and Hindu officers of the Timurid sovereigns of India from 1500 to about 1780 AD*, tr. H. Beveridge and Baini Prashad, 3 Vols, Calcutta, 1911–52, Vol. I, p. 290, for the Persian text of which see Nawwab Samsam al-Daula Shahnawaz Khan, *Ma'asir al-Umara*, eds Maulavi 'Abdur Rahim and Maulavi Mirza Ashraf 'Ali, Vols I and II, Calcutta, 1888–90, Vol. I, p. 154.

[28] *Jahangirnama*, tr. Thackston, p. 460; *Toozuk-i Jahangeeree*, ed. Syud Ahmud, p. 425.

[Asaf Khan] in accordance with the order made over the blinded Sultan Shahryar, Sultan Bulaqi and Tahmuras and Hushang, the sons of Sultan Daniyal [to Riza Bahadur]. He on 25 Jumada I 1037 H. [22 January 1628], put them all to death in one day.[29]

Shahjahan waited outside Agra for the appropriate moment. Finally, on 3 February (7 Jumada II), scrupulously following the instructions of astrologers as to the date and hour that were best for entering the city, he was crowned in Agra.[30] Once on the throne, the new ruler was soon to face serious challenges on the southern fringes of his domains. In October 1629, Khan Jahan Lodi, an Afghan noble of some importance who had been close to Jahangir (but who had chosen to support the candidacy of Dawar Bakhsh), decided to flee Agra and take refuge in the Deccan. Since he had already served as Mughal governor in the region, he was immediately welcomed by Murtaza Nizam Shah II, the much-weakened Sultan of Ahmadnagar. Shahjahan, who greatly feared a generalized rebellion amongst the Afghans who were in his service, decided to react with the utmost harshness. He at once mounted an expedition to the south, and installed his camp at Burhanpur, in the region of Khandesh, where he arrived in March 1630. He was to remain there until March 1632, launching a series of attacks on the forces of Khan Jahan Lodi during the rest of 1630. The rebellious Afghan noble was eventually captured and executed in January 1632.[31]

The presence of the Mughal court in the Deccan seemed to be a clear enough sign that the emperor himself had every intention of closely supervising the governor of that province, Mahabat Khan, in the process of forcing the autonomous Sultanates of the area to submit to Mughal power. An initial campaign against Ahmadnagar, which had chosen to welcome Khan Jahan, went on until 1633, culminating in the siege of the major fort of Daulatabad. In 1635–6, besides formally terminating the existence of the Nizam Shahi dynasty of Ahmadnagar, Shahjahan also managed to 'domesticate' the Sultanates of Bijapur and Golconda. Both these rulers were obliged from that time on to recognize Mughal hegemony and suzerainty, by way of paying a tribute and in the fact that the _khutba_ was henceforth read in the name of Shahjahan, while excluding mention of the Shi'i Imams.

[29] Shahnawaz Khan, _Ma'asir-ul-Umara_, (English tr.), Vol. I, pp. 811–12; Persian text, Vol. I, pp. 713–14.

[30] For a summary of the major events, see Banarsi Prasad Saksena, _History of Shahjahan of Dihli_, reprint, Allahabad, 1968, pp. 56–65; Richards, _The Mughal Empire_, pp. 116–18.

[31] On Khan Jahan Lodi, see Afzal Husain, _The Nobility under Akbar and Jahangir: A study of family groups_, Delhi, 1999, pp. 149–50; and M. A. Rahim, _History of the Afghans in India, AD 1545–1631_, Karachi, 1961.

Nevertheless, the early years of Shahjahan's reign were far from being as simple and linear in character as the rapid summary we have presented above might suggest. Besides many other major problems, including the major famine that ravaged much of western India in 1630–1, the Mughal ruler also had to come to terms with a sort of ghost. For, soon after the execution of the five princes in January 1628, a rumour came to be heard that Sultan Bulaqi had in fact been spared, and that as the legitimate heir to Jahangir, he was in the process of getting together a powerful rebel army in order to challenge the 'usurper' Shahjahan. His escape, according to this view, had been managed with the complicity of Asaf Khan, who had sacrificed another person in the prince's place. The collaboration in the matter of Mahabat Khan, an important noble of Persian origin who had been particularly close to the deceased Prince Khusrau, was also portrayed as being decisive.

At much the same time, rumours also came to be heard that Mirza Baisunghar— another son of Prince Daniyal, who had decided to support Shahryar in the succession struggle after the death of Jahangir—had also survived after the defeat that he and Shahryar had suffered at the hands of Asaf Khan near Lahore. It would, in fact, seem that this cousin of Bulaqi did manage to escape to Badakhshan, where he died. However, someone else managed to pass himself off as the prince, and travelled first to Balkh, and then to Iran, before eventually settling for a time in Istanbul. Here, he seems to have made grandiose plans to depose Shahjahan from the Mughal throne with the help of the Ottoman Sultan Murad IV (r. 1634–40), and even claimed to have the support of the Shaibanids, as well as supporters in Kabul who would revolt at a signal from him. However, the poor figure that he cut at the Ottoman court led to his being identified as an impostor. He was apparently sent to India on the request of Shahjahan, and executed in 1636.[32] The incident is reported in a variant version as follows in an eighteenth-century Mughal text.

In the 9th year [1636], he [Daulat Khan Mayi, governor of Sind] arrested the false Baisunqar and brought him to court. That trickster was an obscure person who gave himself out as the Baisunqar who in Shahryar's battle was the leader of the latter's army (*sardâr-i lashkar*), and who after fleeing to the fort of Kaulas in Telingana died a natural death. The pretended Baisunqar went to Balkh. Nazr Muhammad Khan, the ruler (*wâlî*)

[32] Naimur Rahman Farooqi, *Mughal-Ottoman Relations (A study of political and diplomatic relations between Mughal India and the Ottoman Empire, 1556–1748)*, Delhi, 1989, pp. 6, 26, 46–8. Farooqi bases his account on the chronicle of Mustafa Na'ima (1655–1716), *Târîkh-i Na'ima*, or *Rauzat al-Husain fi Khulâsat Akhbâr al-Khâfiqain*. For a partial translation of this text, see Charles Fraser, *Annals of the Turkish Empire, from 1591 to 1659*, London, 1832; and also the modern edition, *Naîmâ Târîhî*, ed. Zuhuri Danishman, Istanbul, 1967–9, 6 Vols, Vol. III, pp. 1260–4, *passim*.

there wanted to make him a relation by marriage, but as his claims did not prove to be true the connection did not take place. Then he went to Iran, and though Shah Safi did not admit him to his presence, he showed him some favour. From thence he went to Baghdad and Rum. After a long time, willingly and unwillingly, the hand of death seized his collar and brought him to Thatta. Daulat Khan arrested him and sent him to court and he was put to death (*ba qatl rasîd*).[33]

Contemporary European observers, with the exception of the Portuguese (for reasons that will presently become clear), do not pay much attention to the episode of Baisunghar. However, they were far more interested in the legend of Bulaqi, which appears in a wide variety of writings from the seventeenth century. Besides the brief references to Bulaqi in the writings of Johannes de Laet[34] and Peter Mundy,[35] a handful of other interesting versions of this incident can quite easily be cited. The German traveller Mandelslo, after noting that Shahjahan had usurped the throne from his own nephew, tells us that he actually met the prince *Polago* in the Iranian city of Qazwin.[36] For his part, Thomas Herbert is rather more prolix. He thus explains that Jahangir had decided to name Bulaqi as his successor, but that the latter—since he was very young and inexperienced—was quickly outmanoeuvered by Nur Jahan and Asaf Khan, who ordered a certain 'Radgy Bandor' (that is, Riza Bahadur) to kill him while in Delhi. He then closes the history of the 'poor prince' who apparently only managed to reign for three months, but does mention the fact that two other false Bulaqis then appeared, each of them with sufficient charisma to gather together a band of followers.[37] Other writers present minor variants. In the account written in 1638 by an anonymous Italian, native of Piedmont, Asaf Khan once more is given a central role. He writes: 'The dead King made him [Asaf Khan]

---

[33] Shahnawaz Khan, *Ma'asir al-Umara*, (translation) Vol. I, p. 468; Persian text, Vol. II, p. 26. For another version, with some minor additional details, see W. E. Begley and Z. A. Desai, eds, *The Shah Jahan Nama of 'Inayat Khan: An abridged history of the Mughal Emperor Shah Jahan, compiled by his royal librarian*, tr. A. R. Fuller, Delhi, 1990, p. 191.

[34] *De Imperio Magni Mogolis* (1631), tr., and eds J. S. Hoyland and S. N. Banerjee, *The Empire of the Great Mogol: De Laet's Description of India and Fragment of India History*, reprint, New Delhi, 1974, p. 238.

[35] *The Travels of Peter Mundy, in Europe and Asia, 1608–1667*, ed. Richard C. Temple, Vol. II (*Travels in Asia, 1628–1634*), London, 1914, pp. 105, 107, 206.

[36] *Relation du voyage D'Adam Olearius en Moscovie, Tartarie, et Perse, augmentée en cette nouvelle edition de plus d'un tiers, particulierement d'une seconde voyage de Mandelslo aux Indes Orientales*, 2nd edn, 2 Vols, Paris, 1679, Vol. 2, p. 179.

[37] Thomas Herbert, *Relation du Voyage de Perse et des Indes Orientales*, Paris, 1663, pp. 175–9. The edition by William Foster does not include the part relating to the Mughal empire (*Travels in Persia, 1627–29*, New York, 1929).

swear that he would make a certain Sultan Bolaschi the king, since the one who now lives [Shahjahan] had made war on his father [Khusrau] some twenty-five years ago, but he did not keep the promise, and put him in prison and under guard, and when this King was crowned, he ordered that the other [princes] should be killed, amongst whom two were Christians, and Bolachi fled to Persia where he is now.'[38]

The excursus devoted by the French jeweller Jean-Baptiste Tavernier to Bulaqi, whose flight to Iran is recounted by him as an absolute fact, is also of some interest for us. The French traveller refers to the unfortunate prince in the context of the later war of succession (1657–8), and draws his own moral connections between crime and punishment. For Tavernier, the imprisonment of Shahjahan by his own son, Aurangzeb, was simply the return for the injustice that he himself had committed three decades earlier, when he had ordered the assassination of his own nephew Bulaqi.[39] Precisely the same idea may be found in the text of the Italian traveller Gemelli Careri, who recounts the story in the following manner. 'If we now look back into the life of Sciah-Gehan, we shall find that he was punish'd by the Hand of God as he had deserved, for the wrong he had done his Nephew Bulaki, usurping the Crown from him'. He then narrates the succession struggle after the death of Jahangir, concluding with the flight of Bulaqi with the aid of Asaf Khan, who we are assured had promised Jahangir on his deathbed, 'that they would never consent that Bulaki should be put to Death; which he afterwards faithfully perform'd, but not to settle him on the throne'. Careri then concludes his version of the story as follows:

Bulaki receiving this dismal News [of the succession of Shahjahan] by the way, being in consternation had no hopes in safety but in flying; which was easie to be done, because his Enemies thought not proper to pursue him. He wandered about India a long time, becoming a Fachir; but at last tir'd with that painful Employment he retir'd into Persia, where he was nobly receiv'd and entertained by Scia Sofi.[40]

We return here to the idea of a prince who has been transformed into a *qalandar* or *faqîr*, a theme for which Couto already shows a weakness. Later, at the end of the seventeenth century, Niccolò Manuzzi provides us with a version full of fantastic details, and having totally confused the relationships between the principal protagonists, recounts the triumphal entry into Agra of Shahjahan, and

[38] Bibliothèque Nationale de France, Paris, Collection Dupuy 587, 'Partenza del Re Gran Mogor della citta d'Agra per la citta di Laor' (1638), fls 300–12, citation on fls 310v–11.

[39] *Travels in India by Jean-Baptiste Tavernier*, tr. V. Ball and William Crooke, reprint, Vol. I, Delhi, 1995, Book II, Ch. III, pp. 267 et seq.

[40] Surendranath Sen, *Indian travels of Thevenot and Careri*, New Delhi, 1949, pp. 232–3.

the fall of Bulaqi who, so it would appear, had no other option from that moment on but to flee.[41] Manuzzi's text is accompanied by a portrait in the Mughal style of Bulaqi, with the following legend:

This is the portrait of the unhappy prince Sultan Bolaqui, oldest son of Djehanguir; as he wished to live a life of pleasure like his father, this permitted his brother to usurp the throne; on account of which in the chronicles he is no longer permitted the title of king; to save himself he fled in haste to the king of Persia, and remained there until his death.[42]

As we shall see below, the later existence of a person in the Safavid domains who was believed to be the real Bulaqi is usually also accepted by the greater part of the texts written by European travellers, as also in some of the Portuguese sources of the epoch. We do not know, however, to what extent this recurrent rumour of the 'resurrection' of Bulaqi, taken together with the opposition centred around the false Baisunghar, actually affected Shahjahan. We need to know the manner in which such episodes might have conditioned the emperor's actions, both at the level of the assertion of his internal authority and in terms of the external relations of the Mughals, particularly the rather delicate dealings with Safavid Iran. The present state of information does not permit us to pursue the comparison with the well-documented reaction of the Ch'ing emperor Yongzheng (r. 1723–35) to a a rumour concerning a possible revolt both against him personally, and against the Manchu domination of China in general, that came to light in 1728.[43]

The Perspective from Goa

The legend of Bulaqi equally attained some proportions in the Portuguese documentation of the period. In contrast to the other Europeans, in the case of the Portuguese, it is neither through the accounts of travellers nor even through

[41] Niccolao Manucci, *Storia do Mogor or Mogul India*, tr. William Irvine, 4 Vols, reprint, Delhi, 1981, Vol. I, pp. 172–5.

[42] *Storia del Mogol di Nicolò Manuzzi veneziano*, ed. Piero Falchetta, Vol. I, Milan, 1986, p. 98. Few other known portraits of Bulaqi exist; but see Milo C. Beach, *The Grand Mogul: Imperial Painting in India, 1600–1660*, Williamstown, Mass., 1978, pp. 61–3, figure 14, where he appears clearly identified in a group portrait. We are grateful to Saqib Baburi for this and other references.

[43] A certain Zhang Xi, a messenger from a teacher from Hunan called Zeng Jing, attempted to bring around to this cause the Governor-General of the provinces of Shaanxi and Sichuan, General Yue Zhongqi. However, the latter immediately informed Beijing of what had happened, leading to an extremely complex process of inquiry promoted by the emperor himself, as has been studied recently by Jonathan D. Spence, *Treason by the Book*, New York, 2002. In this case too, there is the problem of the authenticity of one personage, a certain Wang Shu, and issues of the proof of identity that require resolution.

the missionary sources that we can follow the trajectory of the rumours. Rather, in the Portuguese case, it is necessary to look to the materials preserved by the state, the *Estado da Índia*, both in terms of the correspondence exchanged between Goa and Lisbon (or Valladolid), and in terms of the reflections of the Portuguese viceroy of that time, and in the minutes of the formal meetings that he held at Goa to discuss the 'Bulaqi affair'.

It was recognized by the early seventeenth century that the huge dimensions of the Mughal empire, and its growing ascendancy over the politics of the Deccan, could have an immediate and rather devastating effect on the Portuguese presence in maritime western India. Through the detailed information that they regularly received from the Jesuits at the Mughal court, taken together with intelligence that was gathered through other channels, the viceroys at Goa from the 1570s on came to acquire the reflex of closely monitoring and evaluating the activities of the Mughals, in particular with regard to their 'external relations'. But they also paid great attention to the internal revolts and the massive movements of Mughal armies, even those that occurred on the somewhat remote frontier with Central Asia. It is therefore scarcely surprising that the Portuguese should also have paid particular attention to processes of transition and imperial succession. In critical situations, when they were faced with a Mughal central power that seemed to them to be particularly adverse to the interests of Goa, the fratricidal struggles for power in Agra, Delhi, or Lahore were important processes for the Portuguese, simply from the viewpoint of safeguarding their own *Estado da Índia*.

Two examples will bring this out clearly enough. In view of the periodic illness of Akbar, taken together with the revolts of Prince Salim, the question of imperial succession in India was amply discussed in the correspondence between Goa and the Habsburgs in the early years of the seventeenth century. In March 1604, Philip III believed that things could turn out very well indeed for the Portuguese. He wrote to Goa: 'The state in which you tell me that Equebar finds himself with his oldest son is what is best for the *Estado*, in view of the intentions of this king. May it please God that as long as he lives this division between them continues, for on his death we may well expect that it will spread throughout his domains'.[44] A year-and-a-half later, the death of Akbar and the succession of Jahangir were followed very closely by the Jesuits who were at that time resident in the Mughal court.[45]

We may also briefly consider the situation in the 1650s, and the Portuguese reaction at that time to the succession of Aurangzeb (r. 1658–1707). This

[44] King to viceroy, Valladolid, 23.III.1604; Arquivo Histórico Ultramarino, Lisbon, Cod. 282, fls 206–7v, citation on fl. 207.

[45] Cf. Alam and Subrahmanyam, 'Witnessing Transition', esp. pp. 108–12.

emperor, the son and successor of Shahjahan, awakened the deepest fears of the Portuguese who thus produced extremely critical images of him. But, once again, the possibility of long-lasting internal wars and of a sort of political 'implosion' gave hope to the administration of the *Estado da Índia*. Thus, the viceroy wrote to Lisbon in 1666: 'The brothers, sons of the Mogor, are at (...) war, and the oldest has left for the parts of Persia, and nothing is known with certainty about him as he was defeated; the other brothers have had various confrontations, the one of who calls himself king is Auranzeb, and he is in possession of the kingdom. They say he is a tyrant and cruel, and not particularly well-disposed towards the Christians'.[46] The profile of Aurangzeb that is set out here naturally meant that the Portuguese were open to an alternative solution. It is in this context that we must understand the instructions given to Gregório Pereira Fidalgo when he was sent on his embassy to Iran in 1696–7. In view of the advanced age of Aurangzeb at that time, the ambassador was asked to advance his contacts with the Mughal prince, Muhammad Akbar, who was in those years exiled in the Safavid court: 'To motivate him in this sense, you will demonstrate to him the great benefits that will follow from our friendship for the pretensions that he may have in Industão as the son of the Mogor, since the latter is so old, it is evident that his life must be of short duration'.[47]

The Portuguese reaction to the rise to the throne of Khurram in the late 1620s, and the movements around Bulaqi, can be seen within the ambit of a very similar set of tensions and motivations. As we shall see, the emergence of the figure of Shahjahan was followed in Goa, as also in Lisbon (and Madrid) with a particular attention. The first actions of the Mughal emperor on coming to the throne already carried a premonition of the difficult relations that he would have with the Portuguese, and with Christianity in general. It would seem that the religious eclecticism of Akbar and Jahangir, which had been at the origin of both dreams and disappointments concerning the possible conversion of the Mughal court, was now giving way to the assertion of a regime with a somewhat more orthodox Islamic character, which was then pushed forward and intensified by Aurangzeb. The period thus sees some actions against the places of worship of

[46] Viceroy to king, Goa, 22.III.1666; Historical Archives of Goa, Panaji (henceforth HAG), *Monções do Reino*, n° 36, fl. 535. The first part of this sentence seems to relate to rumours that Dara Shikoh was still alive, as we know that in 1663–4, someone claiming to be this deceased Mughal prince had appeared in Gujarat and led a brief revolt; cf. M. N. Pearson, 'Shivaji and the Decline of the Mughal Empire', *Journal of Asian Studies*, Vol. 35, No. 2, 1976, p. 226.

[47] Jean Aubin, *L'Ambassade de Gregório Pereira Fidalgo à la cour de Châh Soltân-Hosseyn, 1696–1697*, Lisbon, 1971, pp. 99–128, especially p. 115. Also see P. Pissurlencar, 'Prince Akbar and the Portuguese', *Bengal Past and Present*, Vol. 35, 1928, pp. 63–169.

other religions, and the hardening of the attitude towards Christian missionaries seems to be a part of this more general movement.[48] The Jesuits did maintain their 'Mogor mission', but the ambience had changed from what had obtained in the late sixteenth century.

This reverse, which was both religious and political, was not entirely autonomous of another jolt, this one of a politico-economic nature. We refer here to the destruction of the Portuguese establishment of Hughli in 1632, which, no matter what the precise reasons for it were, does reveal quite clearly the mercantile aspect of the imperial strategy followed by Shahjahan.[49] On account of all this, it is hardly surprising that the image of Shahjahan in the Portuguese texts of the epoch is strongly negative, much worse than those of his father or his grandfather. According to the Jesuits who lived in Agra, this emperor 'has a natural aversion for the Padres and all the *frangis*'.[50] 'Tyrannous' and 'cruel' are two of the most common adjectives that the Portuguese use to characterize the monarch whom they often continued to designate not by his chosen title, but in a somewhat pejorative fashion as 'Sultão Corromo'.

The enthronement of Shahjahan and the first phase of his reign as emperor happen to coincide, *grosso modo*, with the start of the first mandate of the Count of Linhares as viceroy of the Portuguese Indies.[51] D. Miguel de Noronha began to govern in October 1629, more or less at the moment when Khan Jahan Lodi decided to abandon Agra and flee to the Deccan. The march of Shahjahan towards the Deccan, the desertion of the great Afghan noble, as well as the

---

[48] See the interesting discussion in François Bernier, *Travels in the Mogul Empire, AD 1656–1668*, tr. Irving Brock and Archibald Constable, ed. Vincent A. Smith, London, 1934, pp. 286–8.

[49] Cf. Sanjay Subrahmanyam, 'Through the looking glass: Some comments on Asian views of the Portuguese in Asia, 1500–1700', in A. Teodoro de Matos and L. F. Thomaz, eds, *As relações entre a Índia portuguesa, a Ásia do Sueste e o Extremo Oriente. Actas do VI Seminário Internacional de História Indo-Portuguesa*, Macau-Lisbon, 1993, esp. pp. 396–401; Jorge Manuel Flores, 'Relic or Springboard?: A Note on the 'Rebirth' of Portuguese Hughli, ca. 1632–1820', *The Indian Economic and Social History Review*, Vol. 39, No. 4, 2002, pp. 381–95.

[50] 'Relação d'algumas cousas que passarão na Missão do Mogol, des do fim do anno 627 te ao dia presente 13 de Junho de anno 1628'; British Library, London, Addn. Ms. 9854, fls 116–30, published in A. da Silva Rego, ed., *Documentação Ultramarina Portuguesa*, Vol. III, Lisboa, 1963, pp. 187–98, quotation on p. 188.

[51] On this figure, see Anthony Disney, 'On attempting to write an early modern biography: My encounter with the life of Dom Miguel de Noronha, Fourth Count of Linhares (1588–1656)', *Indica*, Vol. 29, No. 2, 1992, pp. 89–106; as also Disney, 'The Fiscal Reforms of Viceroy Linhares at Goa', *Anais de História de Além-Mar*, Vol. III, 2002, pp. 259–75.

reports of the death of Bulaqi are all subjects that are referred to in some detail in the Portuguese documentation of the epoch. Besides, the administration of the Count of Linhares is particularly well-documented in view of the fact that D. Miguel de Noronha—in keeping with royal instructions—maintained a public diary of the events during his government.[52] It is this valuable text, taken together with the letters that one finds in the so-called *Livros das Monções* (Monsoon Codices) and the minutes of the Council of State (*Conselho do Estado*), which permit us to reconstruct the manner in which the Portuguese struggled with the legend of 'Sultão Bolaquim'.

The first time Bulaqi appears in the materials of the *Estado da Índia* may be dated to a document on the 'Neighbouring Kings' (*Reis Vizinhos*) from the end of 1629. Here we find a reference to the disturbances caused by the death of Jahangir, and the fact that the throne belonged by rights to his 'first-born grandson (*neto morgado*) by name Sultão Bulaqui, somewhat above twenty-three years of age'. In this version of events, Jahangir had handed over his grandson to the charge of Asaf Khan but the latter, as soon as the emperor was declared dead, quickly summoned Khurram to the court telling him that he had Bulaqi 'secure in his hands'. Khurram then ascended the throne, 'and Bulaqui has gone away to the borders of the kingdom of the Xaa, and until now they said he was dead, or had been killed, and now in the last two months they say he is alive, and that the Xaa has promised him one of his legitimate daughters, and has given him great succour, and they say that he has returned to the Kingdom of Dely'.[53]

The following reference to Bulaqi that appears in the Portuguese official sources dates to 15 March 1630. On the basis of information that had been sent to him from one of his spies in the 'Mogor's camp', the viceroy made a note in his diary of the advance of Shahjahan in the direction of the Deccan, and further noted that the emperor had left Agra, 'which is an open and defenceless city' (*sic*) out of fear of the reaction of Bulaqi, rather than to really conquer the Sultanate of Ahmadnagar. He then goes on to describe the bloody succession of Shahjahan, and makes it a point to argue that it was Khusrau's son, Bulaqi,

[52] However, the diary of Linhares is incomplete, and three distinct parts exist to it. The first is to be found in the Biblioteca da Ajuda, Lisbon (henceforth BA), Codex 51–VII–12, and deals with the period from 3 March 1630 to 6 February 1631. The second, also unpublished, is to be found in in the Biblioteca Nacional, Lisbon, Codex 939, and covers practically the whole of the year 1631 (9 February to 20 December). The third section has been published as *Diário do 3° conde de Linhares, vice-rei da Índia*, 2 Vols, Lisbon, 1937, and runs from February 1634 to January 1635.

[53] HAG, *Monções do Reino*, liv. 13 (AN 15), published in P. Pissurlencar, 'A Índia em 1629: Relação dos Reis Visinhos do que por ora passa e contão', *Boletim do Instituto Vasco da Gama*, Vol. 7, 1930, pp. 52–61, especially pp. 52, 54.

who was in fact the legitimate heir. The version that had reached Goa had it that it was the wife of Mahabat Khan who had saved Bulaqi, 'by placing another dead man in his place'. The real Bulaqi for his part had fled to Delhi, and still under the protection of Mahabat Khan, had even married one of the latter's daughters. Linhares appears excited at the prospect of a possible alliance between Khan Jahan and the Sultan of Ahmadnagar, and concludes by noting that if Bulaqi seizes power once more, the Dutch would be expelled summarily from Surat.[54]

Two months later, there is further news of Bulaqi. On 12 May, Linhares notes that letters have arrived in Goa from Bengal, either written by or sent through a certain Gaspar Pacheco de Mesquita, who was a particularly important informant who kept the viceroy abreast of developments in that region. These letters claim, he writes, that 'Bolaquim is alive, and that he is much loved and adored by all, and that many people follow him, and that he has put together a very large army, and that the Nababo of Bengal and his son-in-law have taken four large ships and fled out of fear to Massulapatão and that he [Bulaqi] is very soundly situated in those parts'.[55] Then, on 28 August, further letters arrived for the viceroy from a certain Diogo Saraiva, his informant in the court of Ahmadnagar. This time it was reported from Daulatabad 'that Bulaquim, king of the Mogors, is alive, and I have mentioned that it was believed that he was dead, and he is bringing together an army of twenty thousand men to attack the Idalcão ['Adil Khan]'.[56] After trying to render coherent these rather confusing and contradictory rumours, Linhares then spent the rest of the monsoon season in Goa, without receiving any further details concerning the strange peregrinations of Bulaqi. But then, in October, the viceroy received a veritable avalanche of intelligence, which eventually led him to act. We may follow the chronology of events.

On 11 October, a fresh and very happy rumour reached the viceroy. It was said that Shahjahan had died, and this was not surprising since the *banias* had held that according to a prophecy, 'his time of dominance was over'.[57] Linhares reacted to this news with enthusiasm mixed with caution, and three days later, further news arrived from Bijapur: 'I received letters from Vizapor [written on]

---

[54] BA, Cod. 51–VII–12, fls 13v–14. For a Dutch perspective on the events of the period, see the diary of Commissioner Dirck van der Lee, summarized in Om Prakash, 'Archival source material in the Netherlands', pp. 149–50. The Dutch factor notes that the death of Bulaqi had caused 'a certain amount of resentment among both the big and the small'.

[55] BA, Cod. 51–VII–12, fl. 36v.

[56] *Ibid.*, fl. 87.

[57] *Ibid.*, fl. 97. Shahjahan, born in the year 1000 of the Hegiran calendar (1591–2), seems to have possessed a somewhat millenarian aura about him. See, in this context, Wayne Begley, 'The myth of the Taj-Mahal and a new theory of its symbolic meaning', *Art Bulletin*, Vol. 3, 1979, pp. 7–37. However, this particular prophecy appears to be of Vaishnava or Jain origin.

the first of this month, in which they say that Bulaquim, the Mogor King, who had disappeared and who was believed to be dead, was now in the company of the Mellique [Nizam Shah], even though he scarcely had four thousand horsemen, and that his ambassadors were now forty leagues from Vizapor, and that the *baneanes* claimed that his [Shahjahan's] time of dominance was over, for this other one [Bulaqi] had come to take possession of his kingdom, though they say that the peace between the Mogor and the Mellique is being negotiated with great urgency, but for the *Estado* it would be of very great effect if Bulaquim were to seize hold of the kingdom'.[58]

Meanwhile, Diogo Saraiva too had written five times to the viceroy from Daulatabad during the month of October, giving him a close account of various affairs, including the adventures of Bulaqi. Taking all these pieces of information together, the viceroy decided to send a first summary reflection to Portugal on the whole delicate question. This was done in the form of two letters, the first dated 4 November 1630,[59] and the second dated 6 December of the same year.[60] It is really at this moment that Linhares makes the transition from simply collecting floating rumours and scarce information, to seeking out systematic intelligence on the matter in order to formulate a systematic policy in consultation with the Habsburg monarchy. This appears clearly enough in his letter to Diogo Saraiva, written on 6 November:

I am not fully satisfied with what you tell me about Sultam Bulaquim, and it is important that you should dilate on it by writing a longer relation, from the time that he escaped from death, and how and where he went and was hidden, and how he reappeared and at what time, and for what reason, and who he depends on and who helps him, and where he is and with which people, and what he intends to do, and if he is coming there to seek the aid of the King Melique and Canajão [Khan Jahan], and what it is believed the captains of the Mogor Xaajahan will do on his arrival, and whether they want him and will acclaim him as their true King which he is, and also what his ambassador told you of the desire that he had to deal with me concerning various matters, setting them out in order to see if they could be attained; and send me this relation [which should be] very well written and with all the necessary declarations [documentation] that are necessary, and send it to me so that I can send it on to His Majesty.[61]

[58] *Ibid.*, fl. 98.

[59] HAG, *Monções do Reino*, liv. 14 (AN 16), fl. 175. It is probably this letter, or the one that is cited in the note below, that arrived in Lisbon the next year with the title 'Sobre o netto del Rey Jahamguir, que escapou, e estado em que fica'; see Biblioteca Nacional, Lisbon, Cod. 11410, fl. 150, 'Lista de todas as cartas que vierão na via da nao Almiranta deste governo, anno de 1631'.

[60] *Ibid.*, fls 178–178v; published in P. Pissurlencar, ed., *Assentos do Conselho do Estado*, Vol. I, Goa-Bastorá, 1953, pp. 523–5.

[61] BA, Cod. 51–VII–12, fl. 107.

The viceroy thus clearly felt the need to evaluate the rigour of the intelligence that was coming in to him, in order to define a coherent line of action. For, already in less than a year, Bulaqi had been spotted on the border with Iran, in Delhi, Bengal, and in various parts of the Deccan, and the most diverse projects and alliances had been attributed to him. To make matters even more confusing, Linhares received news from Bijapur on 16 November, which he considered to be extremely doubtful, and which claimed that Bulaqi was preparing still another alliance, this one with 'Abdullah Qutb Shah, Sultan of Golconda (r. 1626–72).[62]

Now, the Portuguese viceroy's own diplomatic project came to centre on the idea of an alliance between the Sultan of Ahmadnagar, Khan Jahan Lodi, and Bulaqi, against Shahjahan. His plan was that the *Estado da Índia* would provide various sorts of discreet support to this alliance, allowing the allies, for instance, to use the ports in western India that were under Portuguese control. Based on this view of things, Linhares finally wrote a letter to Bulaqi himself on 2 December, 'telling him that he should choose the direction in which he wanted to proceed, either to the north or to the south, and that I would have him fetched from there in fleets so that he could be secure, and that he should let me know as quickly as possible'.[63] The idea was that the Mughal prince should enter Ahmadnagar territories as rapidly as he could as a measure of security.[64]

The advantages of such an alliance were obvious from the point of view of Goa, both from a political and from an economic perspective. On the one hand, the *Estado da Índia* would thus be able to limit the power of an emperor who was clearly hostile to the Portuguese, and instead have in his place the far more consensual Bulaqi. Throughout this period, Linhares continues to harp firmly on his legitimacy. He calls him the 'true Mughal King' (*verdadeiro Rei Mogor*), insists on the empathy of the populace for this prince, and as importantly (or perhaps even more so), refers to how a great proportion of the most influential Mughal *amîrs* are in fact ready to adhere to his cause. On the other hand, he also suggests that in case of a victory for Bulaqi, it is certain that 'the lands and

[62] *Ibid.*, fl. 110v.

[63] *Ibid.*, fl. 121v; HAG, *Monções do Reino*, n° 16, fls 178–178v. The letter from the viceroy was apparently carried by an 'intelligent Brahmin' (*bramane inteligente*), whom Pissurlencar identified with a certain Ramoji Sinai Kothari; cf. Pissurlencar, *Agentes da diplomacia portuguesa na Índia (hindus, muçulmanos, judeus e parses)*, Bastorá-Goa, 1952, p. 30.

[64] BA, Cod. 51-VII-12, fls 120v, 121. Here too, there is a parallel to be drawn with the projected alliance between the *Estado da Índia* and Prince Akbar at the end of the seventeenth century. In the latter case, the viceroy instructed Gregório Pereira Fidalgo that the exiled son of Aurangzeb should be incited to seize the throne by making use of one of the Portuguese-controlled ports, 'for we have so many doors for him, all between Dio and Goa' (Aubin, *L'ambassade de Gregório Pereira Fidalgo*, p. 115).

customs-houses of Surrate, Cambaja, and Baroche' will be handed over to the control of Goa. Apparently, the envoys from Khan Jahan had already reached an agreement with Bulaqi in this respect.[65]

The month of December 1630 proved absolutely decisive in the matter. On 6 December, the viceroy received letters from the port of Chaul, which would turn out to be crucial for the *dénouement* of the Bulaqi affair in its Portuguese incarnation. Besides the captain of the Portuguese fort, Linhares also received letters from a certain Manuel de Azevedo, stating that Bulaqi was now to be found resident in Upper Chaul (Rewadanda). He had apparently made his way there discreetly from Gogha, in a small vessel and accompanied by a handful of servants. Azevedo sent him a few trusted *bania* intermediaries, with money and some gifts, and these men stated that they knew the prince well and that they could guarantee that it was in fact the real Bulaqi. The captain of the Portuguese fortress of Chaul for his part had also offered the Mughal prince his help, so that he could leave Upper Chaul in a secure fashion.[66] It was claimed however that the local governor of Chaul (*sar-samat*, or in Indo-Portuguese, 'sarssamata') was isolating the *faqîr* Bulaqi from external contacts, and subjecting him to a propaganda campaign against the Portuguese. He had hence placed him in a fortress that was some leagues from the city proper, and was reportedly trying to convince him that the Portuguese were his enemies and that they planned to kill him.[67]

The pressing importance of this news from Chaul led the viceroy to summon a meeting of the State Council on the following day, in order to decide the next step to take.[68] The meeting concluded that a certain Jesuit called Francisco Leão should be asked to leave Goa immediately for Chaul in order to identify Bulaqi. This Padre Leão had been superior of the mission at the Mughal court between 1627 and 1628, and in the context of the court had followed the transition between Jahangir and Shahjahan. He also claimed to know Bulaqi rather well.[69]

But the dream of an alliance between the *Estado da Índia* and the supposed heir to the Mughal throne went up in smoke even before the start of the year 1631. For, on 27 December, viceroy Linhares received a letter from Padre

---

[65] BA, Cod. 51–VII–12, fl. 119.

[66] *Ibid.*, fl. 122v.

[67] *Ibid.*, fls 122v, 123v, 126.

[68] *Ibid.*, fl.122v; also see 'Conselho sobre Soltão Bolaquim que veyo a Chaul de Cima'; Goa, 7.XII.1630; in Pissurlencar, ed., *Assentos do Conselho do Estado*, Vol. I, Doc. 111, pp. 331–3.

[69] Padre Leão was removed from his post in 1628, largely on account of an imprudent conflict that he had with three Venetians who lived at the Mughal court; he also fell out at much the same time with the powerful Asaf Khan (cf. *supra*, n. 50).

Francisco Leão, announcing his arrival in Chaul. The Jesuit had quickly found out that Bulaqi was exchanging letters with Khan Jahan Lodi, and declared that he intended to leave the next day for the fortress where the Mughal prince was thought to be.[70] Two days later, Linhares received a fresh letter. The man whom the Jesuit had visited was not the one whom he had known at the Mughal court. The missionary stated bluntly that the 'Bulaqi' he had seen in Upper Chaul was no more than a blatant impostor.[71] The idea of proof of identity that was used here was thus simple and direct: the testimony of one reliable witness, in this case the Jesuit, was seen as enough to discredit the claims of the man who called himself Bulaqi. Things were not so simple in most other cases of imposture in the sixteenth- and seventeenth-century world.[72]

A few days later, on 12 January 1631, the viceroy ruefully related what had happened to Philip IV in a letter: 'On the twentieth of November of the last year, a veiled man (*hum homem embussado*) arrived in Chaul by sea, with a voice that suggested that he was the said Bolaquim, and he persuaded all the Moors and even the Christians who were there that he was the true Mogor King, and he went to the *Morro de Chaul* on disembarking with much adoration, and veneration, and he was then secured in a fortress that is in the mountains which they call Drugo. I was advised with all speed so that I could have him stay over in the fortress of Chaul, and as I am not given to believing in such matters so quickly, it seemed to me better to first send a Padre of the Company, called Francisco de Leão who had spent many years in educating this prince. Francisco de Leão carried out this task very well indeed, even though it was at risk to his own person. He entered the fort of Drugo, and in a letter of 24 December, wrote to me that this was not Bolaquim.'[73]

The Count of Linhares immediately lost interest in the subject. In the following years, the viceroy preferred to gamble on a delicate strategy of an alliance between Bijapur, Ahmadnagar, and Golconda with the aim of checking the advance of Shahjahan into the Deccan, and thus attempted to guarantee the safety of Goa and the Portuguese fortresses of the *Prov-incia do Norte*. During the rest of his government, it is rather difficult to see any coherent line of development in the shifting logic of the alliances and conflicts between the *Estado da Índia*, Shahjahan, and the Sultanates of the Deccan. An anonymous Italian account written in Goa in 1632 resumes the Bulaqi affair to that point,

[70] BA, Cod. 51–VII–12, fl. 129.

[71] *Ibid.* fl. 129v; HAG, *Monções do Reino*, n° 16, fl. 202v.

[72] Compare Miriam Eliav-Feldon, 'Invented Identities: Credulity in the Age of Prophecy and Exploration', *Journal of Early Modern History*, Vol. 3, No. 3, 1999, pp. 203–32.

[73] Viceroy to king, Goa, 12.I.1631; HAG, *Monções do Reino*, n° 16, fl. 202v. By a scribal error, the letter is dated 12 December 1630.

and already in January of that year, takes note of the new inflection in Portuguese official attitudes on the question: 'The legitimate Bolachino, the true king
of the Empire of the Mogor, persecuted by Corumbre [Khurram] who reigns
now, came as far as Carapatan, 18 leagues from Goa, and they said that he was
coming here, but he went off instead to Persia, which was good for him and
a favour to us, because besides the fact that they could not swear it was him,
it would have given cause [for conflict] to the Mogor who has just become our
neighbour'.[74]

A somewhat similar logic as that which appears in the case of the 'Bulaqi
affair' also appears to work for a time in the case of the 'double' of Baisunghar,
in whom D. Miguel de Noronha also seems to have believed for a time. This
time however, the mirage of an alliance between the *Estado da Índia* and an
alternative to the detested Shahjahan moved from the southern frontier of the
Mughal empire to its northernmost confines. What lent the affair a particular
piquancy was that Baisunghar was one of the three sons of Mirza Daniyal who
had been baptised by the Jesuits in Agra in 1610, an episode that had a great
place in the missionary sources of the period. As might have been predicted,
the conversion of D. Carlos (Baisunghar), D. Filipe, and D. Henrique, was seen
as a prefiguration of the conversion of Jahangir himself, as well as of his whole
court and kingdom.[75]

In a meeting of the State Council dated 6 November 1632, there was a
discussion on whether Portuguese support whould be lent to this Mughal prince,
even if he was now an apostate from Christianity. It was noted that 'in this
interim period which was one in which the army of the Mogor was destroying
the kingdom of the Idalcão [Bijapur], in the kingdom of Cabul which belongs
to the Mogor, there was a rebellion by one of his cousins who had been baptised
by the Padres of the Company, and who was called Dom Carlos, and later he
gave up the faith, and he took control of the said Kingdom, with the help of the
people of the Usbeques, who are the bravest and most feared of all these lands,
because Dom Carlos married a daughter of that King. Because of this, the Mogor
found it necessary to go to the rescue of Cabul, since it is from those parts that
all the horses that make up his army come, besides which he also feared that
Dom Carlos could easily seize hold of the kingdom of Laor, which borders that

---

[74] Biblioteca Casanatense, Rome, Ms. 2681, 'Relatione di alcune cose che succederono
in India nell'anno 1632', fls 142–59, citation on fl. 142v.

[75] For an account of these events, see Arnulf Camps, *Jerome Xavier S. J. and the
Muslims of the Mogul Empire: Controversial works and missionary activity*, Schöneck-
Beckenried, 1957, pp. 8–10; as also Angel Santos Hernandez, *Jeronimo Javier S. J.
Apostolo del Gran Mogol y Arzobispo electo de Cranganor, en la India, 1549–1617*,
Pamplona, 1958, pp. 226–32.

of Cabul, and it is understood that he can do it quite easily because the Mogor is a tyrant and unpopular(...)and Dom Carlos is valiant and liberal'.[76]

At the same time, the references to Bulaqi in the Portuguese sources become less frequent. It is of course true that the years 1632–3 are not as well documented as the preceding ones, since the diaries of viceroy Linhares from the period have not come down to us. But there is still little doubt that the subject of Bulaqi ceased for the most part to interest Goa. For Linhares, the project of an alliance with Bulaqi vanished at much the same time that the idea of profiting from the revolt of Khan Jahan Lodi against Shahjahan began to appear less and less realistic. Finally, we are aware that the Afghan noble was captured in January 1632, and his head taken to the emperor who was at the time in Burhanpur, an episode that the artists who illustrated the celebrated Windsor *Pâdshâhnâma* brought out in rather gruesome detail.[77] Besides, the destruction of the Portuguese settlement of Hughli in 1632 was to pose a challenge to the viceroy that was almost as important as those that he faced in the Deccan, forcing him to strike a balance between the neighbourhood of Goa and Portuguese interests at the eastern extremity of the Mughal empire.

It was only in a letter of 28 February 1632 that Philip IV eventually reacted to the information that had been sent to him from Goa in November and December of 1630. This meant of course that the response from the Habsburg centre was already somewhat out-of-date, since the later developments in Chaul were not taken into account. Even so, there is a curious detail that catches one's eye. The king counsels prudence, noting that 'the *Estado* should always maintain peace with the Mogor', in view of the latter's enormous power. We find the same preoccupation a half-century later, when the Count of Vila Verde was to urge Gregório Pereira Fidalgo to seek an alliance with Prince Akbar, the rebel son of the emperor Aurangzeb.[78] Hence, it is suggested that any negotiation with

[76] 'Sobre a guerra do Mogor suas detreminações e retirada entre aqui a carta sobre as cousas do Melique e tambem a retirada do Turco de Babilonia', Goa, 6.XII.1632; in Pissurlencar, ed., *Assentos do Conselho do Estado*, Vol. I, pp. 556–7, citation on p. 557.

[77] Painted by Abid, *ca.* 1633; for this painting see *The Padshahnama: King of the World*, eds, Milo Cleveland Beach and Ebba Koch, London, 1997, nº 16, pp. 50–1.

[78] 'In all these negotiations that concern Prince Acabar, you will be cautious in two matters(...), the second in trying to find out of if his father, the Great Mogor, has some of his agents in the court, who serve him as spies to observe the dealings of his son, be very careful with these men, and once you get to know them, show them how faithful we are to the Mogor, for if not you will scandalise him, and since he is our very close neighbour and his power embraces our territories, if he is scandalised he may break off with us to the great damage of the *Estado*, which is not in a condition to resist so great an enemy'; Aubin, *L'ambassade de Gregório Pereira Fidalgo*, p. 116.

Bulaqi should be as discreet as possible, so that Shahjahan should not grow suspicious and hence take it upon himself to make war on the Portuguese.

The pragmatic posture of the Habsburg monarch with regard to a possible alliance with Bulaqi is also worth noting. For it would seem that Philip IV was even willing eventually to consider an alliance with a false Bulaqi, that is with 'a man who under his name can lay claim to the kingdom of Mogor'. A 'good' impostor was thus as useful as the real thing.[79] A similar move had been proposed a century earlier by the governor Nuno da Cunha (1529–38), in relation to Sultan Bahadur of Gujarat and his rivals. A contemporary observer—the celebrated Goan Brahmin Krishna—claimed that the governor had tried to promote the case of one of Bahadur's brothers by 'bringing from Dabul a black (*huum negro*) saying he was the brother of the King of Canbaya, and he did him much honour and lavished great expenses [on him]'.[80]

In his own reply to Philip IV, written in the closing days of 1632, D. Miguel de Noronha informed the king of his decision not to proceed further on the question of 'Bulaqi', who Padre Francisco Leão believed had now fled to Iran. In point of fact, after this Portuguese moment, the spectre of Bulaqi travelled north, and we will follow it presently into the Safavid domains. According to some Portuguese sources, Shah Safi (r. 1629–42) covered the man who they saw as an impostor with grants and benefices, giving him an army and even entire charge of Qandahar, which the Safavids had conquered from the Mughals in 1622. Even though he did not wish to involve the *Estado* further in the matter, Linhares coud not help gloating over this: 'If this is so, nothing could be more convenient for us.'[81]

---

[79] Instituto dos Arquivos Nacionais/Torre do Tombo, Lisbon (henceforth IAN/TT), *Livros das Monções*, liv. 30, fl. 7. Also see the version in HAG, *Monções do Reino*, liv. 16 A (AN 18), fl. 3.

[80] Summary of a letter from Krishna to D. João III, ('Sumario das cartas que vieram este anno de 1534 na armada da India…'), in A. da Silva Rego, ed., *As Gavetas da Torre do Tombo*, Vol. X, Lisbon, 1974, pp. 193–4. On Sultan Bahadur and his brothers, see the note by Sanjay Subrahmanyam, 'Irmão de Bahâdur (Badur) que viveu em Goa', in Couto, *Década Quarta da Ásia*, ed. M. Augusta Lima Cruz, Vol. II, pp. 88–9. On Krishna, also see Pissurlencar, ed., *Agentes da diplomacia*, pp. 1–16.

[81] IAN/TT, *Livros das Monções*, liv. 30, fl. 7. Philip IV appears to have understood the new situation in November of the following year, and broadly agreed with the new strategy proposed by Linhares. The king however did not see it as if Bulaqi had been handed over charge of Qandahar, and instead interpreted matters as if the Mughal prince had been put in charge of the same army as had been used by Shah 'Abbas I to conquer Qandahar in 1622; letter dated Lisbon, 12.XI.1633, IAN/TT, *Livros das Monções*, liv. 31, fl. 65. In any event, the version in the Persian sources is quite different, as we shall see below.

In the Court at Isfahan

It was indeed the case that a certain 'Bulaqi' had sought exile in Iran, and was attempting to persude Shah Safi to aid him in a project to regain power at the expense of Shahjahan. The English factor, William Pitt, claimed at much the same time to have lent money to the 'Mogulls brother which fledd into Persia', and stated that he feared a violent reaction from Shahjahan on this account.[82] The Persian sources of the Safavids are in consonance with the Europeans in some measure on this question, but there are also significant points of divergence. The official chronicler of Shah 'Abbas, Iskandar Beg Munshi, provides us a first version of events at the Mughal court which is as follows. After the death of Jahangir, he writes, 'the principal officers of the Mogul state, apparently in accordance with a testamentory disposition made by Jahangir at the time of his death, nominated as his successor Dawar Bakhsh the son of the blind Sultan Khusrau, who was known as Sultan Bolaghi, and minted coins and had the _khutba_ recited in his name'. The other princes are said to have agreed to this, except Shahryar in Lahore. The conflict between Bulaqi and Shahryar is then described, ending with the defeat and blinding of Shahryar. Iskandar Beg now passes to a discussion of the fortunes of Sultan Khurram, and his changing relations with Jahangir. He even suggests that at one point in the 1620s, wearied by his miserable condition, Khurram 'tried to go to Iran and seek assistance from Shah 'Abbas'. At the death of his father, his position is thus portrayed as rather weak, save for the fact that he was supported by Mahabat Khan, who it is stated did not get along with Asaf Khan, the chief supporter of Bulaqi. It was with the aid of this powerful noble and the 'princes of the Deccan' that Shahjahan is said to have marched northwards, gathering up support on the way from 'Chaghatays, Mughals, Afghans and Rajputs'. This unexpected swell of support eventually led to a sharp weakening in the situation of Bulaqi. So, writes Iskandar Beg:

Sultan Bolaghi's fortunes began correspondingly to decline, and his principal officers of state and the wisest heads among his military leaders saw no future for a grandson now that an ambitious natural son of the late emperor was in the contest for the throne. Their loyalty to Sultan Bolaghi wavered, and they began to leave Lahore and go to Agra to join Shahjahan, striving to outdo one another in the race to pledge their fealty and services.[83]

[82] Letter from Dabhol to William Methwold in Surat, 19.V.1636; in William Foster, ed., _The English Factories in India, 1634–1636_, Oxford, 1911, p. 259.

[83] Eskandar Beg Monshi, _History of Shah 'Abbas the Great (Tarikh-i 'Alamara-ye 'Abbasi)_, tr. Roger M. Savory, Boulder, 3 Vols, 1978–86, Vol. II, pp. 1290–3; for the Persian text, see Iskandar Beg Munshi, _Târîkh-i 'Âlamârâ-yi 'Abbâsî_, 2 Vols, ed. Iraj Afshar, Teheran, 1957, Vol. II, pp. 1066–9. For a general reflection on the Safavid

Abandoned by his nobles and troops, Bulaqi was also soon betrayed by his own chief supporter Asaf Khan, who is hence portrayed here not as the initial mastermind behind the operation to place Shahjahan on the throne, but rather as an unwilling accomplice.[84] It is only to ingratiate themselves to Shahjahan that Asaf Khan and his faction kill the five princes: and one of those killed is termed by Iskandar Beg 'Dawar Bakhsh ibn Sultan Khusrau, known as Sultan Bolaghi and entitled Sher Shah'. This interesting last piece of information, concerning the title that Bulaqi allegedly assumed on mounting the throne, is to be found in only one other Mughal source, though not on the coins of the epoch.[85]

However, the information presented by Iskandar Beg in this chronicle is contradicted by another Persian source, paradoxically itself the continuation of this very chronicle by the very same Iskandar Beg and a certain Muhammad Yusuf, and entitled *Zail-i Târîkh-i 'Âlamârâ-yi 'Abbâsî*.[86] The *Zail*, in its account of events of the year 1041–2 H. (1632), contains a detailed account of the affair of 'Sultan Bulaghi', which it may be worth paraphrasing here in some detail, for the light it sheds on a number of questions. The relevant section of the chronicle begins by noting that among the Tarin Afghans (on the border between the Safavid and Mughal domains), there was a 15-year-old boy, who had been brought clandestinely (*duzdîda wa poshîda*) to their leader Sher Khan Tarin, who had decided to employ him as his cup-bearer and lamp-lighter. This boy was said to be the son of the Mughal prince, the late Sultan Khusrau, himself the son of Shah Salim, the son of Jalal-al-Din Muhammad Akbar, the erstwhile ruler

---

chronicling tradition in the period, see Sholeh A. Quinn, *Historical writing during the reign of Shah 'Abbas: Ideology, imitation, and legitimacy in Safavid chronicles*, Salt Lake City, 2000.

[84] For still another version of the succession, in which Asaf Khan is portrayed as having acted in the best interests of the empire, and Dawar Bakhsh is portrayed as somewhat less of a victim than usual, see Muhammad Salih Kamboh, *Amâl-i Sâlih*, eds Ghulam Yazdani and Wahid Quraishi, 3 Vols, Lahore, 1967–72, Vol. I, pp. 169–82.

[85] Compare the titulature used on the surviving coins of Bulaqi, for which see the silver rupee of Dawar Bakhsh: Ashmolean Museum, Oxford, Heberden Coin Room (ex-Thorburn Collection, acquired 1965–6). The coin is minted in Lahore in 1037 H. and carries the legend on the obverse: 'Abu'l Muzaffar Dâwar Bakhsh Bâdshâh'. We are grateful to Shailendra Bhandare of the Ashmolean Museum for his help in this matter. For other discussions, see H. Nelson Wright, 'Dawar Bakhsh', *Journal and Proceedings of the Asiatic Society of Bengal*, 2nd series, Vol. I, 1905, pp. 127–8; and J. G. Delmerick, 'On a silver coin of Dawar Bakhsh', *Proceedings of the Asiatic Society of Bengal*, 1884, p. 60. The title 'Sher Shah' does appear on a *farmân* that is preserved in Bikaner.

[86] Iskandar Beg Munshi and Muhammad Yusuf, *Zail-i Târîkh-i 'Âlamârâ-yi 'Abbâsî*, ed. Suhaili Khwansari, Teheran, 1938, pp. 120–6. The authors are grateful to Muzaffar Alam for his unstinting help with this text.

of Hindustan. The boy's name was apparently Nabdi Mirza, and it is reported that Sher Khan kept him very secretly, so much so that few people knew about him until he was captured by 'Ali Mardan Khan the Safavid governor (*beglerbegî*) of Qandahar during a skirmish with the Tarins. 'Ali Mardan Khan then sent him to the Safavid Shah, with details of the story about him and his royal Mughal origins. The Shah for his part placed him in the custody of the *wazîr* of Isfahan, asked him to keep him in the fort of Tabrak, with the full honours and dignity appropriate for such a prince, until the full truth about him was ascertained.

In the meanwhile, however, another young man, this one about 20 years old, arrived via the port of Surat in the southern Iranian region of Fars. He claimed, for his part, to be none other than Dawar Bakhsh Mirza, the son of Khusrau, and said that he had been crowned with the help of some nobles as the successor of Sultan Salim after the latter's death, on the way to Kashmir (*dar râh-i Kashmîr*). This prince, it is noted, was popularly known not by his formal name, but rather as Sultan Bulaghi (note: not 'Bulaqi'). The authors of the *Zail* remark that Dawar Bakhsh had already been mentioned in the *Târîkh-i 'Âlamârâ-yi 'Abbâsî* in the context of the account of the last years of Jahangir. They sum up the story as follows: at the time of the death of Jahangir (or Salim), Bulaghi (taking advantage of the fact that Prince Khurram was not in the good books of the late emperor, and that he was far away in the Deccan) had approached Lahore and crowned himself as emperor; but when his supporters heard of the approach of a huge army under Khurram, they had all deserted him and run away. Khurram had thus managed to take possession of the Mughal capital, Agra, and had firmly established as the new emperor with the name Shahjahan. Asaf Khan, who is now presented as the main prop of Khurram (in contrast to the earlier version in the Safavid chronicle), and other nobles thought it better to make peace with Bulaghi and other rival princes. He hence persuaded Bulaghi to submit to the new emperor, explained his position to Shahjahan, and tried to have him pardoned. But the emperor would have none of it and ordered Bulaghi's life to be terminated together with that of several other princes. Subsequently, it is said, he was executed (*badarja-i shahâdat*) with five other ill-starred princes. Since this was what was believed in Iran in 1630, when the man claiming to be Dawar Bakhsh had entered the land of Fars, the governor there, Imam Quli Khan, had sent a report about him to the Shah. The Shah had prudently directed that he be received with the appropriate royal dignity, and sent to the court if, after investigation, his story was found to be true. The chronicle continues:

The story that he related about himself at the Bandar ['Abbas] and which I have heard is as follows: 'When Shahjahan ascended the throne, he ordered my execution. I was told by some of my friends about the plot, and also about the night when I was to be arrested. I had a slave of almost the same age as myself. I told him to sleep in my bed in my place. He hesitated initially, but I assured him that no harm would come to him, as it was I and not he who was the target of the emperor. The same night I fled in the darkness towards the jungle, lived on mere grass for fourteen days while wandering in the wilderness, and hiding from people. Then, in the guise of a dervish, I joined a group of the *faqîrs*, and finally arrived in Surat. There, I met the governor (*hâkim*) of the port, and told him the tale of my plight. He was very helpful and friendly, guarded the secret, assisted me with people and money, and advised me to leave for Iran, in order to avoid any harm coming both to me and also to him. With the help of God I set out towards this royal court [Isfahan].

When I arrived at the port of Fars [Bandar 'Abbas], many thought I was a cheat and a liar. Some however noticed the signs of nobility in me, and believed in what I said. I remained suspended between truth and falsehood, fear and hope (*khauf-o-rajâ, sidq-o-kizb*) for quite some time after I entered the province of Fars, until I encountered some people there who had seen me as Sultan on the way to Kashmir. They recognized me, and spread the news about me to others. I was then surrounded by numerous servants (*khidmatgârân*). People from India and Hindu traders came to meet me with whatever help they could extend to me in cash and kind (*naqd-o-jins*).

Imam Quli Khan, in the first instance, believed in my statement, and showed me appropriate respect, but later due to the denial (*inkâr*) of my identity by some traders, he grew suspicious, and accordingly, I declined in his esteem. He dispatched a report about me to the Shah stating his own doubts. In consequence, I was summoned to Isfahan, and there again, I remained suspended between hope and fear. The Shah however was very kind, saw to it that I was shown due respect, that my comfort was ensured and that my requirements were attended to, in keeping with the rules of hospitality.

This extended first person account, in the voice of the man claiming to be Sultan Bulaghi, is a particularly valuable addition to our understanding of what transpired in Iran. It contains many familiar elements, including that of the time spent as a dervish, but also introduces an additional plot-theme, namely that of the substitution (of the slave for the prince).[87] We thus see that even as Linhares sent his Jesuit representative to verify the identity of the claimant, in Iran too, the claims of this 'Bulaghi' were met with scepticism and put to the test. The *Zail* resumes its account by noting that Bulaghi now lived for some time as a guest of an important official, the *nâzir-i buyûtât*. In due course, in the presence of the latter, a couple of Indians visited Bulaghi and verified his claim. Hearing about him, many Multani merchants (*tabaqa-i multâniyân*) who then lived in large numbers in Isfahan, also collected at the prince's residence to pay him their

[87] It is possible to trace the idea of substitution, and the smuggling out of a prince from a palace in a moment of siege, to a series of texts from the Vijayanagara period onwards in south India. We cannot explore this theme here, but see Velcheru Narayana Rao, David Shulman, and Sanjay Subrahmanyam, *Textures of Time: Writing History in South India, 1600–1800*, New Delhi, 2001, as also Robert Sewell, *A Forgotten Empire: Vijayanagar*, London, 1900, pp. 222–31.

respects (*kûrnish*). After about two months, the Shah at last expressed a desire
to meet him. When Bulaghi had his audience with the Shah, he was honoured
with the award of a special horse, and the Shah is said to have remarked: 'Verily,
high birth and greatness are evident on his countenance. From his utterances
too, he seems very sedate and wise; he uses no words without a purpose
(*bi-mahâsal*).'

The Shah then ordered that Bulaghi and Nabdi Mirza, the young boy who had
arrived via Qandahar (and who was also allegedly a son of Sultan Khusrau),
should meet. Perhaps this too was a test, though in this instance, the claims of
not one but both were in question. As it happened, when the two met, they did
not recognize each other. However, they then spent a night together, and mentioned the names of several women from the harems of Khusrau, Shahjahan, and
other princes, hinted at their good and bad qualities in order to test each other's
claims, and to assess how much each of them was familiar with the people who
were mentioned. It then presently became clear to Sultan Bulaghi that this Nabdi
was indeed his brother, and he embraced him with affection (*âghosh-i mihrbânî*).
The Shah ordered that both brothers should henceforth live together.

Later, it is stated, whosoever came from India confirmed that in Hindustan
too the talk about the escape of Bulaghi was widespread, even though—write
the authors of the *Zail*—Bulaghi's story itself sounded rather incredible. It was
really a wonder of the time that he escaped his fate, despite the fact that there
was so vigilant a watch over and guarding of the princes opposed to Shahjahan
by that emperor's well-wishers. What made the story stranger still was that
Bulaghi had nurtured the ambition to be emperor himself, and a royal order had
been issued to terminate his life. So, write the Iranian chroniclers, it is possible
that some of the guards let their vigilance grow slack, or that they themselves
helped him flee and then killed the slave in order to escape the wrath of the king.
Yet, God alone knew the truth of all this.

But the chronicle has not finished with its account of fugitive Mughal princes
and claimants, for it now passes on to the case of the other prince whom we
have encountered above, namely Mirza Baisunghar, the son of the Mughal
prince Daniyal, who had passed away in the time of his father, Akbar. It is
reported in the *Zail* that after Sultan Salim's death, Baisunghar had joined the
supporters of Shahryar, when the latter had fought against Sultan Bulaghi in the
neighbourhood of Lahore. But Shahryar was defeated, and his army was shat-
tered, so that Baisunghar managed to flee towards Kabul with the help of some
of Shahryar's soldiers. On his way there, he heard about the plight of Bulaghi
and the establishment of Shahjahan's power. He then thought it unwise to go
to Kabul, turned towards Balkh instead, and lived there a while among the
Uzbeks and their ruler, Muhammad Khan. But since he was devoid of wisdom,
and was also a mere fugitive, he could be of little real use to the Uzbeks. He

was rather ill-tempered as well and the Uzbeks, for their part, grew indifferent and cold to him. So, with the intention of leaving for the Safavid Shah's court, he is reported to have left for Qandahar, where he met 'Ali Mardan Khan, and stayed there as his guest for some time before he set out for the Shah's court with some of the governor's men. Shah Safi, it is reported, sent a large number of people to receive him in style.

All this had taken place before the arrival in Iran of the man claiming to be 'Bulaghi'. Indeed, when the latter arrived, Baisunghar refused to accept his claim, and since he had a surer position in the esteem of the Shah, he even misbehaved with Bulaghi. Unseemly exchanges took place between the two who claimed to be Mughal princes, and once, in an assembly organized for them to meet and in which the Shah was especially to be present, Baisunghar is reported to have used impolite and unjust words for the other prince, to have shouted at him in anger, and called him a fraud. But Bulaghi maintained his calm, ignored his invectives, and attributing all that he said to his illiteracy and madness (*jahl wa junûn*), then left the assembly. Hearing all about this, the Shah also declined to come there. Still later, at the time of the Shah's march against the Georgian Tahmurs, who had been instigated to rebel against the Safavid sovereign by the brother of Imam Quli Khan and others, Baisunghar sought the Shah's permission to leave his domains. The Shah had no hesitation in allowing him to go back. At this time, Baisunghar submitted that he wanted to return to India in the hope of support to him from the Sultans of the Deccan. He received nothing else besides the 100 *tomâns* that the Shah had earlier sent for him for his expenses in Iran. The *Zail* notes that he was an able young man, but much too proud of his bravery and royal position. He lived during his stay in Iran like an arrogant upstart, with an unbecoming comportment, had little wisdom or sagacity, and was also intolerant and narrow-minded.

The extended and valuable account in the *Zail* does leave a number of crucial questions open. To begin with, it does not by any means resolve our doubts about the genuineness of the man who claimed to be Bulaqi or Bulaghi, as the *Zail* itself admits. There is notably the problem of the relationship between Bulaqi and Baisunghar, the fact that the latter called the former a hoax or fraud, while other evidence (as we have noted above, from his later career with the Ottomans) suggests that it was in fact Baisunghar who was a fraud. If so, why did the Bulaqi of the Safavid court (if he was genuine) not unmask him? A further set of problems concerns the relationship between the man encountered by Padre Leão, and the man who arrived in Bandar 'Abbas from Surat. Were they the same or not? In the case of the claimant in Iran, how do we come to terms with the fact that large numbers of people who had known Bulaqi in the Mughal court came forward to identify him? In any event, it appears that after initial problems, the claimant was accepted by the Safavids as genuine, and we encounter him periodically in the chronicles of the epoch, both in later sections of the *Zail*, and elsewhere.[88]

Besides the narratives in the chronicles, it may also be useful to look briefly at the correspondence that was exchanged between the Safavid monarchs Shah Safi and Shah 'Abbas II, and Sultan Bulaqi. The first set of such letters come to us from around 1632, thus shortly after the arrival of the claimant in Iran. Here, Shah Safi assures the man claiming to be the Mughal prince that he will look after his welfare, and that he is sending a certain Zu'lfiqar Beg Qurchi Baiburdlu to him in this connection. The letter addresses 'Bulaghi' as a genuine Mughal prince, with titles such as *shâhzâda* and *farâzinda-i sarîr-i saltanat*.[89] We also possess a letter from the same period, written by Bulaqi/Bulaghi himself to Shah Safi, though it is unclear whether it precedes the above letter, or is in response to it. In this, the letter-writer terms himself Bulaghi *pâdshâhzâda-i Hindustân* ('descendant of the emperor of Hindustan'), and refers to his own illustrious ancestors from Timur to Humayun (who had sought help from Shah Tahmasp in the sixteenth century). An interesting feature of this letter is its reference to Shi'i holy sites in Iran, whether Karbala, Ardabil, or Najaf, to which the letter-writer claims to have a special attachment. Humble in tone, the purpose of the letter is clearly to flatter Safavid pretensions and suggest that the author is not far from becoming a Shi'i himself. The writer also states that he hopes to put an end to the oppression of the people by Shahjahan with the help of Shah Safi.[90] Portuguese sources, as we have seen above, suggest that in the next few years, the Safavids did give this Bulaghi some resources, allowing him to make a minor nuisance of himself on the Mughal–Safavid frontier. This seems to have lasted only into the mid-1630s however, after which the prince (whether real or false) would appear to have retired to enjoy whatever revenues the Safavids had given him.

The Safavid support for this putative prince was clearly to continue for a time. Still in the time of Shah Safi, we have a further exchange of letters, such as one in November 1640, concerning gifts sent by Sultan Bulaghi to the Shah, including a shield and a sword. The letters of this period suggest a certain familiarity and even intimacy between the Mughal 'prince' and the Safavid ruler, and we know that at much the same time, this Bulaghi accompanied Shah Safi on a visit to Ashraf in the region of Mazandaran.[91] In the same year, 1640,

---

[88] See, for example, *Zail*, pp. 230–40, *passim*.

[89] Cf. Riazul Islam, *A Calendar of Documents on Indo-Persian Relations (1500–1750)*, Vol. I, Teheran, 1979, Doc. Sh. 113, pp. 243–4.

[90] *Ibid.*, Doc. Sh. 113.1, pp. 245–6.

[91] *Ibid.*, Docs Sh. 130 and 131, pp. 276–7. Also see the account of the visit to Ashraf, in *Zail*, pp. 237–8.

Augustinian sources from Iran also inform us of a conflict between members of their order and 'the secretary of Bolaquin, son or nephew of the Great Mogor, successor to that kingdom', over some matters of conversion in Isfahan. Here, the Mughal prince and his entourage are presented as staunch Muslims; 'the Mogors', the Augustinian writer declares, 'profess that they are great observers of their sect'.[92] Two years later, when Shah Safi died and was succeeded by Shah 'Abbas II (r. 1642–66), Bulaghi was amongst those who wrote a letter of condolence and congratulations to the new ruler, leading to a further friendly correspondence between the two as well as an exchange of gifts.[93] In one of these letters, a *ruq'a* drafted by Mirza Muhammad Riza, the recipient Bulaghi is given particularly high titles such as *Nizâm al-saltanat wa'l-khilâfat*, suggesting that by this time any residual doubts concerning his identity had been resolved. These letters must have been written at the time that Bulaghi was resident at Qazwin, and met his various European visitors—as has been noted above. We are also aware that Shah 'Abbas II probably took this 'Bulaghi' along when he mounted his expedition to recover Qandahar from the Mughals in 1648. And when the false rumours of the death of Shahjahan reached Iran in 1658, the same Bulaghi apparently grew keen to ask for the aid of the Safavid monarch in order to regain the Mughal throne, and rushed to Isfahan from Qazwin.[94] This would seem to be the last trace we possess of 'Bulaghi' in the Safavid documents, though we do find some correspondence relating to revenue-grants to his son, Sultan Khusrau.[95]

The Continuity of Tradition

As for the Portuguese, their deep interest in Bulaqi did not really survive the disappointment of the meeting with Padre Leão in December 1630. Even so, Bulaqi was to have one last encounter with the Count of Linhares. On 18 July 1634, the Portuguese viceroy received news from Surat, through the Jesuit Paulo Reimão. He was informed by his correspondent 'that the Mogor king was in Laor

---

[92] See the report from Pietro dei Santi reproduced in Carlos Alonso Vañez, OSA, 'Stato delle missioni agostiniane nelle Indie orientali secondo una relazione inedita del 1640', *Analecta Augustiniana*, Vol. 25, 1962, pp. 291–325, citation on p. 319.

[93] Riazul Islam, *Calendar*, Docs Sh. 134, 135, 136 and 136.1, pp. 281–4.

[94] Muhammad Tahir Wahid Qazwini, *'Abbâs Nâma yâ Sharh-i Zindagânî-yi 22-sâla-yi Shâh 'Abbâs-i sânî (1052–1073)*, ed., Ibrahim Dihgan, Arak, 1951, pp. 234–5, section entitled 'Sharh âmadan-i Sultân Bulâghî ba Dâr al-Saltanat Isfahân'. These moves seem to have been related to a Safavid project to support the prince Murad Bakhsh in 1657–8; cf. Mohammad Quamruddin, *Life and Times of Prince Murad Bakhsh (1624–1661)*, Calcutta, 1974, p. 117.

[95] Riazul Islam, *Calendar*, Docs Sh. 229 and 229.1, pp. 424–5.

to prepare a response to the Persian regarding the affairs of Bulaquim, to whom many of the Mogor's *fidalgos* had gone over, as was the case with Mirzamadafar, who by pretending to depart for Mecca, embarked with a great quantity of riches in a ship in Surrate, and as soon as he reached the high seas, he expelled the pilgrims to Meca in some ship's boats, and those who resisted were thrown into the sea, and he then went off to Persia to join Bulaquim'.[96]

A week later, on 25 July, the viceroy once more had news from Surat through the same Padre Reimão. This time, it was stated that Shahjahan was in Lahore en route to Kashmir, where he hoped to confront Bulaqi. It was claimed that the Mughal prince had decided to openly challenge his uncle, sending him an embassy, 'and as a present, a sword and a bed made of gold, and the embassy told him to choose the one that was more to his taste: the bed on which he could take rest once he had handed over the kingdom, or the sword with what he could expect from it. The Mogor felt this deeply, and wished to kill the envoys, but [instead] had contempt for them, and without deigning to reply prepared himself for war, since the Persian has given much power and help to Bolaqui'.[97]

Then, on 19 January 1635, we have the last echo of the legend of Sultan Bulaqi in the Portuguese sources. That evening, the viceroy Linhares read with some attention a letter that had just arrived from Bijapur, between two unknown correspondents (the recipient clearly is a high-placed Portuguese official, perhaps the Secretary of the *Estado*).[98] Amongst other questions, there was an outline of a proposed alliance between Bulaqi and the *Estado da Índia*:

Sultão Bolaquim asks His Excellency [Linhares] for a royal safe-conduct, [issued] in the name of His Majesty, so that he can stay securely in Goa and from there consult with the captains of the kingdom of the Mogor, and that another such [safe-conduct] should be given to his brother who also escaped,[99] and is with the King of Persia, and once this has been agreed upon, that the lord viceroy should give him passage through one of the ports that he could designate, and to this end he would meet all the accords and conditions that the lord viceroy might desire, carrying this matter out at once. Your Grace should send this messenger for I have agreed to this with the Soltão Bolaquim, and I do not write to His Excellency [directly] for I do not know if he will wish to enter

[96] *Diário do 3º Conde de Linhares. Vice-rei da Índia*, Vol. II, Lisbon, 1937, pp. 146–7.

[97] *Ibid.*, pp. 149–50.

[98] The letter could have been written by one of a number of Portuguese agents at the Bijapur court, such Vicente Ribeiro, Fernão Lopes, Fr. João da Rocha, or a certain Jorge da Costa, who had just arrived in Bijapur as Linhares's envoy in late December 1634.

[99] Is this a reference to the mysterious Mirza Nabdi, whom we have encountered in the *Zail*? According to Mughal chronicles, Bulaqi had only two brothers, Gurshasp (who was killed in January 1628), and Buland Akhtar, who died young; the latter name seems closer to Nabdi, but the association is still far-fetched.

into this affair, and I greatly desire that through the mediation of Your Grace it may come to the knowledge of the lord viceroy, and if he wishes to do this, that I may be informed immediately of the response of the lord viceroy, so that it may be written out in [proper form]. Your Grace should carry out this affair with rapidity.[100]

But the circumstances had changed drastically from those in late 1630. At that time, the Count of Linhares believed in a possible alliance and, in view of the varied origins of the different pieces of intelligence that he had before him, his main preoccupation was with the authenticity of the person, and then, with the feasibility of a political manoeuvre to unseat Shahjahan. Now, in early 1635, Linhares was totally unbelieving. His own viceroyalty was in its final phase, and the viceroy contents himself by noting a last fleeting thought on the subject, two days before concluding his diary for that year and sending it back to Europe: 'I hold this to be a fable, and this Bolaquim seems to be for the Mogores, another king Sebastião for the Portuguese.'

It was the second time that the history of the 'hidden one' (o encoberto) was to cross that of the Mughal emperors. If one is to follow the Jesuits who lived in the court of Akbar, that ruler (who was Shahjahan's grandfather) was much impressed by the figure of Dom Sebastião: 'And he feels deeply for the case of the king Dom Sebastião, and when he talks of that affair, he praises the forceful spirit of the king Dom Sebastião'.[101] Half a century later, we have this interesting comparison from the pen of D. Miguel de Noronha. There are of course various parallels between the different Bulaqis and the different (and false) claimants to being D. Sebastião in the sixteenth century, such as the King of Penamacor, the King of Ericeira, the pastry cook of Madrigal, and the so-called Calabrian.[102] The omnipresence of the legend and the central place of rumour in both cases are fed by the wandering presence of a veiled personage. The tragic component of both stories and of both personages can even reputedly move foreign observers, as the Portuguese were moved by the misfortunes of Bulaqi, and Akbar by those of D. Sebastião. In both cases, we also see the same problems of legitimacy and illegitimacy, the same problem of a popular movement, and the same lack of stability in an early phase of a ruler who had seized power in a disorderly succession.

[100] Diário do 3° Conde de Linhares, Vol. II, p. 265.

[101] Excerpt from a letter written by R. Acquaviva, A. Monserrate, and F. Henriques to the Portuguese captain of Daman, Fatehpur Sikri, March–April 1580; published in Documenta Indica, ed. J. Wicki, Vol. XII, Rome, 1972, Doc. 3, p. 23.

[102] On this subject, see, António Machado Pires, D. Sebastião e o Encoberto, reedn, Lisbon, 1982, esp. pp. 59–64; Jacqueline Hermann, No reino do Desejado: A construção do sebastianismo em Portugal, séculos XVI e XVII, São Paulo, 1998, and the classic work by Miguel D'Antas, Les faux Don Sébastien: Étude sur l'histoire de Portugal, Paris, 1866.

The case of Sultan Bulaqi was certainly not the last of its kind in Mughal India. We find other instances around the brother of Aurangzeb, Shah Shuja' in the 1660s and 1670s, and in the early eighteenth century, such cases of persons pretending to be Mughal princes continue to proliferate, perhaps owing to the fact that very large numbers of princes of royal blood now in fact existed. But certain figures seem to attract particular attention. Thus, as late as 1717, we find an instance of a man (apparently really called 'Aqibat Mahmud), who appeared in the Deccan claiming to be the Mughal prince Muhammad Akbar, and who was eventually imprisoned by the Mughal governor of Arcot.[103] Mughal chroniclers equally mention other incidents concerning the same prince; in the early eighteenth century, the Maratha Raja Shahu is reported to have raised 'commotion' and sought strength by picking up a certain Mu'in-ud-Din who claimed to be a son of Prince Akbar; while a few years later, during the conflicts between the emperor Farrukhsiyar and the Sayyid brothers, Husain 'Ali Khan defied the emperor by returning to court from the Deccan, while claiming to have a son of Muhammad Akbar with him. On this occasion, we are told that 'the emperor's gall-bladder melted with fear' on account of the rival claimant.[104] And later still, after the fall of the Safavid dynasty, men claiming to be princes of that house would appear periodically in India, where on some occasions at least their claims were upheld, as we see with Abu'l Fath Sultan Muhammad Mirza Safavi in the late eighteenth century.[105] Again, in the 1790s, the wandering Mughal prince Mirza 'Ali Bakht 'Azfari' was disconcerted to arrive in the eastern Indian town of Murshidabad, for he found there to his chagrin an impostor who was already in place, claiming to be none other than Mirza Azfari himself.[106] Did such men know the story of Sultan Bulaqi, from almost two centuries before? Or had it passed into folk memory as a more generic theme, even as the legend of Bulaqi itself drew from the same corpus of beliefs and legends pairing kings and renouncers, *faqîrs* who might reveal themselves to be rulers?

The episodes that we have discussed in the preceding pages can, as we have suggested at the outset, be read as part of a larger history of royal 'doubling'

---

[103] On this case, see Sanjay Subrahmanyam, *Penumbral Visions: Making Polities in Early Modern South India*, Delhi, 2001, pp. 128–9.

[104] These incidents may be found in Muhammad Hadi Kamwar Khan, *Tazkirat-us-Salâtîn Chaghtâ*, ed. Muzaffar Alam, Bombay, 1980, pp. 228 and 254.

[105] Giorgio Rota, 'Un Sofi tra i Nababi: L'ultimo Safavide a Lucknow', in Daniela Bredi and Gianroberto Scarcia, eds, *Ex libris Franco Coslovi*, Venice, 1996, pp. 337–80; and also Rota, 'The Man who would not be King: Abu'l Fath Sultan Muhammad Mirza Safavi in India', *Iranian Studies*, Vol. 32, No. 4, 1999, pp. 513–35.

[106] Mirza 'Ali Bakht, *Wâqi'ât-i Azfarî*, eds, T. Chandrasekharan and Syed Hamza Hussain Omari, Madras,1957, pp. 102–3; and for an Urdu translation, Muhammad Husain Mahvi Siddiqi, *Wâqi'ât-i-Azfarî*, Madras, 1937.

in the early modern world, or—as one recent author has put it—as part of the question of how 'identity' and 'credulity' came together in the period, which is termed 'a golden age for impostors and pretenders'.[107] Yet, as we have seen, credulity was always tempered with certain down-to-earth notions of the empirical testing of claims, even if the criteria used differed from one context to another. If the Portuguese viceroy's method was simple enough, and involved sending an accredited eyewitness, the Safavids judged their own claimant by a more complex means, having to do with his civility and mastery of the appropriate etiquette for a prince, including the notion that 'high birth and greatness [were] evident on his countenance'. The problem could also find resolution of another sort if one were cynical enough: we observe this in Philip IV's view that a plausible enough impostor was about as good as the genuine article. As regards the Safavids, we may have some doubts as to whether they thought the man who claimed to be Sultan Bulaghi really was what he declared, for it is interesting that they chose to keep him not at the court in Isfahan (where he would have to meet visitng Mughal dignitaries), but rather in Qazwin. The difference in the treatment of 'Bulaghi' in this period, and Prince Muhammad Akbar later in the seventeenth century is thus marked. Still, true or false, so long as an element of doubt subsisted, such a claimant could always play a role on the chessboard of inter-state politics in the period. To this extent, the Bulaghi who spent the 1630s, 1640s, and 1650s on a comfortable Safavid pension may not have eventually mounted the Mughal throne; but if he was indeed an impostor, he must be deemed a successful one. This success was not predicated though on simple credulity, or on the absence of an empirical spirit, but because ambiguity, bluff, and doubt always had a place in the political systems of the time.

[107] Eliav-Feldon, 'Invented Identities', p. 203.

6

The Company and the Mughals Between
Sir Thomas Roe and Sir William Norris

No man hath proprietye in land nor goods, if hee [the King] please to take it; soe
that all are slaves. Witchcraft, sorcery, juggling, yea, all cunning that the Divell
can teach, is frequent, eaven in the court, wher is wanting noe arte nor wicked
subtility to bee or doe evill; soe that, comparing the vices to some cittyes in Europe,
which I once judged the treasuries and sea of synne, I find them sanctuaryes and
temples in respect of these.

Sir Thomas Roe to Prince Charles, Ajmer (30 October 1616)

Introduction

In recent decades, historians of ideas (above all, political ideas) have returned
to the study of the problem of the Birth of Despotism in the centuries that are
also termed those of European expansion. Here, what is meant is not despotism
as a political 'system' (in the sense that Karl Wittfogel might have construed
it), but rather despotism as a political *topos*, which is usually attributed to
another landscape, on which Europeans projected their fears at the time when
their own political systems were under challenge both at the level of ideas, and
of internal social and political movements.[1] The task is a delicate one, and the
dangers facing the researcher are many, of which we may list a few. In the first
place, the danger of a return to a form of perverse Euro-centricism is very real,
since the greater part of the analyses in question are attempts at explicating what
is a history of European ideas.[2] Armed with what is often a formidable textual

---

[1] Lucette Valensi, *The birth of the despot: Venice and the Sublime Porte*, tr. Arthur
Denner, Ithaca, NY, 1993.

[2] See for example, Joan-Pau Rubiés, *Travel and ethnology in the Renaissance: South
India through European eyes, 1250–1625*, Cambridge, 2000.

erudition, leading back to the medieval Christian tradition (if not the classical representation of the 'Other' in Herodotus), it is thus possible to forget, at least temporarily, that there were really other societies out there, and that they were constituted politically even outside the European imagination. A second danger emanates directly from the literary turn in these studies, since it is for the most part analysts of literature who have led the charge, in view of their superior skills in the analysis of rhetorical tradition. (The first major work in this line is probably Alain Grosrichard's *Structure du sérail* [1979], published at much the same time as Edward Said's *Orientalism*).[3] One result of the literary turn can be that the historical actors disappear, as it were, into a textual miasma, in which process the most banal procedures of historical discipline also fall by the wayside. To be sure, not all literary scholars are equally susceptible to naive ahistoricism, but a sufficiently large number of instances have now been accumulated (including from some of the better-known practitioners such as Stephen Greenblatt or Tzvetan Todorov) for a genuine unease to have set in on this front.

Here we stand then, between the Scylla of overblown literary analysis of texts produced by European expansion, and the ever-present Charybdis of reading these materials at face value, to which their very mass, to say nothing of their congealed power of seduction, draws the archivally-oriented scholar. The materials I address in this essay have in some measure been dealt with before, and some of the earlier treatments have suffered from precisely the problems that I have outlined briefly above. If I have decided to analyse them here once more, it is because it seems to me that some blood can still be squeezed, as it were, out of these turnips, but also for reasons of a more directly political nature. Having been involved on an earlier occasion in the celebration of a centenary (the quincentenary of Vasco da Gama's voyage to East Africa and India in 1998), it has become painfully clear to me that such centenary celebrations carry a rather ambiguous political charge.[4] What, after all, was the English East India Company, the fourth centenary of whose foundation was commemorated in the year 2000? Was it merely a group of merchants, which strayed, in a fit of absent-mindedness, into building a huge and extremely lucrative empire? Or, as certain conspiracy theorists might have it, was it designed from the very start as an exercise in empire-building, which then bided its time for a century-and-a-half, until the right opportunity offered itself? My preliminary response is simple enough. The English Company, from its very inception, was not merely a

---

[3] For an English translation, see Alain Grosrichard, *The sultan's court: European fantasies of the East*, tr. Liz Heron, London, 1998.

[4] The matter is discussed at some length in Sanjay Subrahmanyam, 'Somos el mundo: El discurso de la autarc-ıa en la tierra de los descubrimientos', *Istor*, No. 8, 2002, pp. 165–81.

commercial but a political actor, both in the politics of England (and Europe), and that of Asia. As a political actor, it also produced a political discourse, which was however both somewhat fragmented at any point in time, and shifting over time. One of the major objects of this political discourse was the state that controlled much of India at the time, namely the Mughal empire.

Englishmen and Elephants

In August 1617, some two years into his extended stay in India, the celebrated English courtier and diplomat Sir Thomas Roe (1580/81–1644) wrote to his counterpart, the English ambassador at Istanbul, concerning the Mughal empire (as well as its ruler): 'Neyther will this overgrowne Eliphant descend to Article or bynde himselfe reciprocally to any Prince vpon terms of Equalety, but only by way of fauour admitt our stay so long as it either likes him or those that Gouerne him'.[5] Roe was unhappy with the Mughal state in general, and with its ruler Jahangir in particular, who he felt gave neither his own person, nor the Company and monarch he represented, their entire due. While presenting the Mughal empire as an 'overgrowne Eliphant', he also sought to compare it with other such eastern imperial pachyderms, most notable the Ottomans. In the same letter, he thus addresses some choice sneers at apparent Mughal military might, not dissimilar to what his contemporaries might have done with respect to the Grand Turk. So, in the same letter to Constantinople, we hear:

The King [Jahangir] is at present in what they call an army; but I see no souldiers, though multitudes entertaynd in the qualety. The purpose was the oppression of the united Decan kings, who are perswaded to part with some rotten castles that may pretend a shadowe of yeilding somwhat, for which they are pleasd here to thinck themselves woorthy of the glorious prayses due to an honorable conquest.[6]

What is the historian of cross-cultural encounters to make of such rhetoric? Should we assume that it is no more than a tissue of self-referentiality, produced by autistic Europeans in a landscape that they had no real means of coming to terms with? Or, as recent authors armed with the epistemological might of Renaissance and post-Renaissance studies have begun to insist once more, should we take Roe with the same literal-minded seriousness that Peter Burke has accorded to the French physician François Bernier, who was resident in the

[5] William Foster, ed., *The Embassy of Sir Thomas Roe to India, 1615–19, as narrated in his Journal and Correspondence*, new and revised edition, London, 1926. 1st edn, 1899, 2 Vols The citation is on pp. xxviii–xxix of 1899 edn, and p. xliii of the 1926 edn (which I will hereafter cite unless otherwise stated).

[6] Foster, *The Embassy*, pp. 385–6 f.n.

Mughal domains a half-century after Roe?[7] Before answering these questions, we might do well to ask a rather more basic one: who was this Sir Thomas Roe? The question is easy enough to answer at one level.[8] Born in Leyton in 1580–1, he was the son of a certain Robert Roe, himself the fourth son of Sir Thomas Roe, Lord Mayor of London in 1568. Our Thomas Roe entered Magdalen College, Oxford, in the early 1590s, and was admitted as a student to the Middle Temple in 1597, after which he perhaps spent some time in France. His step-family (his mother having remarried) were the Berkeleys, and possibly through their influence, Thomas Roe was eventually made Esquire of the Body to Queen Elizabeth in the very last years of her reign. At the very outset of the Stuart monarchy, in 1603, he was knighted by James I, and became a close acquaintance of the monarch's children, Prince Henry and Princess Elizabeth. Henry was instrumental in arranging an 'adventure' for Roe, in the region of Guiana, where he spent some time in 1610, exploring one of the branches of the Amazon, and also the mouth of the Orinoco. Here he learnt a little broken Spanish, though (as becomes clear when he is in the Mughal court) he knew no Portuguese. Returning to England in July 1611, Roe was left in somewhat poor straits on account of the death of his patron, Prince Henry (in November 1612), while soon afterwards his other patroness, Princess Elizabeth left for the Palatinate.

As he himself put it, Roe was pretty desperate by 1614. Though briefly Member of Parliament from Tamworth that year, his resources were threadbare. He was to write a few years later from India:

I esteeme it an infinite mercy of God that when I had fully ended and wasted my patrimony and saw no way but scorne (the reward of folly), before I suffred disgrace hee vndertooke mee, and beeing as it were new borne, hee restored mee to a new Inheritance and sett me right, for I doubt not but to equall my wastes.[9]

Besides having run out of money, Roe had also contracted a secret marriage with the daughter of Sir Thomas Cave from Stanford (Northants), who was also the widow of a certain Sir George Beeston. In these circumstances, the East India Company's request to have him sent as ambassador to the Mughal was a godsend. We may recall that the idea of an ambassador at the Mughal court had been mooted by Thomas Aldworth, writing from Ahmadabad in November 1613,

[7] Cf. Peter Burke, 'The philosopher as traveller: Bernier's Orient', in Jás Elsner and Joan-Pau Rubiés, eds, *Voyages and visions: Towards a cultural history of travel*, London, 1999, pp. 124–37.

[8] For the standard biography, see Michael J. Brown, *Itinerant Ambassador: The Life of Sir Thomas Roe*, Lexington, KY, 1970. Also see the more recent account by Colin Paul Mitchell, *Sir Thomas Roe and the Mughal Empire*, Karachi, 2000.

[9] Cited in Foster, *The Embassy*, p. xxii.

and seconded by another Company factor, William Biddulph. Aldworth claimed this was the only way of getting the Company's affairs to be taken seriously, *vis-à-vis* their rivals, the Dutch and especially the Portuguese: 'Their might be a suffitient man be sent in your first shippes that may bee Resident in Agra withe the Kinge, and sutch a one whose person may breade regarde, for they here looke mutch after greate men.' This was no doubt the result of the experience of William Hawkins, who had been at Agra from early 1609 to November 1611, but who had not carried sufficient weight with Jahangir to ensure the stability of the Company's position in Gujarat.[10] In September 1614, Sir Thomas Smythe, Governor of the Company, thus officially proposed sending 'one of extraordinarye partes to reside att Agra to prevent any plottes that may be wrought by the Iesuites to circumvent our trade'. The sending of this envoy would be in keeping with the *farmân* that Jahangir had granted Thomas Best.

However, in debate, several different positions emerged amongst Company circles. Some were against the expense of the envoy, while others thought that sending a merchant was good enough. Still others feared that James I would impose his own candidate, and thus undermine the autonomy of the Company. Finally on 7 October 1614, it was decided to send 'an Embassadour of extraordinarye Countenance and respect'. The first name proposed was Sir John Brooke, whose health was too poor though. Then the name of a certain 'Master Bailie' was mooted, but the proposal met with little enthusiasm. In third place came Sir Thomas Roe 'yf hee may bee had'. Sir Thomas Smythe himself seems to have proposed this name, and he was described as 'of a pregnant understandinge, well spoken, learned, industrious, and of a comelie personage'. King James approved the choice. Roe had instructions from him to impress on the Mughal the greatness of the English monarch, which 'Maketh us even a Terrour to all other Nations; Concluding all with this happines, that Wee be not onlie absolutelie obeyed but universally beloved and admyred of all our People'.

Roe embarked for India on the *Lion*, on 2 February 1615, and reached Surat in six months. During the voyage, it is clear that he was kept at some distance by the commanders of the fleet, so as to avoid a conflict of authority. The fleet eventually arrived at Swally on 18 September 1615; at this time the merchant William Edwards was already at the Mughal court. Roe himself made his way to at Ajmer on 23 December 1615, after briefly visiting the Mughal prince Sultan Parviz at Burhanpur. He was however taken ill on arrival, and was thus able to go the the *darbar* for the first time only on 10 January 1616. A longish stay ensued, to which we shall turn at greater length later. He eventually took leave of Jahangir at Ahmadabad in August 1618, when the monarch was about to move

---

[10] For the voyages immediately preceding the embassy of Roe, see William Foster, ed., *The Voyage of Thomas Best to the East Indies, 1612–1614*, London, 1934.

to Agra. Roe claimed about this time that he was convinced 'after almost three yeares experience of the pride and falshood of these people, that [they] attended only advantage and were governed by privat interest and appetite'. After a further four months in Surat, he left for home on the *Anne* on 17 February 1619, and arrived at Plymouth in August that year, eventually returning to London in September.

Thereafter too, Sir Thomas Roe may be said to have had a fairly reasonable career. Not every one of his contemporaries and friends was so fortunate. Meanwhile, in 1616, after thirteen years in the Tower, Roe's sometime friend Sir Walter Ralegh was released and allowed to make plans to go to Guiana. He set sail in June 1617, but in early January 1618, his subordinates attacked a Spanish settlement, in a major diplomatic *faux pas*. One of those responsible, Keymis, committed suicide on ship rather than return; Ralegh returned to England and was somewhat summarily beheaded in the Palace Yard at Westminster on 29 October 1618.[11] Roe, on the other hand, became Member of Parliament again on his return, and then in 1621 was sent to Istanbul. Here, he is supposed to have secured good conditions for English trade, and also helped block Habsburg overtures to the Sublime Porte while helping cement a treaty between the Ottomans and Poland.[12] He stayed on in the Ottoman domains until Spring 1628, and in June 1629 was sent to help negotiate the peace between Sweden and Poland. In these years, he is reported to have become close to Gustavus Adolphus, and even helped persuade him to invade Germany in 1630.[13] In 1632, Roe's close friend Sir Dudley Carleton (Viscount Dorchester) died, and he began to harbour hopes that he would succeed him as the King's Secretary. Eventually, considered too 'liberal', he was set aside and retired to the country. In 1637, Roe's star rose once more, as he was made Chancellor of the Order of the Garter. He participated in the peace negotiations at Hamburg, Ratisbon, and Vienna, and in June 1640, entered the Privy Council, and also re-entered Parliament as Member from Oxford. In 1641, he was again in Germany as a diplomat. As things worsened for him politically in these last years, Roe eventually decided to pull out from public life, and retired to Bath in July 1643. He died in November 1644.

Roe's account, already known in an incomplete form to his contemporaries, has been used over the years by a number of historians, both of the East India

---

[11] From a vast bibliography on Ralegh, see for example, Stephen Coote, *A play of passion: The life of Sir Walter Ralegh*, London, 1993.

[12] Material on Roe's career in Istanbul may be found in Richard Knolles, *The generall historie of the Turkes*, 4th edn, London, 1632.

[13] For this phase of his life, see Samuel R. Gardiner, ed., *Letters relating to the mission of Sir Thomas Roe to Gustavus Adolphus, 1629–1630*, London, 1875.

Company and of the Mughal court. The latter have in particular drawn upon the Englishman's account to examine the nature of Mughal court rituals, of which some have seen him as a keen observer. His description of the first time he was received by Jahangir, in January 1616, brings out the flavour of his account clearly enough.

I went to court at four in the evening to the *durbar*, which is the place wher the Mogull sitts out daylie, to entertayne strangers, to receive petitions and presents, to give commands, to see and bee seene. To digresse a little from my reception, and declare the customes of the court, will enlighten the future discourse. The King hath no man but eunuchs that come within the lodgings or retyring roomes of his house: his weomen watch within, and guard him with manly weapons. They doe justice on upon another for offences. He comes every morning to a wyndow, called the *jarruco*, looking into a playne before his gate, and showes him selfe to the common people. At noone he returns thither and sitts some howers to see the fight of eliphants and willd beasts; under him within a rayle attend the men of rancke; from whence hee retiers to sleepe among his woemen. At afternoone, he returns to the *durbar* before mentioned. At eight, after supper, he comes downe to the *guzelcan*, a faire court, wher in the middest is a throune erected of free stone wherein he sitts, but some tymes below in a chayre; to which are none admitted but of great qualetye, and few of those without leave; wher he discourses of all matters with much affabilitye.[14]

The tone of irony is not to be missed. Here is an effeminate court dominated by women, where the king 'hath no man but eunuchs' in his intimate surroundings, while his women 'guard him with manly weapons'. This is a court moreover where the decisions are taken in public, 'propounded, and resolved, and soe registred', but even this is not quite to Roe's taste for it means that royal decisions are 'tossed and censured by every rascall'. Besides, there is the issue of the nature of this kingship itself; for even if the king is complimented for 'never refusing the poorest mans complaynt', we are equally reminded that he 'sees with too much delight in blood the execution done by his eliphants'. Two significant passages may be found in the description of the same meeting, which are of some importance for understanding Roe's view of how royal power functions in a Mughal context. After having detailed Jahangir's daily schedule, Roe assures the reader that 'this course is unchangeable, except sicknesss or drinck prevent yt; which must be known, for, as all his subjects are slaves, so is he in a kynd of reciprocall bondage, for he is tyed to observe these howres and customes so precisely that, if hee were unseene one day and noe sufficient reason rendred, the people would mutinie; two days noe reason can excuse, but that he must consent to open his doores and bee seene by some to satisfye others'. This is a powerful thesis indeed, one that moves from a critical view

[14] Foster, *The Embassy*, pp. 84–6.

of royal power, to one of the contract of rulership itself, seen here as 'reciprocall bondage', where the ruler is as unfree as his slavish subjects.

In a slightly later passage, Roe emphasizes the theatrical quality of the Mughal court, and this is a remark that has attracted the attention of a number of recent analysts. Is this a way for King James's ambassador to suggest that the Mughals are somehow unreal, or a way of suggesting affinities between all sorts of courts, which do after all have rituals, ceremonies, and their share of theatre? The passage in question runs: 'This sitting out hath soe much affinitye with a theatre—the manner of the king in his gallery; the great men lifted on a stage as actors; the vulgar below gazing on—that an easy description will informe of the place and fashion'. I would argue however that this is not a light view of play-acting, but intimately linked to the earlier passage. This is a repetitive theatre that must be played out again and again, where no one—not even the king—can change the rules. It is difficult to read in this view of the Mughal court a positive appreciation by an open-minded visiting dignitary, as some scholars have wished to have us believe, the more so since theatre to the early seventeenth-century Englishman most commonly carried with it associations of immorality and tawdriness.

The major aspect of Roe's account is its ability to drive a wedge between the ruler as person, and the Mughal court system. Jahangir, as he emerges in this account, is not an entirely despicable man, and Roe wishes his readers to believe that at a human level a certain complicity grew between him and the Mughal. We have already noted his claim that the so-called _ghusl khâna_ is a place 'to which are none admitted but of great qualetye'; it then turns out that Roe is one of those who can claim this degree of consideration. Similarly, after an occasion in early September 1616, when an exchange of sundry presents had taken place, Roe reports that 'hee [Jahangir] made frolique, and sent mee woord hee more esteemed mee than ever any Francke'; and for his part, the English ambassador declares that 'so drincking and commanding others, His Majestie and all his lords became the finest men I ever saw, of a thowsand humors'.[15] It is all too easy to misread such passages (including one where we learn that Jahangir is 'of countenance cheerfull, and not proud in nature, but by habitt and custome; for a nights he is veary affable, and full of gentle conversation'), and conclude sententiously that 'their initial deep incomprehension about the other's cognitive world impelled each to seek a language in which to achieve a mutual understanding'.[16] In order to do so, we must deliberately shut our eyes to other passages, written by Roe much later, indeed at a time when—according

---

[15] Foster, _The Embassy_ , pp. 225–6.

[16] William R. Pinch, 'Same Difference in India and Europe', _History and Theory_, Vol. 38, No. 3, 1999, pp. 389–407, citation on p. 407.

to a 'learning-by-doing' view of communication—the ambassador and the ruler should have come ever closer cognitively. Yet, here is Roe writing from Ahmadabad to Sir Thomas Smythe, in February 1618:

These Princes and Customes are so Contrarie to ours that I shall travell much in myne owne eies and performe little in yours. Ther is no treaty wher ther is soe much Prid, nor no assurance wher is no fayth. All I can doe is to serve present turnes. The People are weary of us. The King hath no content, who expectes great Presentes and Jewelles, and reguardes no trade but what feedes his unsatiable appetite after stones, rich and rare Peices of any kind of arte.[17]

Or again, in a letter written to James I from Jahangir's camp at much the same time as the above letter:

To the monarch with whom I reside your Maiesties minister I delivered your Royall letters and presents, which were received with as much honor as their barbarous pride and Cust-toomes affoord to any the like from any Absolute Prince, though far inferior to that respect due unto them. I have stroven, sometimes to displeasure, with their tricks of unmeasured greatness rather than to endure any scorne. I dare not dissemble with Your Majestie, their pride and dull ignorance takes all things done of duty, and this yeare I was enforced to stande out for the honor of your free guifts, which were sceazed uncivilly. I have sought to meyntayne upright Your Majesties greatenes and dignitie, and withall to effect the ends of the merchant; but these two sometyme cross one another, seeing ther is no way to treate with so monstrous overweening that acknowledgeth no equall. He [Jahangir] hath written Your Majestie a lettre full of good woords, but barren of all true effect.[18]

Roe's prejudices, from the time of his arrival in India, were clearly in this direction, and we can see that two years' stay has not fundamentally altered his view of the Mughal empire, even if it has nuanced the details, and been given far more local colour over time. The two letters cited above can be read as a direct continuation of another, written to George Abbot, the Archbishop of Canterbury, as early as January 1616:

A discription of the land, customes, and manners, with other accidents, are fitter for wynter nights. They are eyther ordinary, or mingled with much barbarisme. Lawes they have none written. The Kyngs judgement bynds, who sitts and gives sentence with much patience, once weakly, both in capitall and criminall causes; wher some tymes he sees the execution done by his eliphants, with two much delight in blood. His governors of provinces rule by his firmanes, which is a breefe lettre authorising them. They take life and goods at pleasure.[19]

[17] Foster, *The Embassy*, p. 466. A fruitful comparison may be made between Roe's image of the Mughal court and corruption in the court of James I itself, for which see Linda Levy Peck, *Court patronage and corruption in early Stuart England*, London, 1993.

[18] *Ibid.*, pp. 464–5.

[19] *Ibid.*, p. 104.

Here, then, is a key to understanding Roe's presentation of the Mughal to the English reader, an understanding which I would contend is far less subtle than that of the Portuguese and Spanish Jesuits at the Mughal court, and far more apt to drift towards the *topos* of Oriental Despotism: absence of laws, arbitrary royal power and a penchant for blood-lust, absence of private property.[20] Like his chaplain, Edward Terry, also the author of an account on Jahangir's court, Roe presents the nature of power in the Mughal domains as unreasonable, even if it must be tolerated by the Company for reasons of *realpolitik*.[21] Where he differs from Terry, whose lampooning of the Mughal is far cruder and often requires him to contradict Roe in details, is in the fact that the ambassador must use the Mughal ruler to advance himself. Thus, the account of Thomas Roe, while denigrating the Mughal state and what it stands for (its 'habitt and custome'), cannot present the embassy itself as a failure. Rather, the ambassador must appear a man of rare ability and understanding, who manages to insinuate himself into the rank of the intimates of the emperor; in sum a diplomat who is better received than all his rivals, be they the envoys of other European powers, or the Safavids and Ottomans. If the eventual results of this embassy fall short of the Company's requirements, it is the fault of the Mughals, and that too not as individuals but as a court-society. This view, that Roe successfully managed to communicate of himself, explains the subsequent success he had in his public career. In order that such an image be the dominant one, Roe also had to suppress or discredit some of his own critics in the Company, men such as the factors John Brown and William Biddulph, the former the author of a trenchant letter of complaint to London, accusing the ambassador of waste, extravagance, vanity, and dubious private trade, which only earned him sharp censure from the Company. What triumphed eventually was the account of Roe himself, and of his greatest supporter and admirer, the Rev. Edward Terry.

Recent historians have unfortunately displaced the reading of Roe into quite another sphere. Rather than ask what his views of the Mughal political system were, and how they affected his representation both of that empire and of his own embassy, the recent debate has chosen to focus on the problem of 'translatability' or (as historians and sociologists of science might put it) 'commensurability'. Thus, Bernard Cohn has read Roe's account in order to argue that

---

[20] On the Jesuit view of Mughals, see *inter alia*, Muzaffar Alam and Sanjay Subrahmanyam, 'Witnessing Transition: Views on the End of the Akbari Dispensation', in K.N. Panikkar, Terence J. Byres, and Utsa Patnaik, eds, *The Making of History: Essays presented to Irfan Habib*, New Delhi, 2000, pp. 104–40.

[21] Rev. Edward Terry, *A voyage to East-India: Wherein some things are taken notice of in our passage thither, but many more in our abode there, within that rich and most spacious empire of the great Mogol*, London, 1655.

while 'the British in seventeenth-century India operated on the idea that everything and everyone had a "price"', Indians had quite another view of matters.
This opposition is brought out further by him in two lapidary phrases: on the
one hand, 'Europeans of the seventeenth century lived in a world of signs and
corespondences'; and on the other hand, 'Hindus and Muslims operated with
an unbounded substantive theory of objects and persons'.[22] Reproaching the
ambassador for not having attended the learned courses of Professors Marriott
and Inden at the University of Chicago (where such an unbounded substantive
theory might have been explicated), the American scholar thus makes himself
an easy target for other writers, eager to establish that Roe in fact comprehended
pretty much everything in Mughal India, and spoke in a wholly transparent
manner. Thus, William Pinch's recent riposte to Cohn claims the following:

The Mughal darbar and Elizabethan-Jacobean court were differently conceived in many
obvious and subtle ways—certainly in terms of their ritual styles and the objects used
to convey political authority and power, not to mention their traditions of statecraft. But
these were primarily differences of detail, not of substance. The differences were
translatable.[23]

This is manifestly less-than-satisfactory as a formulation. What does it mean
to say that Mughal court culture was 'translatable' to an English reader in Stuart
England? At first sight, it may appear to mean that it was in fact translated, a
claim that is however quite easily dismissed. The reader of Roe's account in
England emerged with a particular view of the workings of power in the Mughal
empire, which cannot be presented as some neutral 'translation'. A second
possibility is to state that, notionally, Mughal concepts were translatable; but
it then remains to specify the real circumstances under which this theoretical
translatability could be put into practice. Here, our problems are certainly not
solved by claiming (as Pinch does, in a telling ahistorical formula) that one can
appeal to concepts that are 'emblematic of all human relationships'. The argument can be advanced further by contrasting Roe's account to that of another
visitor to Jahangir's court.

[22] Bernard S. Cohn, *Colonialism and Its Forms of Knowledge: The British in India*
(Princeton: Princeton University Press, 1996, pp. 18–19 (an essay first published in
1985). Cohn's ideas with respect to Roe were further extended in Kate Teltscher, *India
Inscribed: European and British Writing on India, 1600–1800*, Delhi, 1995.

[23] Pinch, 'Same Difference', p. 404. Pinch criticizes both Cohn and Teltscher, at times
on grounds that are sound; but, as will become apparent, he is extremely selective in
reading Roe as well as in understanding the context. In part, this is because of Pinch's
desire to demote Cohn's view, in favour of his own preferred alternative, namely C. A.
Bayly, *Empire and Information: Intelligence Gathering and Social Communication in
India, 1780–1870*, Cambridge, 1996.

Excursus on Mutribi

The visitor in question was from Central Asia (Samarqand to be precise), a poet and scholar by the name of Mutribi Samarqandi.[24] Over two months, in 1627 (1036 AH), Mutribi was at the Mughal court in Lahore, in the last years of Jahangir's reign, and his work consists of an account of 24 conversations with the Mughal emperor.[25] These conversations were conducted in Persian, a language that both Mutribi and Jahangir spoke with native fluency (Jahangir also knew some Turkish, Arabic, and Braj Bhasha, and perhaps a smattering of Portuguese); Thomas Roe, on the other hand, was obviously constantly obliged to take recourse to interpreters, a fact that he is often discreet about, but which must surely have influenced the very nature of the enterprise of conceptual 'translation' we have spoken of above, when that translation passed literally through language, and was not simply a question of interpreting gestures, visual events, or physical signs. The account of Mutribi's dealings with Jahangir, initially through the mediation of a certain Khwaja Fakhr-al-Din Husain, were penned within a few months after their occurrence, when the recollections were still fresh in the author's mind. The text is of course court literature, and meant to be read by even the Mughals themselves; this had a double significance, for if on the one hand Mutribi (unlike Roe) could not be critical of Jahangir even if he wished to do so, on the other hand, everything he wrote was subject to evaluation (and verification) by the other courtiers. Herein lies one of the greatest problems with Roe's account, one which has been systematically downplayed: we simply do not know how to evaluate the truth-value of his narrative. Save in those instances when the Rev. Terry was present, no other account exists of Roe's dealings, for the Mughal sources more or less entirely ignore him. As for Terry, it is unclear whether his own text can be regarded as an independent one from that of Roe; the two were clearly in close contact, depended on the same interpreters, with Terry sometimes adding his own gloss, in view of his greater hostility to the Mughals.

The meetings between Mutribi and Jahangir are described using the term *wâqiᶜ'a*—'happenings'—and as noted above they are 24 in number. We shall

[24] On Mutribi, see Surinder Singh, 'The Indian Memoirs of Mutribi Samarqandi', *Proceedings of the Indian History Congress, 55th Session, Aligarh, 1994*, Delhi, 1995, pp. 345–54, and Richard Foltz, 'Two Seventeenth-Century Central Asian Travellers to Mughal India', *Journal of the Royal Asiatic Society of Great Britain and Ireland*, Series 3, Vol. VI, No. 3, 1996, pp. 367–77.

[25] For the text, see *Khâtirât-i-Mutribî Samarqandi (being the Memoirs of Mutribi's sessions with Emperor Jahangir)*, ed., Abdul Ghani Mirzoyef, Karachi, 1977. A recent translation, somewhat unsatisfactory, is by Richard C. Foltz, *Conversations with Emperor Jahangir by 'Mutribi' al-Asamm of Samarqand*, Costa Mesa, 1998. I am grateful to Muzaffar Alam, with whom I have extensively discussed this text.

focus on a few of them in order to present their flavour. In the first meeting, Jahangir asks Mutribi why, after spending a month in Lahore, he had only now come to the court. Mutribi answers that he was finishing a text in honour of Jahangir (the *Nuskha-yi Zîba-yi Jahângîrî*), and had only now found a chronogram to close it. On being presented the text, Jahangir is pleased, and asks Mutribi whether he would rather stay in the Mughal court, go back to his homeland, or whether he wanted to make the *hajj* to Mecca and Medina. Mutribi, as an etiquette-bound courtier, says that he is at the ruler's disposal. Jahangir then tells him he has four gifts for him, but that he would give them one after the other. They were, money for his expenses, a *khilᶜ'at* (ceremonial and honorific robe) to wear, a horse and saddle, and a slave to serve him. Which of these did he want first? Mutribi replies in poetry on the importance of money (*zar*), and is at once given a platter full of money, amounting to 1000 rupees. Besides, he is given 500 rupees on the part of Nur Jahan. Though the visitor is from Central Asia and not from India, no cognitive dissonance is reported, nor is any 'noise' to be discerned in the account thus far. True, it may be argued, Mutribi does not have the critical distance of Roe. He is not likely to say, when a dance has been arranged in his honour, 'some whoores did sing and dance'.

The stage has now been set for the subsequent meetings and conversations between Mutribi and Jahangir, which will have a more explicitly comparative and reflective nature for the most part. In the second meeting, the ruler's brother-in-law Asaf Khan (who plays a major and somewhat sinister role in Roe's account), and several other *amîrs* are present. Jahangir now enquires on the state of the burial place of his illustrious ancestor, Timur, in Samarqand, and Mutribi replies that details were to be found in his text, the *Nuskha-yi Zîba*. A discussion ensues, at the end of which Mutribi is given a *khilᶜ'at*, a Kashmiri shawl, a turban, and other gifts; his son Muhammad 'Ali too is given expensive brocade clothes. The horse and the saddle were saved up for the next day. We have now understood that Mutribi represents a window into Central Asia for Jahangir, as a sort of authentic eyewitness (*bayân*) to affairs in Transoxania; but, like the Europeans at the court, he also has a certain potential in the matter of 'wonders'. The next day, some European merchants (*tujjâr-i firang*) who are present at the court, give what are termed 'tributes' (*peshkash-ha*) to Jahangir. A small booklet (*kitâbcha*), four fingers long, fits in the emperor's hand; it has twelve folios, and the paper has a brownish colour. The book is in a small locked box, and calling Mutribi, Jahangir asks him to guess which book it is. The former confesses ignorance, and the emperor opens the box and gives it to him with a stick, and explains that one could write on the paper with it, and also rub the writing off. Mutribi is astonished, and by way of demonstration Jahangir writes a verse in the book, shows it to him, and then rubs it off. Jokingly, he even offers to sell the book and pencil to Mutribi for a rupee. The latter superstitiously refuses, saying that it is magical (*tilism*), and might harm him; besides he does not have any money on him. Jahangir laughingly gives it to him as a gift, assuring him it is harmless. Mutribi reports his intention to carry it back to Turan, and give it to the ruler there, Imam Quli Khan, as a valuable gift from Hindustan.

In the fourth meeting, the intimacy between ruler and visitor has begun to grow. Matters take a literary turn, as Jahangir has by now read Mutribi's book, and even comments on a verse in it. Once more we see, that as with visitors and envoys from the Ottoman domains (Seyyidi 'Ali Re'is at Humayun's court), or Iran, the Mughal ruler has a common set of cultural resources on which to fall back with Mutribi, points of mutual reference that mean nothing to Roe.[26] Again, it is conceivable that this might not have been so. Let us imagine that instead of Roe, the English Company had sent George Strachan, the Scottish polyglot and sometime resident of Baghdad and Isfahan in the 1610s and 1620s.[27] Strachan could doubtless have conversed with Jahangir on far more familiar ground, in view of his knowledge of Persian, Turkish, and Arabic, in a spirit rather closer to that of the Jesuits at the Mughal court. Yet, would the Company have sent such a man, in view of their own search for 'one of extraordinarye partes', that is of high social standing?

A few further aspects of Mutribi's account sharpen the contrast further, demonstrating the distinction between 'insiders' and 'outsiders', a distinction which recent protagonists of the cultural translation thesis continue to obfuscate. Consider the following anecdote relating to Mughal painting. On a certain occasion, Mutribi reports, Jahangir wishes to test him. A freshly made set of portraits from the Mughal ateliers is brought before Mutribi, who sees that they depict the former ruler of Turan, 'Abdullah Khan Uzbek and his son 'Abdul-Momin Khan. As someone who has known these individuals, Mutribi is meant to give his seal of approval to the portraits. However, he tells Jahangir that there are defects in the representation of 'Abdullah Khan's chin, and his son's headgear. At this, the painter is at once summoned, and asked to correct the paintings, which he does by the next day. Another courtier from Transoxania expresses a contrary opinion on 'Abdul-Momin Khan's headgear, but finally Mutribi's view is upheld. This may be contrasted to a celebrated episode in Roe's account, again on the subject of Mughal painting. Here, Jahangir reportedly boasts to Roe that the painters of his atelier can reproduce any European

[26] On Seyyidi 'Ali at Humayun's court, see Seyyidi 'Ali Re'is, *Le miroir des pays: Une anabase ottomane à travers l'Inde et l'Asie centrale*, tr. Jean-Louis Bacqué-Grammont, Paris, 1999; and for a modern Turkish text, Seydi Ali Reis, *Mir'âtü'l-Memâlik*, ed. Mehmet Kiremit, Ankara, 1999.

[27] G. L. Dellavida, *George Strachan: Memorials of a wandering Scottish scholar of the seventeenth century*, Aberdeen, 1956.

portrait; the challenge is taken up, and though Roe notes that the copies were well-done, 'yet I showed myne owne and the differences, which were in arte apparant, but not to be judged by a common eye'.[28] The text has been much commented on, amongst others by historians of Mughal art: for our purposes, the significance of the incident lies in the fact that while Mutribi is concerned to show the meticulous nature of Mughal portraiture and the confidence that was vested in him as a judge of its quality, Roe's is a grudging acceptance of the painter's skills, framed in a story in which the skills that are brought to the fore are his own, for he tells the reader that he does not have a 'common eye'.

The tensions between Jahangir and Roe are most manifest in matters of gifts and money, where the English ambassador shows periodic uncertainty with how to deal with payments as well as how to receive gifts. This may again be contrasted with Mutribi, who negotiates such matters with consummate skill. We see this on the occasion of a celebration, when Mutribi receives two platters of coins, worth 2000 rupees, and other valuables. As a poet, he then recites verses in the court in praise of the emperor, and pleased in turn at the verses, Jahangir for his part gives him more gifts. Yet, the play between gifts and their value, and prices, is not entirely avoided; rather it is very playfully dealt with. Thus, Jahangir asks Mutribi what sort of horse and saddle he wants, and the latter asks rather directly for the most expensive sort. A discussion then ensues on the relative quality of different sorts, and Mutribi finally he receives an Iraqi horse (rather than a less valuable Turkish one), but a saddle of velvet (rather than a more expensive but less durable one in scarlet). Similarly, in the 16th meeting, Jahangir auctions three slaves in the court, while proclaiming (in a semi-serious fashion) that of all the professions, only trade is respectable in the eyes of Islam, an inversion of the usual clichés concerning the culture of the Mughal court.

Yet, these meetings are not entirely devoid of cut and thrust, or repartee between emperor and poet. Thus, in another meeting, Jahangir quite bluntly asks Mutribi whether he thinks white skin is better than black, obviously wishing to test our Central Asian's colour prejudices in respect of Indians. Mutribi replies evasively, saying that it was all a matter of opinion; but Jahangir insists that he wants to know his opinion. Mutribi for his part says that he could only judge by seeing (*bînam wa gûyam*), and so Jahangir advises him to look right and left and decide. On the right, Mutribi finds a dark young Indian princeling (*râjabacha*), who was extremely handsome, but equally, on the left, a fair and handsome boy is standing, who dazzles Mutribi's eyes. How can he now decide? Having looks twice at each, he says to Jahangir, that it is not a matter of dark and fair but of the pleasantness of the countenance. Jahangir is pleased at the tact of the response, and recites a verse in the same sense, to which Mutribi responds

[28] Foster, *The Embassy*, pp. 189–90, 199.

with a supporting *hadîth*, in which the Prophet says that his brother Yusuf was fair, but it was he whose countenance had a more agreeable (literally 'salty') quality (*malâhat*).[29]

There are, hence, two travellers within Mutribi's text, the author himself and Jahangir. If Mutribi makes comparisons between Central Asia and Hindustan, based on what he sees (and the insistent emphasis is on the eye, and its superiority to hearsay), Jahangir transforms himself through Mutribi (and, undoubtedly, scores of others like him) into an armchair traveller. If the wonders and the superiority of Hindustan are brought out, it is by constant contrast to Transoxania, and in effect Mutribi becomes the vehicle for the expression of Jahangir's opinions and prejudices. Yet, the account has a vastly different tone and texture than Roe's account, not only because of the ambassador's preoc-cupation with humiliation (real or imagined), and because of his inability to participate in the court as he might have done in France or Sweden; the key difference is that Roe's account is caught in a matrix of comparing two political systems, and two civilities, whereas this represents a non-issue for Mutribi. We cannot entirely neglect another aspect either (which Cohn too stresses, cor-rectly), namely the distance imposed by layers of interpreters and translators on Roe's dealing with Jahangir. A flagrant instance is that of 13 March 1616, when Roe appears in the *ghusl khâna* with an Italian interpreter, who is kept out; he then pleads that 'I could speak no Portugall, and soe wanted means to satisfie His Majestie'. The interpreter is hence admitted, and Roe communicates to him in what he himself admits is 'broken Spanish'. Jahangir for his part throws a few Portuguese words into his own conversation, and at a later stage in the proceedings, when an altercation arises with Prince Khurram, further interposes a Safavid prince called Mir Miran into the chain of translation. Thus, we eventually have Roe speaking broken Spanish to an Italian interpreter, who translates into Turkish; the Safavid prince then translates this Turkish into Persian.[30] To imagine then, as Roe does, that his arguments carried all before them ('the Jesuite and all the Portugalls side fell in; in soe much that I explaynd my selfe fully concerning them'), requires a certain optimism. It is not incon-ceivable that Roe failed to make much of an impression on the Mughals, which would explain why Jahangir, who—on the accumulated evidence of the period, including Mutribi's account—showed considerable geographical curiosity, as well as curiosity concerning flora and fauna, as well as ethnographic difference, found so little of interest in Roe.

[29] The translation by Foltz, *Conversations*, pp. 48–50, misunderstands much of the text, confounding the expression for adolescent peach-fuzz on the youths' cheeks for their 'candy-green colour'.

[30] Foster, *The Embassy*, pp. 128–31.

From Oxford to Cambridge

After Thomas Roe, the English Company desisted from sending further ambassadors to the Mughal court for the greater part of the seventeenth century. We know of Dutch and even French representatives at the court of Shahjahan and Aurangzeb, and Englishmen who were sent for example to Golkonda, but it was not until the very end of the seventeenth century that another English ambassador sought to follow in Sir Thomas's footsteps.[31] This is Sir William Norris, a rather more obscure character than his precedessor, and in some sense symmetrically located: if Thomas Roe was a rough contemporary of Thomas Hobbes at Oxford, William Norris was at Trinity College, Cambridge, at the same time as Sir Isaac Newton. This section will be concerned with Norris's failed embassy to the court of Aurangzeb, an embassy which in certain respects is in marked contrast both to that of his predecessor, Roe, who turned diplomatic failure into rhetorical success, and later embassies of the eighteenth century (such as that of John Surman), which actually gained the English far greater advantages than in the previous century.

The circumstances surrounding Norris's embassy were already substantially different from those attending the despatch of Roe. From the middle decades of the seventeenth century, English trade to India, which had earlier been on a rather precarious footing, assumed more substantial proportions. Besides Gujarat, which had been the mainstay of their early operations, and Roe's own main concern, the English Company had established factories in Bengal, and also on the Coromandel coast of south-eastern India, where Fort St. George in Madras was established in 1639. In the mid-1660s, the Crown acquired territories in Bombay as part of a negotiation with the Portuguese monarchy, and by this means the Company's implantation both within Mughal territories and outside them had been strengthened. The only serious rival operation that had been mounted, namely Courteen's Association in the 1630s and 1640s, did not prove to have staying power.[32] It was only in the last quarter of the century that other English merchants, taking advantage of the fluid political situation in England, were periodically able to penetrate into Asian waters. The increasingly threadbare character of the Company's monopoly allowed their rivals to engage in

[31] For some examples of Dutch and French envoys, see François de La Boullaye-Le Gouz, *Les voyages et observations du sieur de La Boullaye-Le Gouz*, ed. Jacques de Maussion de Favières, Paris, 1994, and A. J. Bernet Kempers, ed., *Journaal van Dircq van Adrichem's hofreis naar den Groot-Mogol Aurangzeb, 1662*, The Hague, 1941.

[32] No full-length study of Courteen's Association exists to date; but see, for an excellent ringside view of its operations, *The travels of Peter Mundy in Europe and Asia, 1608–1667*, eds, Richard Carnac Temple and L. M. Anstey, 5 Vols, London, 1907–36, especially Vols 3 and 4.

trade on the Cape Route, but also to combine commerce with filibustering. But even here, the nuisance value of the 'interlopers' was probably greater than their real economic clout. In any event, by 1686, it seemed the Old Company had won its battle. Sir Josia Child, its head, was close to the reigning monarch James II, and the 'interlopers' seemed to be in difficulty. But the Glorious Revolution of 1688 changed the politico-commercial map considerably, and a different set of cards was now dealt out to the rival groups. Kirti Chaudhuri and Jonathan Israel have written recently of these changes:

It is not generally appreciated by historians of early modern Europe that 1688 marked not only a 'revolution' in Britain but also one in the Indian Ocean. During 1687–8 the English East India Company, under the leadership of Sir Josia Child, decided to wage a war on the Mughal emperor and demonstrate to the VOC [Dutch Company] that its naval power was more than a match for the Dutch organization. Tactically, the war went badly for the Company but in the long run its strategic aims were fully realized.[33]

In the short run, the news of the defeat that came back to England in 1689 could not have come at a worse time for the Company. A parliamentary committee was set up to look into the Company's affairs, for it was seen as a Jacobite and Tory organization, whose detractors had every reason to want an alternative structure in place of the old merchant oligarchy that held sway. Thus, 10 years after the Glorious Revolution, in 1698, the Old Company was told to wind up its affairs, with its charter ending on 29 September 1701. A New Company was formed, with its merchant members promising much aid to William III. But since the Old Company still dominated in India, where it was well-entrenched, it was thought wiser to send an ambassador to sort things out between the rivals, and also explain matters to the Mughal ruler.

The man chosen was Sir William Norris, a Member of Parliament (MP) from Liverpool who, like Roe, had no previous experience of India before being sent out. In this, the English strategy was quite different (in both cases) from that of the Dutch, who always sent out experienced hands—men like Adrichem, Bacherus, or Ketelaar—rather than innocents, whose main asset would be their social standing and political connections in Europe. Norris eventually set sail from Plymouth on 21 January 1699, and in September that year, his ship anchored off Fort St. George (Madras), where he was given a churlish reception by the governor, Thomas Pitt. His idea was to go to the Mughal port of Masulipatnam, to accede from there to Aurangzeb's camp, in view of the fact that the Mughal

---

[33] K. N. Chaudhuri and Jonathan I. Israel, 'The English and Dutch East India Companies and the Glorious Revolution of 1688–9', in Jonathan I. Israel, ed., *The Anglo-Dutch Moment: Essays on the Glorious Revolution and its world impact*, Cambridge, 1991, pp. 407–38, citation on p. 407.

emperor found himself in the Deccan, still fighting his interminable campaigns of southward expansion. But Norris could not make much headway. In 1700, after nearly a year at Bandar Masulipatnam, he eventually decided to try access to the Mughal royal camp by a westerly route, and set sail for Surat. Eventually, in January 1701, two years after his departure from England, Norris began to make his way overland from Surat to the Deccan, notably to the obscure town of Panhala, where the emperor was. However, while on his way, Norris received destabilizing news from home. It turned out that in his absence, the Old Company has managed to regain ground in London, and even obtained a new Act of Parliament, renewing its existence, and eventually paving for the way for the merger of the two into the United East India Company (a process that was completed only in 1709). Norris was thus in a bad way, with his own legitimacy (as ambassador of the New Company), severely compromised. Eventually, after obtaining little of note, in November 1701, he left the imperial camp, and at last reached Surat overland in March 1702. By now, however, he had also lost credit with the New Company, which considered him a waste of money, since he had by then spent the astronomical sum of some 80,000 pounds. He thus obtained a vessel, the *Scipio*—with difficulty, for his return voyage, sailed to Mauritius, and then while on his way to the Cape, died of dysentery on board the ship on 10 October 1702.[34]

It would appear that Norris had left behind six volumes of materials dealing with the embassy, titled 'Journalls of transactions and observations from the time of His Excellency's leaving England to the 14th of September [1702]'. However, only four of the six volumes are extant, two in the Bodleian Library at Oxford, in the Rawlinson Collection, and two others at the Public Records Office, in London. The first of these volumes runs from Norris's arrival at Porto Novo in September 1699 to early May 1700; and the second runs from 10 December 1700, the date of his arrival at Surat, to 23 April 1701, while at Panhala. The other two volumes are in the Public Records Office, are in fact the fifth and sixth of the series; one runs from 26 September 1701 to 12 March 1702, when Norris eventually returns to Surat, while the last tome continues the chronology to 14 September 1702. Finally, there is a fragment of his journal, concerned with the outward voyage, and dated from the departure from England to 5 January 1699, while at Cape Verde.[35]

[34] Entry for Sir William Norris by Stanley Lane-Poole, *The Dictionary of National Biography*, eds Sir Leslie Stephen and Sir Sidney Lee, Vol. XIV, pp. 589–91.

[35] Bodleian Library, Oxford, Rawlinson Collection, C. 912 and C. 913; the other two volumes are in the Public Records Office, Kew, as C.O. 77/50 and C.O. 77/51. The fragment of his journal is to be found in the British Library, OIOC, Original Correspondence No. 54, dated from the departure from England to 5/1/1699 at Cape Verde.

These rather extensive papers have however been the object of little attention, and certainly Norris did not enjoy the contemporary notoreity of Sir
Thomas Roe.[36] We are however quite well-informed on the subject of Norris
himself. Originally from a Lancashire family, William Norris came from the
branch which resided at Speke Hall on the north bank of the Mersey. His father
was Thomas Norris, who fought on the royalist side in the civil war; while his
mother, Katherine, was the daughter of Sir Henry Garraway. Of the couple's
seven sons and four daughters, the eldest son, also Thomas Norris, inherited
the property in 1686, while William Norris, the second son (born at Speke Hall
in 1657) was first sent to Westminster School in 1672 as King's Scholar, and
then in June 1675 entered Trinity Collage, Cambridge, where he distinguished
himself as a poet, and a scholar of Greek. Norris eventually graduated in 1678,
and was made minor Fellow of Trinity in October 1681, received an MA in 1682,
and was raised to the rank of major Fellow in the same year, in which capacity
he continued till Christmas 1690. A political profile also begins to emerge in
these very years. Thus, in 1686–7, Norris was delegate for the University and
involved in a dispute with James II in which the Vice-Chancellor, Dr John
Peachell, was deprived of his office in May 1687. Thus, in 1688, his sympathies
were clear enough, and it comes as no surprise that in 1689, Norris writes a
Latin poem praising William and Mary and their accession to the throne. In
December 1689, he marries Elizabeth Poxfellen (d. 1713), widow of Nicholas
Poxfellen; his wife, too, was closely connected to anti-Tory politics, in part
through Lord Ranelagh. By the early 1690s, William Norris's position as a Whig
was clear, and his political career was clearly on the ascendant. In 1694, he
helped negotiate the Charter granted to Liverpool by the Crown, and the next
year, succeeded his brother, Thomas, as MP from Liverpool. He was also made
Baronet in December 1698, with the express purpose of elevating his rank for
his mission to India.

Norris's account, which has yet to be published for the most part, can
nevertheless be quite easily contrasted with that of Roe, in terms of its tone and
preoccupations. Where the latter is almost exclusively concerned with Mughal
political society, notably the court and its intrigues but also the doings of princes
of the blood, governors, and the like, Norris is far more of a naturalist and
an observer of society at large, stopping to examine exotic trees and lizards,
and comment on the monsoon winds, as also on marriage processions and
popular festivals. The familiar tension between political observation and ethnography thus surfaces when we contrast these two figures, and is further
strengthened perhaps by their differing circumstances. Roe's political activity

---

[36] The best account to date is H. H. Das, *The Norris Embassy to Aurangzib (1699–
1702)*, condensed and arranged by S. C. Sarkar, Calcutta, 1959.

was more or less incessant in India, whereas Norris had a long, more-or-less forced, stay in Masulipatnam, where he was able to accumulate a rather large number of observations on Indian society, which we will have occasion to comment on later.[37] We must also take into account the fact of a significant gap in Norris's papers at the time when his courtly political activity is most intense; this is for the period from 23 April 1701, while at Panhala, to 26 September of the same year. On the other hand, the parallels between the two men are also striking at times, not least of all their penchant for private trade (Norris's brother Edward, who accompanied him on the embassy, carried back a cargo worth some 87,000 rupees on his account). Not least of all, neither ambassador really succeeded in obtaining what he wanted from the Mughal court, and the embassy ended on a rather sour note on both occasions. However, this did not place the basic functioning of English trade in India under a cloud: embassy or not, the Company continued to conduct business (and more) pretty much as usual after the ambassador had returned, and in the early 1700s even went from strength to strength, with the gradual decline of its main competitor, the Dutch East India Company.

Norris was aware in his own way of the possible comparisons with Roe, who obviously enjoyed a rather good reputation as a diplomat at the end of the seventeenth century. He remarks, for example, on arriving in India: 'It was a little remarkable yt I should land ye same day of ye month on ye Coast of India as Sr Tho: Roe did who was ye only Ambassadour ever sent from England to these parts before Ano 1615 25th 7ber att Suratt he landed.'[38] On landing at Surat, Roe claimed to have been rather badly treated by the local authorities, but Norris did not immediately have much to complain about on his arrival. Rather, the initial impression he gives us of society in Masulipatnam is rather favourable, it being only the local climate that did not agree with him, especially when 'ye Raines begin to be dryd up & ye Morasses wch almost encompass ye Town begin to be swampy'. He was given a house that he describes as 'ye K[ing] of Golcundas pallace when he fled into these parts pursud by ye Mogull(...) & is not only a very hansome stately & pleasant but a convenient house large enough to Reeceive me & all my Retinue with greate ease to every Body. It stands high & comands & over lookes ye whole Town'. Even the local entertainment made a more favourable impression on him than his Oxonian

---

[37] On Masulipatnam in this period, and the English Company's troubles with relation to this port town, see Sanjay Subrahmanyam, 'Masulipatnam Revisited, 1550–1750: A Survey and Some Speculations', in Frank Broeze, ed., *Gateways to Asia: Port Cities of Asia in the 13th–20th Centuries*, London and New York, 1997, pp. 33–65.

[38] Das, *The Norris Embassy*, p. 115.

predecessor: he appreciated 'a Company of Dancinge women who are much prized & admird by everybody & indeed are very nimble & active', as he would later greatly admire a company of jugglers and acrobats.

But over the next few months, his observations on the society itself begin to sharpen, as he begins to enumerate the different groups there: Moors and Gentoos to be sure, but also amongst them Bramines, and other 'casts' and 'sects' on whom he attempts to gather information, apparently through the Company's Indian brokers and agents. On the Brahmins, for example, he has this comment to offer:

Ye Generality of people Great & small are soe ignorant & foolish as to beleive whatever ye Bramines tell them & depend upon it for certainty (…). [The Bramines] themselves are none of ye wisest sort but cunninge enough however in this particular to leade ye Rest of ye people be ye noses & soe their pretended knowledge is very advantageous & bringes ym in greate profitt.[39]

Further, he also has a general theory concerning the historical evolution of the Hindu (or 'Gentoo') religion, for which he has rather more sympathy all in all than for Islam, which he also has occasion to observe at close quarters while at Masulipatnam. Thus:

The account I have been yett able to gett in discoursinge wth their Learned Bramines about their Religion convinces me beyond all contradiction that Christianity was formerly planted here & you may most clearly Trace ye ffootstepps & very foundations of it in ye Traditions they give you of Their Religion, Length of Time havinge worn out both ye Truth & practise of it ye Gentoos beinge now universally given up to Idolatry though some of ye most understanding who have livd amongst ye English seeme to deny it & not to practise it. I shall take another occasion to Treate more largely on this Subject. But already I find it very evident yt In ye Gentoo Religion Christianity is to be Tracd & ye Jewish Religion in ye Moores Practise still retaining severall of their solemnitys particularly ye new moons & sabbaths.[40]

The religion of the Brahmins and other Hindus is thus taken to be a degenerate version of Christianity that the passage of time has 'worn out'; the hypothesis bears a certain resemblance to what earlier Portuguese observers claimed, though they often based themselves on the legend of St. Thomas's apostolate in India. Norris is of course quite anxious to dispel any ideas that he might have any sympathy for the Papists, as we see in his rather odd discussion of the celebration of Muharram in Masulipatnam. Having initially informed the reader that the festival takes place when Muslims commemorate 'ye Death or funerall

[39] Das, *The Norris Embassy*, p. 152.
[40] *Ibid.*, p. 163.

of Mahomett ye Grand Impostor', he goes on to describes the processions, and concludes on this rather interesting and complex note:

I thinke it harde to judge whether ye Moores or Rashbootes are more Ridiculous in their ceremoneys ye Moores favour more of ye papistes & this Ceremony is Like their exposinge ye Relicks off some saint. This I thinke is observable yt there is not ye least clashinge or fallinge out amongst soe many different sects & Casts as there are in this Town. They live quietly & contented amongst one another, each sect & cast enjoyinge his superstition & performinge their Idolatrous worship without any disputes or molestation, & I see no liklyhood of their fallinge out unlesse ye Gentoos & Moores should chance to have a greate feast fall out ye same day & then they must fight it out as boys doe when different parishes meet in walkinge bounds. I heartily pity ym for their Ignorance & mistaken Devotion, but really they might teach Christians this one Lesson who are of different opinions in some points To live quietly & peacably amongst themselves & not Teare one another in pieces.[41]

Here then is an interesting use of the exotic as a mirror, something which Norris is capable of on more than one occasion. Though a classic device, where the traveller turns his distant lens on his own society, the remark while less than Swiftian in its mordancy, yet represents far more than we find in Roe's account. The experience of the Civil War, in which his own father fought (on the losing side), may have left this trace on Norris. Another instance shows this again with some clarity. This is a passage where Norris describes the discriminatory poll tax that Aurangzeb has re-introduced, and what he himself thinks of as its deleterious effects on society. He writes:

If Aurengzebe live 3 or 4 yeares longer by severitys usd in fininge & Taxinge ye gentoos above wht they are able to pay, will oblige most of ym to come over to his own Religion wch he uses all possible meanes to propogate. Though ye Gentoos to give ym their due livd strictly sober lives & not soe much given to frequent ye Whores cast as ye moores, yet doe not approve these methods calling ym Inovations, but ye Mogull who is wholly devoted to Religion uses all methods to plant it, & have all under him strict observers of it. In these 3 monthes yt I have been here I have neither seen nor heard of any Drunkenesse disorder Riott or quarellinge in ye Town. It would be well if European City's would take example.[42]

Like the earlier characterization of Indian sects and castes that live 'without any disputes or molestation', this one too can hardly be defended on empirical grounds. The history of Masulipatnam, and the records that we dispose of, both from the European factories and in Persian, do not authorize such an idyllic vision, where no 'Drunkenesse disorder Riott or quarellinge' may be found; but it is nonetheless interesting that Norris is willing to go so far as to hold out these

[41] Das, *The Norris Embassy*, pp. 165–6.
[42] *Ibid.*, p. 149.

aspects of the Indian society that he observes as a veritable model for their European counterparts. But matters stop there. For, if Norris's vision of late seventeenth-century Indian society admits of a number of positive aspects (despite the unfortunate religious beliefs and practices of the inhabitants), this approbation cannot be extended by him to the state. For the Mughal state to him is the very epitome of despotism and tyranny, where 'the higher authority squeezes ye Lower and ye Mogull squeezes all'.[43] Not only are these taxes heavy, they are collected moreover by a corrupt state, rotten through and through, with a military system that can hardly be taken seriously either. Here, Norris, like Bernier and Manuzzi, indulges in a characteristic fantasy of how few European soldiers it would take to put paid to Mughal might. In a passage on the fighting style of different groups, such as the Rajputs ('Rashboote'), he concludes:

[They carry] a sword & buckler for shew & are nimble & expert in shewinge tricks of activity & divertion, but I make no complement to my country att all when I attest yt 20000 English men well armed would beate all ye Mogulls army both Moores & Gentoos (for they are warlick much alike). Their discipline not much exceedinge their Courage & neither to be mentioned ye same day wth what England produces of both. They have one Art of Warr here as in other places, to protracte it for advantage of ye Cheife Comanders, for they say ye Mogulls Army might in much a shorter time have conquered this country but then they should have been layd aside as uselesse, having little more to doe but keepinge a Rajah or two in good order.[44]

The overall impression is moreover one where the Gentoos, if anything, are even weaker and less suited to making war than the Moors. Norris's view of the Mughal state as a Muslim incubus, draining the resources of a predominantly Hindu society, is of course a classic one, nuanced no doubt by his view that within society itself, Hindus and Muslims can normally co-exist without a great deal of tension. The onus is thus clearly on the state and state power, and Norris, as Christian and Englishman, does leave some rather broad hints in the air on the nature of tyranny and resistance to it. Thus, still commenting on the *jizya*, or differential poll tax,

It is said to be ye Mogull's order yt those yt Refuse or are not able to pay this tax shall be obligd to Turn Moores, wch I dare say if they were put to ye Extremity severall of these poore ignorant people people are soe well satisfyd in ye sort of worship they are born & bred in yt they would suffer death rather than Embrace Mahoumenatism (*sic*), how much more ought wee who by God's good providence are brought up in ye light of ye Gospell & ye knowledge of Jesus Christ, how much more ought wee to be steadfast in our faith if it ever please God to bring us to ye Tryall.[45]

[43] Das, *The Norris Embassy*, p. 149.
[44] *Ibid.*, pp. 124–5.
[45] *Ibid.*, pp. 156–7.

The 'tryall' in question can of course be read in two ways; first as referring to a situation when the Englishmen residents in India become subject to Mughal taxation, and second—and in my view, far more plausibly—as referring to a hypothetical situation in Europe itself, where the people of one religion become subject to a ruler from another. There may be some point in suggesting, therefore, that Norris identifies Aurangzeb, as it were, with the Jacobite threat, made all that much worse by the nature of the state he rules, and the fact that he is a Muslim to boot. But one also senses that the contrast is between peoples who will brook such subjection, and others who will not. Still, on the same subject, Norris has this to offer:

These poore Gentoos are miserably harrassed by ye Moorish Govermt ever Scince ye Mogull conquerd Golcunda & tooke their Kinge prisoner who was one of their cast and used ym kindly, but ye Mogull, who is a great bigott in his own Religion & an Abhorror of their superstition and Idolatry, has already destroyd most of their pagods only for quicknesse sake permitts Jugrenaut wch is ye Cheife & most gainful & will in time bringe ym over to his own Religion though I believe ye Gentoos are 50 for one of ye moores, but an Effeminate people.[46]

Once more, one could point to the flagrant errors of fact and interpretation (the idea that Abu'l Hasan Qutb Shah of Golkonda was to the Gentoos 'one of their cast'), which reflects the cognitive dissonance that runs through the account. But what is of far greater interest is the combination in the portrayal of a tyrannical state run by a 'great bigott' and an 'effeminate people' subject to him, which rehearses a portrayal that would take deeper root in the years to come. It must take an incurable Panglossian to see this sort of situation as one of 'mutual understanding [that] was the outgrowth of proximity, fueled by basic human curiosity, and achieved by means of fortuitous cultural convergences'.[47] At the purely human level, it is of course the case that Norris—like Roe—finds some Indians, and even some Mughal courtiers more to his taste than others. A particular target for his annoyance is the *wazîr* Asad Khan, described by him as 'ye Greatest & Richest man in ye Empire next ye Mogull & most say Richer then He having amassd vast sums of money by very large Incomes & never paying any body wch makes him generally hated'. The usual accusations of lechery and debauchery follow inevitably: 'They tell us he has 30 wives and 800 other women wth him & has change of 3 or 4 every night wch I thinke might be spard considering his age wch is 90 yeares Old'. Norris then concludes, explaining at the same time his own incapacity to make much diplomatic progress: 'It is impossible to believe how dissolute & luxurious ye lives of these

[46] Das, *The Norris Embassy*, p. 157, entry dated November 1699.

[47] Pinch, 'Same Difference', p. 407.

greate men are. The vizier spendinge his whole time with his women, his eunuchs & pandars, who have liberty of accesse at all times & his secretarys in Relation to business but rarely & yt as ye eunuch pleases'. Even if he were to meet him, it would do the ambassador no good, since the *wazîr* allegedly consumes great quantities of 'Hott spiritts wth wch they make themselves drunke every day if they can gett it'.[48] But to Asad Khan is contrasted another figure, namely a certain Yar 'Ali Beg, a high official of the *dîwanî*, to whom Norris pays the most fulsome compliments. Thus:

[In the] midst of ye most base vitious & corrupt court in ye Universe this minister alone is virtuous. The sole businesse of all other ministers is to gripe squeeze all ye money they can from all people by ye basest & Indirect meanes Imaginable openly & barefaced. This man alone despises riches & is above ye Temptation of any bribe can be offerd. Just to ye greatest nicety & firme to ye Intrest he espouses & not to be disobligd, but by suspectinge his Integrity or offering bribery to debauch it, He is courted by everybody & dreaded by all ye corrupt ministers of the court who stand in aw of his virtue & rigid maners. The virtue of ye antient Romans eminently appears in him & seemes a compound of Ffabritius [and] Cato ye Censer.[49]

We would be mistaken however if we believed that this was seen as a redeeming feature of the Mughal system. Rather, notes Norris, 'it is Impossible for one man to stem ye current of vice & corruption or else this good man's example might be very prevalent'. This then is the very uneven struggle between a system, which can only be condemned, and some individuals within it, whose honesty and modestly puritan lifestyle can still be held up, if only to heighten the contrast.

Norris's view of the Mughals assumes a rather ironic dimension in view of the immense luxury and pomp with which the ambassador surrounded himself. We have already noted that the costs of the embassy were eventually judged crippling by the Company itself; Norris himself notes unabashedly that it was his custom to have '14 or 16 good dishes every day' for dinner, and another '6 dishes' for supper. The Italian Niccolò Manuzzi, who had briefly been deputed to aid the embassy, but begged off using the excuse of 'age, blindness and other infirmities', claimed in his *Storia del Mogol*, that Norris 'made a great show, and his expenses were extraordinary', to the point that he was given the nickname of the 'King of England'.[50] The 'pomp and

---

[48] Das, *The Norris Embassy*, pp. 267–8.

[49] *Ibid.*, p. 303. The classical references are to the Roman Republican statesman, Marcus Porcius Cato (234–149 BC), known for his austere scrutiny of Senate officials; and to the Roman general and statesman Caius Fabricius Luscinus (d. 250 BC), famed for his simplicity and probity.

[50] William Irvine, tr., *Storia do Mogor; or, Mogul India, 1653–1708, by Niccolao Manucci, Venetian*, 4 Vols, London, 1907–8, Vol. III, p. 300.

ostentation' to which Manuzzi refers is clear enough when we see how the ambassador presented himself at the Mughal *darbâr*, where he was received for the first time on 28 April 1701. Accompanied by carts with brass cannon, much glassware, two Arabian horses, a state palankeen, several crests and flags, musicians on horseback in livery, troopers and pages, and Norris himself in a 'rich palanquin, with Indian embroidered furniture', the embassy may have impressed observers but it also rendered them suspicious by the largesse that was indiscriminately distributed by way of bribes (with the agents of the Old Company competing to outbribe those of the New). Norris's sour view of the Mughals can only be seen then as a case of the pot calling the kettle black.

A number of the statements made by Norris at various times to Mughal officials can only have increased their sense of suspicion. Besides declaring that his ruler, William III was 'King of England, Scotland, France, and Ireland, the richest and most victorious of all Europe', Norris also made strenuous efforts to separate himself from the Old Company, again a tactic that must have seemed less than credible. We may consider a petition directed by him to Aurangzeb for example, in which he declared:

This New company is distinct from the old one. This New company has no relation whatsoever with the Old company. The Old company is responsible for its obligations, and has no connection with the New company. If the New Company does anything against (the law) or shows any unfairness in its dealings and trade then it is the obligation of our King to answer for that.[51]

In view of the accumulated complaints against English freebooters and pirates in the western Indian Ocean, as well as the assurances already given by Sir Nicholas Waite, the Company representative at Surat on this matter, the position of Norris must have appeared contradictory to his interlocutors in the Mughal court. Who spoke for the New Company, Norris or Waite? Further, what precisely was the status of the Old Company with respect to the King of England? How did William III claim to be King of France at certain moments, while the English Company also admitted (in a list submitted to Ruhullah Khan), that Louis XIV was in fact the King of France? We may well wonder what the Mughal court would have made of an explanation from Norris's embassy, where it was stated that European diplomacy functioned in such a way that 'if by the going of the ambassador, no purpose is reached, and no work is done, and between the Kings no concord is arrived at, then the

[51] British Library, OIOC, Mss. Eur. D. 1075, Type Copy of Correspondence dated 1701, translated from the Persian between Sir William Norris, Ambassador of the New English East India Company, and the Mughal Emperor, from O.C. 57–I, 7572.

ambassador is allowed to depart with honour and respect; but afterwards they declare war'![52]

Conclusion

A comparison of the two embassies sent out by the East India Company to the Mughal court in the seventeenth century should ideally be completed by a framing of these in a still larger context, where one would ideally like to compare the reception and comportment of these embassies with others in Mughal India, whether Dutch, French, Portuguese, or indeed Safavid or Ottoman. This larger task must await another occasion, but even on the basis of our limited examination of materials, certain conclusions seem to impose themselves. It is clear that what has come to be known as the 'Todorov model' of the cross-cultural encounter cannot hold in this case, any more than it does in the initial context in which it was mooted, namely that of the meeting of Cortés and Moctezuma in Mexico.[53] That is, one cannot simply assume an opacity or incapacity to communicate on *a priori* grounds stemming from semiotic incompatibility; few would dare to declare today, with Todorov, that 'Moctezuma is located at a first level of semiotic incapacity: he misunderstands the signals of the other and interprets them badly; his own messages do not attain their goal, for he is incapable of perceiving that the Spaniards are at the same time similar (humans) and different'.[54] But to demolish this model is all-too-easy, and does not address the complex problem of how the Company's ambassadors communicated in a Mughal context, and how they perceived and represented the Mughals. To my mind, the counterproposition, which argues that everything was translatable, or at least as translatable here as in 'all social relations', cannot be acceptable to the historian. To accept such a position is to deny the specificity of the problem at hand, namely one in which England, a medium-sized power from the western end of Eurasia, was seeking to impose its terms on a diplomatic relationship with a far larger power, the Mughals, who also belonged to a religious category that was seen as fundamentally antagonistic to Christianity.

[52] OIOC, Mss. Eur. D. 1075, from O.C. 57–I, 7561. 'The answer of the King of England, the Wearer of Hats, concerning what was demanded of the Ambassador'. The document also contains a brief description of the political structure of Europe, that is not without interest.

[53] Tzvetan Todorov, *The conquest of America: Perceiving the other*, tr. Richard Howard, 1st edn, New York, 1984.

[54] Tsvetan Todorov, 'Cortés et Moctezuma: De la communication', *L'Ethnographie*, vol. LXXVI, Nos 1–2, 1980, pp. 69–83, quotation on p. 83. Compare the account to that in Carmen Bernand and Serge Gruzinski, *Histoire du nouveau monde*, 2 Vols, Paris, 1991–3; Vol. 1: *De la découverte à la conquête, une expérience européenne, 1492–1550*.

To sum the matter up schematically, we might say that the problem we are dealing with here is not one where knowledge is shaped by actual power (for the English had very little power in India, whether at the time of Roe or that of Norris); rather it is one of a will to power where a form of political ethnography, in which various political systems are compared and ranked, has become the standard framework for the ambassadorial account. This was not inevitable, nor had it always been the case, as a comparison of the accounts of Roe or Francisco Pelsaert (the Dutch factor at Agra in the 1620s) with those of the Jesuits at the courts of Akbar and Jahangir shows. The latter's evaluation of Akbar does not, in the final analysis, seem to differ very much from the manner in which they might have judged a Christian monarch in Europe, whereas by the time of Roe, the tone and the nature of the judgement had shifted. This shift seems to crystallize and become standardized over the course of the seventeenth century, whether with Bernier, Norris, or even the thoroughly marginal Manuzzi, who both despised and modelled himself on Bernier. Seen through this prism, exceptional and sympathetic individuals might exist even in the Mughal court, but the framework was one in which Mughal rule itself was political anathema, a form of government so constitutionally corrupt and despotic, that it could only be compared with that of the Ottomans.

This still leaves us with an unanswered question. What if the roles were reversed? Would Mughal ambassadors to England have seen the Stuart court in an analogous way to that in which the Mughals were perceived by Roe or Norris? We cannot answer with any certitude, because the first Mughal (or Indo-Persian) accounts of England date to a period after the seizure of Bengal by the Company, and are very much shaped by those events.[55] The closest comparison we can find is with the Ottomans, for in the eighteenth century, we know of Ottoman accounts of France that can be read against European accounts of the Ottoman empire. Amongst these, we can count the embassy account of Yirmisekiz Çelebi Mehmed Efendi to the court of the young Louis XV in 1720–1;[56] and in the same line of narratives, one may equally number the reports from Revolutionary and Napoleonic France of Morali Seyyid Ali Efendi and Seyyid Abdürrahim Muhibb Efendi, the first dating from the years 1797 to 1802, and the second from 1806 to 1811.[57] These accounts do not seem to me to confirm

---

[55] I have addressed a related question in an earlier essay, reproduced in Subrahmanyam, From the Tagus to the Ganges, chapter 2.

[56] For this account, see Julien-Claude Galland, *Le Paradis des infidèles: Un ambassadeur ottoman en France sous la Régence*, ed. Gilles Veinstein, Paris, 1981.

[57] Morali Seyyid Ali Efendi and Seyyid Abdürrahim Muhibb Efendi, *Deux Ottomans à Paris sous le Directoire et l'Empire: Relations d'ambassade*, trans. Stéphane Yerasimos, Paris, 1998.

the view that when the roles were reversed, the proto-Orientalism of one was simply replaced by the Occidentalism of the other. The reasons for this are surely at least two-fold: the asymmetry of the relationship between the two parties, even in purely commercial terms; and the differing traditions of xenology within which the Ottoman ambassadors and, say, the Venetian or French consuls in the Levant, located themselves.

To return then to the point of departure, our problem in dealing with the East India Company's relations with Mughal India in the seventeenth century lies in our very characterization of the period. Clearly, this is not an epoch when we can assume any direct European domination over south Asia, and so it is naturally tempting to assume that the history of representations too is characterized either by symmetry or by its relatively 'innocent' character. Yet, without wishing to impose a crude teleology on the Company's dealings in India, or assuming that the conquest of the Mughal empire was already written on the wall by 1615, it is important to understand that a form of conflict did exist already by the time of Roe, and even more so by that of Norris. If at times this conflict between Mughals and Europeans expressed itself as open war, as with the Mughal capture of Portuguese Hughli in 1632, or Sir Josia Child's Mughal war of the 1680s, at other times the conflict was far more in the nature of a 'war of images', to borrow—and slightly displace—a phrase.[58] It is with this 'contained conflict' that we must come to terms in understanding the world of our ambassadors, rather than return once more to the time-honoured cliché of the period as a supposed 'Age of Partnership'.

[58] Cf. Serge Gruzinski, *La guerre des images: De Christophe Colomb à 'Blade Runner'* (*1492–2019*), Paris, 1990.

7

Dreaming an Indo-Persian Empire in South Asia, 1740–1800

The Serpent (to Eve): 'I tell you I am very subtle. When you and Adam talk, I hear you say "Why?" Always "Why?" You see things; and you say "Why?" But I dream things that never were; and I say "Why not?" (...)'.

George Bernard Shaw, *Back to Methuselah*

Introduction

Through much of the 1960s and 1970s, students of economic history in the University of Delhi were routinely confronted in their examinations with a characteristic counterfactual proposition: what form would Indian industrialization have taken in the absence of the British colonial state? Answers ranged typically within a rather limited set of possibilities. One tendency was to argue that an independent India (which it was tacitly assumed would be politically coherent and a unitary state), would have developed economically in the nineteenth and early twentieth centuries along the lines of Japan. That is, the state, guided along by an Indian version of the Japanese minister, Matsukata, would have afforded industry a certain degree of protection, the cotton textile and jute industries would have expanded far more rapidly than they in fact did, and crucially, the backward linkages from the expansion of the railway network from the 1860s on would have benefited a domestic Indian iron and steel industry rather than the British one. Thus, with an iron and steel sector and a chemicals industry, that would each have been established a good half-century before the first successful attempts in British India, India by 1914 would have been well on its way to becoming a major industrial power. To this scenario (supported in large measure by the Marxist-nationalist analysis of Indian industrial history by Amiya Kumar Bagchi, published in 1972),[1] was contrasted a rather more

---

[1] Amiya Kumar Bagchi, *Private Investment in India, 1900–1939*, Cambridge, 1972.

pessimistic view, sustained by writers such as Morris David Morris, who argued that India by 1750 was already sufficiently 'backward' in terms of infrastructure and markets, not to be able to achieve industrial growth of the sort outlined above, even in the absence of colonialism.[2] While Morris studiously made it a point to deny that 'values' as such were an obstacle to economic change in India (thus setting himself apart from the older Orientalist and Weberian traditions), he nevertheless did not see much by way of a developmental silver lining, even when the colonial cloud had been cleared away.[3]

If one were to take the first of these tacks, a subsidiary question was then inevitable. Under what conditions would one be authorized to imagine the absence of the colonial state? Here, the favoured scenario was one that imagined the comprehensive defeat of the armies of the English East India Company by the rulers of the state of Mysore (in southern India) in the last quarter of the eighteenth century. These rulers, Haidar 'Ali Khan and his son Tipu Sultan, were thus thought to be capable either on their own (and with a little bit of luck on the battlefield), or with the aid of the French, of defeating the English Company armies, to whom they did in any event give a serious fright over the 1770s and 1780s. Since Tipu also entertained diplomatic relations with revolutionary France after 1789, it was even possible with a dash of fancy to conceive of a 'liberal' monarchy, drawing on a dose of Jacobinism.[4] Citizen Tipu might thus have led a resurgent India into the nineteenth century, rather than dying a martyr (*shahîd*) in the fort of Srirangapatnam in early May 1799.[5]

Other counterfactual scenarios have periodically captured the imagination of historians of south Asia, wishing to conceive of some trajectory other than British colonial domination. These range from constructing a possible victory for the rebels in the anti-British uprising (rather rudely summarized at times as 'the Mutiny') of 1857, to positing a British defeat in the Afghan wars and a

[2] Morris D. Morris, 'Towards a Re-interpretation of Nineteenth-Century Indian Economic History', *The Indian Economic and Social History Review*, Vol. V, No. 1, 1968, with responses by Toru Matsui, Bipan Chandra, and Tapan Raychaudhuri, and a rejoinder by Morris in *IESHR*, Vol. V, No. 4, 1968.

[3] Morris D. Morris, 'Values as an Obstacle to Economic Growth in South Asia: An historical survey', *Journal of Economic History*, Vol. XXVII, No. 4, 1967, pp. 588–607. For a survey of positions in the 'values' debate, also see Sanjay Subrahmanyam, 'Institutions, Agency and Economic Change in South Asia: A Survey and Some Suggestions', in Burton Stein and Sanjay Subrahmanyam, eds, *Institutions and Economic Change in South Asia*, Delhi, 1996, pp. 14–47.

[4] For a critical view of such extrapolations, see Kate Brittlebank, *Tipu Sultan's Search for Legitimacy: Islam and Kingship in a Hindu Domain*, Delhi, 1997.

[5] A version of this view is presented most recently in Irfan Habib, ed., *Confronting Colonialism: Resistance and Modernization under Haidar Ali and Tipu Sultan*, Delhi, 1999.

consequent Russian sphere of influence that extended well south of the Oxus. These scenarios all belong to a certain class of speculation, namely regarding the transformation of social and political outcomes that derive from changes in the sphere of military history.[6] The tradition in South Asian history has, however, shied away from what one may facetiously term 'CIA Counterfactual History', wherein the counterfactual operates on a hinge, which is simply the assassination of a leader, or the premature death of a genial inventor, or its converse—namely the assassination that fails. This may be the result of the strongly anti-Carlylean bias of most south Asian historians, who have been taught for at least three generations to shy away from the idea of history as made (or conversely unmade) by Great Men. This is combined, interestingly enough, with an assumption that we shall have occasion to examine later, namely that in the absence of colonial domination, south Asia would nevertheless have produced a modern state corresponding in terms of territorial extent with either post-1947 India, or with India, Pakistan, and Bangladesh combined. Other territorial outcomes are ruled out as a matter of habit.

This chapter will diverge deliberately from the received tradition of south Asian counterfactuals in many respects, but will nevertheless remain partly true to it, in so far as the counterfactual will hinge partially on a military event. Now, the location of counterfactual propositions on the battlefield has a certain appeal for various reasons. More often than not, the two sides engaged in a battle do not expect the same outcome, though a grand tradition of suicidal battles (wherein the losing side knows it is doomed from the start), is not entirely unknown. There is thus some appeal to taking a complex event that has the probabilistic structure of a chess game, and where there is a sharp divergence in terms of the subjective probabilistic expectation of the nature of outcomes for participants, as the basis for a counterfactual exercise; one has the impression that the historian comes somewhat closer here to seizing the spirit of participants in historical events and processes. No doubt such a conception has its share of illusion about it, but in the final analysis making a counterfactual is after all something of a conjuring act.

A Conqueror from Iran

And so on to our south Asian case. Consider the following piece of high diplomatic correspondence in the Persian language, written in, let us say, the mid-1740s from the city of Hyderabad in the Deccan to the Seat of the Sultanate

[6] See Robert Cowley, ed., *What If?: The World's Foremost Military Historians Imagine What Might Have Been*, New York, 1999; as also Robert Cowley, ed., *What If? 2: Eminent Historians Imagine What Might Have Been*, New York, 2001.

(*Dâr al-Saltanat*) at Delhi, and beginning with the usual *Bi-ismih il asma subhânahu* ('In the Name of the High and Awe-Inspiring').

Commander of the state (*mubâriz al-daula'*) and of exalted heights and fortune, may God strengthen the foundations of your state and height and fortune for ages together. May I present you this letter that carries caravans of prayers with pleasant fragrance, and people with rose-coloured praises. The purpose of this letter is to state the following: That earlier in Shawwal, the month with the mark of virtue and fortune, the sedition-mongering Franks (*fitnasâzân-i-firang*) of the port of Chinnapattan [Madras] had attempted by means of their ill-starred armies to interfere in the matters of the *wilâyat* of Arcot, and had even sent out a force to this end. Boasting of their claims from their ships that ply the circumscribing ocean (*darya-i muhît*), as well as those of Firang and Hind, they opposed the victory-laden armies that had been sent out from the feet of the throne that is the refuge of the Caliphate (*dar pâya-i sarîr khilâfat masîr*). Thus, many of the hat-wearers (*kulah-poshân*) met their doom and departed this life in accordance with the Qur'anic verse, 'No soul knoweth in what land it shall die' [Qur'an 31:34], as their souls were entrusted to the seizer of spirits in keeping with the saying, 'Wheresoever ye be, death will overtake you' [Qur'an 4:78]. Now, having witnessed the face of calamity (*hâdisa*), they have retreated within their fortress, and have pleaded for a new agreement (*shart-nâma*) to be signed with the court of the Caliphate (*dargah-i khilâfat panah*), in which they humbly state that they will walk the road of sincerity and return the territories around the said fortress that they had unjustly usurped from the *khâlisa*. We have informed them besides that in the event of their not complying, the Star of Greatness (*kaukabah-i a'zmat*) shall rise in the direction of their fort.[7]

Such a letter might have been written in, say, 1745 from Nizam al-Mulk Asaf Jah, semi-autonomous governor of Hyderabad, to his sovereign Nadir Shah Afshar, the ruler of a vast Sultanate extending east to west between Bengal and Iran, announcing that the forces of the English East India Company had received a bloody nose and been suitably chastised in their feeble attempts at territorial aggrandizement. But it was not.

Why not indeed, as the Serpent might have said to Eve? The present volume and its intellectual project invite us not only to explore the bylanes of the historical imagination in the so-called 'Cleopatra's Nose' mode (which, truth to tell, pales rather quickly for those who are not nasally fixated), but to ask under what possible combinations of economic, political, and institutional conditions, the relations between the West and the Rest might have been radically different from what they turned out to be in the late eighteenth and nineteenth centuries. My point of departure is ostensibly south Asia, but my story will also run rapidly into an examination of the situation in west Asia and central Asia in the period

---

[7] This letter should by rights be found in Arjun Jaishankar and Eduard Jayson Loman, eds, *Nâdir Shâh Afshâr: Majmû'a-i asnâd wa makâtabât tarîkhi hamrâ ba yâddâsht-ha-i tafsîli*, Malgudi, 1977, pp. 723–4.

that interests me. I posit a relatively small 'perturbation', to espouse the language of natural scientists, which might however have led to a shift, in terms of international political economy, of considerable consequence. I shall attempt here, first, to describe the context of the shift in question, then to address successively its primary and secondary consequences, focusing on the possible permanence of the ripple caused, as it were, in the pond of the historian. The point of departure must nevertheless be made clear, since it may not be shared by everyone (and in certain cases may also lead to the creation of false resemblances).[8] It is evident to me from my reading of the literature of the past decade, and my own research, that the English East India Company did not establish its political dominance over South Asia after 1750 because it possessed superior economic skills, or was in some evolutionary sense more advanced than the rest of the institutional field in which it found itself.[9] As late as 1770, when the conquest of Bengal was more or less complete, the impact of changes in the English manufacturing economy were yet to make themselves felt in terms of Britain's economic relationship to South Asia. Nor was it clear that the English had on offer a superior, or more stable, legal-institutional structure, which could hence seduce the unsuspecting native populace in south Asia by offering them security of property, and the means to progress and prosperity.[10] The reasons for the conquest of south Asia, and its subsequent 'pacification' which went on until the mid-nineteenth century (the so-called 'Mutiny' of 1857–8), must largely lie therefore in the military sphere, not in the narrowest sense of military technology, but in a somewhat larger context. This is why the question that I address here is one of state-building in its most basic configuration, having to do with the wielding of power, and the ability to win not only battles but sustained campaigns, both of a military and a non-military character.

[8] Thus, I believe that the exercise here differs quite substantially from the far more playful, and also largely 'micro-historic' attempt at 'experimental history' in Daniel S. Milo and Alain Boureau, eds, *Alter Histoire: Essais d'histoire expérimentale*, Paris, 1991.

[9] This is one of a number of themes treated in Sanjay Subrahmanyam, *Penumbral Visions: Making Polities in Early Modern South India*, Delhi, 2001. For rather more teleological readings than mine, see C. A. Bayly, *Empire and Information: Intelligence Gathering and Social Communication in India, 1780–1870*, Cambridge, 1997, and Eugene F. Irschick, *Dialogue and History: Constructing South India, 1795–1895*, Berkeley, 1995. Irschick's work is in many respects a mere refinement of Robert E. Frykenberg, *Guntur District, 1788–1848: A History of Local Influence and Central Authority in South India*, Oxford, 1965.

[10] Cf. the rather futile debate between Peter van der Veer, 'The Global History of "Modernity"', *Journal of the Economic and Social History of the Orient*, Vol. XLI, No. 3, 1998, pp. 285–94, and David Washbrook, 'The Global History of 'Modernity'— A Response to a Reply', *JESHO*, Vol. XLI, No. 3, 1998, pp. 296–311.

On 5 January 1739, Joseph-François Dupleix, later to prove that he was no slouch himself in matters of empire-building, wrote from the Bengal town of Chandernagore (where he was appointed to direct commercial affairs by the French East India Company) to the Controller-General of the same Company:

We are on the eve of a great revolution in this empire. The conqueror from Persia, Thamas Coulikan, who also titles himself Nader Cha or Vely Moamet, has entered Indostan. After having taken Candahar, and forced his way through the most difficult routes, it is said that he is near Delhy. The weakness of the Mogol government gives ample grounds to believe that he may very soon be master of this empire. This revolution, if it takes place, can only cause a great disturbance (*un grand dérangement*) to trade. However, it is believed that it can only be advantageous to Europeans, to whom it is said this conqueror accords importance.[11]

Who in fact was Dupleix writing of, as the author of this *grande révolution*, that was imminently to shake up South Asia, and more particularly the Mughal empire? Tahmasp Quli Khan (1698–1747), the object of his attention, was born Nadir Quli Beg, son of Imam Quli Beg, and belonged (according to contemporary Persian sources) to the commoners of the city of Abiward in Iran.[12] In some versions, his father was a member of the humble community of furriers (*pustin-dost*). Brought up initially in a life of indigence, he was adopted by his step father Baba 'Ali Beg, who was head of an Afshar Turk group in that city. Having first imposed himself on his adoptive clan (*ulûs*), who numbered some 40 households, as their leader, Nadir then became the local governor (*ambardâr*) of Abiward, and thereafter rose to higher and higher positions.[13]

[11] Archives Nationales [hereafter AN], Paris, Archives du Ministère des Colonies [hereafter AMC], Correspondance Générale, C^2 76, fl. 221v. On Dupleix, no really satisfactory modern study exists. But see, Alfred Martineau, *Dupleix et l'Inde française*, 4 Vols, Paris, 1920–8; also Marc Vigié, *Dupleix*, Paris, 1993.

[12] For the main contemporary sources by Iranian chroniclers, see Mirza Muhammad Mahdi Astarabadi, *Târîkh-i-Jahângushâ-yi Nâdirî*, ed. 'Abd al-'Ali Borumand, Tehran, 1370/1991; also Muhammad Kazim, *Nâma-yi Âlam-ârâ-yi Nâdirî*, 3 Vols, Moscow, 1960–6. Muhammad Mahdi's chronicle was translated into French already in the eighteenth century; cf. William Jones, tr., *Histoire de Nader Chah, connu sous le nom de Thahmas Kuli Khan, Empereur de Perse*, 2 Vols, London, 1770.

[13] A useful complement to the Iranian chroniclers is the text of Khwaja 'Abd al-Karim ibn Khwaja 'Aqibat Mahmud Kashmiri (or Shahristani), *Bayân-i Wâqi': A Biography of Nâdir Shâh Afshâr and the Travels of the Author*, ed. K. B. Nasim, Lahore, 1970. An early translation is that of Francis Gladwin, *The memoirs of Khojeh Abdulkurreem, a Cashmerian of distinction who accompanied Nadir Shah (...): including the history of Hindostan, from AD 1739 to 1749*, Calcutta, 1788), but it excludes much of the biographical sections on Nadir Shah.

This was the time of the decline of the Safavid dynasty in Iran, and the moment of the temporary rise of the Khalji Afghans from Qandahar to power there.[14] In the 1720s, one of these Afghan warlords, Mahmud Khan (later, Mahmud Shah) laid siege to the Safavid capital of Isfahan, until the relatively weak garrison within surrendered, so that the Safavid Sultan Husain was comprehensively defeated. Plunder, looting, and massacres followed in the heartland of Iran, which contemporary observers portray as a result of the Afghans' narrow sectarian religious prejudices (ta'assub-i mazhab). The Safavid Shah was nevertheless forced to approach Mahmud Khan, and negotiate with him, so that eventually the latter entered Isfahan in triumph, and became the ruler of Iran.[15]

Seen at a more schematic level, a broader shift underlay the emergence of the Khalji Afghans in Iran. In the course of the sixteenth century, a four-part political equilibrium had gradually emerged in the vast space extending from Hindustan via Transoxania and the Iranian plateau, to Anatolia. The western end of the quadrilateral was largely dominated by the Ottomans, who first under Yavuz Sultan Selim (1512–20), and then Sultan Süleyman (1520–66), had come to extend their dominance as far as Baghdad and Basra, besides controlling a good part of the Red Sea littoral. However, from about the 1540s onwards, Ottoman expansionism was clearly unable to make much further headway eastwards, despite a number of costly campaigns and temporary victories.[16] Their opponents to the east were above all the Safavids, a dynasty that had seized power in the closing years of the fifteenth century (and which was thus of far more recent origin, as a political power, than the Ottomans themselves). In their first dynastic phase, extending to the 1520s, Safavid power seems largely to have depended on a particular form of charismatic authority, with the Shah himself being at the head of a Sufi order, and regarded as an infallible, messianic, even invincible, chief.[17] Gradually, however, as the sixteenth century wore on,

---

[14] For an interesting, if minor, source on the period of Shah Husain, see Jean Aubin, ed., L'ambassade de Gregório Pereira Fidalgo Ja cour de Châh Soltân-Hosseyn, 1696–1697, Lisbon, 1971.

[15] For political details, see Laurence Lockhart, Nadir Shah, London, 1938, brought up-to-date in Peter Avery, 'Nâdir Shâh and the Afsharid legacy', in Peter Avery, Gavin Hambly, and Charles Melville, eds, The Cambridge History of Iran, Vol. 7 (From Nadir Shah to the Islamic Republic), Cambridge, 1991, pp. 3–62.

[16] Cf. Salih Özbaran, The Ottoman Response to European Expansion: Studies on Ottoman-Portuguese Relations in the Indian Ocean and Ottoman Administration in the Arab Lands during the Sixteenth Century, Istanbul, 1994); also the useful if problematic discussion in Palmira Brummett, Ottoman Seapower and Levantine Diplomacy in the Age of Discovery, Albany, 1994.

[17] Cf. the important study by Jean Aubin, 'L'avènement des Safavides reconsidéré (Etudes safavides III)', Moyen Orient et Océan Indien, No. 5, 1988, pp. 1–130, to be read

power became routinized and anchored in institutions other than the Turkoman tribesmen who had first brought the Safavids to power. The old bureaucratic tradition of the towns re-established itself, and fiscal resources were marshalled somewhat more systematically in order to permit a viable military system, using both mercenaries and levies.[18] This form of state is clearly visible in the last years of the sixteenth century (under Shah 'Abbas I), and in the early years of the century that followed. Yet, even though their control of the Iranian plateau remained secure, the Safavids were largely unable to transform their core state into a truly expansive empire.[19] Their frontiers with the Ottomans remained mostly stable after the mid-sixteenth century as noted above (despite disputes over the control of towns such as Tabriz), and their neighbours further east— the Mughals—also allowed them limited room for manoeuvre. The major areas left open were, on the one hand, Armenia and Daghestan, and on the other, the marches leading into Transoxania. The Persian Gulf was another possible sphere of expansionary operation, though Safavid ambitions there were specific and rather limited.

It was in Transoxania (Mawarannahr, in Persian usage), that the third, and most unstable, of the four great polities of our quadrilateral was formed by the so-called Shaibanid lineage and its offshoots, descended from Muhammad Shaibani Khan (1451–1510). These Sultans of Sunni persuasion (unlike the Safavids, who became rather fervent, and even violent, Twelver Shi'ites) had emerged into prominence by expelling the main political contenders descended from Tëmur from Central Asia, and managed to hold together a relatively significant polity, centring on such towns as Balkh, Samarqand, Tashkent, and Bukhara, until the first quarter of the seventeenth century. Even at the best of times, however, this so-called 'Uzbek' polity was subject to alternating processes of fission and fusion, largely mediated through its complex system of appanages.[20] The most successful phase of centralization appears to have been in the last quarter of the sixteenth century, under 'Abdullah Khan (d. 1598), who

---

together with Aubin, 'Révolution chiite et conservatisme: Les soufis de Lâhejân, 1500–14 (Etudes safavides II)', *Moyen Orient et Océan Indien*, No. 1, 1984, pp. 1–40.

[18] Cf. Jean Aubin, 'Etudes safavides I: Shâh Ismâ'îl et les notables de l'Iraq persan', *Journal of the Economic and Social History of the Orient*, Vol. II, No. 1, 1959, pp. 37–81.

[19] See the important discussion in Kathryn Babayan, 'The Waning of the Qizilbash: The Temporal and the Spiritual in Seventeenth-Century Iran', Princeton University, Ph.D. dissertation, 1993; also the schematic reconsideration in John Foran, 'The long fall of the Safavi dynasty: Moving beyond the standard views', *International Journal of Middle East Studies*, 24, 2, 1992, pp. 281–304.

[20] Cf. *inter alia*, Richard C. Foltz, *Mughal India and Central Asia*, Karachi, 1998, and R. D. McChesney, *Central Asia: Foundations of Change*, Princeton, 1996.

annexed a good part of Khorasan from the Safavids, and Badakhshan from the Mughals, but also reunified otherwise divided appanages within the Uzbek fold. A series of bloody struggles followed his death, eventually leading to the emergence of a bicephalous state, centering on Balkh and Bukhara. This model of divided state power (with brief intervals, in which attempts at reunification were made), persisted into the latter part of the seventeenth century, and was, if anything, exacerbated further in the early eighteenth century after the death in 1702 of Subhan Quli Khan. Nevertheless, it is noteworthy that in the seventeenth century, the Transoxanian polities were still vigorous enough to resist external aggression, as we see from the case of the Mughal campaign against Balkh in the 1650s.

The fourth corner of our rather lopsided quadrilateral is defined then by the Mughals, a dynasty of Timurid and Chinggiskhanid descent, which had opportunistically seized power in north India in the mid-1520s after being expelled from Transoxania. In the course of the sixteenth century, Mughal power consolidated itself over the rich alluvial plains of the Indus and the Ganges (in the area called Hindustan in the epoch), and eventually began to make substantial inroads down the Indian peninsula. Despite some limited territorial adventures against the Uzbeks (as noted above), and the Safavids (centring above all on the fortress of Qandahar and other parts of what is today Afghanistan), the balance of power in the Mughal north-west remained broadly stable, once the Mughals under Akbar (1556–1605) had eliminated the rival Mughal polity centerd at Kabul in the 1580s. The two open frontiers for the Mughals were, to a limited extent, the east and north-east (extending into northern Burma, and the Brahmaputra valley), and above all the south, where Mughal aggrandizement continued until the eighteenth century.[21]

The four polities described rapidly above were rivals, to be sure, but also shared significant elements in common. They were all influenced in good measure by the Persian and Persianate culture that had been a pole of attraction since the beginning of the first millennium CE. A common vocabulary of statecraft had gradually been hammered out, in the violent synthesis provoked by the irruption of the Mongol polity first into south-central Asia, and then parts of Iran, in the early centuries of the second millennium CE. The four polities described above thus patronized similar elites, appreciated similar poetry and calligraphy, and thus permitted the circulation across this considerable space of poets, divines, architects, specialists on legal questions, and warriors-on-hire. Thus, a poet and musician from Samarqand could find himself welcomed in the 1620s in the court of the Mughal emperor, Jahangir, and might immediately be

---

[21] For a general consideration, see Muzaffar Alam and Sanjay Subrahmanyam, eds, *The Mughal State, 1526–1750*, Delhi, 1998.

able to accede to the courtly discourse of the Mughals, even if it was not exactly the same as in Central Asia.[22]

Nevertheless, we should be aware that these four polities were rather unequally constituted. The Ottomans and the Mughals by about 1600 clearly commanded the most immediate prestige, and also the greatest financial and human resources. The Mughal domains were the most populated (about three times the Ottomans, at a rough guess), and state revenues here were also the greatest of the four. The circulation of elites thus tended to be asymmetric: more Iranians gravitated towards Mughal India and the Ottoman state, than the other way around.[23] At the same time, Iran (or 'Ajam) had a greater accumulated historical prestige from Sassanid times, and Transoxania too boasted centres (such as Bukhara or Samarqand) that had an enormous long-term significance, both in religious and more general cultural terms.

In the eighteenth century, the situation we have described above was challenged in fair measure by the re-emergence of a fifth political centre that had long been used as a military resource by some of the others, namely Afghanistan.[24] It was from a base in Afghanistan that the early Delhi Sultanate had been constituted in the twelfth century, first through the activities of the polity centred at Ghazna, then through the activities of the Mamluks and free tribesmen dependent on the Mu'izzi state at Ghur. However, the consolidation of the Sultanate at Delhi by the middle decades of the thirteenth century shifted the centre of gravity, rendering Afghanistan 'marginal' in this scheme of things. Afghan groups then gravitated periodically to the centre of the Sultanate, at times successfully seizing power there, as was the case of the Lodis in the fifteenth century.[25] But once the Mughals were well-established in north India, they made it a point to crush any opposition from the Kabul and Qandahar regions, dealing in a ruthless fashion, for example, with the so-called Raushaniyya movement in the late sixteenth and early seventeenth centuries, and also showing little sympathy for the religious opposition that centred around Khushhal Khan Khatak in the mid-seventeenth century.

[22] Cf. *Khâtirât-i-Mutribî Samarqandî (being the Memoirs of Mutribi's sessions with Emperor Jahangir)*, ed. Abdul Ghani Mirzoyef, Karachi, 1977; English translation by Richard C. Foltz, *Conversations with the Emperor Jahangir by 'Mutribi' al-Asamm Samarqandi*, Costa Mesa, 1998.

[23] Cf. the analysis in Sanjay Subrahmanyam, 'Iranians Abroad: Intra-Asian elite migration and early modern state formation', *The Journal of Asian Studies*, Vol. LI, (2), May 1992, pp. 340–62.

[24] Cf. Jos J. L. Gommans, *The Rise of the Indo-Afghan Empire, c. 1710–1780*, Leiden, 1995.

[25] On these, and related, questions, see D. H. A. Kolff, *Naukar, Rajput and Sepoy: The ethnohistory of the military labour market in Hindustan, 1450–1850*, Cambridge, 1990.

In sum, so long as the imperial power that controlled Hindustan was strong, the north-western periphery had little chance of asserting itself. But this state of affairs changed in the late decades of the seventeenth century, and the beginning of the eighteenth century, as the Mughal state began to assume a rather modified character. Now, these changes, often defined under the rather broad head of Mughal 'decline', have been the subject of great controversy in the past two decades. Before that, two modes of explanation tended to dominate. One, which reflected the Whiggish historiographical preferences of the nineteenth and early twentieth centuries, tended to see Mughal 'decline' as a matter of lack of character where the rulers were concerned. Lacking the 'right stuff' from which great emperors like Akbar and Shahjahan were made, it was argued that the later Mughal princes were molly-coddled in the harem, given to debauchery, excessively fond of music and the arts, and thus incapable of being the vigorous warrior-leaders that such an empire required. In presenting such an analysis, historians delved into the writings of chroniclers from the early eighteenth century, who often were crushingly contemptuous in their judgements of rulers such as Muhammad Shah (1719–48).[26] Later historians, often of a Marxist bent of mind, shied away from such personality-oriented explanations, and instead presented early eighteenth-century Mughal 'decline' in systemic terms, stemming from what they termed a great 'agrarian crisis' of the late seventeenth century.[27] This crisis, so they argued, derived in turn from the over-exploitation of the peasantry by the fiscal apparatus that the Mughals had developed in the late sixteenth century. While remarkably sophisticated for its time, this apparatus was, in the view of historians such as Irfan Habib and Athar Ali, eventually destined to grind the productive apparatus into the dust (killing the goose that laid the golden eggs, as it were).[28] The system of revenue assignments (*jâgîrdâri*) was symptomatic of a fiscal structure that was more concerned with short-term benefits to the surplus class, than with improving the productivity of the peasant economy in the longer term. Thus, these authors argued, from the last years of the seventeenth century, and the reign of Aurangzeb-

---

[26] For a minor example in this genre, see Anon., *Wâqi'ah-i Kharâbî-yi Dehlî dar 'ahd-i Muhammad Shâh az wurûd-i Nâdir Shâh wâlî-yi Irân*, ed. Sharif Husain Qasemi, Delhi, 1990.

[27] For a compromise between the two approaches, see Zahir Uddin Malik, *The Reign of Muhammad Shah: 1719–1748*, Bombay, 1977.

[28] M. Athar Ali, M., 'The Passing of Empire: The Mughal Case', *Modern Asian Studies*, Vol. IX, No. 3, 1975, pp. 385–96; also Athar Ali, 'Recent Theories of Eighteenth-Century India', *Indian Historical Review*, Vol. XIII, Nos 1–2, 1986–7; Irfan Habib, *The Agrarian System of Mughal India (1556–1707)*, Bombay, 1963, and Habib, 'Potentialities of capitalistic development in the economy of Mughal India', *The Journal of Economic History*, Vol. XXIX, No. 1, 1969, pp. 32–78.

'Alamgir (r. 1658–1707), the Mughal agrarian economy entered into a downward spiral, with peasant revolts following one another in rapid succession.[29]

More recent work casts serious doubt on this analysis. It is less and less clear that the agrarian economy of northern India had entered a crisis of productivity in the early eighteenth century. Rather, it would seem that conflicts had begun to brew between sections of the high Mughal elite, and an entrenched interme- diary class of rural gentry (the *zamîndârs*), who resented the attempts of the central authority to penetrate into the rural areas, gathering information and making up detailed cadasters, as well as attempting to regulate matters that had hitherto been within the autonomous domain of local or regional decision- making. Faced with the centralizing ambitions of the late seventeenth-century Mughal state, resentful *zamîndârs* thus attempted alliances with some parts of the upper elite against others, making use of the ever-present potential for factional conflict along 'ethnic' or sectarian lines that existed among the grandees (*umarâ'*) of the court.[30] Over a period of several decades, and by about 1720, this eventually led to a process of decentralization. New regional polities began to form under the still-present carapace of Mughal sovereignty, of which the cases of Awadh (in northern India), Bengal, and Hyderabad (in the Deccan), are the most flagrant. Central Mughal armies, sometimes led by princes of the blood, were still powerful enough to settle succession disputes or prosecute expansion in marginal zones, but they were simply unable to bring provincial governors (who in turn were allied to regional and local power-brokers) to book. A particularly spectacular case of this logic is that of Chin Qilich Khan, later to be known as Nizam al-Mulk Asaf Jah (d. 1748).[31] As a powerful and well- connected member of the Mughal nobility (whose father had already been a prominent member of the Mughal aristocracy), Nizam al-Mulk seems to have attempted to exercise various options within central Mughal politics (as a great Turani *amîr*), before deciding in the 1720s that his only avenue was the creation of a regional polity. It was in these circumstances that he entered definitively into the Deccan, and after 1724, made the city of Hyderabad the centre of his extensive operations. If on the one hand, he negotiated from Hyderabad with the Mughal court and with neighbouring political structures (such as the Marathas), on the other hand, he deftly controlled developments to the south, in Mysore and Arcot. This balancing act was rewarded with great success into the late 1740s,

[29] It is also useful in this context to consult Satish Chandra, *Parties and Politics at the Mughal Court, 1707–1740*, 3rd edn, New Delhi, 1979.

[30] See the important work by Muzaffar Alam, *The Crisis of Empire in Mughal North India: Awadh and the Punjab, 1707–1748*, Delhi, 1986.

[31] Cf. Yusuf Husain, *The First Nizam: Life and Times of Nizam-ul-mulk, Asaf Jah I*, 2nd edn, Bombay, 1963.

and only then began to crumble, above all under the onslaught of the demands of European *arrivistes*, based in the coastal enclaves of south-eastern India.

As for the Mughal north-west, as late as 1720, the region, notionally under the charge of the Mughal governors of the Punjab remained relatively quiet, even though central Punjab itself witnessed considerable unrest with the early attempts by Sikh *zamîndârs* to claim greater autonomy, culminating in the important but unsuccessful rebellion led by Banda Bahadur. In contrast, as we have briefly seen earlier, the Safavid state proved far more fragile in the period, and was unable (unlike the Mughals) to contain problems by renegotiating political and institutional arrangements with regional satraps. Perhaps the smaller scale of the Safavid state was the major disadvantage here; at any rate, problems in the frontier zone around Qandahar proved impossible to contain, and worked their way rapidly to the political centre. As the Khalji Afghans seized control of the political centre, other regional leaders too made a bid for power. Among them was a certain Malik Mahmud Sistani, governor of the province of Nimroz, who—taking advantage of the the dominance of the Afghans, the imprisonment of Shah Sultan Husain, and the confusion in the cities of Khorasan—arrived in Mashhad in about 1723 and declared himself autonomous ruler. Most of the cities of Khorasan, which were not yet under Afghan control, came under that of Malik Mahmud, and Nadir Quli Beg too saw this as an opportunity. Leaving Abiward, he arrived in Mashhad to join the service of Malik Mahmud, and within a few years soon rose up in favour. However, Nadir's obvious ambitions led to conflicts between the two, forcing Nadir Quli then to resort, for a time, to a sort of social banditry in the area around Mashhad. Malik Mahmud now grew uneasy, and attempted to re-engage Nadir Quli in his service, but to no avail. Instead, Nadir managed to make common cause with Shah Tahmasp (son of the deposed Sultan Husain Safavi) who had earlier fled Isfahan and taken refuge in Mazandaran. Together, they then defeated Malik Mahmud Sistani, captured and killed him; thus, his territories came into the control of the surviving Safavid prince. In appreciation of this, Nadir Quli was appointed *qurchi-bâshi* and given the title of Tahmasp Quli Khan under the restored Safavid dispensation.

A complex phase now follows, with a series of battles between Shah Tahmasp and the Afghans, the defeat of the latter, and the death in battle of Ashraf Shah, cousin and successor of Mahmud Shah Khalji. After a gap of seven years, the Safavids thus returned fully to power, and the power of Nadir Quli, now titled *sipah-sâlâr* and *mîr-i-shamshîr* and a major military commander, grew apace. His next set of activities brought him into conflict with the Ottomans; for once the battles with Ashraf Shah in Fars were over, Tahmasp Quli clashed with the Pasha of Hamadan and the Ottoman armies. His efficiency as a military commander increased over this phase, as did his reputation for near-invincibility, as he managed to wrest control over the territories of Iraq from the Ottomans, who retreated to Baghdad. Shah Tahmasp now grew increasingly uneasy in respect of Tahmasp Quli Khan, who had meanwhile moved towards Azarbaijan, captured Tabriz from the Ottomans, and brought the lands south of the river Ars into his control.[32] Thereafter, he signed a truce with the Ottomans, and returned to Khorasan, where he defeated local rebel Turkomans, as well as the Abdali Afghans. By now, Tahmasp Quli was on the lookout for allies, and he managed in the aftermath of this campaign to incorporate the Abdalis into his army, and then returned to Mashhad and the Safavid court.

It was only a matter of time before this *éminence grise* showed his hand. It is interesting to note, though, that Tahmasp Quli proceeded in stages. First, he forced the Shah to abdicate, and to place his two-month old son on the throne. At around the same time, Tahmasp Quli Khan had married the sister of Shah Sultan Husain, and he thereafter went on to marry off the daughter of Sultan Husain (and sister of Shah Tahmasp) to his older son Riza Quli Khan. Having cemented his own legitimacy through such alliances, he also took care to place his own chosen men as governors of all the provinces of Iran, before returning to fight the Ottomans around Baghdad.

These campaigns, as also others against the Baluch and the natives of Daghestan, were once more broadly successful, with the Ottoman governor of Baghdad being obliged to retreat within the town's fort. Eventually, after a siege, the old part of Baghdad fell into Iranian hands. Relief forces arrived from Anatolia under the celebrated Topal Osman Pasha, who had been a well-known Ottoman commander on the European front, and on this one occasion, the forces commanded by Tahmasp Quli met a reverse, as he was obliged to retreat to Hamadan from Baghdad in order to regroup. Then, in a second encounter, the Qizilbash (or 'Red-Caps', the soldiers under Tahmasp Quli's command), managed to overcome the Ottomans, and forced them to retreat to Kaikuk. Topal Osman Pasha himself was killed in this campaign, and the leaderless Ottoman army fell apart.

With this decisive victory, in 1733, against an enemy still possessing great prestige, Tahmasp Quli Khan's position was considerably strengthened. For one, chroniclers report that he amassed limitless wealth, though in a brilliant act of propaganda, he also set fire to a good part of the loot that had been gathered, to show his own contempt for the alleged softness of the Ottomans. Meanwhile, news from Iran arrived that Muhammad Khan Baloch, governor of Fars, had imprisoned the agents of Tahmasp Quli, and was planning to capture Isfahan and eastern Iraq, and also deliver the deposed and imprisoned Shah Tahmasp from captivity. Tahmasp Quli Khan grew anxious at this, and consulted his generals; he eventually had to sign a peace treaty with Ahmad Pasha at

---

[32] Khwaja 'Abd al-Karim, *Bayân-i Wâqi'*, p. 13.

Baghdad, and rush back to Fars. Here, he confronted the powerful army of Muhammad Khan, based at Shiraz. Accounts suggest that Muhammad Khan's army was larger and better supplied, but that the very news of the arrival of Tahmasp Quli spread terror, causing the opposing army to scatter overnight. Muhammad Khan thus found himself in the morning with only 3000 men, and had to flee the battlefield towards Lar. Shiraz fell into the hands of Tahmasp Quli, and he once more got the better of a dangerous rival.

The Defeat at Karnal

Chroniclers and newsletter-writers of the period, whether writing in Persian or in European languages, are near-unanimous by the mid-1730s in portraying Tahmasp Quli Khan as a sort of irresistible force. If, on the one hand, they refer to his military efficiency and tactical mastery, they also speak of his calculated use of terror, in which he resembles Tëmur (without however resorting to the celebrated pyramids of skulls of the fourteenth-century conqueror).[33] In the case of one of his opponents, Muhammad Khan Baloch, for instance, he was eventually captured alive, tortured, and had both his eyes gouged out with a knife. On being imprisoned, it is reported that Muhammad Khan knew he would only have a worse fate thereafter, and so killed himself the same night.

Tahmasp Quli Khan's military mastery is demonstrated not only in his successful campaigns against the Ottomans (no mean fighting force even in the late 1720s or early 1730s), but also in his campaigns in Armenia and Georgia. Having overcome both his internal and external enemies, he could now aspire at last to the throne. In order to do this, we are aware that he convoked an assembly of various Iranian notables, chiefs, and elders at the plain of Mughan, and having executed two of them publicly, left them with little choice but to ask him to get rid of the fiction of Safavid sovereignty. Tahmasp Quli Khan, of course, had his marital link with the Safavids to assure his notional legitimacy, but he also made it a point to prepare a *mahzar* (a document to be signed by a sort of 'popular' assembly), stating that he was consenting to take on this responsibility only on the insistence of the people. The chiefs were asked to put their seals on the *mahzar*, and he then assumed the throne. These events may be traced to 1736 (or 1148 AH).[34]

It was now that Nadir Shah (the title that Tahmasp Quli Khan assumed) could get on with larger projects. In order to do so, he first arranged matters with the

[33] See, for instance, Jean Aubin, 'Comment Tamerlan prenait les villes', *Studia Islamica*, No. 19, 1963, pp. 83–122.

[34] Khwaja 'Abd al-Karim, *Bayân-i Wâqi'*, pp. 21–2. Contrast Jones, tr., *Histoire de Nader Chah*, Vol. I, pp. 355–65.

Ottomans and Georgia, and only then turned his attention to Qandahar to settle with the Ghilzai Afghans. With an army of 80,000 men, Nadir crossed the mountains to Qandahar, setting out from Iran in November 1736.[35] Nadir Shah's gaze was clearly turned eastward by now, to the Indo-Gangetic plain, and his first (and characteristically methodical) step was to consolidate his situation in Afghanistan through the construction of a new town, which he named Nadirabad, in the vicinity of Qandahar fort (which was totally razed after it fell in March 1738). We are now on the eve of the expeditions to Hindustan.

A *casus belli* was soon found in order to declare war on the Mughals, namely that they were aiding and sheltering rebel Afghans. Nadir Shah thus sent an ambassador, Muhammad 'Ali Khan Afshar to the court of Muhammad Shah at Delhi, but no clear response was forthcoming. When it became clear that matters would advance no further, Nadir Shah decided to leave Qandahar for Kabul. Sharza Khan, commander of Kabul tried, to resist him with some of the townsmen and *mansabdârs*, but a lack of war material and the absence of assistance led him to strike a bargain for his own life and that of the townsmen. He thus handed the fort over to Nadir Shah, preserving his life and goods. Meanwhile, Nadir's son Riza Quli Mirza was summoned from Balkh, and appointed deputy ruler of Iran (*nâ'ib al-saltanat*) in his father's absence. Having thus secured matters on the home front, Nadir Shah inspected his army, left behind the injured and the infirm, and proceeded towards Peshawar. The Mughal governor of Kabul, Peshawar, and Ghazna, who was resident at Peshawar, came out to fight, but his army was routed while he himself was wounded, and fell into the hands of the Qizilbash.

We are now in late 1738, and it was only at this stage that the Mughal emperor and his principal nobles seem to have begun to suspect the plans of Nadir Shah. They set about belatedly preparing for war, and the emperor decided to join forces with the great regional power-holders such as Nizam al-Mulk Asaf Jah from Hyderabad (one of the leaders of the so-called Turani faction in Mughal politics, as noted earlier), and also asked the main court-notables such as Khan-i-Dauran and Qamar al-Din Khan to exert themselves.[36] Again, Burhan al-Mulk, governor of Awadh, was asked to arrive as soon as possible at the court. For his part, Nadir Shah, having settled matters in Peshawar, moved from there towards Lahore in early January 1739. Zakariya Khan, governor of Lahore, apparently felt unable to face Nadir Shah, and on the advice of his companions and officials, submitted to the invader, and thus saved his city from attack. Nadir Shah entered Lahore, amassed 2 million rupees in cash, and from that town set

[35] Peter Avery, 'Nâdir Shâh and the Afsharid legacy', pp. 37–8.

[36] For Khan-i-Dauran, see Zahir Uddin Malik, *A Mughal Statesman of the Eighteenth Century: Khan-i Dauran, Mir Bakhshi of Muhammad Shah, 1719–1739*, Bombay, 1973.

out soon thereafter for the Mughal capital of Shajahanabad-Delhi. To cite the French East India Company reports of the period:

While Nadercha extended his conquests in the Indies, Mametcha basked in Delhi in the fullest of security, either on account of the little knowledge that was given to him of his affairs, or because a false notion of his own power made him consider the King of Persia as an enemy who was little to be feared. The news of the fall of Lahore awoke him from his lethargy, and threw the court in Dely, and the people, into the deepest throes of discouragement. Still, preparations were made with one of the most powerful armies in terms of men which have ever been heard of, to oppose Nadercha, who advanced rapidly towards that city.[37]

As the mammoth Mughal armies for their part began to advance towards the north-west, the plain of Karnal, at some distance from Shahjahanabad, was fixed as the potential battleground. The battle itself, on 24 February 1739, turned out to be something of an anti-climax. The Mughal forces were disunited, and in disarray despite their great numerical strength, Burhan al-Mulk having arrived belatedly from Awadh.[38] The main brunt of the fighting on the Mughal side was taken on by Khan-i Dauran and by Burhan al-Mulk, the latter atop an elephant and with 4000 horsemen and about 1000 foot-soldiers. Observers noted though that the Awadh army had taken about a month to travel to Karnal, and that the soldiers seemed to have lost the habit of campaigning; at least one sarcastic contemporary stated besides, that the Mughal soldiers were also anxious to preserve their horses, as their employment depended on them. Initially, the Qizilbash beat a tactical retreat, but then regrouped and attacked. In the Mughal camp, confusion prevailed as some of the major commanders declared that combat was not appropriate on that day. At length, it was decided that since Nizam al-Mulk Asaf Jah was the most accomplished amongst them all in combat, the overall charge should be assigned to him. This was despite the fact that his loyalty was in doubt, since he had left 50,000 men behind in the Deccan, and had come north with only 3000 men. Asaf Jah now advised Muhammad Shah that since Burhan al-Mulk had repeatedly asked for aid, and since Khan-i Dauran was in charge of the right wing, he should go to his aid on the northern front. Khan-i Dauran accordingly rushed to the battlefield in consonance with the imperial order, but without having fully prepared his troops. He was a popular commander, and so many people followed him despite the inadequate preparation, ready to lose their lives. Eight to nine thousand horsemen collected to go along.

Nadir Shah, for his part, had assigned the left wing to Fath 'Ali Khan and Lutf 'Ali Khan, while the middle was in charge of Nasrullah Mirza. He himself, with 4000 horsemen and *jazâ'irchi* (heavy musketeers), descended on the

---

[37] AN, AMC, Correspondance Générale, C² 76: fls 181–98, citation on fls 183–83v.
[38] Khwaja 'Abdul Karim, *Bayân-i Wâqi'*, p. 26.

battlefield. It thus turned out that the two Mughal *amîrs*, Khan-i Dauran and Burhan al-Mulk were left to fight against the ruler of Iran, with his musketeers and his 27,000 experienced Qizilbash horsemen, while the Mughal commanders had neither aid, nor proper artillery, nor adequate muskets. A contemporary chronicler, Khwaja 'Abd al-Karim Sharistani writes of this engagement:

Perhaps the other nobles thought that after the death of these two, they would emerge to meet the enemy. At any rate, despite the small size of the Mughal army, the absence of an arsenal and overall bad strategy and arrangement of the forces, the army of Hindustan fought with bravery. But one cannot fight musket-balls with arrows.[39]

Matters are described in a similar manner by French Company reports, in turn based on the despatches of a certain Joseph Devolton, a French deserter and 'doctor', who was in Mughal service in these years.[40] Here then is their description of the forces that came face to face in the battle of Karnal in February 1739:

[The army] of Mametcha [Muhammad Shah] according to the first letters of Seigneur Voulton and the Persian newsletters, which are nearly unanimous, was of two hundred thousand horsemen, and five hundred thousand foot soldiers or infantry (*fantassins*), besides five thousand war-elephants. The artillery was proportionate to the size of this army, it was made up of seven thousand cannon, or *fauconnaux*, but if one is to follow the last letter sent by Seigneur Voulton, this army was even stronger, [for] he estimates it at four hundred thousand horse, seven to eight hundred thousand foot-soldiers, ten thousand cannon, two thousand war-elephants, and thirty thousand camels, on the back of which is mounted a sort of falconet (*fauconneau*).[41]

In sum, we are dealing with a vast Mughal army, 200,000 (or even as many as 400,000) horsemen, some 500,000 (or perhaps 700,000–800,000) foot-soldiers, and very large numbers of elephants and artillery. Contrasted with this is the tightly disciplined force of Nadir Shah.

The army of Nadercha was made up of no more than eighty-thousand horsemen, one part of them Caselbatches [Qizilbash] and Georgians, twenty thousand infantry-men, two

---

[39] The account by Khwaja 'Abd al-Karim, *Bayân-i Wâqi'*, though partly apologistic, is nevertheless useful. Compare Jones, *Histoire de Nader Chah*, Vol. I, pp. 441–52.

[40] Joseph Devolton was born at Saint-Amand, in Bar-le-Duc; he was married to Jeanne Tarabillon at Pondicherry on 3 November 1729. In 1736, he was employed by the governor Benoît Dumas as an intermediary with the Mughals. Earlier, he had been a French soldier, but had deserted the Pondicherry garrison. In November 1740, he was pardoned by the Company in consideration for his actions after his desertion. He was still at the Mughal court in 1744, and appears to have ended his life at Kotah. Cf. Laurence Lockhart, 'De Voulton's Not-icia', *Bulletin of the School of Oriental Studies*, Vol. IV, No. 2, 1926–8, pp. 223–46.

[41] AN, AMC, Correspondance Générale, C² 76, fls 184– 84v.

hundred and fifty piece of field-cannon and twelve pieces of sizeable artillery; but these troops were determined, war-hardened, and led by a chief who knew how to manoeuvre them properly.

The army of Mametcha on the other hand had no one at its head, the Generals were divided amongst themselves, the soldiers brought together in haste, without discipline, and so dispirited that a single horseman from the army of Nadercha, whom the Persian newsletters term *Loutchis* would make a thousand horsemen of Mametcha tremble, for they were unprepared for the very appearance of these *Loutchis*. They have a cap on their heads that is a foot and a half tall, covered with sheepskin, with a woollen dress in the Hungarian style (*à la heiduc*), culottes, and leather boots, they are armed with a sabre, a matchlock (*un fuzil à meiche*) and a hatchet.[42]

Devolton then drives his point home, contrasting the disciplined and highly organized and experienced fighting force of Nadir Shah with that of the Mughals.

The army of Nadercha had both food-supplies and munitions in abundance. That of Mametcha lacked everything. It is not the habit in India to have established supply-depots and suppliers, [and] the horseman like the foot-soldier is obliged to arrange from his pay for his supplies, his powder, and his shot, and of the last they carry as little as they can. A foot-soldier is regarded as well-armed when he has three rounds of shot, so that often after the first volley he can no longer fight. It is true that the cavalry alone [really] fights in this land, and that the infantry is little used.

He concludes then, and the French East India Company's writers conclude with him:

These things that are well-known make the rapidity of the conquests of Nadercha more understandable.

The Mughals suffered a heavy defeat and numerous casualties, including some amongst the highest ranks of the nobility. Thus, after some hours of fighting, Khan-i Dauran was left with only a few commanders and some 2000 horses. His own brother, Muzaffar Khan, was shot by a musketeer and died, while a number of others, including some of the closest associates of the general, were also killed in a similar manner. Burhan al-Mulk's men too fought, and they too were victims of the musket. Many of them fled, and Burhan al-Mulk (or Sa'adat Khan) himself was wounded twice by musket-shot and eventually captured alive by the Qizilbash with some of his followers.[43] Khan-i Dauran for his part was seriously wounded, and retreated to the camp of the emperor. Mughal sources insist despondently that their soldiers were brave and full of loyalty (*halāl-namaki*), but also admit that they were badly let down by the absence of an

---

[42] AN, AMC, Correspondance Générale, C² 76, fls 184v–85.

[43] Jones, tr., *Histoire de Nader Chah*, Vol. I, pp. 445–7.

efficient artillery (*topkhâna*), together with the lack of rapid mobility. In contrast, the soldiers of Nadir Shah not only fought with muskets, but retreated and advanced with rapidity, and so very few of them were wounded or killed.

At the very end of the day, the forces of Asaf Jah and Qamar al-Din Khan belatedly reached the remnants of the army of Burhan al-Mulk. By this time, Nadir Shah went back to his own camp, as did the Mughal emperor Muhammad Shah. The next day, the gravely-wounded Khan-i Dauran died, while the captured Burhan al-Mulk was handed over by Nadir Shah into the charge of Mustafa Khan Shamlu, and eventually returned to the Mughal camp, and thence to Shahjahanabad, where he died a week later. The day after, the Mughal army went through the motions of preparing for battle, but negotiations for peace were begun, with the Mughal emperor recognizing that he had had the worst of it. Nizam al-Mulk Asaf Jah eventually came to the camp of Nadir Shah and negotiated in person the terms of the agreement, and also agreed to send the Mughal emperor the following day to the tent (*khaima*) of Nadir Shah.

French Company sources add curious details on the nature of the negotiations between Nizam al-Mulk and Nadir Shah. They write (basing themselves once more on the eyewitness account of Devolton):

Nezamelmoulouk, on seeing famine menace the camp, decided in order to save a very large number of those whom he learnt Nadercha had not massacred, to go and meet him with ten persons, amongst which number Seigneur Voulton declares he was present. For the meeting and the general details, one is obliged to have recourse to the account of Seigneur Voulton, though it is incomplete and exaggerated, since the Persian newsletters do not deal with it.

Here then is the conversation between that king-maker and *éminence grise* Nizam-ul-Mulk, and Nadir Shah, as it comes down to us.

Nezamelmoulouk was very well-received by Nadercha, and once the Prince had made him sit down, he posed the following questions, according to Seigneur Voulton.

'For the last four years, I have sent my ambassadors to your Emperor, to ask him to pay that which is due to Persia; why has he retained my people, and my letters, without responding, and why has he obliged me to take the trouble of coming so far?'

Nezamelmoulouk responded, 'I have always been in the Deccan, I only came last year to Dely in order to bring this affair to a conclusion, but the Empire was not in a position to do what you had asked for'. He added, 'The pressing desire that we had to see you, made us neglect everything so as to have, at any price, the honour of kissing your feet' (An Asiatic expression).

Nadercha smiled at this compliment, and showed him the papers from Persia; first, the account of a throne that had cost nine *courous* of Rupees; he then said to him, 'Is it true that Thamour, King of Persia, handed it over to Dely?'

Nezamelmoulouk agreed that this claim was just.

'The grandfather of Mametcha, and uncle of Geanguier [*sic*] (continued Nadercha) had asked Persia to help him with ten thousand men, at a time when he needed them to reclaim his throne; Persia sent them to him, and met all his expenses on the condition that he would reimburse them; this has not been done. Is this reimbursement just?'

Yes, responded Nezamelmoulouk.

'According to the alliance agreed to between the two Empires (added Nadercha) each was supposed to aid the other. Persia was involved in a cruel war that ruined it, and you were asked for the same help that you had been given. You did not reply; I have borrowed considerable sums on which I pay interest, in order to recover from the Turks those provinces of Persia that they had seized; it is your fault that the Empire of Persia is ruined on account of the little assistance that you have given. Who will reimburse me for all this?'.

'Allow me', replied Nezamelmoulouk, 'to write to my master, and pardon us for what happened in the past. My head is in your hands, do with me what you please. I submit to your orders'.

Nadercha then said to him, 'I am touched by what you say to me. I will spare your Emperor and his troops, whom I had the intention of putting to the sword. I order you [instead] to go to him and say on my behalf that he should come and meet me between the two armies, and that we shall make peace as I see fit'.

Nezamelmoulouk returned to his camp, and gave an account of this meeting to Mametcha.[44]

This extremely complex and confused account, in which Devolton moves from the history of the celebrated Central Asian conqueror Timur (on whom more below), to that of Humayun's exile in Persia, does not seem particularly reliable. It does nevertheless demonstrate that, despite Mughal rhetoric, they were obliged to accept the terms that Nadir Shah laid down, which we see even more clearly the next day, when Muhammad Shah himself had to make his way to the Iranian camp to meet Nadir Shah. Contemporary chroniclers report that on the arrival of the Mughal emperor, Nadir Shah came out of his tent to receive him; both sat on one long seat (*masnad*), and a *qahwachi* (coffee-maker) brought a cup of *qahwa* first to Nadir Shah, who then with his own hands presented it to Muhammad Shah, saying that now that he was there, he was like his brother. He also stated from the outset that Muhammad Shah could keep the Sultanate of Hindustan to himself, for what he, Nadir Shah, wanted for the most part was tribute in cash and kind (*naqd-o-jins*).

The Dealings in Delhi

This is the crucial moment, at which we may operate what I shall term the counterfactual 'switch'. But before we enter into that exercise, let us briefly

[44] AN, AMC, Correspondance Générale, C² 76, fls 186–87v.

survey what *did* in fact take place thereafter. The truce was now made public in the Mughal camp, and detailed negotiations continued for a day or two. Eventually, it was decided that the Mughal emperor would send back his army to the different parts of Hindustan, while he himself would remain camped there with 2000 men in the vicinity of Nadir Shah's army. Three days later, they were to depart together to Shahjahanabad, and Nadir Shah would be the guest (*mihmân*) of the emperor of Hindustan for two months and would then return to the capital of his own Sultanate. In fact, matters took longer than had been foreseen. It was thus only on 20 March 1739 that Nadir Shah made his entry into Shahjahanabad, where he was lodged in the Red Fort, and where he remained until 16 May. During this period, Mughal sovereignty was temporarily suspended, and it was only on 12 May that Muhammad Shah was officially restored to the throne by permission of Nadir Shah.

In the course of these two months, a number of incidents took place, which we need not enter into in detail here. These include the marriage between one of Nadir Shah's sons and a Mughal princess, as well as the collection of a huge sum of money, for which the French reports give us the following account in *karors* (the *karor* being equivalent to 10 million rupees):[45]

• Value of the elephants, horses, artillery, and other war-materials taken after the battle	5
• Gold and silver taken from the royal treasury	15
• Jewels	8
• A decorated bed	7
• The Peacock Throne	9
• In vessels and other decorated objects	11
• In cash and jewels from the wives and children of Muhammad Shah	3
• From the looting in the city of Delhi	10
• Tax on the city's inhabitants	10
• From the *wakîls* and servants of the Rajas, Nawwabs, and *umara'*	10
• Taken from Qamar al-Din Khan	16
• From the estates of Burhan al-Mulk and 'Ali Ahmad Khan	7
Total (in *karor* rupees)	111

Exaggerated though these figures may seem, they do not differ in their order of magnitude from the sums given in other sources. Khwaja 'Abd al-Karim Shahristani, for example, puts the value of goods and money taken at well over 80 *karor* rupees, and similar numbers are cited by other texts.[46] Part of this

---

[45] AN, AMC, Correspondance Générale, C² 76, fls 194v–95.

[46] Peter Avery, 'Nâdir Shâh and the Afsharid legacy', p. 41.

plunder was collected from the inhabitants of Delhi, as noted above, after clashes between them and the Qizilbash. These clashes occurred a day after Nadir Shah's entry into the city, and began with the rumour that the Mughal emperor had deceitfully killed Nadir Shah, severing his head from his body. Chroniclers note that a commotion resulted in the city, and people fell on the Qizilbash and killed some 3000 of them. In retaliation, Nadir Shah ordered a 'general massacre' (*qatl-i 'âmm*), in which it was estimated by the *kotwâl* (warden) of Shahjahanabad that some 20,000 people were killed, and all sorts of jewels, hoards, and cash fell into the hands of the Iranian soldiers.[47]

In the final arrangement between the two rulers, it was decided that the areas beyond the river Atak, such as Peshawar, Kabul, Ghazna, and the Bangash country, as well as Thatta and Bhakkar, along with the revenues of the four *mahals* of the Punjab, which were earmarked for the expenses of Kabul province, would be given over to Nadir Shah's control. The rest would remain with Muhammad Shah. Now, what is entirely remarkable is the fact that after the battle of Karnal, with the exception of the disturbances at Delhi, no further resistance was shown to Nadir Shah, save on his return journey (and that too largely by the Afghans, and to a limited extent the Jats). On the contrary, as French reports make clear, his authority was largely accepted, even as far as Bengal. Thus:

The rapidity of the conquests of this Prince had spread so much astonishment in the rest of the Empire, that it submitted on simply receiving orders. This sense of vertigo (*cet étourdissement*) even attained Mouxoudabat [Maqsudabad ie. Murshidabad] which is 300 leagues distant from Dely, and even though Nadercha did not send any troops to Bengal, and his orders had not even penetrated there, his authority was recognized there was soon as they were informed that he was master of Dely. SafrasKam [Sarfaraz Khan], Nabab, had him proclaimed King of India at Mouxoudabat on 4 April, the prayers were conducted in his name, and rupees were struck in his coin, [so that] the Dutch even received a hundred thousand coins struck with this mark.[48]

In fact, the French are quite categorical, that no one really believed that Nadir Shah would leave Hindustan, but rather that having displaced the Mughal emperor, he would take over the reins of the administration himself. This transition would be facilitated, it was thought, by a number of factors. First, the Iranians were familiar, broadly speaking, with the sort of administrative

---

[47] Khwaja 'Abd al-Karim, *Bayân-i Wâqi'*, pp. 38–9. For a description of the city at this time, see Stephen P. Blake, *Shahjahanabad: The Sovereign City in Mughal India 1639–1739*, Cambridge, 1991; a key text is Dargah Quli Khan, *Muraqqa'-i Dehlî*, ed. Nurul Hasan Ansari, Delhi, 1982.

[48] AN, AMC, Correspondance Générale, C² 76, fls 193– 93v.

arrangements that existed in the Mughal empire. They used broadly similar systems of state accounting (*siyâqat*), and kept state papers in same language, namely Persian. The only major difference was the persistence in the Mughal case of a large number of specific Indian usages, that subsisted from the time of Raja Todar Mal, in the late sixteenth century. It is thus with great puzzlement that they note how 'this Prince [Nadir Shah], master of Dely, for whom it would have required no more than his simple orders for his authority to be recognized in the rest of the Empire, when one least expected it, took the decision to reestablish Mametcha [on the throne] and to return to Persia'. Further, it was also generally held that Nadir Shah would arrive at an arrangement with Nizam-ul-Mulk Asaf Jah, with whom he entertained relatively good relations. Indeed, the French reports go even further than this and state: 'Many people believe that it is Nezamelmoulouk who, annoyed with Condoram [Khan-i Dauran], engaged this Prince to come to India.' We shall return presently to the possible nature of arrangements between the two.

However, none of this happened. Instead, as we know, Nadir Shah proceeded back via Afghanistan to Iran, where he declared a sort of tax holiday for three years. He then went on to campaign for several years in central Asia, reducing the surviving Uzbek Khanates with the same ease as he had dealt with the Mughals, and eventually went as far as Khwarizm, before returning once more to Iran. In general, contemporaries frequently expressed great wonder at the precision and foresight with which each of Nadir Shah's campaigns was organized, the campaign against central Asia being planned for example while Nadir Shah was on his return from Delhi to Nadirabad. Khwaja 'Abd al-Karim Shahristani, who accompanied him to Transoxania, was also struck by the discipline that he had inculcated into his troops, and their ability to make long forced marches under the most difficult conditions.[49] Besides discipline, it would also appear that Nadir Shah and his close associates (such as Tahmasp Khan Jala'ir), had become expert in the matter of logistics, calculating with great exactitude the needs of the army at various stages, and how to raise these resources. In central Asia, Nadir Shah acted pretty much as he had in northern India, deposing rulers, but then restoring them after a short interval. This was the case in Bukhara, where his dealings were with Abu'l Faiz Khan. Once more, Nadir Shah's reputation preceded him, and the residents of Bukhara seem to have offered little resistance. They persuaded Abu'l Faiz Khan to agree to submit, and he accordingly sent a message with some gifts. An arrangement was thus rapidly arrived at here, as in the bulk of the Central Asian cities.

---

[49] For a discussion, see Muzaffar Alam and Sanjay Subrahmanyam, 'Empiricism of the Heart: Close Encounters in an Eighteenth-Century Indo-Persian Text', *Studies in History*, (N.S.), Vol. XV, (2), 1999, pp. 261–91.

In view of these continued campaigns, the reports of the French Company were obliged to paint Nadir Shah in a rather different light. They thus noted, after his departure from Delhi:

The Persian newsletters attribute the widest conceivable view of the world to this Prince. They say that his intention is to go and besiege Constantinople, and to subject the Turks, and that thereafter he will enter Europe by force and force it to follow the law of Mahomet, and that he will then come back to conquer China. After such a long trajectory, he will doubtless need to rest. Nevertheless, one can attribute to him even more than to Alexander, the famous phrase to the effect that he came to India more to travel, than to fight.[50]

In later years, Nadir Shah went on to continue his campaigns in Daghestan, and against the Ottomans, until his eventual assassination on the night of 30 June 1747.[51] After his return from India, he did make some supplementary demands on the Mughals, but did not actually return to the plains of Hindustan. The mantle was picked up in the next decade by the Abdali Afghans, who precipitated a further crisis by their incursions into the Mughal polity in the late 1750s and early 1760s (of which the high-water mark is the Third Battle of Panipat in 1761). The Mughals by now felt the noose tightening around them, as the Afghan incursions were accompanied by a new threat that emerged in the east, and the south, namely the English East India Company. English Company officials for their part, on at least one significant occasion, admitted that it was on seeing Nadir Shah take Delhi with such ease in 1739 that their own dreams of an empire had been sublimated, and taken concerete form.[52]

The Counterfactual

But what if Nadir Shah had indeed stayed on? It is possible, of course, that not much would have changed if we imagine a scenario in which, say, he was assassinated in Delhi in 1739 or 1740, with his sons deciding thereafter to withdraw to the safer lands of Iran. But rather than enter into such a dull sequence, I propose an alternative view, in which Nadir Shah might simply have displaced the Mughal emperor, after cementing marriage ties between his own family and that of the Mughals (thus following the model that he had with the

[50] AN, AMC, Correspondance Générale, C² 76, fl. 197v. Also compare James Fraser, *The History of Nadir Shah formerly called Thamas Kuli Khan*, 2nd edn, London, 1742.

[51] For a view of events around this time, see Père Louis Bazin, 'Mémoire sur les dernières années du règne de Thamas-Kouli-Kan...' and 'Seconde lettre...contenant les révolutions qui suivirent la mort de Thamas Kouli-Kan', in *Lettres édifiantes et curieuses, écrites des missions étrangères*, Vol. IV, Paris, 1780, pp. 277–364.

[52] Cf. William Bolts, *Considerations on India Affairs Relating to the Present State of Bengal and Its Dependencies*, London, 1772.

Safavids). This would have enabled the Iranians then to construct a new political formation, linking north India, Afghanistan, and the Iranian plateau. In order to do so, they would arguably have been able to make use of the very large pool of specialist bureaucratic manpower (the so-called *munshî* class) that Mughal India possessed in far greater measure than Iran.

How precisely could this have worked? Let us return to the fateful scene described by Devolton, in which Nadir Shah and Nizam al-Mulk sit down at the negotiating table. Consider the two concrete historical references used in these circumstances by Nadir Shah, even if they come down to us in a confused version through Devolton. The first concerns Timur, called 'Thamour Roi de Perse', in the French account, who had, in fact, paid one significant visit to India, in the course of a military campaign in 1398–9. The ruler of Delhi at that time was a member of the Tughluq dynasty that had ruled over a good part of northern India since the 1320s. Timur made it a point to call his expedition a 'holy war' (*jihâd*), in spite of the fact that his opponents were Muslims like himself, and in the text of the 'Victory Declaration' (*Fath-Nâma*) that he issued in March 1399, after the conquest and sack of Delhi, he put matters as follows:

In the year that we decided to leave on a campaign and in a holy war to the land of infidels (*diyâr-i kufr*) in certain regions of Hindustan, we were told that since Sultan Firoz Shah had passed from this life to the hereafter, some of the slaves that he had purchased against gold had refused to hand over Delhi and the lands of Islam to his descendants, and that they had taken to tyranny and oppression; they had made rapine and pillage their rallying signs...closed the doors to the passage of merchants, and taken brigandage to its height.[53]

What is of particular significance is that this rhetoric was not treated as some empty claim. The legend of Timur took root in India, and despite the bloody massacre that he perpetrated in Delhi, the rulers of India a half-century later were appealing to his descendants in Herat to arbitrate between them.[54] Nadir Shah could well have taken courage from this abject letter addressed to Mirza Shahrukh (grandson of Timur) by Fath Khan, an exiled Tughluq prince at the Vijayanagara court in the 1440s.

When the victorious train of His Highness the Sahib-Qiran [Timur, Master of the Conjunction] came to the land of Hindustan, there was none among our renowned Sultans then alive to make obeisance and render fealty to him. In their ignorance, Mallu [Khan]

---

[53] Aubin, 'Comment Tamerlan prenait les villes'. For this campaign and its context, see Beatrice Forbes Manz, *The rise and rule of Tamerlane*, Cambridge, 1989, pp. 71–3, *passim*.

[54] I am obliged to disagree here with the reading advanced by Irfan Habib, 'Timur in the Political Tradition and Historiography of Mughal India', in Maria Szuppe, ed., *L'héritage timouride: Iran-Asie centrale-Inde, XVe-XVIIIe siècles*, Aix-en-Provence, 1997, pp. 297–312.

and Sarang [Khan] created a disturbance and effaced the foundation of the dynasty. This humble one has suffered much misfortune in exile (*diyâr-i ghurbat*) for a long time now but hopes that the servants of the royal threshold will summon me to the court so that perhaps through His Majesty's good fortune, I may be restored to my native land (*watan-i mâluf*).[55]

The precedent established by Timur, and of which Nizam-ul-Mulk could well have reminded Nadir Shah if necessary, was thus one in which the charismatic fallout of a dramatic act of conquest could efface older, and seemingly deeply entrenched, systems of legitimacy. This memory of Timur seems at least in part to have facilitated the actions of Babur in conquering northern India in the early sixteenth century.

A possible counterargument, in which the relatively unassailable position of the Mughals in terms of legitimacy (even if not military power) would be stressed, might refer to another moment that equally appears in Devolton's account, when Babur's son Humayun was driven out to Iran by Sher Shah in the late 1530s, but then returned a decade later with Safavid aid. The significance of this incident in the context of our discussion is however open to doubt, and this for several reasons. First, Sher Shah was not an external conqueror but rather represented a sort of 'conservative' return to the earlier Afghan sovereignty that had existed in northern India. Himself a native of Bihar (though of Afghan origin), Sher Shah thus represented a resurgence of forces that continued to subsist even after the Mughal conquest of the 1520s, rather than a new beginning. This character becomes even more marked under his two successors Islam Shah and Muhammad Shah 'Adli, and can be thought to have facilitated the return of Humayun, and then the accession of Akbar in the mid-1550s.

The situation in the late 1730s was entirely different. Nadir Shah represented a new beginning, a form of sovereignty that rested on a combination of personal charisma and institutional innovation, rather than appealing to the traditional (dynastic or 'ethnic') sources of legitimacy. While such a form of power undoubtedly contained seeds of instability, it also opened up radical possibilities, and we may arguably see Nadir Shah as a precursor in this respect of Napoleon Bonaparte, rather than merely as a latter-day Timur.[56] Thus, had the negotiations

---

[55] Maulana Kamal al-Din 'Abd al-Razzaq Samarqandi, *Matla'-i Sa'dain wa Majma'-i Bahrain*, Vol. II, Parts II and III, 2nd edn, ed. Muhammad Shafi', Lahore, 1949, pp. 849–50; translation in W.M. Thackston (selected and tr.), *A Century of Princes: Sources on Timurid History and Art*, Cambridge (Mass.), 1989, p. 321.

[56] Certainly, it seems more reasonable to compare Napoleon to Nadir Shah rather than to Tepedelenli Ali Pasha of Ioannina (1744–1822), on whom see Katherine E. Fleming, *The Muslim Bonaparte: Diplomacy and Orientalism in Ali Pasha's Greece*, Princeton, 1999.

between Nadir Shah and Nizam al-Mulk taken a different turn, the following scenario is imaginable. The Turani faction in the Mughal nobility, of which Nizam al-Mulk was the most important member, would have proposed to Nadir Shah that Mughal power was at an ebb, with the emperor Muhammad Shah notably lacking credibility, and beset by public rumours concerning the propriety of his comportment. Were Nadir Shah to take over Hindustan, he would find himself master of an area which had resources far exceeding those of the ecologically limited Iranian plateau. Besides, it could be argued, no conqueror who had taken booty from Hindustan had ever really benefitted from it in the medium or long term. Those who did well, in the long run, were those who settled in the Indo-Gangetic plain, making use of its rich agricultural and artisanal resources. Indeed, this argument was made quite explicitly by Khwaja 'Abd al-Karim Shahristani in the mid-eighteenth century, who wrote:

Having observed the condition of the residents of Turan and the Arab lands, I am surprised to see that in these lands worldly wealth does not last long, contrary to the case of Hindustan. Why is this so? This is in spite of the fact that Amir Timur Sahib-i-Qiran, had taken the treasures and buried wealth of Iran, Rum and Hindustan to Turan. All this was scattered in no time. And in the time of the Pious Caliphs, the booty (_kharâj_) from Rum, Yemen, Iran, Abyssinia, Egypt the Maghreb and Sind, and even some from Turan and other countries, had been taken to the Hijaz, where too all this did not remain. Apparently, an explanation for this would be the excessive generosity of these people, or else that they do not have the talent (_salîqa_) to keep wealth intact. [On the contrary] in the lands of Hindustan, in spite of several raids by Turks and Tajiks, and despite the fact that none of the Indian Sultans have brought anything from Turan and Iran, and also in spite of the fact that there are few mines of gold and silver, the country is distinguished (_mumtâz_) over others in the possession of an excess of money, goods and jewels (_wafûr-i zar-o-bisyâri-ye mâl-o-jawâhir_). Very probably, the reason for the gold and silver being in abundance is the income from the Frankish ships that bring most of the cash (_naqd_) and take away a variety of goods from India.[57]

If Nizam al-Mulk had indeed addressed such an offer as we have imagined to Nadir Shah, it would have naturally required a _quid pro quo_. The main target of an alliance between Nadir Shah and Nizam al-Mulk would undoubtedly have been, in the first instance, the Marathas in the Deccan. At this time still largely reliant on cavalry in warfare, and relatively slow to move to the use of infantry drilled in firearms, a military alliance between the Iranians and the Deccani forces based in Hyderabad would surely have proven a potent mix for the Marathas to combat. Thus, the logic of events, once one proceeds on the counterfactual route, would suggest to start with an arrangement between the new sovereign Indo-Persian dispensation and the powers in the Deccan, by

[57] Khwaja 'Abd al-Karim, _Bayân-i Wâqi'_, p. 73.

which Nizam al-Mulk would be left with a relative fucntional autonomy once south of Malwa (which becomes the implicit frontier between the two political formations), but where the Hyderabad state comes to be schooled in the new techniques of state-building imported from Iran and central Asia. Nizam al-Mulk might have continued to treat Nadir Shah and the throne of Delhi as sovereign, while continuing to exercise a good deal of functional autonomy; a tributary (*peshkashi*) arrangement might have sealed matters to their mutual satisfaction. But in turn, it is likely that the new Indo-Persian administration of Delhi would have acted far more decisively in the Deccan in the 1750s than the Mughals actually did.

In northern India itself, the Muslim and Persianized elites of Awadh, Bihar, and Bengal could, in these circumstances, quite easily have made common cause with Nadir Shah's dispensation, since they were already strongly marked by Persian culture, and dominated by an Irani (rather than a Turani) elite. This would have arrested the further development of autonomous political poles in northern India, of a type that occurred in the 1740s and 1750s, as Awadh gradually detached itself from the real tutelage of Delhi. One may imagine some opposition being put up by the Bengal governors, and indeed a few rumours of this had already reached the ears of the French in 1739. Thus, they mention the following incident at Murshidabad, soon after the *khutba* (Friday prayer) had been read there in Nadir Shah's name, and coins struck for him by Sarfaraz Khan:

It is true that at Mouxoudabat, they soon regretted this decision, [and] there was even talk for a certain time of bringing out from the fortress, in order to make him mount the throne, a Prince of royal blood called Carimcha, who was imprisoned there during the reign of Mametcha, and who was supposed to be blind, though it was said he could actually see quite well; it is said that this Prince refused the proposition that was presented to him. It is certain though that this attempt at rebellion had no real consequence.

The new Delhi dispensation would undoubtedly have had to consolidate its hold over the two maritime provinces of Gujarat and Bengal, if it were to have any long-term possibility of survival. One imagines that in a situation in which Maratha power was limited through a strategic alliance with Nizam al-Mulk, gaining control over Gujarat anew would not have been too difficult, while the Nawabs of Bengal after 1740 would undoubtedly have had to be dealt with using rather more explicit military pressure. In contrast, it would probably have been necessary to limit expansionary ambitions in the north, that is with respect to Transoxania and Khwarizm. The campaigns that Nadir Shah did conduct there in the 1740s, even if they were profitable in the very short term, were also rather costly in terms of manpower. The scenario that is proposed here is rather that of the consolidation of a large swathe of territory, extending from Tabriz in the west to Bengal in the east, with the rough borders in respect of southern India of the empire of Jahangir. Further south then would have been an area where a political regime with a certain degree of autonomy (but nevertheless benefitting from the military support of the Afsharid state), subsisted.

What militate in favour of such a construction are above all, two aspects. First, it is clear that Nadir Shah's army was far and away the most efficient of that of his contemporaries in south, west, and central (as indeed, south-east) Asia. It was based on tight discipline, a mix of firearms and mobile light cavalry, and the doing away of a number of conspicuous archaic features that still dominated warfare in the Mughal style. As it happens, after the 1760s, other states in south Asia also took up this model (as we see with the Marathas, or Mysore under Haidar 'Ali and Tipu Sultan), but probably only under belated Afghan influence.[58] But the Nadir Shahi apparatus is clearly the first to take up the idea of well-supplied, directly paid troopers, who depend directly on the ruler in the model of a professional standing army.

The debility of the Iranian political edifice, as it stood, stemmed from its imperfect articulation with a bureaucratic and fiscal system. The problem here was that Nadir Shah inherited a rather weak state system from the Safavids, who never controlled their provinces with any degree of care, and whose system was also hollowed out from within on account of very extensive 'tax-shelters' afforded within the so-called *auqâf* provision (where foundations could be created to protect property from taxes). In contrast to Safavid Iran, both urban and rural property in Mughal India were far better defined in relation to the fiscal system. Also, a very extensive bureaucracy existed in Mughal India, whose members inhabited a world where the dominant culture was already mixed with that of Iran. A political change of the type that we have imagined would probably have led to a re-Persianization of north Indian elite culture, which had begun to drift by the early eighteenth century in the direction of vernacular languages and regional practices. But this is a transition that is far more plausible, and notionally would have been far more smooth, than that which the English Company and the Crown in fact introduced.

Conclusion

Would such a military and political system have deterred the English Company in its territorial adventurism? An argument can certainly be made for this, with

---

[58] Jos J. L. Gommans, 'Indian Warfare and Afghan Innovation During the Eighteenth Century', *Studies in History*, (N.S.), Vol. XI, No. 2, 1995, pp. 261–80; also Stewart Gordon, 'The limited adoption of European-style military forces by eighteenth century rulers in India', *The Indian Economic and Social History Review*, Vol. XXXV, No. 3, 1998, pp. 229–45.

support from a number of different directions. Let us consider first the short and medium terms, and then the long term, including what Philip Tetlock and his collaborators have called 'second-order counterfactuals' (or reversions).[59] In the first place, it is crucial to consider the political and economic position of the English Company itself, which was in fact remarkably fragile in about 1740. Even if the English Company had made great strides in respect of its great rival, the Dutch Company, in the years after 1680 so far as trade on the Cape Route was concerned, the 'country trade' still had only tenuous foundations, which were in turn dependent on the vicissitudes of private fortunes in Britain, and the nature of the volatile diamond market.[60] Further, in the 1740s, the French under Dupleix were about to launch a major political and commercial offensive, which would have direct implications both for Calcutta and, above all, for Madras. Much hinged therefore on the English Company's ability to tap into local sources of finance, and to work the networks of private trade that linked them to the powerful bazaar interests in south Asia. In order to do this, the Company needed to have credibility, and credibility depended in turn crucially on military success.

Arguably, the key phase in this matter was the 1740s, as the British took advantage of the succession wars at Arcot, and the growing power there of the Marathas (both the Peshwas, and other semi-independent warlords like the Ghorpades), to make deep inroads into peninsular India. It was here that Robert Clive cut his teeth, as it were, and it was from a south Indian base that the Bengal campaigns of the 1750s were eventually launched. A balance of power such as the one which we have proposed, with a centralized Afsharid dispensation in the north and east, and a rejuvenated Hyderabad (and Arcot) in the south, would have posed enormous problems for such projects of colonial expansion, since each step was predicated on an earlier one. Not least of all, since the Company faced considerable political opposition in Britain itself, it would arguably have been extremely difficult to build a consensus amongst the Court of Directors to launch a costly offensive against substantial forces under an efficient political leadership in the south Asian subcontinent.[61]

For, in respect of Bengal, the British were considerably encouraged by the fact that in 1756–7, the central Mughal administration did not react to developments

[59] See Philip Tetlock and Aaron Belkin, eds, *Counterfactual Thought Experiments in World Politics: Logical, Methodological and Psychological Perspectives*, Princeton, 1996.

[60] Cf. Søren Mentz, *Den engelske gentlemankøbmand i funktion: Madras og City of London, 1660–1740*, Ph.D. thesis, University of Copenhagen, 1999.

[61] In this context, it is useful to turn to slightly later debates on the question of expansion in India, eg., in Jim Phillips, 'Private Profit and Imperialism in Eighteenth-Century Southern India: The Tanjore Revenue Dispute, 1775–7', *South Asia*, (N.S.), Vol. IX, No. 2, 1986, pp. 1–16.

in the Nawabi, thus allowing Clive and his small armies a field day. In military terms, none of the Company's armies until the 1790s came even faintly close to the degree of efficiency that Nadir Shah's forces possessed already by the 1730s. Indeed, even in the 1790s, their successes against Tipu Sultan were in the context of relatively limited forces, and rather modest fiscal resources when compared to those available in northern India. In the absence of the networks of *bania* finance, it is difficult to see on what basis the colonial expansion wars of the years from 1740 to 1790 could have been supported.[62] And such networks responded closely to political circumstances, credit being a direct function of credibility.

The effects, which have been posited, essentially concern the first 60 years or so following our 'counterfactual switch'. To resume, what is proposed here is a large political structure, with a powerful standing army on the Iranian model, underpinned by a fiscal-bureaucratic structure that would draw on the centuries of Mughal expertise. Such a military-fiscal structure would possess enough credibility to hold the vast networks of banking and credit in northern India to it, while in the Deccan a semi-autonomous (but nevertheless linked) dispensation would some into being, drawing not only on Khattri and Kayastha fiscal expertise (as the Hyderabad state did, in any event), but on a further extension of the centralized administration that Nizam al-Mulk had already begun to put into place in the coastal regions in the early 1730s.

It is evident that in the absence of a base in the Karnatak and Bengal, further British expansion in south Asia would have been relatively difficult, if not impossible. Certainly their position in western India did not allow them much margin for manoeuvre, and the inroads made under Warren Hastings into Awadh in the 1770s depended directly on the British position in Bengal. However, it can be argued that this would have had very little direct impact in the first instance on the history of Britain itself. There is more or less a consensus in the historiography, as I understand it, that the Industrial Revolution and attendant changes in the metropolis on the one hand, and colonial expansion on the other, were largely independent events. Thus, one can well imagine changes in the economic and social structure of Britain proceeding roughly unchanged to 1800, no matter how events turned out in south Asia. The course of matters in the nineteenth century is another matter, for we are aware that the eventual financial domination on a world scale of London was very much linked to its ability to manipulate its colonies overseas. Would Britain then have been able gradually, in the course of the decades after 1800, to assert an informal control over south Asia of the type that was exercised over parts of North Africa and Latin America (as also the Middle East, including Iran)? Much depends here

---

[62] Cf. Lakshmi Subramanian, *Indigenous Capital and Imperial Expansion: Bombay, Surat and the West Coast*, Delhi, 1996.

on how one imagines the economic and social counterpart of the political developments that we have set out for south Asia.

In this context, two other features of the possible synthesis that we have posited require mention. First, there is the religious question. Iran under the Safavids, and until the first half of the seventeenth century, was as we know subject to a rather extreme form of Shi'ism, which Shah Isma'il and his successors had put in place. This contrasted markedly with the far more accomodating style of Islam that the Mughals practised for the most part. It is noteworthy however that by the early eighteenth century, matters had changed in Iran, and that Nadir Shah is never accused even by his detractors (who were many), of sectarian prejudices of a type that had been in vogue a century earlier. Thus, the re-Persianization of which we have spoken, that might have taken place in northern India, is unlikely to have been part of a process of Islamization, which (had it happened) could have disturbed the delicate political balance with the bulk of the subjects in northern India, who were in fact not Muslims. A second feature concerns the idea of institutional change. What we have proposed here is not a radical change, say the adoption of an entirely different legal system, or the sudden transformation of artisanal manufacture into factory production, or the adoption of 'democratic' political institutions. The counterfactual still posits a monarchical system, functioning under a more-or-less Islamic aegis (although at the liberal end of the spectrum), presiding over a largely peasant economy with a significant artisanal production and quite considerable overseas trade. What has changed in our counterfactual is that some of the best elements of two such neighbouring systems (those of India, and Iran) are here conjugated in a novel fashion on account of a particular type of political intervention. Such a system would, I would tend to argue, have been able to protect itself politically for at least three-quarters of a century longer from British imperialism than the Mughal empire in fact did. If indeed this had turned out to be the case, other changes might have followed suit. It is certain, for one, that the measures put in place by the Company between 1760 and 1830, both in the economic sphere (which led, almost certainly, to the de-industrialization of some parts of India), and in that of culture (where patronage to a number of 'native' institutions was withdrawn, and the ground prepared for what was to follow after Macaulay), would not have had the effect they did.

The consequences for Iranian history, where formal colonization did not in fact occur in any case, are also interesting to conceive. For, after the rule of the Afsharids and the Zands, we come to the involuted and weakly-articulated state of the Qajars, that presides on the one hand over a rather static economy, and on the other hand over the gradual provincialization of culture in the name of Iranian 'patriotism'. The larger world of Persian culture, and the role played in it by Mughal India, tends to be set aside, with results that are visible into the present day. Had it been possible, from the middle decades of the eighteenth century, to articulate the relationship with northern India differently, with greater possibilties for the circulation of elites, and mutual influences rather than the barriers that came to be installed in about 1800, it is likely that the institutional bases of Iranian politics would have been very different from what they have turned out to be.

Thus, what has been proposed here is a 'switch' with lasting effects, certainly in the medium term, and perhaps into the long term as well. To put matters simply, it is my view that British domination over south Asia was (as Arthur Wellesley might have said), a 'damned close-run thing', and that matters would have taken a radically different turn between the 1740s and 1770s. In short, I would disagree with those who would claim that sooner or later, something called 'the British empire' would have come around to India; that it was all a matter of time really. The British empire such as it was in 1800 was largely constructed from its south Asian basis and cannot be conceived of being independent of it. The logic of rule over the American colonies did not necessararily lead in the direction of expansion in Asia, and the two must be seen as largely independent processes. Further, it is my view that the changes that have been posited here, had they come into effect, would have been difficult to reverse in the course of the nineteenth century. Had south Asia escaped formal colonization in the latter half of the eighteenth century, it is difficult to see the British gaining much more than informal control (and influence) over it in the course of the first half of the nineteenth century. This might not have affected the dominant economic position of Britain in the nineteenth century, but it would certainly have had long-term economic and cultural consequences for south Asia. In place of *The Moor's Last Sigh*, for example, we might have had a powerful and resurgent Persian literature, wherein the cultural resources of south Asia would have been added to those of Iran, Afghanistan, and those parts of Central Asia (Tajikistan, parts of Uzbekistan) where that language is still largely dominant.

While completing a first version of this chapter, I had occasion to see a French film of the director Cédric Klapisch, entitled *Peut-être* ('Perhaps'). Here, a socially marginal and poorly-off young man, who is in two minds as to whether to have a child with his girlfriend (who wants one), is projected 70 years into the future while attending a New Year's Eve party at the end of 1999. The Paris he encounters is totally transformed, with all the buildings buried in sand up to the third floor. Camels and donkeys dominate local transport, though the occasional bicycle-airplane taxi is available to visit the suburbs. The real premise of the story is however located not at this scenic level. Rather the problem is a 'philosophical' one. For, in 2070, the hero's descendants (a 70-year old son played by Jean-Paul Belmondo, and a 40-something grandson) are literally disappearing bit by bit (a piece of an arm, or a leg, etc), precisely because their 'perhaps' progenitor is unable to decide whether or not actually to conceive his children. If he returns to 1999/2000, and goes through with his decision not to have children, they will definitively disappear. On the other hand, they may well be totally reconstituted, and the missing pieces may return, if only he goes through with the act of conception.

The plot is admittedly untidy, and full of loopholes; so is counterfactual history. I am aware of several problems in the scenario such as I have presented it, which take us back in a deterministic direction, where the only thing that could have happened is that which really did happen. Let me list some of the possible objections, beyond those of both Indian and Iranian nationalist historians, who would probably horripilate at the scenario that has been set out above. Indian nationalist historians (including those attached to the Hindu extremist party currently in power, the BJP), would consider this extension and shoring up of 'Muslim' rule even worse, if anything, than the colonial rule that in fact followed from the second half of the eighteenth century. As for Iranian historians, who have largely been brought up to look down on south Asia, they might arguably prefer to guard their pristine purity within the existent boundaries than dream of an empire whose 'Iranian' (as opposed to Persianate) character would in any event have become diluted over time. Other objections of a less blatantly nationalistic character might be added to those mentioned above. First, it may be argued, Nadir Shah was really a warrior-conqueror not an administrator; it would have been well-nigh impossible for him to put in place a structure such as the one that I have described. The objection is partly an issue of 'personality type', and here I venture that the role of the entourage and larger milieu of Nadir Shah (such men as Mirza Mahdi Astarabadi, Tahmasp Khan Jala'ir, and so many others) must also be taken into consideration. The dominant Marxist school of historians of Mughal India would argue that the changes that I have posited would not have affected the 'primary contradiction' between peasants and elite, which in their view determined the fate of the Mughal empire, and made its decline inevitable to permit the later Rise of Capitalism. Second, it may be argued that the Mughals had too much legitimacy and too great a hold over the south Asian imagination to be displaced so easily. Here, historians of a rather more romantic inclination would seize upon the nostalgia that existed for the Mughals after 1857, neglecting perhaps to note that this nostalgia was partly a function of the profoundly alien character of British rule in India. This is a subject that has become unfashionable in recent literature, where many historians insist that the British in the nineteenth century were practically indistinguishable from Indians in white-face, and that what has unjustly been termed 'colonialism' is in fact really all about 'dialogue'. I must beg to differ, pointing to the profound cultural, political, social, and economic consequences of British rule, particularly after 1830 or so. These consequences were the result of a deep divide between rulers and ruled, which was radically different in nature from that which the Mughals practised (and which, in my view, the Afsharids too would have followed). I am sure that had the Afsharids seized power on a permanent basis, a number of pretenders would have arisen from within the Mughal fold, but as such it seems perfectly conceivable that in 1740 the Mughal dynasty could be set aside by another group from within the Persianate world.

Finally, it may be argued by sceptics that the sort of large imperial political structure that I have posited would have been structurally too unwieldy, and much too hard to hold together over a long period of time. I am relatively sympathetic to this view, since the nineteenth century was in general less kind to territorially contiguous empires than it was to dispersed ones. At the same time, I cannot help but believe that the weight that such an objection instinctively carries, only shows once more the limits to which the historical imagination can be stretched. But, as noted above, it may well be argued that had the English Company not taken first Bengal, then the Karnatak, then the North-Western Provinces (later termed the United Provinces), the British empire in much of south Asia and even elsewhere (based as it was on using Indian troop-levies, and financed in good part by Indian capital-markets), would have been inconceivable.[63] The British empire was after all not even a distant gleam in anyone's eye in 1740. Rather, what seemed at least possible (if not likely), was a great empire built from a base in south-west Asia. To quote once again one of our contemporary texts on Nadir Shah then: 'They say that his intention is to go and besiege Constantinople, and to subject the Turks, and that thereafter he will enter Europe by force and force it to follow the law of Mahomet, and that he will then come back to conquer China.' But, as for a Muslim Europe in the eighteenth century, that must surely be the subject of another counterfactual, related to, but perhaps not identical with, that posed in this volume by Ira Lapidus.

The scenario I present here is certainly not a 'last chance' counterfactual to 'stop the West' in its conquest of South Asia, for as I have outlined at the outset, other counterfactual exercises have extended the possibilities chronologically at least as far as 1799 (or even 1857) in terms of the relationship between south Asia and the West. Nor is it an issue of a return to personality-oriented history, with Nadir Shah being presented in larger-than-life terms as one of the forgotten Great Movers of history. Rather, the true motivations for this particular exercise have to my mind been two. First, it was my intention to conceive a counterfactual that destabilizes not merely the 'Rise of the West',

---

[63] For a sample of writings on the question, see Michael H. Fisher, ed., *The Politics of British Annexation of India, 1757–1857*, Delhi, 1993; also C. A. Bayly, *Indian Society and the Making of the British Empire: The New Cambridge History of India, Vol. II. 2*, Cambridge, 1988.

but the comfortable assumptions of Indian and Iranian nationalist historiographies, which assume a stable and robust teleology leading to the creation of those nation states. Second, I have in mind an 'aesthetic' motivation, for the counterfactual switch here does *not* work on the usual counterfactual clichés: assassinations and conspiracies, reversals of battles when the king falls off his elephant, or James Watt and Isaac Newton being dropped on their heads as babies. The point is that the Iranian forces of Nadir Shah actually won the key battle, as well as the earlier campaigns, and entered Delhi in triumph. Then they turned back. This seems to me to be, *a priori*, a rather improbable event. Yet it happened. Since historical truth was thus stranger than counterfactual fiction, it seems only reasonable then to favour the probable over the improbable, even if we find ourselves confronted as a consequence, whether we like it or not, with a counterfactual scenario. Does this reveal a deep-rooted nostalgia on the historian's part for empires, or a visceral anti-Western bias? *Peut-être*, as Cédric Klapisch might say. For my part, I would argue that a Panglossian social science that is incapable of conceiving of anything but unhappy outcomes, once one deviates from the actual historical trajectory, has already chosen to show its hand. Historians and social scientists, even before they are put on the psychoanalyst's couch, are a rather transparent tribe, all in all.

8

Afterword

During the century that followed the first small beginning made in India, the English in the island settled whether King or Parliament should be ruler (...) It was a century in which something was achieved. But it is depressing for a Western mind to turn in the same period from Europe to India, not only because the degree of cruelty and human misery is on the whole greater, but because there is no sign of growth in any desirable or even definite direction.

Philip Woodruff, *The Men who Ruled India* (1953)[1]

Sometime in the closing decades of the sixteenth century, in all probability in the late 1580s or early 1590s, the Ottoman chronicler Seyfi Çelebi put down his geographical description of the countries to the east, in the posthumously titled 'Book of the History of the Monarchs of the Countries of India, Khitay, Kashmir, 'Ajam, Kashgar etc'. The text as it is written hardly constitutes one of the literary marvels of the epoch, and its interest resides mainly in the fact that it is a compendium of Ottoman xenology which is not directed to the west, which is to say the countries of the Mediterranean littoral, but instead to the east, a far more uncommon procedure. The sixth chapter (*fasl-i-sâdis*) dealing with the sovereigns of Hind other than Jalaluddin (which is to say the Mughal emperor Akbar, 1556–1605) begins with the monarchs of the Deccan, but moves on soon enough to Pegu (in Burma), then to Sri Lanka (Serendib), and eventually to the Sultanate of Aceh (*Açï vilâyeti*) in western Indonesia.[2] For a brief moment, we are given a glimpse of how the 'Lands below the Winds' (*zîrbâdât*) of south-east Asia

---

[1] Philip Woodruff, *The Men who Ruled India: The Founders*, London, 1953, p. 48. This work by a member of the Indian Civil Service remains an important ideological statement justifying British colonial rule, even after that rule had ended.

[2] Joseph Matuz, ed. and tr., *L'ouvrage de Seyfî Çelebî, historien ottoman du XVIe siècle*, Paris, 1968, pp. 120–1.

appeared, not to some Italian or Catalan observer, but to the Sunni co-religionists of the Aceh Sultans from the eastern Mediterranean, who ostensibly supported them in their *jihâd* against the infidel Portuguese in the epoch. The results are not edifying. Having told us that 'Aceh is located in the middle of an island but it is a vast place; its Padshah is Sunni and a Muslim, and is called Muhammad Shah', Seyfi moves on to his real interest, which is in the elephants of Aceh. The rest of the description of Aceh is thus simply an exoticist composition on its marvellous elephants, as if its people have no interest either for Seyfi or for his imagined reader. Seyfi looks out, but one wonders sometimes whether he would not have done better to let his geographical imagination stay at home. Yet, the same chronicler is capable of producing a more-or-less reasonable (if at times slightly eccentric) history of Mughal rule in India since the time of Babur, including the flight of Humayun to Iran, his death and the subsequent battle between Akbar and the *kâfir* Hemu, as well as the difficulties between Akbar and his half-brother Mirza Hakim. One does occasionally find a truly astonishing passage such as the following one, but this is the exception rather than the rule.

Humayun remained some days in Delhi. Then he took the road and went to the hospice of Somnath (*Deyr-i Somnâta*). This hospice of Somnath, may God turn from it, was the Ka'ba of the infidels. All the types of animals that God had created had been made into images in gold and silver by the infidels and placed there. Humayun destroyed the hospice of Somnath, which had been a temple, and he seized the animals in gold and silver. Then, he went to the city of Agra, which is also a great city of Hind. Then he went to the Ganges.[3]

Now, the imprint that geography leaves on history is suggestive and even tantalizing, but deeply problematic. A long tradition of geographical determinism is to be found not only in the humanities and social sciences as they have emerged in recent times, but in far older writings, such as those of the medieval Perso-Arabic traditions.[4] While it may no longer be popular, as it once was in Persian chronicles on south Asia, to attribute qualities to human communities on the basis of the quality of the air and water (*âb-o-hawâ*) they consumed, and whether they lived in excessive heat or biting cold, the spectre of a geographically-driven comparative world history is still with us.[5] One solution to the excesses of the genre is to limit and discipline the comparison, and thus investigate to what extent the comparison of the historical trajectory of two

[3] *Ibid*, p. 108.

[4] For the Persianate tradition, see for example, Richard M. Eaton, *The Rise of Islam and the Bengal Frontier, 1204–1760*, Delhi, 1994, pp. 167–71.

[5] David S. Landes, *The Wealth and Poverty of Nations: Why some are so rich and some so poor*, New York, 1998.

distant spaces can help shed new light on the two spaces themselves, as well as on the exercise of comparison as such. The general rule in such exercises has been the national comparison, thus Japan and Germany in the nineteenth century (the staple of many a university examination), or more recently, China and India.

The chapters brought together in the present work have been conceived as a partial response to the challenge posed by the intellectual project of a reflection on the ongoing encounters between South Asia and Europe at the time of the Mughals. While the challenges posed by this particular theme in 'connected history' (rather than a more traditional comparative history) are no doubt specific in character, they also bear comparison to other such exercises, notably that seeking to link the histories and 'destinies' of the northern and southern shores of the Mediterranean in the early modern period. Several historians of the Indian Ocean have, especially since the 1980s, sought to draw upon the mould of Mediterranean studies to define their own field, and the classic reference has inevitably been to *The Mediterranean* of Fernand Braudel, not so much in its first edition of 1949, but rather to the second edition from 1966, which was eventually very successfully and elegantly translated into English by Siân Reynolds (in 1972), earning its author worldwide, if somewhat belated, fame. As it happens, the recent publication in the form of a single volume, entitled *Autour de la Méditerranée*, of a number of Braudel's major articles concerning the Mediterranean, allows us to track the evolution of his thought on this sea and its littoral, and it is rather useful for our purposes. Braudel's researches appear to have begun definitively in 1927, the year in which he registered for a thesis with the perfectly conventional title, 'Philippe II, l'Espagne, et la Méditerranée', with the Mediterranean given a modest enough third place, rather than the primacy that it was later to have. This project allowed him, in 1928, to commence research at the Simancas Archives in Spain, and at the Biblioteca Nacional and the Archivo Historico Nacional in Madrid. Indeed, it has been noted that the Spanish sources occupied a central position even in later incarnations of the project, despite the wide range of other archives explored. One notices the interest expressed already at this date in the history of groups such as the New Christians and the *moriscos*, but also in the constitution of transcultural networks of espionage. Thus, a brief remark concerning Istanbul at the epoch of Süleyman the Magnificent is significant: 'There existed at Constantinople an interloper colony of renegades, who sold Christian Europe more or less exact news concerning the Oriental world. The same informers worked for the diverse Christian nations.'[6] These renegades, who served as information agents, and cross-cultural brokers, have since been the object of

[6] Fernand Braudel, *Les Écrits de Fernand Braudel autour de la Méditerranée*, eds, Roselyne de Ayala and Paule Braudel, Paris, 1996, pp. 27–8.

attention of a number of historians, who have thus been able to bring out with numerous nuances the complexity such themes as the circulation of humans in the Mediterranean, outside of the problematic strait-jacket of the idea of 'merchant diaspora'. The concrete geographical reality of the Mediterranean, on which Braudel laid so much emphasis in the opening chapters of his later *magnum opus*, is in fact difficult to make any sense of for the historian, in the absence of the idea of the constitution of the Mediterranean as a social space, for which the ceaseless circulation of humans was a *sine qua non*. Some of these were ambassadors, who went as self-conscious representatives of one power and culture to another; thus, the celebrated cases of, say, the Frenchmen Ogier Ghiselin de Busbecq or Nicolas de Nicolay in the mid sixteenth-century Ottoman domains.[7] Others brought back visions of irreducible difference, that they considered essential no matter what the apparent similarities. Thus, it would seem that any of the major mercantile cities of the Mediterranean—Marseilles, Venice, Dubrovnik, or Izmir (Smyrna)—had something in common at first glance in the sixteenth and seventeenth centuries, whether in terms of the languages spoken, the goods and currencies exchanged, or the manner in which the mercantile quarters were organized.[8] But scratch the surface, and one would find the true marks of asymmetry, not least of all in the repeatedly asserted difference (amongst European writers of the epoch), of the manner in which political power and economic transactions articulated 'east' and 'west' (which is probably better glossed 'north' and 'south' in the Mediterranean). The account of Friar Jean Thenaud, guardian of the Convent of the Cordeliers d'Angoulême, and who accompanied André Le Roy, French envoy to the Egypt of Sultan Qansuh al-Ghauri (in 1512) is symptomatic:

There are Baasas and agents for particular nations such as the Turks, Jamiens, Moresgabins, Indians, Persians and still others. We were told that in Cairo one can find two hundred merchants with a fortune worth a million in gold, and two thousand more who are worth a hundred thousand seraphs, but they do not dare to show their possessions and treasure for fear of the daily tyranny that the Souldan, and the *amîrs* and Mamluks, practise on the rich.[9]

Texts such as these would later coalesce, it has been argued convincingly by Lucette Valensi and others, in an image of the 'Oriental Despot', which was

[7] See, for example, Nicolas de Nicolay, *Dans l'Empire de Soliman le Magnifique*, eds, M. C. Gomez-Géraud and S. Yérasimos, Paris, 1989.

[8] On Izmir (Smyrna), see the useful monograph by Daniel Goffman, *Izmir and the Levantine World, 1550–1650*, Seattle, 1990.

[9] Charles Schefer, ed., *Le voyage d'outremer de Jean Thenaud (Égypte, Mont Sinay, Palestine) suivi de la Relation de l'Ambassade de Domenico Trevisan auprès du Soudan d'Egypte, 1512*, Paris, 1884, p. 48.

focused quintessentially on the figure of the Grand Turk, or the Ottoman Sultan.[10] But it is important in this context to avoid the hasty attribution of some essence to the hierarchizing capacity of the western observer. On the contrary, the emergence of the image of the Turk was a slow process, that may have begun in the political circumstances surrounding the capture of Constantinople by Fatih Mehmed in 1453.[11] Even if the Turk was a powerful trope (and real threat) in the sermons of Girolamo Savonarola (1452–98) and his contemporaries in the late fifteenth century, it is is only a century later that the public discourse produced by a series of returning Venetian consuls to the Porte permitted the fixing of key elements, and the clear definition of the central idea (for instance) that the Ottomans lived off war, and that in its absence they would inevitably enter into decline. These elements interacted with the philosophical reflections, and political theorizing, of observers from Guillaume Postel to Montesquieu, eventually to engrave in stone perceptions of socio-political difference that persisted into later centuries.

But this is only a small part of the story of the dynamic of circulations and connections in the early modern Mediterranean. One tendency in the historiography, at times latent, at others quite explicit, is to argue that both the nature of economic ties and the asymmetry of images were reversed radically, and in a parallel fashion, between the medieval centuries, and those studied by Braudel. It is undoubtedly true that for an earlier period, say, the eleventh–thirteenth centuries, readers of Shelomo Dov Goitein's magisterial work, *A Mediterranean Society* (whose five volumes have not received quite the attention of those of Braudel), would recognize the possibility that quite another history of the Mediterranean, with a different set of regional foci, and indeed of *dramatis personae*, might be written.[12] At the same time, as recent historians such as Mark R. Cohen have pointed out, it is necessary to rethink the Golden Age perspective on the medieval Mediterranean world that seems to underlie Goitein's apparently empiricist approach. This vision of an 'Islamic interfaith utopia', that preceded the seizure of power in the sea by the Christian powers (to which Lepanto eventually set the seal), and thus the inevitable rise of not only northern economic hegemony over the southern littoral, but of victory in the 'war of

---

[10] Lucette Valensi, *Venise et la Sublime Porte: La naissance du despote*, Paris, 1987.

[11] One of the best-known works in this context remains that of Steven Runciman, *The Fall of Constantinople, 1453*, Cambridge, 1965.

[12] S. D. Goitein, *A Mediterranean Society: The Jewish Communities of the Arab World as Portrayed in the Documents of the Cairo Geniza*, 5 Vols, Berkeley, 1967–88. Useful work in the same tradition is found in Olivia Remie Constable, *Trade and Traders in Muslim Spain: The Commercial Realignment of the Iberian Peninsula, 900–1500*, Cambridge, 1994.

images', needs to be nuanced considerably.[13] Looking over the extensive spaces covered in the Mediterranean by the 'Geniza community' in its heyday, we also have a second possible model. This one, attributable in its origins to Eliyahu Ashtor, but then thoughtlessly repeated by a number of recent writers, would argue that the medieval Mediterranean was already a sort of 'world economy', but one dominated by its south-eastern littoral. This dynamic 'industrial core' would ostensibly have dominated the northern 'periphery' until a reversal occurred in late medieval and early modern times, with the rise of the Italian port-cities, and parts of Iberia as centres of economic dynamism.[14] One part of this thesis goes back to older, and in part quite legitimate, debates concerning the 'real' origins of key financial and accounting institutions that are to be found in medieval Italy and Iberia.[15] But whereas the 'origins' debate concerns the transmission of very specific forms of knowledge, and mercantile practice, the 'world systems' perspective mechanistically applies anachronistic and inappropriate criteria to study a space such as the Mediterranean. Basic questions remain unanswered though. Should we think of every coherent socio-cultural space (or 'world system') as constituted by a core and a periphery? Should we imagine that areas that produce manufactures are always destined to be 'cores' in such spaces? Is our repertoire of models so impoverished that we have no other means of conceptualising a space such as the Mediterranean, or *a fortiori*, the Indian Ocean?

I would suggest that we need to go beyond simple binary models that split the Mediterranean east and west (or north and south), models that also reflect the old Pirennian preoccupation of the struggle between Crescent and Cross as the basic dynamic of Mediterranean history. These are useful models to approach what we might call the 'Mediterranean imagination' (and thus, conversely, the imagined Mediterranean), but they are deeply unsatisfactory for other purposes. In the sixteenth century, for example, the 'western' Christian powers were anything but a unified bloc politically, even if very occasionally their interests came together. Nor did the interests of the 'eastern' Mamluks and Ottomans coincide, wishful thinking aside.[16] Instead, it is of significance that

---

[13] Mark R. Cohen, *Under Crescent and Cross: The Jews in the Middle Ages*, Princeton, 1994.

[14] See for example E. Ashtor, *The Levant Trade in the Later Middle Ages*, Princeton, 1973. For the perils of such an approach, see the caricatural account in Janet Abu-Lughod, *Before European Hegemony: The World-System, AD 1250–1350*, New York, 1989.

[15] This debate has been revisited recently in Jack Goody, *The East in the West*, Cambridge, 1996, pp. 49–72.

[16] Jean Aubin, 'La crise égyptienne de 1510–12: Venise, Louis XII et le Sultan', *Moyen Orient et Océan Indien*, t. VI, 1989, pp. 123–50.

when the early sixteenth-century Maluk Sultan Qansuh al-Ghauri's strategic
and diplomatic calculations failed, the major consequence was to exacerbate
the internal political struggles in the Sultanate, and permit the conquest of
Egypt, not by the Christians but by the very Sunni neighbours of the Mamluks,
the Ottomans.

The lines of political and cultural division that begin first to overlap and then
solidify in the late eighteenth century (and above all in the aftermath of the
Napoleonic expeditions) appear far more inchoate at an earlier time. Further,
as the Ottomanist historian, Cemal Kafadar has pointed out, our vision of the
Mediterranean in the sixteenth century still suffers from the very unequal use
that has been made of different archives and resources in the various Mediterranean languages. He thus notes the importance of the Ottoman Turkish mercantile presence in such ports as Ancona, Dubrovnik and even Venice in the
latter half of the sixteenth century, and emphasizes—contrary to the conventional position in the historiography—that 'there is no evidence that any action
on the part of the Ottoman government or the religious authorities was aimed
at stopping Ottoman merchants from trading with foreigners within or outside
the empire'.[17] Since the letter-books and papers of these merchants have scarcely
been used by historians, we remain largely confined to the idea that trade was
entirely the domain of those from the 'west'. Rather, he goes on to argue, even
Ottoman cultural history must be reconsidered, outside of a paradigm of stasis
until the late eighteenth century, when (according to Bernard Lewis, as well as
a number of others) the French Revolution made its first great inroads into this
ostensibly conservative Sunni Muslim society.[18]

The purpose of this brief excursus into Mediterranean history has been to lead
the reader in the direction of three conclusions. First, to suggest that the early
modern historiography of this area even three-quarters of a century after Braudel
began his project remains heavily biased in the direction of not merely the
'northern', but more striking still, the 'Latin' archives, in Italian, Spanish, and
French. This is not merely an empirical question but one of rethinking at a
conceptual level the problem of objects of research that have a tendency to
'disappear' (thus, Muslim merchants in the Mediterranean after 1500), and
geographical areas that have a tendency to remain distressingly murky (notably,

[17] Cemal Kafadar, 'A Death in Venice (1575): Anatolian Muslim Merchants Trading
in the Serenissima', *Journal of Turkish Studies*, Vol. X, 1986, pp. 191–218; also see
Kafadar, 'The Ottomans and Europe', in Thomas A. Brady (Jr), Heiko A. Oberman, and
James D. Tracy, eds, *Handbook of European History 1400–1600: Late Middle Ages,
Renaissance and Reformation*, Vol. I, Leiden, 1994, pp. 589–635.

[18] Cemal Kafadar, 'The Question of Ottoman Decline', *Harvard Middle Eastern and
Islamic Review*, Vol. IV, Nos 1–2, 1997–8, pp. 30–75.

in the example we have chosen, the Adriatic and the Balkans). A similar problem continues to haunt the historiography of South Asia, albeit with slightly different consequences. A second issue that remains to be thought through is a chronological one. Should we read the logic of Mediterranean (and Indian Ocean) history as one of a pendulum, or do our conceptual resources permit us to do more than this? Or, to pose the question differently, is there any fashion of reading Goitein other than as a mirror image of Braudel? Certainly, the empirical riches are there to permit us glimpses of other constructs, but a further clue is given to us by the missing link in Goitein's own work, namely his so-called 'India book', which remained incomplete. Were we to reintegrate the Indian Ocean materials that the Geniza preserves with those on the Mediterranean, we might be presented not with a 'Mediterranean society', but one that ran from Spain and Sicily to western India, and even perhaps south-east Asia. A new form of connected history might then become feasible. A third issue is a cultural one. For beyond the quality of sunlight, olive oil, and wine, beyond the idea of a Mediterranean material civilization that united Baalbeck and the Provence, the most immediate resonances of the popular idea of Mediterranean unity lie in the cultural sphere. Yet, even supposing they are true, we cannot take these congruences for granted, assuming that they exist as structural givens, in the absence of agents of contact and exchange. This must bring us back to the issue of not only the famous 'merchant diasporas', but to other sorts of agents. In sum then, the set of questions regarding 'encounters' opened up by Braudel may have an excessively familiar air about it today, but not all the answers have been found; and perhaps more important, many of the right questions have not been asked.

The case of Mughal dealings with Europe is both similar to and quite distinct from Ottoman dealings with the Habsburgs. Some of the same defining vectors are certainly to be found, notably the emergence of a notion of radical political difference, summed up in the idea of Oriental Despotism that is opposed to a more rationally organized European absolutism. Again, the problem of the 'Ottoman discovery of Europe', and the curiosity or lack thereof shown by Ottoman xenologists in regard to their western neighbours does parallel issues raised by authors such as A. J. Qaisar, on the South Asian 'response' to a number of stimuli provided by the Europeans.[19] If one focuses on processes such as these, it appears that the problematic that has been at the centre of this work is no more than that of the east–west axis of the Mediterranean, stretched a few thousand kilometres in the two directions. But important distinctions also existed and cannot be set aside quite so easily. The 'encounter' with India had a

[19] Ahsan Jan Qaisar, *The Indian Response to European Technology and Culture, AD 1498–1707*, Delhi, 1982.

specificity about it, not least of all because of the mix of 'Moors' and 'Gentiles' to be found even in the Mughal domains. Theoretical formulations, whether those of Bernier or Manuzzi, had to come to terms with the layered nature of the Mughal sovereign system, with the idea of a Gentile population groaning under the Moorish yoke to be found already in the early sixteenth-century letters of Alfonso de Albuquerque. Besides, hostility to the Mughal state was mixed with much admiration in regard to artisanal and others skills, even if the image of India in Europe fell rather short of that of China.

These were tensions that would be dealt with in rather different ways in the nineteenth century, as the Mughal state progressively lost its hold over the Indian subcontinent and the English East India Company gradually asserted its control over both towns and countryside. Initially portraying themselves as successors to Mughal power, the English Company and then the Crown would eventually claim for themselves the role of liberators, freeing 'Hindus' from centuries of 'Islamic rule', but also more generally rescuing the population from a social and political structure that imposed nothing (in the words of Philip Woodruff) but 'cruelty and human misery'. The nature of the colonial knowledge of the latter period is a complex and much-debated subject, to which the present collection of studies can make no particular claim to contributing. What is certain, however, is that one cannot persist in seeing the centuries from 1500 to 1700 as a period when 'a robust confidence in European secular ideals, ideas, institutions and arts', gave way via the 'opening of Asia to the European mind' to a happy situation of a 'wondering doubt about their [Europe's] superiority and permanence'.[20] Such doubts, when they were expressed, remained the opinion of a relatively small minority. Rather than truly seeing the 'civilizations of Asia' as being 'the equal of contemporary Europe and as having a continuous history that went back to antiquity', most European reacted with degrees of distrust and disdain to what they perceived as institutions and cultures that were vastly inferior to their own. Familiarity, in this instance at least, bred contempt. To what extent that contempt facilitated conquest is a question that remains to be addressed.

---

[20] Donald F. Lach, *Asia in the Making of Europe: Volume II, A Century of Wonder*, Book III, Chicago, 1977, pp. 563–6.

Index